This is a significant and landmark book for pastors and preachers seeking to reach Chinese people. With remarkable breadth of scholarship, Dr Hann Tzuu Tan makes accessible key Chinese festivals and cultural norms and then leads us to see ways of making our scriptural preaching culturally aware without forsaking gospel truth. Whether you are Asian, or a Westerner like me who preaches to people from Chinese backgrounds, I highly commend this book and pray that God uses it to enable greater relevance in preaching to win many Chinese for Christ.

Bishop Paul Barker, PhD
Assistant Bishop, Anglican Diocese of Melbourne

For preachers and evangelists, this volume is a gold mine. Written by a preacher, evangelist and entrepreneur, the reader's eyes will be opened and hearts will be warmed as well. The subject of contextualization has been treated many times over, but the treasure in this book is a classic case study in a Chinese cultural context. The reader will also be rewarded by several illustrations from local church ministry. And although Dr Hann Tzuu Tan's primary intention is situated in a Chinese culture, this thorough treatment will be useful in other contexts as well.

John W. Nyquist, PhD
Professor Emeritus of Mission and Evangelism,
Trinity Evangelical Divinity School, Deerfield, Illinois, USA

God's commitment, as demonstrated on the day of Pentecost, is that everyone may hear the gospel in their own language. Languages are more than mere words. They are carriers of culture. In this book, Hann Tzuu Tan explores how the gospel currently is, and may in the future be, preached meaningfully to Chinese people in the light of their three traditional, annual, religious festivals. In doing so, he not only carefully examines the meaning of the festivals but sets his research in the context of recent discussions about contextualization and the nature of the gospel. Furthermore, his investigations lead him to explore a number of key theological themes such as the spirit world and the nature of spiritual warfare. This will prove of major help both to scholars seeking to understand Chinese culture and preachers who have a longing to make Christ known. Clearly and objectively written by an insider who has a passion for the gospel.

Rev Derek Tidball, PhD
Former Principal, London School of Theology, UK
Research Supervisor, Spurgeon's College, London, UK

When reading through Dr Hann Tzuu Tan's study, *The Beasts, the Graves, and the Ghosts: A Study of Contextualized Preaching during Chinese Festivals*, the reader can tell right away that Dr Tan is an articulate scholar, a capable researcher, a reflective Bible teacher, a sincere practitioner, and a faithful disciple of Christ.

The issue of contextualized preaching among Chinese churches has been ambiguous due to different levels of understanding and perceptions towards Chinese festivals and cultures. Dr Tan's book attempts to tackle and resolve the issue, and it is indeed achieved!

This book is full of extensive qualitative research, in-depth and insightful interviews, sound biblical teachings, genuine theological reflections, substantive objective analysis, and practical convincing conclusions. The six principles derived from the research are profound in reference to empirical usage for pulpit ministry among the Chinese churches.

Whether for apologetic purpose, theological education, pulpit ministry or to expand one's understanding of contextualized preaching among Chinese festivals and cultures, Dr Tan's book is unquestionably a reliable source to explore. I highly recommend it.

Rev Joshua Ting, DMin
General Secretary,
Chinese Coordination Centre of World Evangelism (CCCOWE)

The Beasts, the Graves, and the Ghosts

A Study of Contextualized Preaching during Chinese Festivals

Hann Tzuu Joey Tan

MONOGRAPHS

© 2020 Hann Tzuu Tan

Published 2020 by Langham Monographs
An imprint of Langham Publishing
www.langhampublishing.org

Langham Publishing and its imprints are a ministry of Langham Partnership

Langham Partnership
PO Box 296, Carlisle, Cumbria, CA3 9WZ, UK
www.langham.org

ISBNs:
978-1-78368-789-3 Print
978-1-83973-027-6 ePub
978-1-83973-028-3 Mobi
978-1-83973-029-0 PDF

Hann Tzuu Tan has asserted his right under the Copyright, Designs and Patents Act, 1988 to be identified as the Author of this work.

All rights reserved. No part of this publication may be reproduced, stored in a retrieval system or transmitted, in any form or by any means, electronic, mechanical, photocopying, recording or otherwise, without the prior written permission of the publisher or the Copyright Licensing Agency.

Requests to reuse content from Langham Publishing are processed through PLSclear. Please visit www.plsclear.com to complete your request.

Unless marked otherwise, all Scripture quotations taken from the New American Standard Bible®, Copyright © 1995 by The Lockman Foundation. Used by permission. BibleWorks 9.

Hebrew version is from WTT Leningrad Hebrew Old Testament, BibleWorks 9.

Greek version is from BNT BibleWorks NT (NA27), BibleWorks 9.

British Library Cataloguing-in-Publication Data
A catalogue record for this book is available from the British Library

ISBN: 978-1-78368-789-3

Cover & Book Design: projectluz.com

Langham Partnership actively supports theological dialogue and an author's right to publish but does not necessarily endorse the views and opinions set forth here or in works referenced within this publication, nor can we guarantee technical and grammatical correctness. Langham Partnership does not accept any responsibility or liability to persons or property as a consequence of the reading, use or interpretation of its published content.

Contents

Acknowledgements xv
Abbreviations xvii
Approach on Chinese Literature, Translation, and Transliteration xix
Chapter 1 1
   Introduction
      1.1 Background to the Study 1
      1.2 The Study of Chinese Culture 5
          1.2.1 Han Chinese 6
          1.2.2 Malaysian Chinese 10
          1.2.3 Chinese Christians in Malaysia 14
      1.3 Aim of the Research 16
      1.4 Objectives of the Study 16
      1.5 Research Methodology 17
      1.6 Research Questions 17
      1.7 Significance of the Study 18
      1.8 Delimitations of the Study 19
          1.8.1 Three Major Chinese Festivals as Focus of Study 19
          1.8.2 Interviewing Six Experienced Chinese Preachers 20
      1.9 Definition of Terms 23
          1.9.1 Culture 23
          1.9.2 Gospel 26
          1.9.3 Evangelicalism 33
          1.9.4 Contextualization 36
          1.9.5 Worldview 37
          1.9.6 Religion 39
          1.9.7 Worship 42
          1.9.8 Annual Festivals 44
          1.9.9 Chinese Festivals 44
          1.9.10 Spring Festival 45
          1.9.11 Qing Ming Festival 46
          1.9.12 Hungry Ghost Festival 46
          1.9.13 Symbols 47
      1.10 Outline of the Study 47

Chapter 2 49
Literature Review on Issues of Contextualization
    2.1 The Ecumenical Movement in the Twentieth Century 49
    2.2 The Emergence of Contextualization 54
    2.3 Definitions of Contextualization..58
    2.4 Approaches to Contextualization 60
    2.5 Syncretism 66
    2.6 Examples of Contextualization from the New Testament 71
        2.6.1 Paul's Preaching in Lystra (Acts 14:8–20)..........................72
        2.6.2 Paul's Areopagus Address in Athens (Acts 17:16–34) 75
    2.7 Contextualized Preaching...77
    2.8 Contextualization in the Chinese Cultural Context 81
    2.9 Summary 87

Chapter 3 89
Confucianism, Taoism, Buddhism, and Chinese Folk Religion
    3.1 Confucianism 90
        3.1.1 Texts and Major Tenets of Confucianism 90
        3.1.2 The Religious Dimensions of Confucianism 94
    3.2 Taoism 96
        3.2.1 Philosophical Taoism 97
        3.2.2 Religious Taoism...101
    3.3 Buddhism 104
        3.3.1 The Early Development of Buddhism 104
        3.3.2 Buddhism in China 108
        3.3.3 Buddhist Influence on the Chinese View of the Afterlife..115
    3.4 Chinese Folk Religion..119
    3.5 Summary 124

Chapter 4 125
Research Methods
    4.1 Qualitative Field Research of Three Chinese Festivals.................126
        4.1.1 Qualitative Field Research as a Research Method 126
        4.1.2 Selecting Dates and Field Sites of Observations 130
    4.2 Qualitative Interviews with Chinese Preachers 131
        4.2.1 Qualitative Interviewing as a Research Method...............131
        4.2.2 Semi-Structured Interviews with Chinese Preachers.........133
        4.2.3 Selection of Interviewees...134

Chapter 5 139
   Exploratory Study of the Three Festivals
     5.1 Field Research on the Spring Festival 139
         5.1.1 Finding 1: Chinese Legends and Chinese Zodiac
         Remain Part of the Atmosphere of the Spring Festival......141
         5.1.2 Finding 2: Seeking Good Fortune Is Emphasized
         during the Spring Festival 150
         5.1.3 Finding 3: Asking Deities for a Blessing Is Important
         during the Spring Festival 157
         5.1.4 Finding 4: The Lion Dance Is Still Prevalent during
         the Spring Festival 163
     5.2 Field Research on the Qing Ming Festival 168
         5.2.1 Finding 1: The Chinese Worship Their Deceased
         Ancestors during the Qing Ming Festival, but the
         Practices are Slightly Different Depending on the Setting 169
         5.2.2 Finding 2: The Chinese Believe That the Needs of a
         Deceased Family Member Are Similar to the Needs
         of a Living Person 179
         5.2.3 Finding 3: The Chinese Believe that the Deceased
         Still Need Protection and Help from Deities....................186
     5.3 Field Research on the Hungry Ghost Festival 189
         5.3.1 Finding 1: The Chinese Believe Ghosts Are the Spirits
         of Deceased Persons...191
         5.3.2 Finding 2: The Chinese Worship the Ghosts Due to Fear 198
         5.3.3 Finding 3: The Chinese Believe the Hungry Ghost
         Festival Is the Time of Charitable Giving to Both the
         Hungry Ghosts and the Needy in Society 205
         5.3.4 Finding 4: Its Utilitarian Character Is One of the
         Prominent Features of the Hungry Ghost Festival............207
     5.4 Summary 210

Chapter 6 211
   Chinese Preachers' Perceptions and Practices of Contextualized
   Preaching at Three Chinese Festivals
     6.1 The Chinese Preachers Agree That Contextualized Preaching
     Is Important..211
     6.2 Regarding the Spring Festival 213

    6.2.1 The Chinese Preachers Generally Agreed that the Celebration of the Spring Festival Is Compatible with the Christian Faith..........213
    6.2.2 Some Beliefs and Practices Associated with the Spring Festival Are Contrary to the Christian Faith..........216
    6.2.3 The Concept of Renewal Could Be Used as a Cultural Contact Point for Contextualized Preaching during the Spring Festival..........218
    6.2.4 The Concept of Reunion Could Be Used as a Cultural Contact Point for Contextualized Preaching during the Spring Festival..........220
    6.2.5 Suitable Biblical Passages for Preaching during the Spring Festival..........221
6.3 Regarding the Qing Ming Festival..........223
    6.3.1 It Is Permissible to Celebrate the Qing Ming Festival with the Practice of Tomb Sweeping but not with the Practice of Ancestral Worship..........223
    6.3.2 The Emphasis on Filial Piety Could Be Used as a Cultural Contact Point for Contextualized Preaching during the Qing Ming Festival..........225
    6.3.3 The Resurrection of Jesus Christ Is a Suitable Topic for Contextualized Preaching during the Qing Ming Festival..........226
6.4 Regarding the Hungry Ghost Festival..........227
    6.4.1 The Celebration of the Hungry Ghost Festival Is Incompatible with the Christian Faith..........227
    6.4.2 Preaching about Salvation from God during the Month of the Hungry Ghost Festival Is Appropriate..........228
    6.4.3 Preaching the Biblical Truth about Ghosts Is Important during the Hungry Ghost Festival..........229
6.5 Summary..........230

Chapter 7..........231
Theological Reflections of the Cult of the Dead and the Spiritual Realm
7.1 Theological Reflections on the Cult of the Dead..........232
    7.1.1 The Cult of the Dead in the Ancient Near East..........233
    7.1.2 The Cult of the Dead in the Ancient Greco-Roman World..........237
    7.1.3 Christianity and Chinese Ancestor Worship..........239
    7.1.4 Theological Reflections on the Issue of the Afterlife..........246

  7.2 Theological Reflections on the Spiritual Realm 259
    7.2.1 The Reality of the Evil Spiritual Powers.........................259
    7.2.2 The Difference between the Concepts of Ghosts
      and Demons 268
    7.2.3 The Origin of Evil Spiritual Powers....................................274
    7.2.4 Christ's Supremacy and Spiritual Warfare.......................284
  7.3 Summary 290

Chapter 8 ....**291**
Principles for Formulating Contextualized Preaching to Chinese People
  8.1 Principle 1: Contextualization is important in preaching,
    even when the Chinese preacher shares the same cultural
    background with the audience 292
  8.2 Principle 2: Contextualized preaching includes both
    affirmation and confrontation 295
  8.3 Principle 3: The theme of harmony is appropriate for
    contextualized preaching among the Chinese, particularly
    during the Spring Festival 296
    8.3.1 The Biblical Concept of Shalom and the Theme
      of Harmony..299
    8.3.2 The Doctrine of Reconciliation and the Theme
      of Harmony..301
  8.4 Principle 4: The theme of filial piety is appropriate for
    contextualized preaching among the Chinese, particularly
    during the Qing Ming Festival..305
    8.4.1 Emphasis on Filial Piety in Both the Old Testament
      and the New Testament 307
    8.4.2 Jesus the Son of God as a Perfect Model of Filial Piety.....311
    8.4.3 Honoring God Takes Precedence over Honoring Parents .314
    8.4.4 Biblical Filial Piety Honors Both Father and Mother 317
  8.5 Principle 5: Preaching about the spiritual realm is
    appropriate during the Hungry Ghost Festival 319
  8.6 Principle 6: Choosing an appropriate metaphor for
    contextualized preaching in the Chinese culture is essential........321
  8.7 Summary 325

Chapter 9 ....**327**
Summary, Conclusions, and Recommendations
  9.1 Summary 327
  9.2 Conclusions 330

  9.3 Recommendations 333
  9.4 Concluding Remarks 334

Appendix 337
 The Gospel of Jesus Christ: An Evangelical Celebration
  Preamble 337
  The Gospel 339
  Unity in the Gospel 341
   Affirmations and Denials 342
   Our Commitment 345

Bibliography 347
 Bibles 347
 English Works Cited 347
 Chinese Works Cited 388

List of Tables

Figure 5.1.1: Thousands of Red Chinese Lanterns Hanging Everywhere..........144

Figure 5.1.2: Red Chinese Lanterns outside the Main Prayer Hall.................144

Figure 5.1.3: Two Pots of Tangerine Plants Wrapped with Red Cloth............145

Figure 5.1.4: Tangerine Plant Decorated with Red Packets 145

Figure 5.1.5: Couplets Written on Red Paper 146

Figure 5.1.6: Red Decorative Items, Pinwheels, and Toys 146

Figure 5.1.7: Firecrackers for Sale 147

Figure 5.1.8: Decorative Monkey Figures on the Trees..............................148

Figure 5.1.9: Decorative Monkey Figures on the Trees..............................148

Figure 5.1.10: Decorative Monkey King Items for Sale..............................149

Figure 5.1.11: The Monkey Statue is Popular with the Visitors...................149

Figure 5.1.12: Buddha Statues, Buddha Lockets, and Chinese Lucky Charms for Sale 150

Figure 5.1.13: Lucky Wood Carvings and Wooden Chanting Beads..............151

Figure 5.1.14: Lucky Charms and Chanting Beads for Sale 151

Figure 5.1.15: Chinese Gourd Charms for Sale 152

Figure 5.1.16: Sets of Items Symbolizing Chinese New Year Blessings 152

Figure 5.1.17: Fortune Telling..154

Figure 5.1.18: Container of Oracle Sticks in the Prayer Hall 154

Figure 5.1.19: A Bridge to Enable Those Who Want to Change Their Luck...155

Figure 5.1.20: Buddhist Monks Performing the Ceremonies of Blessings 156

Figure 5.1.21: Lotus Wishing Candles..156

Figure 5.1.22: People Worshipping Deities..157

Figure 5.1.23: Tian Hou..158

Figure 5.1.24: Bodhisattva Avalokitesvara...158

Figure 5.1.25: Shui Wei Sheng Niang...159

Figure 5.1.26: Smaller Statue of Bodhisattva Avalokitesvara......................160

Figure 5.1.27: Wen Chang Di Jun 161
Figure 5.1.28: God of Wealth 161
Figure 5.1.29: God of Marriage 162
Figure 5.1.30: Medicine Buddha with Healing Water 163
Figure 5.1.31: Lion Dance 165
Figure 5.1.32: Lion Dance Band 166
Figure 5.1.33: The Lion Gave Out Candy to Children 166
Figure 5.1.34: The Public Taking Pictures with the Lion 167
Figure 5.2.1: People Observing the Qing Ming Festival at
   the Petaling Jaya Chinese Cemetery 169
Figure 5.2.2: People Observing the Qing Ming Festival at
   the Gui Yuan Crematorium 170
Figure 5.2.3: People Observing the Qing Ming Festival at the Kwong
   Tong Cemetery Pagoda Columbarium 170
Figure 5.2.4: Turtle-Back Tomb Style 172
Figure 5.2.5: People Repainting the Tombstone 173
Figure 5.2.6: People Repainting an Inscription on a Tombstone 173
Figure 5.2.7: Sacrificing in Front of the Tombstone 174
Figure 5.2.8: Joss Papers on Top of the Tombstone 174
Figure 5.2.9: Urns in a Columbarium Block 176
Figure 5.2.10: Altar in Front of a Columbarium Block 176
Figure 5.2.11: A Centralized Burning Furnace 177
Figure 5.2.12: A Centralized Worship Place outside the Pagoda 177
Figure 5.2.13: Candles, Joss Sticks, Food, and Drink on the Altar 178
Figure 5.2.14: Joss Paper Furnace at Pagoda 178
Figure 5.2.15: Roasted Pork, Steamed Buns, and
   Fruits Offered to the Deceased 180
Figure 5.2.16: Sticky Rice Dumplings and Other
   Foods Offered to the Deceased 180
Figure 5.2.17: Food with Chopsticks and Spoons Provided 181
Figure 5.2.18: Vegetarian Food Offered to the Deceased 181

Figure 5.2.19: Chinese Tea and Rice Wine Offered to the Deceased 182

Figure 5.2.20: Bags of Joss Paper 184

Figure 5.2.21: Joss Paper Box 184

Figure 5.2.22: Coloured Joss Papers on the Grave 185

Figure 5.2.23: A Paper Double-Storey House, a Paper Van,
and a Pair of Paper Servants 185

Figure 5.2.24: A Paper Shopping Mall, Joss Paper Boxes, and Joss Papers 186

Figure 5.2.25: Hou Tu Shrine 187

Figure 5.2.26: Hou Tu Temple 188

Figure 5.2.27: Ksitigarbha Bodhisattva (Di Zang Wang 地藏王) 188

Figure 5.3.1: The Canopy of the Hungry Ghost Festival in the SS2 Park 191

Figure 5.3.2: Layout of the Canopy 191

Figure 5.3.3: One Whole Raw Pig and One Whole Raw Goat on Red
Wooden Racks and Other Foods 193

Figure 5.3.4: A Table with Five Cone-Shaped Mountains 194

Figure 5.3.5: The Main Ghost-Worshipping Altar with the "Bridge" 194

Figure 5.3.6: A Paper Four-Storey Apartment 195

Figure 5.3.7: A Paper Taxi and a Paper Bus 196

Figure 5.3.8: A Paper Boat 196

Figure 5.3.9: Nightly Live Performance for Hungry Ghosts Entertainment 198

Figure 5.3.10: A Chinese Devotee Performing Prayers to the Deities 199

Figure 5.3.11: Da Shi Wang, the Golden Boy, and the Jade Girl 201

Figure 5.3.12: Hell Guards and Hell Patrols in Front of Da Shi Wang 202

Figure 5.3.13: Taoist Deity Fa Zhu Gong and Thirteen Banners 203

Figure 5.3.14: A Taoist Priest Leading a Chanting Ceremony 205

Figure 5.3.15: Rice of Peace and Other Foods 206

Figure 5.3.16: A Chart Board with Donation Information 207

Figure 5.3.17: The Three Taoist Star Gods 208

Figure 5.3.18: The God of Wealth 208

Figure 5.3.19: The Joss Paper Pineapple 209

Acknowledgements

I am grateful to God for the unfailing love that he has shown me. This book would not have been possible without his grace. My director of studies, Dr Derek Tidball, deserves a special word of thanks for his constant encouragement, thoroughness, helpful guidance, and careful supervision of my thesis. He has been a great model of scholarship for me. My special thanks to Dr Roger Standing, my supervisor, for his timely help and encouragement. Both Dr Tidball and Dr Standing spent endless hours reading the manuscript and making notations. I am profoundly grateful for their efforts. I would also like to thank my advisor Dr Ka Lun Leung, who is familiar with the background of this study and has offered numerous insightful suggestions. Thanks to Dr Paul R. Woods and Dr Joshua T. Searle for being my thesis examiners and providing valuable suggestions and corrections. Thank you to the interviewees for their participation and sharing their experiences and thoughts in this study.

I would like to acknowledge my sincere gratitude to Langham Partnership for its support of my PhD study. I was honored to be a recipient of a John Stott Scholarship in Biblical Preaching. I also wish to record my gratitude to individuals and institutions whose assistance and support made the completion of this study possible. I would like to thank the faculty and staff at Spurgeon's College for their unfailing help. My special appreciation goes to Denver Seminary, in which I had a few months of fruitful research as an International Visiting Scholar. My appreciation is extended to Hong Kong Alliance Seminary, Tyndale House in Cambridge, Wheaton College in Illinois, China Graduate School of Theology in Hong Kong, and Ridley College in Melbourne for their role and resources in my research.

I also owe special thanks to the council members and my colleagues in Malaysia Bible Seminary for helping me in many different ways. There are many people I am also indebted to, but I cannot mention all their names here; I am deeply grateful to all of them. Lastly, a special word of gratitude goes to my wife, Dr Yap Chen Sing, whose encouragement and love have enabled me to carry out this research.

Abbreviations

AFER	African Ecclesial Review
AFS	Asian Folklore Studies
AJPS	Asian Journal of Pentecostal Studies
AJT	Asia Journal of Theology
ANQ	Andover Newton Quarterly
BBR	Bulletin for Biblical Research
BSac	Bibliotheca Sacra
BETS	Bulletin of the Evangelical Theological Society
BibInt	Biblical Interpretation
CBQ	The Catholic Biblical Quarterly
CTM	Concordia Theological Monthly
DDD	Dictionary of Deities and Demons in the Bible
Did	Didaskalia
DJG	Dictionary of Jesus and the Gospels
EJT	European Journal of Theology
ER	The Ecumenical Review
ERT	Evangelical Review of Theology
EvQ	Evangelical Quarterly
ExAud	Ex auditu
HALOT	The Hebrew and Aramaic Lexicon of the Old Testament
HolBD	Holman Bible Dictionary
IBMR	International Bulletin of Missionary Research
Int	Interpretation
IRM	International Review of Mission
JBL	Journal of Biblical Literature
JBQ	Jewish Bible Quarterly

JCR	Journal of Chinese Religion
JES	Journal of Ecumenical Studies
JETS	Journal of Evangelical Theological Society
JFM	Journal of Family Ministry
JIABS	Journal of the International Association of Buddhist Studies
JQR	Jewish Quarterly Review
JSNT	Journal for the Study of the New Testament
JSOT	Journal for the Study of the Old Testament
JSRNC	Journal for the Study of Religion, Nature and Culture
JTSA	Journal of Theology for Southern Africa
LQ	Lutheran Quarterly
LSJ	Greek-English Lexicon
Missiology	Missiology: An International Review
NDBT	New Dictionary of Biblical Theology
NIDOTTE	New International Dictionary of Old Testament Theology and Exegesis
OBMR	Occasional Bulletin of Missionary Research
PRJ	Puritan Reformed Journal
PRSt	Perspectives in Religious Studies
RelSRev	Religious Studies Review
RevExp	Review and Expositor
SANACS	Society of Asian North American Christian Studies Journal
SEÅ	Svensk Exegetisk Årsbok
StudWorldChr	Studies in World Christianity
SwJT	Southwestern Journal of Theology
TynBul	Tyndale Bulletin
TRINJ	Trinity Journal
TSFJ	The Spurgeon Fellowship Journal
TTE	(The) Theological Educator
VC	Vigiliae christianae
VT	Vetus Testamentum
WesTJ	Wesleyan Theological Journal
WTJ	Westminster Theological Journal
WW	Word and World
ZAW	Zeitschrift für die alttestamentliche Wissenschaft

Approach on Chinese Literature, Translation, and Transliteration

With regard to primary sources of Chinese literature used, Chinese publication details will be cited. There are various translations in classical literature on Chinese philosophy, such as *The Analects* and *The Classic of Filial Piety*; translations cited and used vary according to my selection deemed to be the most appropriate for the content. There are two major romanization systems in transliteration of Chinese characters, which are the Wade-Giles and Hanyu Pinyin. The most widely used system today, which is Hanyu Pinyin, was chosen to be used in this book. A new Chinese character or word introduced shall be written first in Pinyin (without tone markings) and then in traditional Chinese characters. The names of persons and places are also given in Hanyu Pinyin form followed by Chinese characters in parentheses, except for the names that have a more commonly used English translation (such as Confucius instead of Kong Zi). Similarly when introducing a Chinese quote, otherwise noted in the footnote or text, traditional Chinese characters of the quote shall be written with simple explanations of the quote.

CHAPTER 1

Introduction

The development of strategies for world evangelization calls for imaginative pioneering methods. Under God, the result will be the rise of churches deeply rooted in Christ and closely related to their culture. Culture must always be tested and judged by Scripture.[1]

1.1 Background to the Study

Christianity has grown unprecedentedly during the past few decades in Latin America, Africa, and some parts of Asia. China has been part of this amazing phenomenon as well.[2] The rapid growth in the number of Christians in mainland China over the last fifty years has been remarkable. It is impossible to say exactly how many Christians there are in China today, because the estimates vary widely. However, based on government information and the work of China-focus researchers, Jason Mandryk estimates the figure is around 105 million.[3] The Chinese church is one of the fastest growing Christian churches in history. Moreover, as Phillip Jenkins rightly points out, "Christianity has also made rapid progress in the Chinese diaspora, the flourishing network

---

1. "The Lausanne Covenant," in *Let the Earth Hear His Voice*, ed. J. D. Douglas (Minneapolis: World Wide, 1975), 3-9 (6).

2. Daniel H. Bays, *A New History of Christianity in China* (Oxford: Wiley-Blackwell, 2012), 205.

3. Jason Mandryk, *Operation World: The Definitive Prayer Guide to Every Nation*, 7th ed. (Downers Grove, IL: IVP, 2010), 215.

of Chinese communities scattered around the Pacific Rim, in nations like Indonesia, Malaysia, and Singapore."[4]

On the other hand, ethnically speaking, the Chinese remain the largest mission field in the world today. In mainland China alone, there are around 1.4 billion people; and if we include the millions of overseas Chinese living throughout the world, approximately one in every four or five human beings is Chinese.[5] According to Mandryk, in the world today there are about 1,213 million people whose first language is Chinese.[6] However, Chinese Christians represent only a small percentage of the worldwide Chinese population. A great number of Chinese still lack the knowledge of Christ's name and salvation.[7]

The Chinese church today faces several challenges. One of the major ones is how to make the message of salvation relevant to the still strongly influential traditional Chinese cultural ways of thinking and living.[8] From the perspective of many Chinese non-believers, Christianity is still associated with Western imperialism, which is perceived to be a threat to their culture; and any who convertes to Christianity is no longer considered truly "Chinese."[9] In the 1920s, some anti-Christian intellectuals in China protested, "One more Christian, one less Chinese."[10] After almost a hundred years, a similar mindset still remains in the minds of many Chinese today. Hwa Yung is right when he remarks concerning Asian missions, "unless genuine efforts are made at contextualizing the proclamation of the gospel and the practice of the faith, Christianity will continue to be widely perceived as a Western religion."[11]

---

4. Phillip Jenkins, *The Next Christendom: The Coming of Global Christianity* (Oxford: Oxford University Press, 2002), 70.

5. David J. Hesselgrave, *Communicating Christ Cross-Culturally* (Grand Rapids, MI: Zondervan, 1978), 172.

6. Mandryk, *Operation World*, 1.

7. Thomas Wang and Sharon Chan, "Christian Witness to the Chinese People," in *Perspectives on the World Christian Movement: A Reader*, 3rd ed., eds. Ralph D. Winter and Steven C. Hawthorne (Pasadena, CA: William Carey Library, 1999), 639-645 (639).

8. Miikka Ruokanen and Paulos Huang, "Preface," in *Christianity and Chinese Culture*, ed. Miikka Ruokanen and Paulos Huang (Grand Rapids, MI: Eerdmans, 2010), ix–xvii (xiii).

9. Jonathan Hill, *History of Christianity* (Grand Rapids, MI: Zondervan, 2006), 404.

10. Hwa Yung, "Strategic Issues in Missions – An Asian Perspective," in The Study of Evangelism: Exploring a Missional Practice of the Church, ed. Paul W. Chilcote and Laceye C. Warner (Grand Rapids, MI: Eerdmans, 2008), 374-383 (380).

11. Yung, "Strategic Issues in Missions," 380.

Making the gospel understood and culturally relevant to the Chinese is extremely important for the Chinese church today.

Since the 1970s, culture has been a major issue on the agenda of world mission. The Bangkok Conference of the World Council of Churches (WCC) on "Salvation Today," which was held at the end of 1972 and into 1973, emphasized the need for the recognition of cultural identity as shaping the voice of those answering and following Christ: "Culture shapes the human voice that answers the voice of Christ."[12] After the Lausanne Congress on World Evangelization in 1974, the evangelical constituency as a whole began to acknowledge the central importance of culture for the effective communication of the gospel.[13] The Lausanne Covenant, which was agreed to by 2,300 people from 150 nations at the 1974 Lausanne Congress, recognized the need for the church to take culture seriously. The Covenant indicated that Christians are bound to have a double orientation, toward Christ and toward culture. Every believer in Christ has the responsibility to develop a biblical attitude to both Christ and culture.[14] At the Lausanne Congress, Pablo M. Perez said, "Culture as a most vital factor in the effective communication of the Gospel of Jesus Christ can no longer be ignored or passed off lightly."[15] As John Stott later indicated, one's cultural background is bound to affect one's perception of the gospel.[16] A few years after Lausanne, the Willowbank Report was produced by a consultation on "Gospel and Culture" in January 1978. The Willowbank Report declared, "No Christian witness can hope to communicate the gospel if he or she ignores the cultural factor." The report stated that "messengers of the gospel need to develop a deep understanding of the local culture, and a genuine appreciation of it."[17]

---

12. World Conference on Salvation Today, Bangkok, "Culture and Identity: Report of Section I of the Bangkok Conference," *IRM* 62 (1973): 185–197 (188).

13. John Stott, "Foreword," in *Down to Earth: Studies in Christianity and Culture*, ed. Robert T. Coote and John Stott (Grand Rapids, MI: Eerdmans, 1980), v–x, (vii).

14. John R. W. Stott, *Lausanne Occasional Paper No. 3: The Lausanne Covenant, An Exposition and Commentary* (Minneapolis: World Wide, 1975), 26.

15. Pablo M. Perez, "Response to Dr. Ralph D. Winter's Paper," in *Let the Earth Hear His Voice*, 255–258 (255).

16. John Stott, "The Significance of Lausanne," in *The Study of Evangelism: Exploring a Missional Practice of the Church*, ed. Paul W. Chilcote and Laceye C. Warner, 305–312 (310).

17. Lausanne Committee for World Evangelization, "The Willowbank Report," in *Down to Earth*, ed. Coote and Stott, 308–339 (319).

Paul Hiebert asserts that the gospel must always be understood and expressed within human cultural forms. It is impossible to communicate the gospel apart from human thought patterns and languages.[18] In fact, in order to communicate the gospel effectively, Christians need to have both a knowledge of the Bible and a knowledge of their own cultures.[19] Luzbetak perhaps overstates the case when he adopts a similar but valid position: "The only way man is able to communicate is in the specific context of his actual cultural experience. He can know, love, and serve God and his fellowmen only in that limited context. Man views and is able to understand and interpret the world, and all that is beyond this world, only in the terms of his cultural or subcultural experience."[20]

In the light of this, more research is necessary concerning the relevance of the cultural context of the Chinese people for the preaching of the gospel. One of the most effective ways to obtain knowledge of Chinese culture is to study how it celebrates its festivals. With their long history and rich heritage, most traditional Chinese festivals are important for retaining the core values and inheritance of Chinese culture. As a form of cultural ritual, festivals are of particular importance in studying cultures. Hiebert points out that at the heart of cultural behaviour are rituals. Rituals play a central role in most societies because they dramatize in visible expression the deep beliefs, feelings, and values of a society.[21] He believes that rituals, such as festivals, are a vital key to understanding people's worldviews, because they visibly reenact the deepest beliefs, feelings, and values of a culture.[22]

Consequently, research into the practice of contextualized preaching at particular Chinese festivals is critical in exploring how the gospel can be effectively communicated among the Chinese. By definition contextual preaching means "preaching that responds intentionally and dynamically to the social and cultural location within which the preacher prepares and preaches

---

18. Paul G. Hiebert, *Anthropological Insights for Missionaries* (Grand Rapids, MI: Baker, 2004), 30.

19. Paul G. Hiebert, *Cultural Anthropology* (Grand Rapids, MI: Baker, 1983), xx.

20. L. J. Luzbetak, "Unity in Diversity: Ethnotheological Sensitivity in Cross-Cultural Evangelism," *Missiology* 4 (1976): 207–216 (209).

21. Paul G. Hiebert, *Transforming Worldviews: An Anthropological Understanding of How People Change* (Grand Rapids, MI: Baker, 2008), 82–83.

22. Hiebert, *Transforming Worldviews*, 98–99.

sermons."²³ Chinese churches consider preaching a primary means of communication. Thus, it is important for preachers who are working among the Chinese to effectively encode the gospel message for the Chinese at major Chinese festivals.

After all, preaching is a communication event which always happens in a particular time and place. Craddock says that a sermon as a spoken word is socially owned, having its life at a particular time and place among a group of participants.²⁴ Therefore, discerning the season and communicating the gospel appropriately and effectively are important to a preacher. As David J. Schlafer points out, preaching is not a religious monologue but a sacred conversation in which the voices of Scripture, culture, congregation, and preacher all take part. Moreover, Schlafer believes that special occasions need a place in the dialogue.²⁵ In order to proclaim the gospel in relevant and transformative ways for particular communities, preachers not only need to become skilled biblical exegetes but also need to be adept in "exegeting" local congregations and their contexts.²⁶

1.2 The Study of Chinese Culture

Chinese culture defines how the Chinese live their lives materially, socially, and spiritually. It denotes the essence of what it means to be "Chinese" and manifest the features of the "Chinese way of life."²⁷ However, one should question if understanding the Chinese culture in general is possible. After all, the Chinese are the largest ethnic group in the world with an extensive history of civilization. As Kam Louie points out, even the concept of "Chinese" is sometimes difficult to define. Debates have continued for decades regarding what

---

23. John S. McClure, *Preaching Words: 144 Key Terms in Homiletics* (Louisville, KY: Westminster John Knox, 2007), 17.

24. Fred B. Craddock, *Preaching* (Nashville, TN: Abingdon, 1985), 31–32.

25. David J. Schlaffer, *What Makes This Day Different: Preaching Grace on Special Occasions* (Cambridge: Cowley, 1998), 7.

26. Leonora Tubbs Tisdale, *Preaching as Local Theology and Folk Art* (Minneapolis: Fortress, 1997), xi.

27. Xinzhong Yao and Yanxia Zhao, *Chinese Religion: A Contextual Approach* (London: Continuum, 2010), 3.

it means to be Chinese.[28] The possibility of oversimplifying today's Chinese culture by simply describing basic characteristics must be carefully borne in mind and taken into account. This study, therefore, acknowledges the great subculture diversities among the Chinese living in different parts of the world.

1.2.1 Han Chinese

It is important to note that the Chinese people to which this study refers are the Han Chinese. Generally speaking, the Han Chinese can be divided into two groups: Chinese people who live in the People's Republic of China and Chinese people who live outside the People's Republic of China.[29] The Han Chinese form the overwhelming majority of China, accounting for 90 percent of the population,[30] along with about 100 million people from ethnic minorities.[31] Numerous large Han Chinese communities also appear across the globe.[32] The Chinese who live outside mainland China can be further divided into the following subgroups.

The first subgroup of Chinese outside China includes nationals of China living or studying abroad. They may return to China eventually or choose to settle and become naturalized in their adopted country.[33] Those settled outside the borders of China are called "mainland Chinese Diaspora," and many are Chinese intellectuals.[34] It should be noted that some analysts insist that the term *Chinese Diaspora* should refer only to new Chinese migrants "who still have close links with China which they still politically identify with,"[35]

---

28. Kam Louie, "Defining Modern Chinese Culture," in *The Cambridge Companion to Modern Chinese Culture*, ed. Kam Louie (Cambridge: Cambridge University Press, 2008), 1–19 (7–8).

29. "Definitions," in *The Encyclopedia of the Chinese Overseas*, ed. Lynn Pan, 2nd ed. (Singapore: Editions Didier Millet, 2006), 15–17 (15).

30. Mandryk, *Operation World*, 214.

31. Paul Hattaway, *Operation China: Introducing all the Peoples of China* (Passadena, CA: William Carey Library, 2000), 1.

32. Jacques Gernet, *A History of Chinese Civilization*, trans. J. R. Foster and Charles Hartman, 2nd ed. (Cambridge: Cambridge University Press, 1996), 6–7.

33. "Definitions," in *The Encyclopedia of the Chinese Overseas*, 15.

34. Paul R. Woods, "Towards a Contextualized Spirituality for Chinese Diaspora Christians" (unpublished master of theology dissertation, Spurgeon's College, 2006), 6–11.

35. Chee Beng Tan, "Migration, Localization, and Cultural Exchange: Global Perspectives of Chinese Overseas," in *Migration, Indigenization, and Interaction: Chinese Overseas and Globalization*, ed. Leo Suryadinata (Singapore: World Scientific Publishing, 2011), 15–38 (20).

while others use the term to refer to all Chinese people living overseas.³⁶ On the other hand, a Chinese slang term for those who choose to return to China after their study abroad is *hai gui* 海歸, meaning "coming back from overseas." In Chinese, this term is pronounced similarly to the term for *sea turtle* (*hai gui* 海龜).

The second subgroup of Han Chinese living outside mainland China is those who reside in Hong Kong and think of themselves as Hong Kong people.³⁷ Hong Kong is one of the most densely populated regions in the world. About 95 percent of the seven million population in Hong Kong is Chinese, among them the majority is Cantonese Han.³⁸ Once a colony of the British Empire and now a special administrative region of China, Hong Kong has many cultural facets that can be traced to Chinese roots and Western influences.³⁹ Overall, Hong Kong features the traditional customs of southern China.⁴⁰ Buddhism and Taoism are the two major religions practised by the majority in Hong Kong; Buddhist and Taoist rituals are the most prevalent practices in the traditional ceremonies for birth, marriage, funeral, and seasonal celebrations.⁴¹

The third group is those who live in Taiwan.⁴² Approximately 96 percent of the population in Taiwan is Chinese. The migration of the Chinese from mainland China to Taiwan can be traced back to the sixteenth century.⁴³ The folk religion brought to Taiwan by these early settlers from the province of

---

36. Enoch Wan, "Mission among the Chinese Diaspora: A Case of Migration and Mission," *Missiology* 31 (2003): 35–43 (35).

37. "Definitions," in *The Encyclopedia of the Chinese Overseas*, 15.

38. Mandryk, *Operation World*, 252.

39. Kam Louie, "Introduction – Hong Kong on the Move: Creating Global Cultures," in *Hong Kong Culture: Word and Image*, ed. Kam Louie (Hong Kong: Hong Kong University Press, 2010), 1–7 (2).

40. 陳蒨, "香港的民間傳統風俗" (Traditional Folk Customs in Hong Kong), 於香港史新編, 下冊 (*Hong Kong History: New Perspectives, vol. 2*), 王賡武編 (香港 [Hong Kong]: 三聯書店, 1997), 841–857 (841).

41. Gail Law, *Chinese Churches Handbook* (Hong Kong: CCCOWE, 1981), 55.

42. "Definitions," in *The Encyclopedia of the Chinese Overseas*, 15.

43. 董芳苑, "就臺灣民間信仰之認識論基督教宣教的場合化" (The Understanding of Taiwanese Folk Beliefs on the Contextualization of Christianity), 臺灣神學論刊 *(Taiwan Journal of Theology)* 3 (1981): 31–66 (33).

Fujian and Guangdong is still overwhelmingly popular today.[44] Moreover, the Confucian tradition also resonates with folk religions in Taiwan.[45]

Another group of Chinese includes those who are Chinese by descent and unequivocally identify themselves as overseas Chinese or Chinese overseas.[46] Today at least forty million Chinese live overseas worldwide.[47] About 80 percent of them live in Asia, 15 percent in North and South America, and 5 percent in other countries.[48] These overseas Chinese have adjusted socially and culturally to their respective locations.[49] Although the common Chinese term for overseas Chinese people is *hua qiao* 華僑, they often refer to themselves as *hua ren* 華人, *han ren* 漢人, or *tang ren* 唐人.[50] In general terms, *hua* 華 or *zhong hua* 中華 refers to "China or Chinese," and *ren* 人 means "people." *Han* 漢 refers to Han Chinese, the word derived from the Han dynasty (206 BCE–220 CE), and *tang* 唐 is derived from the Tang dynasty (618–907 CE).[51] Both the Han dynasty and Tang dynasty are considered as golden ages in Chinese history.

Across the globe, cultural diversity is noticeable among different Chinese communities.[52] For example, in comparison with overseas Chinese communities, the influence of traditional Chinese beliefs has been reduced to some extent in mainland China due to political movements and campaigns.[53] After the May Fourth Movement of 1919, traditional Chinese culture, particularly

---

44. Gary Marvin Davison and Barbara E. Reed, *Culture and Customs of Taiwan* (West Port, CT: Greenwood, 1998), 37.

45. Davison and Reed, *Culture and Customs*, 34.

46. "Definitions," in *The Encyclopedia of the Chinese Overseas*, 15.

47. Dudley L. Poston, Jr. and Juyin Helen Wong, "The Chinese Diaspora: The Current Distribution of the Overseas Chinese Population," *Chinese Journal of Sociology* 2 (2016): 348–373 (349).

48. Wan, "Mission among the Chinese Diaspora," 3.

49. Chee Beng Tan, "People of Chinese Descent: Language, Nationality and Identity," in *The Chinese Diaspora: Select Essays*, vol. 1, ed. Ling Chi Wang and Gung Wu Wang (Singapore: Times Academic, 1998), 29–48 (29).

50. Yit Seng Yow, *Chinese Dimensions: Their Roots, Mindset and Psyche* (Subang Jaya, Malaysia: Pelanduk, 2006), 7.

51. Yow, *Chinese Dimensions*, 7.

52. Tsu-Kung Chuang, *Ripening Harvest: Mission Strategy for Mainland Chinese Intellectuals in North America* (Paradise, PA: Ambassadors for Christ, 1995), 1.

53. Woods, "Towards a Contextualized Spirituality," 7–8.

Confucianism, has been challenged in many ways.[54] Furthermore, under the Communist regime, the Cultural Revolution in the 1960s, which lasted for a decade, dismantled the Chinese cultural tradition at an intense rate.[55] By contrast, for the last few decades, Chinese intellectuals in Hong Kong and Taiwan are enthusiastically promoting traditional Chinese culture.[56]

This research, however, agrees with Hesselgrave that it is still possible to describe a traditional Chinese worldview in order to understand the Chinese in general.[57] Although Chinese people living in different parts of the world have some differences due to local situations and influences, culturally speaking, they are still more similar than dissimilar. Throughout the course of Chinese civilization, most people would agree that the mainland Chinese and the overseas Chinese are both co-heirs of a much greater traditional Chinese cultural heritage, which includes elements of Confucianism, Taoism, and Buddhism.[58] Even though the traditional culture in mainland China encountered many challenges and faced some radical criticism during the Cultural Revolution, devotion to traditional values is being reaffirmed after the dismissal.[59] As a matter of fact, mainland China has experienced a wave of revival in the study of Confucianism since the 1990s.[60] Buddhism has also made rapid progress in modern China today.[61] Moreover, both mainland Chinese and overseas Chinese celebrate major Chinese festivals, including the Spring

---

54. Pan-Chiu Lai, "Chinese Culture and the Development of Chinese Christian Theology," *StudWorldChr* 7 (2001): 219–240 (219).

55. Xuefu Wang, "On Becoming a Religious Therapist in Chinese Culture," *Pastoral Psychology* 61 (2012): 1007–1024 (1008).

56. 莊祖鯤, 契合與轉化: 基督教與中國文化更新之路 (*Conformation and Transformation: The Renewal of Christianity and Chinese Culture*) (多倫多 (Toronto): 加拿大恩福協會, 1997), 189. According to Tsu-Kung Chuang (莊祖鯤), after the 1980s some intellectuals in mainland China hold a more positive attitude toward traditional Chinese culture. See 莊祖鯤, 契合與轉化, 192–194.

57. Hesselgrave, *Communicating Christ Cross-Culturally*, 172.

58. Woods, "Towards a Contextualized Spirituality," 7.

59. Theresa Chu, "Catholicism, Chinese Traditional Values and Marxist Thought: Searching for a Common Ground," *Missiology* 8 (1985): 337–346 (338).

60. 石衡潭, 東風破:《論語》之另類解讀 (*An Alternative Interpretation of* 〈) (濟南 (Jinan): 山東畫報出版社, 2009), 10.

61. Mandryk, *Operation World*, 223.

Festival and the Qing Ming Festival. As for the Hungry Ghost Festival, it is still being celebrated in some areas of China, especially in southern China.[62]

1.2.2 Malaysian Chinese

Malaysia is a country composed of two distinct regions, West (Peninsular) Malaysia and East Malaysia. West Malaysia is situated at the southeastern-most point of mainland Asia, neighboring Thailand to the north and Singapore to the south. East Malaysia (Sarawak and Sabah) is located on the northern third of the island of Borneo.[63] Malaysia is a multicultural and multireligious country of thirty million people, in which approximately 24.6 percent are Chinese.[64] By percentage of total population, Malaysia has the largest ethnic Chinese minority population in the world.[65] The Chinese population in Malaysia is usually referred to as Malaysian Chinese or Chinese Malaysian, and in Mandarin they today call themselves *hua ren* 華人.[66]

Migration of the Chinese to Malaysia can be traced to as early as the fifteenth century, during the Ming dynasty of China when eunuch Zheng He 鄭和 commanded expeditionary voyages to Southeast Asia.[67] In 1409, Zheng He arrived at Melaka with his voyage fleet, and he made six more such journeys. Accordingly, more Chinese started to migrate to Malaysia

---

62. According to Mu Peng, for example, the Hungry Ghost Festival is still being celebrated in the province of Hunan in China. See Mu Peng, "The Invisible and the Visible: Communicating with the Yin World," *Asian Ethnology* 74 (2015): 335–362 (335).

63. Mandryk, *Operation World*, 555–562.

64. D. Kanyakumari, "Malaysia's population to number 30 million on Thursday," *The Star*, 26 February, 2014, http://www.thestar.com.my/News/Nation/2014/02/26/Malaysia-30-mil-population/.

65. Carolyn Cartier, "Diaspora and Social Restructuring in Postcolonial Malaysia," in *The Chinese Diaspora: Space, Place, Mobility, and Identity*, ed. Laurence J. C. Ma and Carolyn Cartier (Lanham, MD: Rowman & Littlefield, 2003), 69–96 (70).

66. Tan Chee-Beng, "Socio-Cultural Diversities and Identities," in *The Chinese in Malaysia*, ed. Lee Kam Hing and Tan Chee-Beng (Oxford: Oxford University Press, 2000), 37–70 (37). As Tan points out, before the independence of Malaysia, Malaysian Chinese regarded themselves as *hua qiao* 華僑. Today they reject the label *hua qiao* 華僑, because *qiao* 僑 means "sojourner" in a foreign country who may return to their origin.

67. 蕭遙天, "中華文化的本質特徵及對馬來西亞的貢獻" (The Essential Characteristics of Chinese Culture and Its Contribution to Malaysia), 於馬華文化探討 (*Essays On Malaysian Chinese Culture*), 賴觀福編 (吉隆坡(Kuala Lumpur): 馬來西亞留臺校友會聯合總會, 1982), 5–16 (13). Chinese migration abroad was interwoven with maritime and commercial development. See "Migration," in *The Encyclopedia of the Chinese Overseas*, 48.

after Zheng He's expeditions.[68] For centuries, however, only small Chinese settlements existed in Malaysia.[69] Waves of Chinese emigration to Malaysia began in the eighteenth century,[70] mainly due to economic hardship and domestic disruption in China.[71] In the period from the 1850s to the 1940s, about twenty million Chinese from southern China emigrated to Malaysia and other countries in Southeast Asia, a region which was called *Nanyang* 南洋, meaning "South Seas" in Chinese.[72] As a consequence, the Chinese immigrants to Malaysia were mainly from the provinces of southern China, and comprised five main dialect groups: Cantonese, Hokkien, Hakka, Teochew, and Hainanese.[73] Being an expatriate community, these Chinese immigrants are conservative in terms of maintaining their traditions. Overall, they "expressed a strong desire to preserve their cultural identity,"[74] and formed their own communities and brought with them the gods they worshipped in their home villages in China.[75] The majority of Malaysian Chinese today are the decendants of these Chinese immigrants from southern China.[76]

In the present day, Malaysian Chinese still hold strongly to their Chinese cultural identity[77] because the cultural past and the continuity "give meaning

---

68. 李明安, 馬禮遜宣教策略的探討 (Robert Morrison: The Study of His Mission Strategy) (Kuang: MBS, 2018), 93–94.

69. N. J. Ryan, *The Cultural Heritage of Malaya*, 2nd ed. (Kuala Lumpur: Longman Malaysia, 1971), 17.

70. Kay Kim Khoo, "The Emergence of Plural Communities in the Malay Peninsula before 1874," in *Multiethnic Malaysia: Past, Present and Future*, ed. Teck Ghee Lim, Alberto Gomes, and Azly Rahman (Petaling Jaya: SIRD, 2009), 11–31 (21).

71. Lukas Tjandra, "Folk Religion among the Chinese in Singapore and Malaysia" (unpublished doctoral dissertation, Fuller Theological Seminary, 1988), 3.

72. Brian Bernards, *Writing the South Seas: Imagining the Nanyang in Chinese and Southeast Asian Postcolonial Literature* (Seattle: University of Washington Press, 2015), vii.

73. Barbara Watson Andaya and Leonard Y. Andaya, *A History of Malaysia*, 2nd ed. (Basingstoke: Palgrave, 2001), 140.

74. Yen Ching-hwang, "Historial Background," in *The Chinese in Malaysia*, ed. Lee Kam Hing and Tan Chee-Beng (Oxford: Oxford University Press, 2000), 1–36 (12).

75. Tjandra, "Folk Religion among the Chinese," 3.

76. 李靈窗, 馬來西亞華人延伸、獨有及融合的中華文化 (The Continuity, Uniqueness and Mixing of Chinese Culture in Malaysia) (福州 (Fu Zhou): 海峽文藝出版社, 2004), 11.

77. 廖建裕, "亞細安華社與華族文化的變遷" (ASEAN Chinese Society and the Changes of Chinese Culture), 於中華文化之路: 中華文化邁向二十一世紀國際學術研討會論文集 *(The Road to Chinese Culture: An International Symposium of the 21st Century Chinese Culture)*, 林水檺與何國忠編 (吉隆坡 (Kuala Lumpur): 馬來西亞中華大會堂聯合會, 1995) 101–125 (111).

and pride" to them.⁷⁸ They make a great deal of effort to keep their Chinese cultural heritage alive. As Thomas In-Sing Leung indicates, compared to Chinese in other Southeast Asia countries, the efforts that Malaysian Chinese put into preserving their cultural heritage are remarkable.⁷⁹ In fact, many Chinese scholars are deeply impressed by the efforts and passions of Malaysian Chinese in maintaining their cultural identity and tradition.⁸⁰

Even though Islam was declared to be the official religion in Malaysia and by law all Malays are Muslim, other religions are allowed to be practiced in peace in any part of the federation.⁸¹ Most Malaysian Chinese still retain their Chinese religious tradition.⁸² They prefer "a religion which links them to their ancestors and fulfils their religious needs, which at the same time expresses Chinese identity."⁸³ Regarding Chinese religious tradition, obviously there has been much cultural continuation among the Malaysian Chinese.⁸⁴

Malaysian Chinese often refer to their traditional religious affiliation as *bai shen* 拜神, meaning "worshipping deities."⁸⁵ They practice a mixture of Confucianism, Taoism, and Buddhism. They also integrate Chinese folk religious practices with these three Chinese religions.⁸⁶ To a small degree, religious localization did occur among the Chinese migrants in Malaysia. The Malay cult of *keramat*, for instance, had been incorporated into the Chinese

---

78. Tan Chee-Beng, "Socio-Cultural Diversities," 65.

79. 梁燕城, 文化中國蓄勢待發 (Cultural China Is Developing) (臺北 (Taipei): 宇宙光, 2006), 88.

80. 張秀明, "東南亞華人的文化認同," 於華僑華人研究文集: 紀念中國華僑華人歷史研究所成立20周年 (北京: 新華書店, 2005), 141-155 (145).

81. Peter Rowan, *Proclaiming the Peacemaker: The Malaysian Church as an Agent of Reconciliation in a Multicultural Society* (Oxford: Regnum, 2012), 53-56.

82. Rachel Sing-Kiat Ting and Alvin Lai Oon Ng, "Use of Religious Resources in Psychotherapy from a Tradition-Sensitive Approach: Cases from Chinese in Malaysia," *Pastoral Psychology* 61 (2012): 941-957 (942-943).

83. Tan Chee-Beng, "The Religions of the Chinese in Malaysia," in *The Chinese in Malaysia*, ed. Lee Kam Hing and Tan Chee-Beng (Oxford: Oxford University Press, 2000), 282-314 (310-311).

84. Tan Chee-Beng, "Introduction: After Migration and Religious Affiliation," in *After Migration and Religious Affiliation: Religions, Chinese Identities and Transnational Networks*, ed. Tan Chee-Beng (Singapore: World Scientific, 2014), xvii-xxxii (xxi).

85. Tan Chee-Beng, "The Religions of the Chinese in Malaysia," 282.

86. Kang San Tan, "Evangelical Missiology from an East Asian Perspective: A Study on Christian Encounter with People of Other Faiths," in *Global Missiology for the 21ˢᵗ Century: The Iguassu Dialogue*, ed. William D. Taylor (Grand Rapids, MI: Baker Academic, 2000), 295-306 (297).

concept of earth god, resulting in the addition of the Sino-Malayan earth deity Na Du Gong (拿督公) of the region.[87] The cult of *keramat* is a product of Islamic mysticism which worships saints (*keramat*), and the concept of *keramat* was transformed into Chinese as Na Du Gong (or Datuk Kong).[88]

On the other hand, Malaysian Chinese play a significant role in urbanization processes in Malaysia.[89] As Voon rightly points out, "The Chinese were inseparably connected with the initial and subsequent development of many towns that literally grew out of the jungle."[90] For example, the founding of Kuala Lumpur, the capital of Malaysia, was closely associated with the pioneering efforts of the Chinese traders and workers.[91] Today, the urbanization level of the Malaysian Chinese community is more than 86 percent. Of the entire Chinese population in Malaysia, about 30 percent live in the Klang Valley, a region including Kuala Lumpur, Petaling Jaya, and some other component districts in Selangor.[92]

As for educational attainment, there is a remarkable improvement among the Chinese in the post-independence period of Malaysia. For example, more than 30 percent of Malaysian Chinese who were born between 1936 and 1940 had never been to school and 46 percent of them obtained only primary education. Forty years later, for the Chinese who were born between years 1976 to 1980, more than 99 percent had been to school and 73 percent of them received at least upper secondary education.[93]

---

87. Tan Chee-Beng, *Chinese Religion in Malaysia: Temples and Communities* (Leiden: Brill, 2018), 66–67.

88. Lee Yok Fee and Chin Yee Mun, "Datuk Kong Worship and Chinese Religion in Malaysia: Reflections of Syncretism, Pragmatism and Inclusiveness," in *After Migration*, 147–165 (152).

89. Nai Peng Tey, "Demographic Trends and Human Capital: The Case of Malaysian Chinese," in *Malaysian Chinese and Nation-Building: Before Merdeka and Fifty Years After*, vol. 1, ed. Phin Keong Voon (Kuala Lumpur: Centre for Malaysian Chinese Studies, 2007), 307–338 (313).

90. Phin Keong Voon, "Pioneers, Entrepreneurs, and Labourers: Building the Social and Economic Foundations of Statehood," in *Malaysian Chinese and Nation-Building*, 43–94 (59).

91. Voon, 59–63.

92. Nai Peng Tey, "Demographic Trends," 313–314.

93. Nai Peng Tey, "Demographic Trends," 320.

1.2.3 Chinese Christians in Malaysia

Christianity has had a long history in Malaysia. Roman Catholicism first came to the region in 1511, when the Portuguese conquered Melaka. In the seventeenth century, the Dutch conquered Melaka and brought Protestant Christianity to the region.[94] Malaysia's first Protestant church, Christ Church Malacca, was built in 1753.[95] As for mission works in East Malaysia, they mainly began during the rule of James Brooke, a British soldier and adventurer who became Rajah of Sarawak. James Brooke ruled Sarawak from 1841 to 1868, and he was convinced that his divine calling was to introduce civilization, commerce, and Christianity into Borneo.[96] In 1847, the Borneo Church Mission (Anglican) started work among the Dyak.[97]

Chinese Protestant churches were established in the early nineteenth century. In 1815, Robert Morrison of the London Missionary Society (LMS) sent William Milne and his young family to Melaka to establish a base for the mission. Milne arrived in Melaka in May 1815 and soon started to preach the gospel to the local Chinese in Chinese temples.[98] In 1818, Morrison and Milne founded the Anglo-Chinese College in Melaka. Beside instructing missionaries and others in oriental cultures and languages, the college also served as a school to teach English and Christian faith to Chinese youth.[99] Milne, together with the first Chinese Protestant minister Liang Fa (梁發), established a printing press in Melaka. Since then, Christianity began to take root among the Chinese society in Malaysia.[100]

---

94. John Roxborogh, *A History of Christianity in Malaysia* (Singapore: Genesis, 2014), 1–10.

95. Daniel K. C. Ho, "The Church in Malaysia," in *Church in Asia Today: Challenges and Opportunities*, ed. Saphir Athyal (Singapore: The Asia Lausanne Committee for World Evangelization, 1996), 266–298 (271).

96. Jin Huat Tan, *Planting an Indigenous Church: The Case of the Borneo Evangelical Mission* (Oxford: Regnum Books International, 2011), 14–15.

97. Kim Sai Tan, "Chinese Christians in Malaysia," in *Malaysian Chinese: An Inclusive Society*, ed. Centre for Malaysian Chinese Studies (Kuala Lumpur: Centre for Malaysian Chinese Studies, 2011), 111–142 (112).

98. Roxborogh, *A History*, 13–15.

99. Robert Hunt, "Christian Schools in Malaysia: An Assesment in History," in *The Pursuit of God's Cause: A Collection of Essays on the Life and Impact of the Evangelical Church in Malaysia* (Petaling Jaya: NECF, 1998), 187–242 (191).

100. 羅曼華編, 華人教會手冊 (*Chinese Churches Handbook*) (香港 (Hong Kong): 世界華人福音事工聯絡中心,1981), 184. Unfortunately, two hundred years after Milne began to preach the gospel to the Malaysian Chinese, Chinese Christians in the region only

Chinese literary productions produced by LMS in Melaka include the Morrison Chinese Bible, the first Chinese news magazine entitled *The Monthly Total Record of the Inspection of Worldly Custom* (察世俗每月統計傳), *A Dictionary of the Chinese Language*, and over a hundred other titles.[101] After the First Opium War (1839–1842), with the opening of the five treaty ports in China, a large number of Chinese from southern China were immigrating to Malaysia. These Chinese immigrants soon became a significant mission field for the early Christian missionaries in Malaysia.[102]

On the other hand, the immigrations of Chinese Christians from China also contributed to the developments of Chinese churches in Malaysia.[103] In 1882, the British North Borneo Company, with the help of Swiss Basel Mission missionary Rudolph Lechler, recruited a hundred Chinese Hakka Christians to Kudat, Sabah to help develop the territory. Later in 1886, the first Basel Christian Church in Sabah was founded.[104] Between 1901 and 1902, Methodist Pastor Wong Nai Siong (黃乃裳) led three batches totaling 1,118 Chinese from southern China to Sibu, Sarawak. Two-thirds of these Chinese migrants were Christians.[105] Sibu eventually became one of the major centres of Chinese Methodists in Malaysia.[106] In 1938, the Baptist congregation in Alor Setar was also founded by the immigrants from southern China.[107]

Today there are about 5,000 Christian churches of various traditions and denominations in Malaysia. Kim Sai Tan estimates the number of congregations where those of Chinese heritage are in the majority is about 1,600 (includes only non-Catholic churches),[108] and about 1,200 of these Chinese congregations are Chinese speaking or bilingual (Chinese and English).[109]

---

represent about 4.2 percent of the whole Malaysian Chinese population today. See 陳偉柏,"大馬華人民間信仰者歸信基督教的初探," 教牧期刊24 (2008), 135–159 (156).

101. Kim Sai Tan, "Chinese Christians in Malaysia," 119.

102. Lee Kam Hing, "The Christian Brethren," in *Christianity in Malaysia: A Denominational History*, ed. Robert Hunt, Lee Kam Hing, and John Roxborogh (Petaling Jaya: Pelanduk, 1992), 107–141 (110).

103. Tan Chee-Beng, "The Religions of the Chinese in Malaysia," 303.

104. Kim Sai Tan, "Chinese Christians in Malaysia," 127.

105. Tan Chee-Beng, "The Religions of the Chinese in Malaysia," 304.

106. Tan Chee-Beng, 305.

107. Tan Chee-Beng, 303.

108. Kim Sai Tan, "Chinese Christians in Malaysia," 114.

109. Kim Sai Tan, 114–115.

According to the 2010 Census, Christianity comprise 9.2 percent of the total population of Malaysia. Of these Malaysian Christians, including members of Catholic churches and all other denominations, 706,479 were Chinese (about 11 percent of 6,392,636 Chinese).[110]

1.3 Aim of the Research

The aim of this study is to investigate the principles involved in formulating contextualized preaching for the Malaysian Chinese during the Spring Festival, the Qing Ming Festival, and the Hungry Ghost Festival. It uses qualitative research to investigate experienced Chinese preachers' perceptions and practices regarding contextualized preaching during these three festivals, as well as studying the celebrations of the festivals through field research. The study examines religious beliefs, cultural values, and practices associated with these three festivals. It also evaluates them in the light of any relevant biblical teaching. The study seeks to distinguish what particular aspects of beliefs or practices of these festivals are contradictory to Christian convictions and which aspects can be used to contextualize the preaching of the gospel effectively. Moreover, this research aims to identify a cluster of theological issues for Chinese Christians in dealing with these traditional festivals.

1.4 Objectives of the Study

This study aims to achieve the following objectives:
1. To investigate experienced Chinese preachers' perceptions and practices with regard to contextualized preaching during three major Chinese festivals: the Spring Festival, the Qing Ming Festival, and the Hungry Ghost Festival.
2. To identify biblical principles in shaping a response to religious beliefs, cultural values, and practices associated with these three festivals.

---

110. Department of Statistics Malaysia, *Population and Housing Census of Malaysia 2010: Population Distribution and Basic Demographic Characteristics* (Putrajaya: DSM, 2010), 9.

3. To clarify the principles involved in formulating contextualized preaching to the Chinese people based on the findings and analysis of this study.

1.5 Research Methodology

In order to facilitate the research, two research methods were used in this study to allow different yet complementary research questions to be asked. First, the exploratory study of the Spring Festival, the Qing Ming Festival, and the Hungry Ghost Festival was done through field observation combined with an examination and analysis of relevant and influential texts. Data collection was undertaken through observation of some festival celebrations, visits to libraries and archives, and an analysis of relevant documents.

Besides an exploratory study of the festivals, second, a series of semi-structured, face-to-face interviews also took place with six experienced Chinese preachers. By this method, this research strived to gather and analyse their perceptions and practices regarding preaching during the Spring Festival, the Qing Ming Festival, and the Hungry Ghost Festival, and to identify principles and ways to encode the gospel message for these festivals. The research interviews were conducted in Chinese.

1.6 Research Questions

The overarching research question that the study focused on is as follows: What are experienced Chinese preachers' perceptions and practices with regard to contextualized preaching during the Spring Festival, the Qing Ming Festival, and the Hungry Ghost Festival? Under the overarching question, six sub-questions worked as guidance for this study. There are the following:
1. How do experienced Chinese preachers perceive contextualized preaching during the Spring Festival, the Qing Ming Festival, and the Hungry Ghost Festival?
2. What are experienced Chinese preachers' experiences of preaching during the Spring Festival, the Qing Ming Festival, and the Hungry Ghost Festival?
3. According to experienced Chinese preachers, which aspects of the religious beliefs, cultural values, and practices associated with the

Spring Festival, the Qing Ming Festival, and the Hungry Ghost Festival are in harmony with the Christian faith?

4. According to experienced Chinese preachers, which aspects of the religious beliefs, cultural values, and practices associated with the Spring Festival, the Qing Ming Festival, and the Hungry Ghost Festival are contrary to the Christian faith?

5. According to experienced Chinese preachers, which elements of the religious beliefs, cultural values, and practices associated with the Spring Festival, the Qing Ming Festival, and the Hungry Ghost Festival, either contrary to or in harmony with the Christian faith, can be used to contextualize the preaching of the gospel effectively?

6. According to experienced Chinese preachers, what theological resources can be used in contextualizing the preaching of the gospel during the Spring Festival, the Qing Ming Festival, and the Hungry Ghost Festival?

1.7 Significance of the Study

In studying Malaysian Chinese culture, besides studying the teachings from Chinese classics, focusing on the customs is also very important.[111] This study argues that research on contextualized preaching during Chinese festivals will contribute to a better understanding of contextualization of the gospel in the Chinese culture. Through studying Chinese festivals, greater insight will be gained into the way Malaysian Chinese people think, as well as a better understanding of their worldviews, core values, and beliefs. The overall importance of this study is to gain knowledge of preaching the gospel in culturally relevant ways to the Malaysian Chinese during specific Chinese festivals, especially the Spring Festival, the Qing Ming Festival, and the Hungry Ghost Festival.

This study will look not only for similarities between Christianity and Malaysian Chinese culture, but the differences between them as well. As Hesselgrave points out, understanding the differences between Christianity

---

111. 王錦發, "大馬華人與中華文化" (Chinese Malaysian and Chinese Culture), 於中華文化之路: 中華文化邁向二十一世紀國際學術研討會論文集 (*The Direction of Chinese Culture: Essays on Chinese Culture toward the 21st Century*), 林水檺與何國忠編 (吉隆坡 (Kuala Lumpur): 馬來西亞中華大會堂聯合會, 1995) 263–273 (270).

and other religions can be an important factor for the effective communication of the gospel.[112] Moreover, this research can be valuable for Chinese Christians. It will give them new insights in deciding how to deal with traditional Chinese festivals, and which cultural aspects should be abandoned and which should be retained. Finally, this work is significant for the development of contextual theology for the Chinese church, since many theological issues will be discussed in light of both biblical teaching and the Chinese cultural context.

The observations made in this study, however, are specific to the observations and interviews undertaken and should not too readily be generalised and taken to represent the Chinese people, including overseas Chinese, as a whole. Shelly Chan in her recent work *Diaspora's Homeland* has helpfully reminded us of the complexity of studying Chinese people in China and globally.[113] Thus, cultural heterogeneity of the Chinese around the world should be taken into consideration to avoid any inappropriate generalisation in this study.

1.8 Delimitations of the Study

1.8.1 Three Major Chinese Festivals as Focus of Study

Chinese festivals are quite numerous, but three of them, namely the Spring Festival, the Qing Ming Festival, and the Hungry Ghost Festival, are the focus of discussion in this study. The Chinese traditional festivals are celebrated according to the lunar calendar. From a general point of view, there are two main categories among Chinese festivals. They are the "festivals of the living" and the "festivals of the dead." Festivals of the living are for celebration while festivals of the dead are memorials for the deceased and ancestral worship.[114] Of all the festivals of the living, Spring Festival is the biggest celebration. In

---

112. David J. Hesselgrave, "Christian Communication and Religious Pluralism: Capitalizing on Differences," *Missiology* 18 (1990), 131–138 (134–135).

113. Shelly Chan, *Diaspora's Homeland: Modern China in the Age of Global Migration* (Durham: Duke University Press, 2018), 6–8.

114. Daniel Tong, *A Biblical Approach to Chinese Traditions and Beliefs*, new ed. (Singapore: Genesis, 2012), 31.

fact, it is the most significant of all the Chinese festivals.[115] It is also the most celebrated by Chinese people worldwide.

On the other hand, the Qing Ming Festival and the Hungry Ghost Festival are considered the most important rituals among the festivals of the dead. The Qing Ming Festival is important to the Chinese because of its emphasis on ancestral worship and on filial piety, one of the core values of Chinese culture. The other Chinese festival which should not be neglected is the Hungry Ghost Festival because it is strongly related to the beliefs of Chinese Buddhism, Taoism, Chinese folk religion, and even Confucianism.

Within the Malaysian context, the Spring Festival, the Qing Ming Festival, and the Hungry Ghost Festival are the three most important festivals to the Chinese who observe traditional religious beliefs. All three festivals are being celebrated on a large scale in Malaysian Chinese society. These festivals, as Chee-Beng Tan rightly indicates, "are major occasions for worshipping deities and ancestors, and even ghosts."[116]

1.8.2 Interviewing Six Experienced Chinese Preachers

This study essentially adopts an *emic* perspective. The Christian linguist Kenneth L. Pike, in 1954, used the terms *etic* and *emic* to contrast human behaviour. Pike explained, "the *etic* view is an alien view – the structuring of an outsider. The *emic* view is domestic, leading to units which correspond to those of an insider familiar with and participating in the system."[117] Pike coined the terms *etic* and *emic* by utilizing the last half of the terms *phonetic* (concerning the raw sound of a language) and *phonemic* (concerning the structural units in the sound system of a language) which are used in linguistics.[118] According to Charles H. Kraft, an *emic* perspective is the "folk perspective" of inside participants in a given culture. On the other hand, an *etic* perspective is that of outside analysts.[119] As Hoebel and Weaver point out,

---

115. Choon San Wong, *An Illustrated Cycle of Chinese Festivities in Malaysia and Singapore* (Singapore: Jack Chia-MPH, 1987), 45.

116. Tan Chee-Beng, "The Religions of the Chinese in Malaysia," 293–294.

117. Kenneth L. Pike, "Language and Life: A Stereoscopic Window on the World," *BSac* 114 (1957): 141–156 (145).

118. Kenneth L. Pike, "My Pilgrimage in Mission," *IBMR* 21 (1997): 159–161 (161).

119. Charles H. Kraft, *Christianity in Culture: A Study in Dynamic Biblical Theologizing in Cross-Cultural Perspective* (Maryknoll, NY: Orbis, 1981), 293.

emic is the inside view, while *etic* is the view from an observer who is not, by training and living, thoroughly enculturated in the culture observed and being written about.[120] Parshall believes *etic* understandings are alien and often fail to adequately deal with issues that are crucial to insiders. On the other hand, *emic* perspectives provide a view that is grappling for answers from within, and such an approach is vastly superior to a purely *etic* one.[121]

All six Chinese preachers who were interviewed in this study are considered as "insiders" or experts on Chinese cultural matters who also have a clear understanding of the Chinese festivals. Three of the interviewees selected are Malaysian Chinese preachers. Since all the field research observations were conducted among Chinese communities in Malaysia, interviewing preachers from the Chinese churches in this region is considered most appropriate. The other three interviewees selected for this study are preachers in Hong Kong. These Hong Kong preachers were selected due to their extensive preaching experience and their practical knowledge of dealing with Chinese religious beliefs and customs from a Chinese Christian perspective. All three of them have some publications on the related subjects, and their publications are considered as helpful sources for Malaysian Chinese Christians. In respect of involving Hong Kong interviewees, however, further clarifications are needed.

First and foremost, this study by no means assumes that Malaysia and Hong Kong are identical in every aspect. After all, Malaysia is a Southeast Asiaian country with Chinese as minority, and Hong Kong is a special administrative region of China with Chinese as the overwhelming majority. However, it is worth mentioning that there are some similarities between Malaysian Chinese and Hong Kong Chinese. First, they were once both subject to British colonial control, and people in these two areas are to some degree westernized, yet Chinese traditional culture continues to have an evident influence on the Chinese in both areas. Second, both Malaysian Chinese culture and Hong Kong Chinese culture can be traced to roots in southern China. Third, both the majority of Malaysian Chinese and Hong Kong Chinese practice Chinese religious traditions.

---

120. E. Adamson Hoebel and Thomas Weaver, *Anthropology and the Human Experience* (New York: McGraw-Hill, 1979), 523.

121. Phil Parshall, *New Paths in Muslim Evangelism* (Grand Rapids, MI: Baker, 1980), 41–42.

Besides the similarities of their Chinese cultural background, there are two main reasons to include experienced Hong Kong preachers in this study. The fact that this study is focusing only on preaching during three major Chinese festivals is the first main reason. Similar to the context of Malaysian Chinese communities, the Spring Festival, the Qing Ming Festival, and the Hungry Ghost Festival have been celebrated on a large scale in Hong Kong as well. Even though some minor localization of the festivals is unavoidable, overall it is believed that elements of the religious beliefs, cultural values, and practices associated with these three festivals remain the same in Malaysia as well as in Hong Kong. The field observations in this study, combined with an examination and analysis of relevant and influential texts, are supportive evidence to this claim.

The second reason for interviewing experienced Hong Kong preachers is to value their possible contribution to this study, because Hong Kong is considered as one of the main sources of Chinese Christian cultural links for Chinese Christians in Malaysia.[122] Christianity in Hong Kong has a history that dates back to the 1840s.[123] Today, Chinese churches in Hong Kong play an important role within worldwide Chinese churches.[124] Even the headquarters of the Chinese Coordination Centre of World Evangelism (CCCOWE) is based in Hong Kong. Hong Kong's regional and global influences should not be ignored in Chinese Christianity. As Mandryk indicates, Hong Kong "continues to be the source of many missionaries as well as a hub for financing ministry, outreach, discipling, media and literature ministries to the Chinese-speaking world in particular."[125] Thus, interviewing Chinese preachers from Malaysia as well as from Hong Kong provides a better understanding of Chinese preachers' perceptions and practices regarding contextualized preaching during the Chinese festivals. While a more extensive piece of research that included Taiwan and Singapore would provide a more comprehensive account of Chinese preachers' perceptions and practices regarding contextualized preaching during the Chinese festivals, this expansion is beyond the scope of this study. Although this study will rely more on

---

122. Tan Chee-Beng, "The Religions of the Chinese in Malaysia," 309. According to Tan, Taiwan is the other one.

123. 羅曼華編, 華人教會手冊, 56.

124. 呂焯安, "香港小型教會發展初探," 教牧期刊 15 (2003): 3–65 (3).

125. Mandryk, *Operation World*, 253.

emic perspectives, it will reflect critically upon these perspectives in light of biblical teaching and other possible *etic* perspectives. After all, Hiebert suggests that the best approach of cultural study seems to use both *emic* and *etic* approaches.[126]

1.9 Definition of Terms

1.9.1 Culture

Raymond Williams said that the term *culture* is one of the two or three most complicated words in the English language because the term has now come to be used for important concepts in several distinct intellectual disciplines and in several distinct and incompatible systems of thought.[127] In fact, there is long-running, shifting, international discussion about the concept of culture.[128]

The word "culture" originally comes from the Latin *colere*, which can mean anything from cultivating and inhabiting to worshipping and protecting.[129] According to Williams in *Keywords*, "culture in all its early uses was a noun of process: the tending of something, basically crops or animals. By the sixteenth century, the meaning of culture extended from 'the tending of natural growth' to 'a process of human development.'"[130]

In the eighteenth century, as Eagleton points out, culture became synonymous with the term *civilization*. Civilization was mainly a French notion. As a synonym of civilization, culture belonged to the spirit of Enlightenment, emphasizing the general process of intellectual, spiritual, and material progress.[131] This Enlightenment view of culture is represented as a progressive, cumulative, distinctively human achievement.[132] Culture in this sense was engaged in a great struggle to overcome the resistance of traditional cultures,

---

126. Hiebert, *Cultural Anthropology*, 54.
127. Raymond Williams, *Keywords: A Vocabulary of Culture and Society* (London: Fontana, 1983), 87.
128. Adam Kuper, *Culture: The Anthropologists' Account* (Cambridge, MA: Harvard University Press, 1999), ix.
129. Terry Eagleton, *The Idea of Culture* (Malden, MA: Blackwell, 2000), 2.
130. Williams, *Keywords*, 87.
131. Eagleton, *Idea of Culture*, 9.
132. Kuper, *Culture*, 5.

with their superstitions, irrational prejudices, and fearful loyalties to cynical rulers.[133]

According to Eagleton, the notion of culture changed around the turn of the nineteenth century in Germany.[134] German philosopher Johann Gottfried Herder argued that it is necessary to speak of cultures in the plural: the specific and variable cultures of different nations and periods, but also the specific and variable cultures of social and economic groups within a nation.[135] Herder insisted that culture means not some grand and unilinear narrative of universal humanity, but a diversity of specific life-forms. In a sense, Herder was against the Eurocentrism claim of superiority of European culture.[136] This notion of culture was widely developed during the Romantic era in Germany. Thus the word culture, or *kultur* in German, was used to emphasize national and traditional cultures. Whether used generally or specifically, culture in this sense indicates a particular way of life, whether of a people, a period, a group, or humanity in general.[137]

In 1871, English anthropologist Edward Burnett Tylor provided a definition of culture which is considered one of his great contributions to the discipline of anthropology. Tylor proclaimed that culture is "that complex whole which includes knowledge, belief, art, morals, law, custom, and any other capabilities and habits acquired by man as a member of society."[138] According to Tylor, culture comprises learned capabilities and habits of human beings. These human attributes are learned and learnable and are therefore passed on socially and mentally rather than biologically.[139] As Roger and Felix Keesing point out, the concept of culture adopted by nineteenth-century anthropologists has spread to other fields of thought with profound impact and has been one of the most important and influential ideas in twentieth-century thought.[140]

---

133. Kuper, 7.
134. Eagleton, *Idea of Culture*, 9.
135. Williams, *Keywords*, 89.
136. Eagleton, *Idea of Culture*, 12.
137. Williams, *Keywords*, 89.
138. Edward B. Tylor, *Primitive Culture: Researches into the Development of Mythology, Philosophy, Religion, Language, Art, and Custom* (London: John Murray, 1871), 1.
139. Gerald A. Arbuckle, *Culture, Inculturation, and Theologians: A Postmodern Critique* (Collegeville, MN: Liturgical, 2010), 2.
140. Roger M. Keesing and Felix M. Keesing, *New Perspectives in Cultural Anthropology* (New York: Holt, Rinehart, and Winston, 1971), 19–20.

One of the contributions of this notion of culture is that it distinguishes the transmission of culture from the biological heritage of humans. Cultures as learned behaviours are passed on from one generation to another. They are transmitted by the society, not by genes.[141] Geert Hofstede and Gert Jan Hofstede point out that culture as "software of the mind" derives from one's social environment. They believe culture is "learned, not innate." Every person carries within him or herself patterns of thinking, feeling, and potential acting that were learned throughout their lifetime within social environments.[142] Ken Gnanakan illuminates this clearly when he uses Indian culture as an example: "Culture is not biologically transferred. An Indian baby adopted by Swedish parents cannot be expected to automatically demonstrate Indian culture. It has to grow up in the Indian culture assimilating that particular worldview in order for it to truly depict the distinctive of Indian culture."[143]

According to Tylor's definition, moreover, culture is a "complex whole," within which unity and harmony are key assumptions.[144] Today, many scholars define culture similarly. Richard Niebuhr, for example, believes culture comprises "language, habits, ideas, beliefs, customs, social organization, inherited artifacts, technical process, and values."[145] Gerry Phillipsen, likewise, says culture is "a socially constructed and historically transmitted pattern of symbols, meanings, premises, and rules."[146] Hiebert has concisely summarized the concept of culture as follows: "the more or less integrated systems of ideas, feelings and values and their associated patterns of behaviour and products shared by a group of people who organize and regulate what they think, feel and do."[147] All these definitions have much in common with Tylor's. They consider culture as a "complex whole."

---

141. Eugene A. Nida, *Customs, Culture and Christianity* (London: Tyndale, 1954), 28.

142. Geert Hofstede and Gert Jan Hofstede, *Cultures and Organizations: Software of the Mind* (New York: McGraw Hill, 2005), 3–4.

143. Ken Gnanakan, "Christ, Culture and Christianity in India," in *Doing Theology in Context: Festschrift in Honour of Dr. Bruce J. Nicholls*, ed. Sunand Sumithra (Bangalore: Theological Book Trust, 1992), 67–78 (71).

144. Arbuckle, *Culture*, 2.

145. H. Richard Niebuhr, *Christ and Culture* (New York: Harper & Row, 1975), 32.

146. Gerry Phillipsen, *Speaking Culturally: Exploration in Social Communication* (Albany: State University of New York, 1992), 7.

147. Hiebert, *Anthropological Insights*, 30.

The present study adopts a definition of culture following the Willowbank Report, because the definition rightly highlights the fact that culture is a multifarious system. According to the Willowbank Report,

> culture is an integrated system of beliefs (about God or reality or ultimate meaning), of values (about what is true, good, beautiful and normative), of customs (how to behave, relate to others, talk, pray, dress, work, play, trade, farm, eat, etc.), and of institutions which express these beliefs, values and customs (government, law courts, temples or churches, family, schools, hospitals, factories, shops, unions, clubs, etc.) which bind a society together and give it a sense of identity, dignity, security, and continuity.[148]

1.9.2 Gospel

"At one level, what one takes to be the gospel is whatever lies at the heart of one's preaching," Paul Scott Wilson says.[149] The gospel is the heart and life-giving force of Christian belief. Ted Peters calls the gospel the Christian identity principle because it identifies what is Christian.[150] Indeed, the gospel is essential to the ministry of the church and gives basic shape to everything the church does.[151] Timothy Keller comments, "Every form of ministry is empowered by the gospel, based on the gospel, and is a result of the gospel."[152] But what is the gospel? This is perhaps the most important question we can ask today.[153] This question, however, is not an easy one. Greg Gilbert says if we ask one hundred evangelical Christians what is the gospel, we would likely receive about sixty different answers.[154]

---

148. Quotation from 312–313 of "The Willowbank Report" in *Down to Earth*, 308–339.
149. Paul Scott Wilson, *Setting Words on Fire: Putting God at the Center of the Sermon* (Nashville, TN: Abingdon, 2008), 55.
150. Ted Peters, "What Is the Gospel?," *PRSt* 13 (1986): 21–43 (21).
151. Millard J. Erickson, *Christian Theology*, 2nd ed. (Grand Rapids, MI: Baker, 2001), 1069.
152. Timothy Keller, *Center Church: Doing Balanced, Gospel-Centered Ministry in Your City* (Grand Rapids, MI: Zondervan, 2012), 36.
153. Scot McKnight, *The King Jesus Gospel: The Original Good News Revisited* (Grand Rapids, MI: Zondervan, 2011), 23.
154. Greg Gilbert, *What Is the Gospel?* (Wheaton, IL: Crossway, 2010), 18.

Various understandings of the gospel prevail today. James I. Packer asserts that the task of laying out the contents of the gospel in full is complicated, because "the material is abundant, varied, and occasional."[155] John Piper rightly reminds us that there are two extremes we need to avoid when defining the word "gospel." He explains, "One extreme would be to define the Christian gospel so broadly that everything good in the Christian message is called gospel, and the other would be to define the Christian gospel so narrowly that the definition cannot do justice to all the uses in the New Testament."[156]

Graeme Goldsworthy defines the gospel as "the event (or the proclamation of that event) of Jesus Christ that begins with his incarnation and earthly life, and concludes with his death, resurrection and ascension to the right hand of the Father. This historical event is interpreted by God as his preordained programme for the salvation of the world."[157] According to Goldsworthy, "If something is not what God did in and through the historical Jesus two thousand years ago, it is not the gospel."[158] He thinks one should not confuse the gospel with the need for the gospel (sin and judgment), the means of receiving the benefits of the gospel (faith and repentance), or the results of the gospel (regeneration, conversion, sanctification, and glorification). Goldsworthy believes these elements are important but are not themselves the gospel.[159]

Others want to define the gospel in broader dimensions. Jacob A. Loewen lists five reasons why it is important to see the gospel in its broadest as well as deepest dimensions: (1) The biblical message is multifaceted. (2) In every Christian's spiritual journey, different facets of biblical truth come into prominence at different times. (3) Different cultures will find different facets of the gospel more meaningful than others. (4) Different cultural backgrounds and their concomitant presuppositions will cause people to hear differing content from the gospel message. (5) Christian community in each culture must take the responsibility for contextualizing the gospel in their own setting.

---

155. James I. Packer, "The Gospel: Its Content and Communication – A Theological Perspective," in *Down to Earth*, 97–114 (110–111).

156. John Piper, *God Is the Gospel: Meditations on God's Love as the Gift of Himself* (Leicester: Inter-Varsity Press, 2005), 26.

157. Graeme Goldsworthy, *Gospel-Centered Hermeneutics* (Nottingham: Apollos, 2006), 58.

158. Goldsworthy, 59.

159. Goldsworthy, 59.

Therefore, they need a deep conviction that God is speaking specifically and directly to them.[160] Samuel Escobar, at the 1974 Lausanne Conference, warned evangelicals to avoid the temptation of reducing the gospel.[161] John Piper proposes understanding the gospel as the good news of our full enjoyment of the glory of God in the face of Christ. He declares, "The Christian gospel is not merely that Jesus died and rose again; and not merely that these events appease God's wrath, forgive sin, and justify sinners; and not merely that this redemption gets us out of hell and into heaven; but that they bring us to the glory of God in the face of Jesus Christ as our supreme, all-satisfying, and everlasting treasure."[162]

Another recent attempt to explain the gospel in wider dimensions was undertaken by Greg Gilbert. According to Gilbert, four issues lie at the heart of the gospel: "We are accountable to the God who created us. We have sinned against that God and will be judged. But God has acted in Jesus Christ to save us, and we take hold of that salvation by repentance from sin and faith in Jesus." Thus he summarizes the gospel in four words: God, man, Christ, and response.[163]

Sensing the need for a fresh articulation of the gospel of Jesus Christ,[164] a group of evangelical leaders who would go for a more traditional definition decided to draft a wide-ranging statement. In June 1999, *Christianity Today* published a reference document, "The Gospel of Jesus Christ: An Evangelical Celebration."[165] In this document, the drafting committee framed an opening statement of commitment to evangelicalism, followed by a series of

---

160. Jacob A. Loewen, "The Gospel: Its Content and Communication – An Anthropological Perspective," in *Down to Earth*, 115–130 (118–122).

161. Escobar sees the danger of presenting a saving work of Christ message without the consequent ethical demands. See Samuel Escobar, "Evangelism and Man's Search for Freedom, Justice and Fulfillment," in *Let the Earth Hear His Voice*, 303–326 (310).

162. Piper, *God Is the Gospel*, 167.

163. Gilbert, *What Is the Gospel?* 32.

164. In 1999, David Neff underscored that many evangelicals do not have thorough understanding of the gospel. See David Neff, "A Call to Evangelical Unity," *Christianity Today* 14 (June 1999): 49.

165. "The Gospel of Jesus Christ: An Evangelical Celebration," *Christianity Today* 14 (June 1999): 51–56. The drafting committee included J. I. Packer, John N. Akers, Timothy George, John Ankerberg, R. C. Sproul, Harold Myra, David Neff, John Armstrong, Thomas C. Oden, D. A. Carson, Scott Hafemann, Keith Davey, Maxie Dunnam, Erwin Lutzer, and John Woodbridge. See "Introduction," in *This We Believe: The Good News of Jesus Christ for the World*, ed. John N. Akers, John H. Armstrong, and John D. Woodbridge (Grand Rapids, MI: Zondervan, 2000), 18.

affirmations and denials with respect to the gospel.[166] The document proclaims, "The heart of the gospel is that our holy, loving Creator, confronted with human hostility and rebellion, has chosen in his own freedom and faithfulness to become our holy, loving Redeemer and Restorer. The Father has sent the Son to be the Saviour of the World."[167] Concerning the overall content of the gospel, this research affirms the proclamations written in "The Gospel of Jesus Christ: An Evangelical Celebration."[168]

One of the key issues in the contemporary discussion of the gospel is the place of the doctrine of justification by faith. In *The King Jesus Gospel*, McKnight criticizes contemporary evangelicals who have reduced the gospel to merely the plan of salvation. McKnight believes this problem exists because of the Reformation. According to him, the centre of gravity of the gospel after the Reformation was shifted toward the need for personal salvation.[169] McKnight considers that the plan of salvation, or justification by faith, is not the whole gospel. He believes that many evangelicals wrongly equate the word εὐαγγέλιον (gospel) with the word σωτηρία (salvation) and have thus created a "salvation culture" and have mistakenly assumed salvation is a "gospel culture."[170] For McKnight, the gospel is the saving story of Jesus that completes the story of Israel.[171]

N. T. Wright makes a similar critique. He points out that in many church circles today the gospel is merely a description of how people get saved. Wright says in older theology this would be called *ordo salutis*, an order of salvation.[172] Wright thinks that this is a misunderstanding of the gospel[173] and says, "Justification by faith is not what Paul means by the 'the gospel.' It is implied by the gospel; when the gospel is proclaimed, people come to faith and

---

166. R. C. Sproul, *Getting the Gospel Right: The Tie That Binds Evangelicals Together* (Grand Rapids, MI: Baker, 1999), 98.

167. Committee on Evangelical Unity in the Gospel, "The Gospel of Jesus Christ: An Evangelical Celebration," in *This We Believe*, 239–248 (241).

168. Committee on Evangelical Unity in the Gospel, "The Gospel of Jesus Christ." See also the appendix in this work.

169. McKnight, *King Jesus Gospel*, 71.

170. McKnight, *King Jesus Gospel*, 29–30.

171. McKnight, 111.

172. N. T. Wright, *What Saint Paul Really Said: Was Paul of Tarsus the Real Founder of Christianity?* (Grand Rapids, MI: Eerdmans, 1997), 40–41.

173. The most recent discussion of Wright's understanding of the gospel is found in N.T. Wright, *The Day the Revolution Began* (London: SPCK, 2016).

so are regarded by God as members of his people. But 'the gospel' is not an account of how people get saved."[174] Wright further criticizes some Christians' traditional approach of putting justification at the centre of theology. He believes such an approach will always be in danger of sustaining some sort of individualism.[175] For N. T. Wright, the gospel is a fourfold announcement concerning Jesus: (1) In Jesus of Nazareth, specifically in his cross, the decisive victory has been won over all the powers of evil, including sin and death themselves. (2) In Jesus's resurrection the New Age has dawned, inaugurating the long-awaited time when the prophecies would be fulfilled, Israel's exile would be over, and the whole world would be addressed by the one creator God. (3) The crucified and risen Jesus was, all along, Israel's Messiah, her representative king. (4) Jesus was therefore also the Lord, the true king of the world, the one at whose name every knee would bow.[176]

On one hand, both McKnight's and Wright's reminders are much needed. Equating the whole gospel with only the doctrine of justification is indeed inappropriate. It is important to remember that there is an irreducible complexity to the gospel, and it cannot be tamed into a single simple formula.[177] On the other hand, this research affirms the significance of the doctrine of justification. The doctrine of justification is one of the central components of the gospel, albeit it may not constitute the whole gospel. It is obvious that the apostle Paul himself emphasizes the concept of justification in the gospel. For example in Galatians 3:13–14, Paul stresses the intercanonical theme of the law court. Jesus takes the curse of the law for us.[178] In Romans 8:30, Paul also mentions justification explicitly when he gives an overview of the process of salvation.[179] John Stott says, "Justification (its source God and his grace, its ground Christ and his cross, and its means faith alone, altogether apart from works) is the heart of the gospel and unique to Christianity."[180] Karl Barth

---

174. Wright, *What Saint Paul Really Said*, 132–133.
175. Wright, 157–158.
176. Wright, *What Saint Paul Really Said*, 60.
177. Keller, *Center Church*, 39.
178. Keller, 39.
179. Wayne Grudem, *Systematic Theology: An Introduction to Biblical Doctrine* (Leicester: Inter-Varsity Press, 1994), 722.
180. John R. W. Stott, *Authentic Christianity: From the Writings of John Stott*, ed. Timothy Dudley-Smith (Downers Grove, IL: InterVarsity Press, 1995), 171.

even declares in his *Church Dogmatics*, "There never was and there never can be any true Christian Church without the doctrine of justification."[181] A right understanding of justification is therefore the dividing line between the biblical gospel of salvation by faith alone and all false gospels of salvation based on good works.[182]

As mentioned previously, *gospel* is not a simple term. Various biblical writers, for example the apostle John and the Synoptic writers, express the gospel in somewhat different ways. According to Keller, for instance, John emphasizes the individual dimension of the gospel, while Synoptic writers emphasize the corporate dimensions.[183] Although this research will not elaborate extensively on the content of the gospel, it will undertake a brief overview of the basic doctrinal core of the gospel. The immediate task is to identify the material content of the gospel by turning to the Bible. The Greek Old Testament and the New Testament supply the noun εὐαγγέλιον (gospel) seventy-seven times and the verb εὐαγγελίζω (preach the gospel) seventy-seven times.[184] Many biblical texts are useful for examining the concept of the gospel.[185] However, some have suggested that the best place to start is 1 Corinthians 15.[186]

Commentators offer varied opinions on the structure of 1 Corinthians 15,[187] but most of them agree that this passage mainly refers to the gospel message.[188] In 1 Corinthians 15:1, Paul says to the Corinthians, "the gospel which

---

181. Karl Barth, *Church Dogmatics, IV: The Doctrine of Reconciliation*, ed. G. W. Bromiley and T. F. Torrance (Edinburgh: T&T Clark, 1956), 523.

182. Grudem, *Systematic Theology*, 722.

183. Keller, *Center Church*, 39.

184. Piper, *God Is the Gospel*, 25. For example in Luke 4:18–21, Jesus proclaims that he would εὐαγγελίσασθαι (preach the gospel) to the poor.

185. John 3:16; Rom 1:1–5; 5:8–11; 1 Cor 1–11; 2 Cor 5:18–21; Eph 2:8–9; Col 2:13–14; etc.

186. To fully understand the meaning of the gospel, McKnight suggests the best place to begin is 1 Corinthians 15. See McKnight, *King Jesus Gospel*, 46. D. A. Carson also discusses the gospel of Jesus Christ solely based on 1 Corinthians 15. See D. A. Carson, "The Gospel of Jesus Christ: 1 Corinthians 15:1–19," *TSFJ* (Spring, 2008): 1–11.

187. See Kenneth L. Chafin, *1, 2 Corinthians*. The Communicator's Commentary (Waco, TX: Word, 1985), 178–190. See also Joseph A. Fitzmyer, *First Corinthians: A New Translation with Introduction and Commentary*, The Anchor Yale Bible (New Haven, CT: Yale University Press, 2008), 540; Roy E. Ciampa and Brian S. Rosner, *The First Letter to the Corinthians*, The Pillar New Testament Commentary (Nottingham: Apollos, 2010), 741–742.

188. Ciampa and Rosner, *First Letter to the Corinthians*, 742–753. See also Fitzmyer, *First Corinthians*, 540–554; Chafin, *1, 2 Corinthians*, 178–181.

I preached to you." The Greek text reads, "τὸ εὐαγγέλιον ὃ εὐηγγελισάμην ὑμῖν," which can be translated as "the gospel I *gospeled* to you." In 1 Corinthians 15:2, Paul says, "the word which I preached to you." The Greek text reads, "τίνι λόγῳ εὐηγγελισάμην ὑμῖν," which can be translated as "the word which I *gospeled* to you." Thus in 1 Corinthians 15:1–2, Paul tells the Corinthians that he is going to talk specifically about the gospel.[189]

In 1 Corinthians 15:3–5, Paul details the main points of the content of the gospel. Through four clauses introduced by the Greek word ὅτι (that), Paul lists four main points: the death of Christ for our sins, his burial, his resurrection, and his appearance to Peter and to the Twelve.[190] In this passage, Paul underlines several facts of the gospel for his readers. First and foremost, Paul reminds them that the gospel is a message about Jesus Christ and what he has done for us, rather than a message primarily about us and how we can be saved.[191] For Paul, the gospel is indisputably Christ-centred. As John Stott explains, "The gospel is not preached if Christ is not preached, and the authentic Christ is not proclaimed if his death and resurrection are not central."[192] This christological stance includes Christ's person as well as his death and resurrection.[193] Second, Paul reminds the Corinthians that the death and resurrection of Jesus Christ are in accordance with the Scriptures.[194] Paul is pointing the readers to the entire Old Testament's witness to the atonement.[195] Third, Paul reminds the readers that Jesus Christ not only died but died "for our sins." Our sins and the death of Christ are intimately connected, and his death is expiating and atoning. For Paul, the death of Christ is not merely historical fact but also a religious doctrine.[196]

---

189. McKnight, *King Jesus Gospel*, 48–49.

190. Fitzmyer, *First Corinthians*, 541.

191. Ciampa and Rosner, *First Letter to the Corinthians*, 745.

192. John R. W. Stott, *Evangelical Truth: A Personal Plea for Unity, Integrity and Faithfulness*, rev. ed. (Downers Grove, IL: InterVarsity Press, 2003), 27.

193. Carson, "Gospel of Jesus Christ," 2.

194. Ciampa and Rosner, *First Letter to the Corinthians*, 746.

195. McKnight, *King Jesus Gospel*, 52. Chris Wright reminds us that the Bible as a whole, in all its canonical parts, contributes to the gospel. See Chris Wright, "According to the Scriptures: The Whole Gospel in Biblical Revelation," *ERT* 33 (2009): 4–18 (4).

196. Robert S. Candlish, *Studies in First Corinthians 15: Life in a Risen Savior* (Grand Rapids, MI: Kregel, 1989), 31–33. According to John Stott, "The death and resurrection of Jesus were not only historical events; they had a theological or saving significance." See Stott, *Evangelical Truth*, 28.

Based on 1 Corinthians 15:1–11, John Stott highlights six aspects helpful for summarizing the gospel:[197] (1) The gospel is christological. The priority truths of the gospel are the events of the death and resurrection of Jesus Christ (1 Cor 15:3).[198] (2) The gospel is biblical. The death and resurrection of Jesus were corroborated by both the Old Testament and the New Testament (1 Cor 15:3–4). (3) The gospel is historical. The resurrection was a datable historical event (1 Cor 15:3–8). (4) The gospel is theological. The death and resurrection of Jesus Christ were not only historical events but had a theological significance (1 Cor 15:2). (5) The gospel is apostolic. The gospel message was received and transmitted by the apostles and belongs to the apostolic tradition (1 Cor 15:11). (6) The gospel is personal. The death and resurrection of Christ are not only historical and theological but also the way of individual salvation (1 Cor 15:1–2). The understanding of the gospel adopted in this research accords with Stott's six statements. Moreover, the view of the gospel in this research is summarized by the following statement from Stephen I. Wright: "A gospel that is faithful to the living Lord of Scripture will speak both of the historical story of Jesus and of how His transforming power remains for us not only as individuals, but as communities, and for the world itself."[199]

1.9.3 Evangelicalism

The term *evangelical* etymologically refers to the gospel.[200] The English word evangelical is a transliteration of the Greek word εὐαγγέλιον, which was employed by the writers of the New Testament to mean "good news." English translators of the New Testament usually translate εὐαγγέλιον as "gospel." Evangelical religion has always focused on the gospel of salvation brought to sinners by Jesus Christ.[201] Thus evangelicalism, simply defined, is a move-

---

197. Stott, *Evangelical Truth*, 27–29. Carson later adds two more aspects: The gospel is universal ,and the gospel is eschatological. See Carson, "The Gospel of Jesus Christ," 7–8.

198. Or as Gilbert says, "The cross must remain at the center of the gospel." *What Is the Gospel?*, 110.

199. Stephen I. Wright, *Alive to the Word: A Practical Theology of Preaching for the Whole Church* (London: SCM, 2010), 129.

200. Sproul, *Getting the Gospel Right*, 33.

201. Mark A. Noll, "What Is Evangelical?," in *The Oxford Handbook of Evangelical Theology*, ed. Gerald R. McDermott (Oxford: Oxford University Press, 2010), 19–32 (20–21).

ment associated with the gospel. Derek Tidball rightly claims, "Evangelicals are 'gospel' people."[202]

John Stott believes that evangelicalism is original, apostolic, New Testament Christianity. The evangelical faith, in fact, can be traced back to the New Testament's gospel.[203] Evangelicalism is faithful to the heritage of Christian belief present throughout history.[204] However, Mark Ellingsen points out that the question of when evangelicalism began as a movement is disputed among scholars.[205] Some date the beginning of the evangelical movement to the time of the Reformation, when Martin Luther and his followers used the terms *evangelical* and *reformer* interchangeably. Evangelical became synonymous with Protestant, one who protested against the corruptions of the late-medieval Western church and sought reformation of the church.[206] Others trace the origins of the movement to seventeenth-century Puritanism and Pietism and consider Johann Arndt, Philip Jakob Spener, August Hermann Francke, and the Moravians as the evangelical pioneers.[207]

One of the most significant books about the history of evangelicalism is David W. Bebbington's *Evangelicalism in Modern Britain: A History from the 1730s to the 1980s*.[208] Bebbington attests that evangelicalism as a popular Protestant movement began in Britain in the 1730s.[209] According to

---

202. Derek Tidball, *Who Are the Evangelicals?: Tracing the Roots of Today's Movements* (London: Marshall Pickering, 1994), 11.

203. Stott, *Evangelical Truth*, 14.

204. Stanley J. Grenz, *Revisioning Evangelical Theology: A Fresh Agenda for the 21st Century* (Downers Grove, IL: InterVarsity Press, 1993), 16–17.

205. Mark Ellingsen, *The Evangelical Movement: Growth, Impact, Controversy, Dialog* (Minneapolis: Augsburg, 1988), 123.

206. Noll, "What Is Evangelical?," 21.

207. Noll, 24.

208. David W. Bebbington, *Evangelicalism in Modern Britain: A History form the 1730s to the 1980s* (London: Unwin Hyman, 1989). Larsen praises Bebbington for his book, saying, "David Bebbington made as significant and substantial a contribution to scholarship as the author of any book could ever hope for." See Timothy Larsen, "The Reception Given *Evangelicalism in Modern Britain* since Its Publication in 1989," in *The Emergence of Evangelicalism: Exploring Historical Continuities*, ed. Michael A. G. Haykin and Kenneth J. Stewart (Nashville, TN: B&H Academic, 2008), 21–36 (36).

209. Bebbington, *Evangelicalism*, 1. Mark A. Noll takes a similar position. See Mark A. Noll, *The Rise of Evangelicalism: The Age of Edwards, Whitefield and the Wesleys* (Downers Grove, IL: IVP Academic, 2003). However, some scholars disagree with Bebbington. For example, McGowan believes that evangelicalism existed since the sixteenth century, but was viewed as a new movement when orthodoxy was challenged. See A. T. B. McGowan, "Evangelicalism in Scotland from Knox to Cunningham," in *Emergence of Evangelicalism*, 63–83 (83).

Bebbington, the emergence of the movement started in Wales in 1735, and soon England followed. The key figures in this period were Howel Harris and Daniel Rowland in Wales and George Whitefield and John Wesley in England.[210] Almost at the same time, the American evangelical movement started with the eighteenth-century Great Awakening, which is associated with Jonathan Edwards and George Whitefield.[211]

From one point of view, Bebbington is correct to date the beginning of evangelicalism as a movement to the eighteenth century. According to Tidball, "evangelical" identified groups of Christians who had a particular approach to the gospel and the Christian life. These evangelical Christians were associated with the revival in the eighteenth century.[212] Hutchinson and Wolffe claim, "Evangelicalism as it developed from the 1730s onwards showed strong continuities with the past, but nevertheless also manifested a distinctive and innovative combination of characteristics."[213]

In the nineteenth century, evangelical Protestants were the largest and most influential Christian group in the United States, Britain, and Canada. During the nineteenth century, Methodists, Baptists, Presbyterians, Congregationalists, and Episcopalians shared broadly evangelical convictions. Lutherans, as well as German and Dutch Reformed, were also influenced by evangelical teachings.[214]

Evangelicals were instrumental in the expansion of Christianity in the nineteenth and twentieth centuries. The growth of non-Western evangelicals in the latter half of the twentieth century and early part of the twenty-first century is astonishing.[215] For the past few decades, evangelicalism has undergone a significant resurgence worldwide. Evangelicalism indeed is becoming

---

210. Bebbington, *Evangelicalism*, 20. Tidball takes a similar view and claims that evangelicalism became a more easily identified stream with the rise of John Wesley and George Whitefield in eighteenth-century Great Britain. See Tidball, *Who Are the Evangelicals?*, 32–33. The Haykin and Stewart volume *Emergence of Evangelicalism* again is the most thorough discussion of this point.

211. Tidball, *Who Are the Evangelicals?*, 54–56.

212. Tidball, 11–12.

213. Mark Hutchinson and John Wolffe, *A Short History of Global Evangelicalism* (New York: Cambridge University Press, 2012), 26.

214. Noll, "What Is Evangelical?," 29.

215. Mandryk, *Operation World*, 3.

a global phenomenon.[216] According to Mandryk, the number of evangelicals worldwide has increased from 89 million in 1960 to 546 million in 2010.[217]

Evangelicalism has always been characterized by diversity.[218] In fact, evangelicalism as a living movement has never been a fixed and immutable entity.[219] Today, evangelicalism has become "an immense tree with all sorts of shoots and branches which often seem to have little in common, yet which clearly draw off the same roots."[220] Bebbington identifies four characteristics that lie at the heart of the movement and distinguish evangelicalism from other movements: conversionism, biblicism, activism, and crucicentrism. Conversionism is the belief that human beings need to be converted and born again. Biblicism refers to a high regard for the Christian Scriptures as the ultimate authority. Activism is the commitment to energetic practice that arises from the belief that the gospel needs to be spread urgently. Crucicentrism stresses the reconciliation of humanity to God achieved by the death of Christ on the cross.[221] Bebbington's definition of evangelicalism is well accepted and consistently employed by numerous scholars who have studied evangelicalism.[222] These four key features of evangelicalism suggested by Bebbington will provide a foundational understanding of the term in this research. Moreover, these characteristics reveal underlying presuppositions that will shape this study.

1.9.4 Contextualization

The term *contextualization* first appeared in the discussions of the Theological Education Fund (TEF) of the World Council of Churches.[223] The 1972 TEF report, *Ministry and Context*, emphasized the significance of contextualization

---

216. Tidball, *Who Are the Evangelicals?*, 8–11.
217. Mandryk, *Operation World*, 6.
218. Tidball, *Who Are the Evangelicals?*, 19.
219. Tidball, 31.
220. Tidball, 11–12.
221. Bebbington, *Evangelicalism*, 2–19. Tidball apparently supports Bebbington's approach. See Tidball, *Who Are the Evangelicals?*, 14. McGowan, on the other hand, indicates that "equal weight cannot be accorded to each characteristic and that other characteristics might well have justified inclusion." See McGowan, 64.
222. Timothy Larsen, "Defining and Locating Evangelism," in *The Cambridge Company to Evangelical Theology*, ed. Timothy Larsen and Daniel J. Treier (New York: Cambridge University Press, 2007), 1–14 (1).
223. Eugene S. Heideman, "Syncretism, Contextualization, Orthodoxy, and Heresy," *Missiology* 25 (1997): 37–49 (39).

for the mission of the church. The report stated, "Contextualization should be the focal concern because through it alone will come reform and renewal. Contextualization of the gospel is a missiological necessity."[224] The report argued that contextuality is the capacity to respond meaningfully to the gospel within the framework of one's own situation.[225] The term *contextualization* was originally used to express the tension between two realities: (1) the universal truths expressed in the Bible, and (2) the world of diverse and everchanging cultures.[226]

There are many different perceptions of what the term *contextualization* is about. Today it is used within a number of theologically related disciplines and by thinkers from a wide range of philosophical and theological perspectives.[227] There is not yet a universally accepted definition of the term *contextualization*, only a series of proposals.[228] A detailed discussion about the definitions of contextualization and its concerns will be presented in chapter two.

1.9.5 Worldview

The term *worldview* is a calque of the German word *Weltanschauung*.[229] The concept of worldview is widely used in many Christian circles today, with various understandings.[230] As James W. Sire defines it, "A worldview is a commitment, a fundamental orientation of the heart, that can be expressed as a story or in a set of presuppositions (assumptions which may be true, partially true or entirely false) which we hold (consciously or subconsciously, consistently or inconsistently) about the basic constitution of reality, and that

---

224. World Council of Churches, "Ministry in Context: The Third Mandate Program of the Theological Education Fund (1970–1977)," in *Classic Texts in Mission and World Christianity*, ed. Norman E. Thomas (Maryknoll, NY: Orbis, 1995), 175–176 (175).

225. Bruce J. Nicholls, *Contextualization: A Theology of Gospel and Culture* (Downers Grove, IL: InterVarsity Press, 1979), 21.

226. M. Pocock, G. Van Rheenen, and D. McConnell, *The Changing Face of World Mission* (Grand Rapids, MI: Baker, 2005), 321.

227. Dean Flemming, *Contextualization in the New Testament: Patterns for Theology and Mission* (Nottingham: Apollos, 2005), 18–19.

228. David J. Hesselgrave and Edward Rommen, *Contextualization: Meanings, Methods, and Models* (Nottingham: Apollos, 1989), 35.

229. David K. Naugle, *Worldview: The History of a Concept* (Grand Rapids, MI: Eerdmans, 2002), 64–66.

230. Charles H. Kraft, *Worldview for Christian Witness* (Pasadena, CA: William Carey Library, 2008), 11.

provides the foundations on which we live and move and have our being."[231] Sire believes that a worldview lies deep in the self – "the central operating chamber of every human being."[232] According to E. Adamson Hoebel and Thomas Weaver, worldview "is a shared perspective on, and philosophy or ideology about, the natural world, including such things as humanity, gods and religion, animals and spirits, and other aspects perceived by the individual."[233]

Charles H. Kraft points out that a worldview is "the central systematization of conceptions of reality to which the members of the culture assent and from which stems their value system." Kraft believes that a people's worldview is their basic model of reality.[234] At one level, a people's worldview provides them with the most pervasive and influential lens in terms of which reality is perceived and interpreted.[235] Worldview, according to Kraft, is also "the deepest level of presuppositions on which people base their lives."[236]

According to Dayton and Fraser, worldviews act as a *gestalt* within which all other understanding of the world takes place. They point out that every people group has its own distinctive philosophy and religious commitments that give specific content to its worldview.[237] Ruth Julian points out that worldview includes categories of reality, assumptions, and preunderstandings about reality, values in society, and emotions allowed or not allowed in society.[238]

Based on anthropology, Hiebert defines worldview as "the foundational cognitive, affective, and evaluative assumptions and frameworks a group of

---

231. James W. Sire, *Naming the Elephant: Worldview as a Concept* (Downers Grove, IL: InterVarsity Press, 2004), 122.

232. James W. Sire, *The Universe Next Door*, 5th ed. (Downers Grove, IL: InterVarsity Press, 2009), 20.

233. Hoebel and Weaver, *Anthropology*, 523.

234. Kraft, *Christianity in Culture*, 53–54.

235. Kraft, *Worldview for Christian Witness*, 18.

236. Charles H. Kraft, *Issues in Contextualization* (Pasadena, CA: William Carey Library, 2016), 14.

237. Edward R. Dayton and David A. Fraser, *Planning Strategies for World Evangelization* (Grand Rapids, MI: Eerdmans, 1980), 150–151.

238. Ruth Julian, "Ground Level Contextualization," in *Local Theology for the Global Church: Principles for an Evangelical Approach to Contextualization*, ed. Matthew Cook, et al. (Pasadena, CA: William Carey Library, 2010), 57–74 (59).

people make about the nature of reality which they use to order their lives."[239] Hiebert further lists six cultural and social functions of worldviews:

1. Worldviews provide us with mental blueprints that shape how we understand the world and how we take action.
2. Worldviews give people emotional security by providing emotional reinforcements for their fundamental beliefs.
3. Worldviews validate the deepest cultural norms in a society.
4. The worldview of a particular society helps to integrate people into the culture.
5. Worldviews monitor cultural changes.
6. Worldviews give psychological reassurance that reality is truly as we see it, thus providing a sense of peace and of being at home in the world.[240]

1.9.6 Religion

The English term *religion* is derived from the Latin term *religio*, which originially was used only as an adjective in ancient Roman times to describe a higher power or a taboo. The term later came to delineate the inner piety of individual worshippers.[241] Not until the seventeenth century did the idea of religion as a distinct and differentiable social domain became solidified in Europe, after the religious conflicts in the wake of the Reformation.[242]

Although the study of gods and religious mythology can be traced back to the philosophers of ancient Greece,[243] the comparative study of religion from the scientific and comparative perspective only began in the late nineteenth

---

239. Hiebert, *Transforming Worldviews*, 25–26.
240. Hiebert, 25–30.
241. Mayfair Mei-hui Yang, "Introduction," in *Chinese Religiosities: Afflictions of Modernity and State Formation*, ed. Mayfair Mei-hui Yang (Berkeley: University of California Press, 2008), 1–40 (13).
242. Peter Beyer, "Social Forms of Religion and Religions in Contemporary Global Society," in *Handbook of the Sociology of Religion*, ed. Michele Dillon (Cambridge: Cambridge University Press, 2003), 45–60 (47–48).
243. William Cenkner, "Religions," in *The New Dictionary of Theology*, ed. Joseph A. Komonchak, Mary Collins, and Dermot A. Lane (Dublin: Gill and Macmillan, 1987), 862–868 (863).

century.²⁴⁴ Friedrich Max Müller, a Sanskrit scholar and philologist, is considered to be the father of the science of religion.²⁴⁵ Müller first sketched his vision of a scientific investigation of religion in 1867, and expanded the principles in 1873 in his *Introduction to the Science of Religion*.²⁴⁶ Müller believed that all human beings are by nature religious. Furthermore, he advocated the creation of a comparative and historical science of religion and proposed a more sympathetic study of non-Christian religions.²⁴⁷

The term *religion*, nevertheless, is difficult to define because in modern discussion scholars tend to have different definitions for it, and some definitions are contradicted by others.²⁴⁸ Max Weber, one of the greatest sociologists and philosophers, even argued that a definition of religion could only be attempted at the conclusion of extensive investigation.²⁴⁹ For the last few decades, more and more people have recognized the complexity and difficulty of defining religion.²⁵⁰ As Stewart Elliott Guthrie attests, "Even within the West and within individual disciplines, almost the only agreement on religion is that there is no agreement."²⁵¹

Generally, there have been two approaches to defining *religion*: the substantivist (also called essentialist) approach and the functionalist approach. The substantivist approach defines religion in terms of its belief content,²⁵² and it identifies the essentials of religion.²⁵³ Edward Burnett Tylor, for ex-

---

244. Bryan S. Turner and Oscar Salemink, "Introduction: Constructing Religion and Religions in Asia," in *Routledge Handbook of Religions in Asia*, ed. Bryan S. Turner and Oscar Salemink (Abingdon: Routledge, 2015), 1–14 (1).

245. James C. Livingston, "Study of Religion," in *The Dictionary of Bible and Religion*, ed. William H. Gentz (Nashville: Abingdon, 1986), 880–881 (880).

246. Marjorie Wheeler-Barclay, *The Science of Religion in Britain, 1860–1915* (Charlottesville: University of Virginia Press, 2010), 51.

247. Wheeler-Barclay, *Science of Religion*, 64–69.

248. Andrew Kerr Rule, "Religion, Religious," in *Evangelical Dictionary of Theology*, ed. Walter A Elwell (Grand Rapids, MI: Baker, 1984), 930–931 (930).

249. Max Weber, *The Sociology of Religion*, trans. Ephraim Fischoff (Boston, MA: Beacon, 1993), 1.

250. Anthony C. Thiselton, *A Concise Encyclopedia of the Philosophy of Religion* (Grand Rapids, MI: Baker Academic, 2002), 255.

251. Stewart Elliott Guthrie, "Opportunity, Challenge and a Definition of Religion," *JSRNC* 1 (2007): 58–67 (61).

252. Beverley Clack and Brian R. Clack, *The Philosophy of Religion: A Critical Introduction* (Cambridge: Polity, 1998), 1.

253. Russell T. McCutcheon, *Studying Religion: An Introduction* (Abingdon: Routledge, 2014) 23.

ample, defined religion simply as the "belief in spiritual beings."[254] The other approach is functionalist, in which religion is "defined in terms of what it is alleged that all religions do or what the social function of religion is alleged to be."[255] Emile Durkheim, a functionalist, defined religion as follows: "A religion is a unified system of beliefs and practices relative to sacred things, that is to say, things set apart and forbidden – beliefs and practices which unite into one single moral community called a Church, all those who adhere to them."[256] One of the more recent examples of functional definition is offered by Keith E. Yandell. He defines religion as "a conceptual system that provides an interpretation of the world and the place of human beings in it, based on account of how life should be lived given that interpretation, and expresses this interpretation and lifestyle in a set of rituals, institutions, and practices."[257]

In this study, the concept of religion is viewed in its broad sense according to Paul G. Hiebert's *Cultural Anthropology*. As Hiebert states, "religion encompasses all specific beliefs about the ultimate nature of reality and the origins, meaning, and destiny of life, as well as the myths and rituals that symbolically express them."[258] Such understanding of religion has a virtue of being broadly applicable in most cultures because it includes a great variety of thoughts and practices. Furthermore, this definition of religion is believed to be genuinely value-neutral, thus appropriate for studying Chinese context.

In the late nineteenth century and early twentieth century, the modern academic methodologies of study of religion were introduced into China.[259] Classical Chinese has no exact term corresponding to the modern Western notion of religion.[260] *Zong jiao* 宗教, the modern Chinese term for the word *religion*, was rendered from the Japanese kanji *shukyo* (宗教) at the end of

---

254. Clack and Clack, *Philosophy of Religion*, 1.

255. Keith E. Yandell, *Philosophy of Religion: A Contemporary Introduction* (London: Routledge, 1999), 16.

256. Emile Durkheim, *The Elementary Forms of Religious Life*, trans. Karen E. Fields (New York: Free Press, 1995), 44.

257. Yandell, *Philosophy of Religion*, 16.

258. Hiebert, *Cultural Anthropology*, 371–372.

259. He Guanghu, "Thirty Years of Religious Studies in China," in *Social Scientific Studies of Religion in China : Methodology, Theories, and Findings*, ed. Fenggang Yang and Graeme Lang (Leiden: Brill, 2011), 23–46, 24.

260. Robert L. Winzeler, *Anthropology and Religion: What We Know, Think, and Question*, 2nd ed. (Plymouth: AltaMira), 2.

nineteenth century.²⁶¹ Two aspects need to be highlighted in this regard. First, the absence of the word *religion* in classical Chinese does not deny the existence of religious activities in ancient China.²⁶² As Robert L. Winzeler attests that although some societies lack a word for religion in their own language, most anthropologists today have no doubt about the universality of religion.²⁶³ In fact, archaeologists have found evidence of religious activities such as divination and making offerings to powers of nature even during the Prehistory Period of China.²⁶⁴ The discoveries of great quantities of Chinese-inscribed oracle bones reveal religious activities, such as divinations and sacrifices to the ancestors, during the Shang dynasty and the Zhou dynasty.²⁶⁵

Second, the term *zong jiao*, although borrowed from Japanese, reveals a specific Chinese perspective of religion. The Chinese word *zong* 宗 designates features of family lineage, transmission, and devotion.²⁶⁶ As for the word *jiao* 教, the Chinese character is composed of two parts, *xiao* 孝 (filial piety) and *wen* 文 (culture), meaning the teachings from the past or instruction given by ancestors.²⁶⁷ Therefore, one of the most significant features of Chinese understanding of religion is the embodiment of ancient tradition.²⁶⁸

1.9.7 Worship

The English word *worship* indicates *worth-ship*, signifying the worthiness of an individual to receive special honor.²⁶⁹ Over the centuries, the noun and verb form of the word have changed in meaning significantly. Although the word *worship* often had God as its object, it was also frequently used to

---

261. Mayfair Mei-hui Yang, "Introduction," 11. Although the compound of the Chinese words *zong jiao* 宗教 had already been used by Chinese Buddhists in the tenth century, it was not what is meant by the modern Chinese term *zong jiao*. See Yao and Zhao, *Chinese Religion*, 27.

262. Yao and Zhao, *Chinese Religion*, 28.

263. Winzeler, *Anthropology and Religion*, 3.

264. Daniel L. Overmyer, *Religions of China: The World as a Living System* (Long Grove, IL: Waveland, 1986), 24–25.

265. Edward L. Shaughnessy, "The Religion of Ancient China," in *The Handbook of Ancient Religions*, ed. John R. Hinnells (Cambridge: Cambridge Univeristy Press, 2007), 490–536 (493–495).

266. Yao and Zhao, *Chinese Religion*, 32.

267. Yao and Zhao, 34–35.

268. Yao and Zhao, 43.

269. Everett F. Harrison, "Worship," in *Evangelical Dictionary of Theology*, 1192–1193 (1192).

connect with "the condition of deserving honor or a good reputation or with the source or ground of that honor."²⁷⁰ In the English Bible, "worship" is used to render the Old Testament Hebrew term שָׁחָה meaning "to bow down" or "to do homage,"²⁷¹ and the New Testament Greek term προσκυνέω, meaning almost the same as שָׁחָה but deriving from a root meaning "to kiss."²⁷² This theme of prostration in the Bible "emphasizes how worshippers are totally overwhelmed by God's glory, otherness, and worthiness."²⁷³ Theologically speaking, worship illustrates a response of adoration evoked in one who has encountered the presence of God.²⁷⁴ The word "worship" is also used to translate the Hebrew term עָבַד, which literally means "to serve."²⁷⁵ As Michael J. Quicke explains, "Worshippers are not just knocked prostrate before God's greatness; they are also set up on their feet to serve him."²⁷⁶ The focus of biblical worship, therefore, is the expression of the divine-human relationship.²⁷⁷

In Chinese tradition, the key word to understand Chinese worshipping deities, ancestors, or ghosts is *ji* 祭. Etymologically, *ji* 祭 symbolises an animal sacrifice to gods.²⁷⁸ The upper part of the Chinese word *ji* 祭 represents a hand with meats, while the lower part of the word represents gods.²⁷⁹ Food always plays an important role in Chinese worshipping. In fact, according to *The Book of Rites*, the origin of worship is offering foods to gods (夫禮之初, 始諸飲食).²⁸⁰

---

270. D. A. Carson, *Worship by the Book* (Grand Rapids: Zondervan, 2002), 18.

271. Warren Wiersbe, *Real Worship: Playground, Battle Ground, or Holy Ground?*, 2nd ed. (Grand Rapids, MI: Baker, 2000), 20.

272. John R. McRay, "Worship," in *Dictionary of Bible and Religion*, 1122–1124 (1122).

273. Michael J. Quicke, *Preaching as Worship: An Integrative Approach to Formation in Your Church* (Grand Rapids, MI: Baker, 2011), 70.

274. Margaret Mary Kelleher, "Worship," in *The New Dictionary of Theology*, ed. Joseph A. Komonchak, Mary Collins, and Dermot A. Lane (Dublin: Gill and Macmillan, 1987), 1105–1106 (1105).

275. David G. Peterson, "Worship," in *New Dictionary of Biblical Theology*, ed. T. Desmond Alexander and Brian S. Rosner (Leicester: Inter-Varsity Press, 2000), 855–863 (856).

276. Quicke, *Preaching as Worship*, 70.

277. Kelleher, "Worship," 1105.

278. 詹鄞鑫, 神靈與祭祀: 中國傳統宗教綜論 (*Spirit of God and Sacrifices: A View of China's Traditional Religion*) (南京 [Nanjing]: 江蘇古籍出版社, 2000), 173.

279. 麥兆輝著, 顧瓊華譯, 尊天敬祖: 當代華人基督徒對祭祖的回應 (*Revering God and Respecting Ancestors : A Contemporary Christian Chinese Response To Ancestral Practice*) (香港 [Hong Kong]: 浸信會出版社, 2014), 18-19.

280. 詹鄞鑫, 172.

1.9.8 Annual Festivals

According to R. J. Smith, most societies periodically set aside portions of time for celebration. He explains, "These recurring moments of special significance, with celebrations that fill them, are called festivals."[281] Annual festivals are calendrical rites in a society.[282] They are found almost everywhere in the world, and they usually adopt practices from greater traditions. Anthropologists believe that people always express the particular beliefs of the local community in annual festivals.[283]

Anthropologically speaking, annual festivals are categorized as rites of intensification. Festivals publicly reaffirm the existing social and religious order, and they are sometimes called rites of restoration or renewal. They generate strong emotions which provide participants with a feeling of familiarity.[284] Like other rites of intensification, festivals help people "remember who they are, re-create a world order, give people a sense of identity and belonging, relate them to the transcendent, and indoctrinate insiders and outsiders alike to the true values and perceived realities of a society."[285]

1.9.9 Chinese Festivals

Chinese festivals are living expressions of popular values and beliefs in Chinese culture.[286] The Chinese people celebrate many different festivals. The Han Chinese, which are the largest Chinese ethnic group, celebrate approximately one hundred festivals each year.[287] In Chinese culture, major festivals are called *jie* 節. In addition to *jie* 節, two other Chinese terms also refer to "festival." Festivals that celebrate the birthdays of gods and goddesses are called *dan* 誕. Festivals that only worship gods or goddesses for a particular

---

281. Robert Jerome Smith, "Festivals and Celebrations," in *Folklore and Folklife: An Introduction*, ed. Richard M. Dorson (Chicago: University of Chicago Press, 1972), 159–172 (159).

282. Hiebert, *Cultural Anthropology*, 372–374.

283. Paul G. Hiebert, R. Daniel Shaw, and Tite Tienou, *Understanding Folk Religion* (Grand Rapids, MI: Baker, 1999), 314.

284. Hiebert, Shaw, and Tienou, 311–312.

285. Hiebert, Shaw, and Tienou, 300–301.

286. Derk Bodde, *Festivals in Classical China: New Year and Other Annual Observances during the Han Dynasty 206 B.C.–A.D. 220* (Princeton, NJ: Princeton University Press, 1975), 2.

287. 康新民, "民間節日文化價值初探" (A Probe into the Cultural Value of Folk Festivals), 於中國民間文化:民俗文化研究 (*Folk Culture in China: Research on the Customs of China*), 上海民間文藝家協會編 (上海 [Shanghai]: 學林出版社, 1991), 143–148 (143).

reason are called *jiao* 醮. *Jiao* 醮 are usually celebrated by a local community and may not be held annually.²⁸⁸ This study focuses on three major Chinese festivals: the Spring Festival (Chun Jie 春節), the Qing Ming Festival (Qing Ming Jie 清明節), and the Hungry Ghost Festival (Zhong Yuan Jie 中元節).

1.9.10 Spring Festival

The Spring Festival is the most important Chinese festival and is also known as Chinese New Year,²⁸⁹ Lunar New Year, or Chun Jie 春節. The Chinese mark the beginning of a new year according to the lunar calendar by celebrating this important festival. The Spring Festival also celebrates the coming of the spring season.²⁹⁰ It normally falls in February, when spring, with its new life and growth, is welcomed with this festival.²⁹¹ The Spring Festival is closely related to many Chinese legends, myths, and folklore. According to the legends of ancient China, this festival originated from the legend of an enormous beast known as *nian* 年獸 (Year). This beast would come each year to the villages after its long hibernation through the winter. Every year the beast would cause massive destruction and much bloodshed until the villagers discovered that "Year" was intimidated by the colour red and by fire crackers.²⁹² From then on, the villagers learned to use the colour red, fire crackers, and the loud noises of cymbals and drums to chase away the beast.²⁹³ For their own safety, family members gather together, and all the lights in their homes are brightly lit. The colour red is also used for their lanterns and their clothing. Children are also given red packets for their protection.²⁹⁴

---

288. 蔡志祥, "香港的傳統中國節日: 節、誕、醮的比較研究" (Traditional Chinese Festivals in Hong Kong: A Comparative Study of Festivals), 華南研究 *(The South China Research)*, 1 (1994), 1–23 (3–9).

289. From ancient to modern times, celebrating the beginning of the calendar year has played an important role in many cultures. For example, the ancient Babylonians celebrated the new beginning of the calendar year with the Akitu Festival, which lasted for twelve days. See E. O. James, *Seasonal Feasts and Festivals* (London: Thames & Hudson, 1961), 80–89. The Persians had a New Year's festival called Nevruz (New Day), which Eberhard believes had a great influence on some customs of the Chinese New Year. See Wolfram Eberhard, *Chinese Festivals* (New York: Henry Schuman, 1952), 57.

290. Xiang Wei, *Chinese Customs* (New York: Better Link, 2008), 9.

291. Tong, *Biblical Approach*, 31–32.

292. Tong, 32.

293. Poh Boon Sing, *The Christian in the Chinese Culture* (Serdang: Good News Enterprise, 1986), 69.

294. Tong, *Biblical Approach*, 32.

Moreover, the dragon dance and the lion dance are often performed during Chinese New Year to scare away evil spirits.

1.9.11 Qing Ming Festival

Commonly celebrated on the 104th day after the winter solstice, Qing Ming 清明 is the annual visit to the ancestors' tombs.[295] Qing Ming is also known as the Clear and Bright Festival or Tomb Sweeping Day. It is a time for remembering the deceased. Visitations to the cemetery are made, tombs are cleaned and cleared of weeds, and food is offered to the ancestors.[296] To show loyalty and piety toward the deceased, ritual offerings are brought to the tomb as sacrifices. The sacrifices may include specific food such as pork, duck, and chicken, steamed buns, and fruits as well as paper effigies.[297] Ancestors are worshipped in the hope of a good yield of harvest later in the year.[298]

1.9.12 Hungry Ghost Festival

The celebration in the seventh month of the lunar calendar is known as the Hungry Ghost Festival.[299] The Chinese believe that the ghosts or the spirits of the dead are freed from hell and roam around the world looking for food during this month.[300] Chinese people suppose that it is very important to appease the ghosts, especially those spirits that do not have any descendants or anyone to make offerings to them.[301] Therefore food and tea are offered and incense and joss papers are burned to satisfy and calm their spirit of vengeance. These offerings can be seen at the road sides.[302] Candles and paper imitations of items are also burned during the celebration of the Hungry Ghost Festival.[303]

---

295. Salinthip Veeravanitkul, "Burning Money: Exploring the Annual Qing Ming Celebration among the Thai-Chinese and Their Consumption Meanings" (unpublished MA diss., University of Nottingham, 2006), 13.
296. Sing, *Christian in the Chinese Culture*, 70–71.
297. Veeravanitkul, "Burning Money," 14.
298. David Hock Tey, *Chinese Culture and the Bible* (Singapore: Here's Life Books, 1988), 124.
299. Tong, *Biblical Approach*, 47.
300. Tong, 47–48.
301. Frena Bloomfield, *The Book of Chinese Beliefs: A Journey into the Chinese Inner World* (London: Arrow, 1986), 54.
302. Sing, *Christian in the Chinese Culture*, 71.
303. Wong, *Illustrated Cycle*, 130.

1.9.13 Symbols

By definition a symbol is "an object, sound, action, or idea to which people assign arbitrary meaning."[304] As A. H. Mathias Zahniser explains, any word, gesture, action, or object can be a symbol.[305] Every culture has its own system of symbols. Each symbol is endowed with meaning. Born into a particular culture, an individual will learn the cultural symbol systems and their meanings.[306] Generally speaking, all festivals contain symbolic objects and actions. Zahniser affirms that "all cultures use symbols and ceremonies to bring life into harmony with faith."[307] In other words, symbols abound in cultures.[308] Therefore this study will take into account various symbols employed during the Chinese festivals.

1.10 Outline of the Study

After this introduction, chapter 2 will present a literature review of issues on contextualization. The first two sections will focus on the ecumenical movement and the emerging significance of contextualization in the twentieth century. The third section will review definitions of contextualization. There will then follow sections that discuss the importance of contextualization, various approaches to contextualization, and the concerns regarding syncretism. The seventh section will present examples of contextualization from the New Testament. The last section of chapter 2 will present in broad outline the concerns of the relationship between preaching and culture.

In chapter 3 a literature review will be undertaken focusing on the teachings of Confucianism, Taoism, Buddhism, and Chinese folk religion, all of which have significant influences on the worldview of Chinese people in general. The material in this chapter presents the conceptual basis for the research that was performed regarding the Chinese festivals.

---

304. Brain M. Howell and Jenell Williams Paris, *Introducing Cultural Anthropology: A Christian Perspective* (Grand Rapids, MI: Baker Academic, 2011), 186.

305. A. H. Mathias Zahniser, *Symbol and Ceremony: Making Disciples Across Cultures* (Monrovia, CA: MARC, 1997), 13.

306. Malefijt, *Religion and Culture*, 8.

307. Zahniser, *Symbol and Ceremony*, 3.

308. Zahniser, 214. The main discussion of Zahniser's book is about learning to adopt indigenous symbols and ceremonies for cross-cultural discipling without syncretism.

Research methodologies will be explained in chapter 4. The exploratory study of the three festivals was done through anthropological observation combined with an examination and analysis of relevant and influential texts. Moreover, a series of semi-structured face-to-face interviews were used to collect data from experienced Chinese preachers.

Chapter 5 reports the findings and analysis of the exploratory study regarding the Spring Festival, the Qing Ming Festival, and the Hungry Ghost Festival. It explored the religious beliefs, cultural values, and practices associated with the three festivals. Their implications for understanding the Chinese worldview will be explored in the light of the teachings of Confucianism, Taoism, Buddhism, and Chinese folk religion.

Chapter 6 presents a qualitative analysis of the in-depth interviews of six Chinese preachers who have years of experience of preaching among Chinese communities. The purpose of this field study is to determine Chinese preachers' perceptions and practices with regard to contextualized preaching during the Spring Festival, the Qing Ming Festival, and the Hungry Ghost Festivals.

Chapter 7 will attempt to reflect critically and identify biblical principles in shaping a response to the religious beliefs, cultural values, and practices associated with the Spring Festival, the Qing Ming Festival, and the Hungry Ghost Festival. After discussing the findings from the field research and the conceptions of the interviewees with regard to contextualized preaching during Chinese festivals, chapter 8 will try to clarify the principles involved in formulating contextualized preaching to the Chinese people. A summary, conclusions, and recommendations will be made in chapter 9.

CHAPTER 2

Literature Review on Issues of Contextualization

The present chapter reviews major issues concerning contextualization. The first section briefly surveys the ecumenical movement in the twentieth century, because the term *contextualization* was originally coined in ecumenical circles. The second section reviews the emergence of the term *contextualization* since its conception in the 1970s. The third section examines the definitions of contextualization. In the fourth section, the importance of contextualization will be discussed. The fifth section investigates different approaches to contextualization. The sixth section focuses on the discussion of syncretism. The seventh section seeks to uncover examples of contextualization within the New Testament. The last section discusses the importance of cultural relevance in preaching.

2.1 The Ecumenical Movement in the Twentieth Century

One of the great facets of modern church life is the ecumenical movement.[1] The term *ecumenism* is derived from the Greek word οἰκουμένη. In the New Testament, οἰκουμένη refers to the whole world: "This gospel of the kingdom shall be preached in the whole world" (Matt 24:14). Today *ecumenism* designates "a modern Christian movement concerned with the unity and renewal

---

1. Derek Tidball, *Who Are the Evangelicals?: Tracing the Roots of Today's Movements* (London: Marshall Pickering, 1994), 170.

of the church and its relationship to God's reconciling and renewing mission throughout creation."[2] Simply speaking, the phrase *ecumenical movement* is dedicated to the quest for the visible unity of the body of Christ.[3]

Evangelicalism has played an important role in ecumenism. Derek Tidball reminds us never to underestimate the evangelical contribution to ecumenism.[4] Norman Goodall points out that evangelicals significantly contributed to the emergence of the ecumenical movement. He comments, "In the dawn of the modern 'ecumenical era' the terms *evangelical* and *ecumenical* were accepted as belonging together."[5] From one point of view, evangelicalism is pivotal in the development of ecumenism.[6]

The evangelical revival in the eighteenth and nineteenth centuries indeed gave birth to a number of organizations that later provided favourable ground for the propagation of ecumenical ideas. These organizations include the Young Men's Christian Association, the Evangelical Alliance, the Young Women's Christian Association, and the World's Student Christian Association.[7] Timothy L. Smith indicates that the evangelicals of the nineteenth century led the way in cultivating interdenominational relationships. The Evangelical Alliance and D. L. Moody's undenominational evangelism were great landmarks of ecumenical progress.[8] In particular, the founding of the Evangelical Alliance in 1846 has long been recognized as one expression of ecumenism, as it was formed to promote interdenominational cooperation.[9] Likewise, Moody's Student Volunteer Movement was one of the major factors

---

2. Michael Kinnamon and Brian E. Cope, "General Introduction," in *The Ecumenical Movement: An Anthology of Key Texts and Voices*, ed. Michael Kinnamon and Brian E. Cope (Geneva: WCC, 1997), 1–8 (1).

3. Charles Hill, "The Ecumenical Movement," in *Zondervan Handbook to the History of Christianity*, ed. Jonathan Hill (Grand Rapids, MI: Zondervan, 2006), 435.

4. Tidball, *Who Are the Evangelicals?*, 174.

5. Norman Goodall, "Evangelicalism and the ecumenical movement," *ER* 15 (1963): 399–409 (399).

6. William J. Abraham, "Church and Churches: Ecumenism," in *The Oxford Handbook of Evangelical Theology*, ed. Gerald R. McDermott (Oxford: Oxford University Press, 2010), 296–309 (297).

7. Millard J. Erickson, *Christian Theology*, 2nd ed. (Grand Rapids, MI: Baker, 2001), 1144.

8. Timothy L. Smith, "An Historical Perspective on Evangelicalism and Ecumenism," *Mid-Stream* 22 (1983): 308–325 (319–320).

9. John Briggs, "The First Industrial Nation," in *Introduction to the History of Christianity*, ed. Tim Dowley (Minneapolis: Fortress, 1995), 518–537 (536).

leading to the 1910 Edinburgh World Mission Conference,[10] which is often considered a seminal moment in the rise of ecumenism.[11]

The majority of the participants of the 1910 Edinburgh Conference were Protestant and broadly evangelical. According to Brian Stanley, the original title of the Conference was "Third Ecumenical Missionary Conference," because it followed two previous large Protestant missionary gatherings. The first occurred in London in 1888, and the second transpired in New York in 1900. However, the organizers of the 1910 Edinburgh Conference ultimately decided to drop the word *ecumenical*.[12] As Barry Till indicates, the Edinburgh Conference started on an interdenominational basis, which became the principle of the twentieth-century ecumenical movement.[13] Therefore, the 1910 Edinburgh Conference is usually regarded as the beginning of the modern ecumenical movement.[14]

At the 1910 Edinburgh Conference, first steps were taken toward interdenominational missionary cooperation.[15] After the Conference, connections between churches at the international level grew significantly, and national councils of churches were founded in various parts of the world.[16] In 1921, the International Missionary Council (IMC) was formed, the direct result of the work of the Continuation Committee from the Edinburgh Conference.[17] IMC was established by the delegates of seventy mission organizations based in Western Europe, North America, Southern Africa, and Australia.[18] Many of these delegates were from a conservative evangelical or fundamentalist tradition.[19] The 1910 Edinburgh Conference also spawned the World Conference

---

10. Michael Kinnamon, *Truth and Community: Diversity and Its Limits in the Ecumenical Movement* (Grand Rapids, MI: Eerdmans, 1988), 100.

11. Abraham, "Church and Churches," 300.

12. Brian Stanley, "The World Missionary Conference, Edinburgh 1910: Sifting History from Myth," *Touchstone* 28 (2010): 7–18 (8).

13. Barry Till, *The Churches Search for Unity* (Harmondsworth: Penguin, 1972), 193.

14. Erickson, *Christian Theology*, 1144.

15. A. Wind, "The Protestant Missionary Movement from 1789 to 1963," in *Missiology: An Ecumenical Introduction: Texts and Contexts of Global Christianity*, ed. A. Camps et al. (Grand Rapids, MI: Eerdmans, 1995), 237–252 (244).

16. Charles Hill, "The Ecumenical Movement," in *Zondervan Handbook*, 435.

17. Charles Hill, 435.

18. A. Wind, "The Protestant Missionary Movement," 237–252 (246–247).

19. Till, *Churches Search*, 246.

on Life and Work and the World Conference on Faith and Order.[20] These two strands united to form the World Council of Churches (WCC), which constituted a provisional committee in 1938. The WCC's first assembly met in Amsterdam on 23 August 1948. Initially, 147 churches became members of the WCC.[21] John R. Mott, the chairperson at 1910 Edinburgh Conference, was made honorary president of the WCC.[22] Eventually, the WCC became the most visible expression of the ecumenical movement.[23]

When the WCC was established in 1948, many evangelical mission societies within the IMC preferred not to be linked directly with the WCC.[24] The IMC evangelical wing was suspicious of the WCC, "regarding it as 'unsound' on questions of the authority and inerrancy of the Bible and, generally speaking, unscriptural and 'liberal' in its theology."[25] As Goodall explains, "Long before the formal inauguration of the World Council of Churches there were developments in the ecumenical movement, its organizations and programmes, which began to give anxiety to some evangelicals on the ground that the central task of evangelism was being obscured or distorted by preoccupation with social and political affairs."[26] By the 1920s, the fundamentalist-modernist rift had surfaced.[27] Evangelicals were concerned with the increasing influence of modernists in the ecumenical movement, especially the modernists' promotion of social engagement as evangelism, otherwise known as the social gospel.[28] The social gospel focuses on the materialistic salvation of the community rather than the individual.[29] Moreover, some

---

20. Abraham, "Church and Churches," 300.

21. Till, *Churches Search*, 232.

22. Stanley, "World Missionary Conference," 10.

23. Tom Stransky, "Criticism of the Ecumenical Movement and of the WCC," in *Dictionary of the Ecumenical Movement*, ed. Lossky and others (Grand Rapids, MI: Eerdmans, 1991), 252–256 (252).

24. Alan J. Bailyes, "Evangelical and Ecumenical Understandings of Mission," *IRM* 85 (1996): 485–503 (486–487).

25. Till, *Churches Search*, 246.

26. See Goodall, "Evangelicalism," 407.

27. Michael J. McClymond, "Mission and Evangelism," in *Oxford Handbook*, 296–309 (349).

28. A. Scott Moreau, *Contextualization in World Missions: Mapping and Assessing Evangelical Models* (Grand Rapids, MI: Kregel, 2012), 33.

29. Billy Graham, "Why Lausanne?," in *Let the Earth Hear His Voice*, ed. J. D. Douglas (Minneapolis: World Wide, 1975), 22–36 (26).

claims within the ecumenical movement in the 1920s and 1930s also drove evangelicals increasingly away from ecumenical circles.[30] For example, W. E. Hocking's *Re-Thinking Mission: A Laymen's Inquiry After One Hundred Years* (1933) was "a proposal for Christians to join with non-Christians and affirm a common religiosity in the face of secularism."[31] This controversial publication argued that all religions are equal manifestations of truth and parallel ways of salvation; therefore, the traditional goal of mission, conversion to Christianity, should be abandoned.[32]

However, during the Ghana assembly in 1958, the majority of the IMC made fundamental decisions in favour of merging with the WCC. The IMC officially merged with the WCC in 1961 during the third assembly of the WCC in New Delhi.[33] Thus the IMC first became the Division on World Missions and Evangelism (DWME) and then the Commission on World Mission and Evangelism (CWME) within the WCC in 1973. Fearing that mission would be lost in the larger organization, a number of evangelicals left when the IMC merged with the WCC.[34]

The 1960s was the period in which secularity emerged in the ecumenical movement. Some in the WCC circles claimed that the world provided the agenda for the church and that God guides the church through secular trends instead of through Scripture or church tradition.[35] Most conservative evangelicals claimed that the WCC celebrated the idea of secularization as proof of its apostasy.[36] Other critics believed that the WCC had compromised biblical authority and adopted a social-political understanding of the gospel.[37] Evangelicals claimed that WCC programmes minimized or even ignored the importance of verbally proclaiming the gospel to the millions who had never heard the name of Christ. Because of the perceived loss of the WCC's

---

30. Moreau, *Contextualization*, 33.
31. McClymond, "Mission and Evangelism," 349.
32. Gerald D. Gort, "Syncretism and Dialogue: Christian Historical and Earlier Ecumenical Perception," *Mission Studies* 6 (1989): 9–22 (14).
33. Wind, "Protestant Missionary Movement," 237–252 (247–248).
34. Moreau, *Contextualization*, 33.
35. McClymond, "Mission and Evangelism," 349.
36. David J. Bosch, "Ecumenicals and Evangelicals: A Growing Relationship?," *ER* 40 (1988): 458–472 (462).
37. Ellingsen, *Evangelical Movement*, 287.

commitment to direct evangelism, many evangelical Christians remain aloof from the WCC.[38]

Generally with regard to the ecumenical movement, evangelicals have always insisted that fellowship is impossible without agreement on certain basic items of belief, such as the supreme authority of the Bible, the deity of Jesus Christ, salvation as a supernatural work of regeneration and justification by grace through faith, and the second coming of Christ. Evangelicals' most common reservations about the ecumenical movement are theological. It appears to the evangelical that the ecumenical movement has often settled for the lowest common denominator. As a result, the evangelical suspects that some members of the ecumenical fellowship may not be genuine Christians. Therefore, many evangelicals have been cautious about the degree to which they are willing to engage in ecumenism.[39]

2.2 The Emergence of Contextualization

Although *contextualization* is a modern term, a long history lies behind the practice it designates.[40] After surveying early church history, Harvie M. Conn concluded that "contextualization is not a new discovery."[41] Concerns over issues of contextualization are ancient, going back to the early church as it struggled to break loose from its Jewish cultural trappings and to communicate the gospel to the Greco-Roman world of the Gentiles.[42] Even in the New Testament era, missionaries had to find effective ways to communicate the gospel in other cultures within the Roman Empire, applying the biblical teaching in light of pagan practices and considering challenges they never faced in their own cultural contexts.[43]

---

38. Stransky, "Criticism," 254.

39. Erickson, *Christian Theology*, 1148–1149.

40. Justin S. Ukpong, "Contextualisation: A Historical Survey," *AFER* 29 (1987): 278–286 (285).

41. Harvie M. Conn, "Contextual Theologies: The Problem of Agendas," *WTJ* 52 (1990): 51–63 (55–62).

42. Darrell L. Whiteman, "Contextualization : The Theory, the Gap, the Challenge," *IBMR* 21 (1997): 2–7 (2).

43. M. David Sills, "Paul and Contextualization," in *Paul's Missionary Methods: In His Time and Ours*, ed. Robert L. Plummer and John Mark Terry (Leicester: Inter-Varsity Press, 2012), 196–215 (197).

As a neologism, however, the term *contextualization* was coined in 1972 by Shoki Coe and the Theological Education Fund (TEF) committee of the WCC. Coe, a renowned Taiwanese theologian, became the director of the TEF committee in 1971 during the Third Mandate of TEF. A year later, the TEF committee decided to call for reform in theological education.[44] Coe believed that reform and renewal can only occur when theological educators engage in a double wrestle – responding to the imperative call of the gospel and tackling the challenges of the times.[45] The TEF committee sought forms of theological expression deeply rooted in local culture and aimed to develop structures for education and ministry appropriate to concrete missiological situations. For this reason, as Bergquist says, "the single, guiding thrust of the TEF's Third Mandate is summed up by the term *contextualization*."[46] The 1972 TEF report, *Ministry in Context*, clearly states, "Contextualization should be the focal concern because through it alone will come reform and renewal. Contextualization of the gospel is a missiological necessity."[47]

According to Shoki Coe, the TEF prefers to use the word *contextualization* instead of *indigenization*. The words *indigenous*, *indigeneity*, and *indigenization* derive from a nature metaphor that means taking root in the soil. Coe explains that through the word *contextualization*, the TEF tried "to convey all that is implied in the older term *indigenization* but seek to press beyond for a more dynamic concept which is open to change and which is also future-oriented."[48] The TEF committee believes that the term *contextualization* is conceptually wider and better than *indigenization*. Because contextualization refers to a dynamic rather than a static reality, this word acknowledges the changing nature of reality.[49] Contextualization includes the concerns of

---

44. Simon S. M. Kwan, "From Indigenization to Contextualization: A Change in Discursive Practice Rather than a Shift in Paradigm," *StudWorldChr* 11 (2005): 236–250 (237).

45. Shoki Coe, "Theological Education: A Worldwide Perspective," *Theological Education* 11 (1974): 5–12 (7).

46. James A. Bergquist, "TEF and the Uncertain Future of Third World Theological Education," *Theological Education* 9 (1973): 244–253 (251).

47. World Council of Churches, "Theological Education Fund, from Ministry in Context: The Third Mandate Program of the Theological Education Fund (1970–1977)," in *Classic Texts in Mission and World Christianity*, ed. Norman E. Thomas (Maryknoll, NY: Orbis, 1995), 175–176 (176).

48. Shoki Coe, "In Search of Renewal in Theological Education," *Theological Education* 9 (1973): 233–243 (241).

49. Kwan, "From Indigenization," 238.

traditional local cultures but looks more deliberately toward the future, toward issues of social revolution and human justice.[50] In fact, the term was introduced to emphasize "the development of local theologies in the context of radical social and political change within a given culture, particularly in the Third Word."[51]

The fact that *contextualization* was coined in ecumenical circles left many evangelicals immediately suspicious. Initially, some conservative evangelicals hesitated to adopt the new term.[52] For example, James O. Buswell III expressed his concern about replacing the older term *indigenization* with *contextualization*. He preferred to preserve terms such as *indigenous, indigeneity*, and *indigenization* for modern use.[53] Some chose to adopt the term *contextualization* but rejected the meaning prescribed by the TEF initiators.[54]

Evangelicals made an explicit response to the term *contextualization* at the Lausanne Congress on World Evangelization in 1974, and came to adopt it, albeit defining it in their own distinctive way. In Lausanne, one of the study groups discussed the issue of contextualization. Chaired by M. Bradshaw, the study group produced a report entitled, "The Gospel, Contextualization, and Syncretism Report" and defined contextualization in light of evangelical convictions. The committee identified two sides of contextualization: "Meaningful communication in forms that are real to the person and his full response to the Lord in repentance and obedience of faith that affects his whole lifestyle, his attitudes, and his values, etc."[55] Later in 1978, a Lausanne Consultation on Gospel and Culture, which met in Willowbank, Bermuda, highly emphasized the importance of contextualization and the need of local Christians to assume the responsibility to contextualize the gospel in their

---

50. Bergquist, "TEF and the Uncertain Future," 251.

51. Dean Flemming, "The Third Horizon: A Wesleyan Contribution to the Contextualization Debate," *WesTJ* 30 (1995): 139–163 (139).

52. Moreau, *Contextualization*, 34.

53. James O. Buswell III, "Contextualization: Theory, Tradition and Method," in *Theology and Mission: Paper Given at Trinity Consultation No.1*, ed. David J. Hesselgrave (Grand Rapids, MI: Baker, 1978), 87–111 (93–97).

54. Hesselgrave and Rommen, *Contextualization: Meanings, Methods, and Models* (Nottingham: Apollos, 1989), 33.

55. William J. Larkin, Jr., *Culture and Biblical Hermeneutics: Interpreting and Applying the Authoritative Word in a Relativistic Age* (Grand Rapids, MI: Baker, 1988), 153.

own languages and cultures.⁵⁶ The Willowbank Report decrees, "By common prayer, thought, and heart-searching, in dependence on the Holy Spirit, expatriate and local believers may learn together how to present Christ and contextualize the gospel with an equal degree of faithfulness and relevance."⁵⁷ The term *contextualization* eventually became widely adopted and is now used widely across the theological mission spectrum.⁵⁸

Latin American theologian C. René Padilla, for example, stresses that the theology of the gospel must be contextualized.⁵⁹ Padilla underscores an urgent need to manifest the universality of the gospel that is not bound by a particular culture but shows the many sided wisdom of God.⁶⁰ Similarly, Brian Wintle indicates that a properly done theology will always be contextual. He says, "Unless a person who is thinking theologically is rooted in his context and thinks from that perspective, his theology will not be truly relevant."⁶¹ Darrell L. Whiteman considers the term *contextualization*, compared with older terms such as *adaptation, accommodation,* and *indigenization,* as more dynamic and more adequate to describe current mission trends. He believes that *contextualization* helps our understanding of the relationship between gospel, church, and culture.⁶² According to Ukpong, the emergence of the idea of contextualization in the twentieth century "has led to a positive search for new Christian expression forms that will consciously take seriously new cultural contexts with which Christianity comes in contact."⁶³ The idea has helped Christians move "away from a conception of the gospel as a-cultural to an understanding of how the gospel necessarily becomes translated into the

---

56. Lausanne Committee for World Evangelization, "Willowbank Report : Report of a Consultation on Gospel and Culture," *IRM* 67 (1978): 211–221 (214–215).

57. Lausanne Committee for World Evangelization, "The Willowbank Report" in *Down to Earth: Studies in Christianity and Culture*, ed. Robert T. Coote and John Stott (Grand Rapids, MI: Eerdmans, 1980), 308–339 (320).

58. Eugene S. Heideman, "Syncretism, Contextualization, Orthodoxy, and Heresy," *Missiology* 25 (1997): 37–49 (39).

59. C. René Padilla, "The Contextualization of the Gospel," *JTSA* 24 (1978), 12–30. See also Dwight Honeycutt, "Contextualization: A Valuable Missiological Concept," *TTE* 36 (1987): 9–15 (11).

60. Padilla, "Contextualization," 28.

61. Brian Wintle, "Doing Theology in Context: A Biblical Case Study," in *Doing Theology in Context: Festschrift in Honour of Dr. Bruce J. Nicholls*, ed. Sunand Sumithra (Bangalore: Theological Book Trust, 1992), 13–23 (13).

62. Whiteman, "Contextualization," 2.

63. Ukpong, "Contextualisation," 278.

various forms and expressions where it takes root."⁶⁴ Today *contextualization* has become a blanket term for a variety of theological models.⁶⁵

2.3 Definitions of Contextualization

With various perspectives, scholars from different schools of thought have diversely defined *contextualization*.⁶⁶ Shoki Coe says, "Contextuality . . . is that critical assessment of what makes the context really significant in the light of the *missio Dei*. It is the missiological discernment of the signs of the times, seeing where God is at work and calling us to participate in it."⁶⁷ For Coe, the method of contextualization involves a continual interplay between Scripture and the ever changing context in which it must be interpreted.⁶⁸

Byang H. Kato and Bruce J. Nicholls are among the first evangelical Christians who overcame reservations and adopted the ecumenical-coined word *contextualization*, with their own definitions. According to Kato, *contextualization* means making concepts or ideas relevant in a given situation. In reference to Christian practices, Kato understands the term to mean "an effort to express the never changing Word of God in ever changing modes for relevance."⁶⁹ Meanwhile, Nicholls defines *contextualization* as "the translation of the unchanging content of the gospel of the kingdom into verbal form meaningful to peoples in their separated cultures and within their particular existential situations."⁷⁰ To Nicholls, contextualization is cross-cultural communication of the gospel. He indicates that contextualization has three foci: the encultured gospel of the Bible, the messenger or communicator who

---

64. Brian M. Howell, "Multiculturalism, Immigration and the North American Church," *Missiology* 39 (2011): 79–85 (80–81).

65. David J. Bosch, *Transforming Mission: Paradigm Shifts in Theology of Mission* (Maryknoll, NY: Orbis, 1991), 527.

66. O. S. Olagunju, "An Evaluation of Bevans' Models of Contextual Theology and Its Contributions to Doing Theology in the 21st Century Church," *Ogbomoso Journal of Theology* 17 (2012): 37–57 (40).

67. Shoki Coe, "Contextualizing Theology," in *Mission Trends No.3*, ed. Gerald H. Anderson and Thomas F. Stransky (Grand Rapids, MI: Eerdmans 1976), 19–24 (21–22).

68. Ray Wheeler, "The Legacy of Shoki Coe," *IBMR* 26 (2002): 77–80 (78).

69. Byang H. Kato, "The Gospel, Cultural Context and Religious Syncretism," in *Let the Earth Hear His Voice*, 1216–1223 (1217).

70. Bruce J. Nicholls, "Theological Education and Evangelization Report," in *Let the Earth Hear His Voice*, 646–648 (647).

belongs to another culture, and the receiver of the gospel who responds from within the context of his own culture.[71] Both Kato and Nicholls stress the unchanging content of the gospel while defining contextualization.

Krikor Haleblian defines contextualization as "that discipline which deals with the essential nature of the gospel, its cross-cultural communication, and the development and fostering of local theologies and indigenous church forms."[72] Haleblian is obviously influenced by Bruce C. E. Fleming. Fleming suggests understanding contextualization according to three aspects: supracultural, transcultural, and cultural. The three aspects suggested by Fleming are all included in Haleblian's definition.[73]

Dean Flemming, on the other hand, emphasizes the dynamic process of contextualization. For Flemming, contextualization seeks to express the gospel authentically in the local context and, at the same time, transforms the context. He considers contextualization as "the dynamic and comprehensive process by which the gospel is incarnated within a concrete historical or cultural situation."[74] Moreau also sees contextualization as a process. He defines contextualization as "the process whereby Christians adapt the forms, contents, and praxis of the Christian faith so as to communicate it to the minds and hearts of people with other cultural backgrounds. The goal is to make the Christian faith as a whole – not only the message but also the means of living out of our faith in the local setting – understandable."[75]

Nevertheless, one of the most concrete definitions of Christian contextualization comes from Hesselgrave and Rommen. In fact, their understanding of contextualization will be employed throughout this study. Hesselgrave and Rommen, emphasizing all the activities involved in carrying out the Great Commission, define contextualization essentially as it was defined in the Lausanne movement, as "the attempt to communicate the message of the person, works, Word, and will of God in a way that is faithful to God's

---

71. Nicholls, *Contextualization*, 53.

72. Krikor Haleblian, "The Problem of Contextualization," *Missiology* 11 (1983): 95–111 (96–97).

73. Bruce C. E. Fleming, *Contextualization of Theology* (Pasadena, CA: William Carey Library, 1980), 73–74.

74. Dean Flemming, *Contextualization in the New Testament: Patterns for Theology and Mission* (Nottingham: Apollos, 2005), 19.

75. Moreau, *Contextualization*, 36.

revelation, especially as it is put forth in the teachings of Holy Scripture, and that is meaningful to respondents in their respective cultural and existential contexts."[76]

2.4 Approaches to Contextualization

For many evangelicals, the main question is how to implement contextualization.[77] It is critical to know how "to achieve a contextualization resulting in a theology both meaningful to the receptors and faithful to God's message,"[78] because theology must speak from, and is relevant to, real people in their specific culture, place, and time.[79] We shall now proceed to examine some of the approaches advocated. Nicholls categorizes two different approaches to contextualization: existential contextualization and dogmatic contextualization. According to Nicholls, existential contextualization is popular in ecumenical circles. This approach involves the interaction of two basic principles: the essential relativity of text and context and the dialectical method of the search for truth. Existential contextualization assumes that the Bible is culturally conditioned and has only relative value. This approach relies on multiple biblical theologies, each conditioned by the writer's own community of faith. Nicholls gives an example of existential contextualization through the approach of S. Wesley Ariarajah of Sri Lanka.[80] Ariarajah insists that the Bible does not have ultimate authority in theology because the Bible itself is cultural conditioned. He remarks that all scriptures, including the Bible, are "the confessional materials that reflect the faith and belief of the people who composed them at a given time."[81]

---

76. Hesselgrave and Rommen, *Contextualization*, 200.

77. Ruth Julian, "Ground Level Contextualization," in *Local Theology for the Global Church: Principles for an Evangelical Approach to Contextualization*, ed. Matthew Cook et al. (Pasadena, CA: William Carey Library, 2010), 58.

78. Tite Tienou, "Contextualization of Theology for Theological Education," in *Evangelical Theological Education Today: Agenda for Renewal*, ed. Paul Bowers (Nairobi: Evangel, 1982), 42–52 (42).

79. Laurie Green, *Let's Do Theology: Resources for Contextual Theology* (London: Mowbray, 2009), 13.

80. Nicholls, *Contextualization*, 24–28.

81. S. Wesley Ariarajah, "Towards a Theology of Dialogue," *ER* 29 (1977): 3–11 (9).

An alternative approach, which Nicholls embraces and advocates, is dogmatic contextualization. This approach "begins with an authoritative biblical theology whose dogmatic understanding is contextualized in a given cultural situation."[82] Nicholls' binary taxonomy – existential contextualization and dogmatic contextualization – rightly acknowledges the prime significance attached to the two poles of contextualization. However, some have criticized that his approach as too simplistic. His binary taxonomy excludes the significant number of theologians who attempt to balance the two poles in some way.[83]

Hesselgrave proposes a tripolar schema to understand different approaches to contextualization, namely apostolic contextualization, prophetic contextualization, and syncretistic contextualization. On a continuum between biblical revelation and cultural consideration, he identifies these three contextualizing approaches used by four theological orientations: orthodoxy, neo-orthodoxy, neoliberalism, and liberalism. According to Hesselgrave, the orthodox position commits to a fully authoritative Bible, seeking to teach biblical truth by didactic method. This approach to contextualization is labeled as apostolic contextualization, since the emphasis is on contextualizing apostolic faith. The approach used by both neo-orthodoxy and neoliberalism is called prophetic contextualization. This approach emphasizes the prophetic insight of the contextualizer and the cultural, political, and social circumstances in which the contextualizer is located. Prophetic contextualization seeks to discern truth by a dialectical method. According to Hesselgrave, although neo-orthodoxy and neoliberalism practice the same approach, neo-orthodoxy tends to emphasize the insights gained from reflection on Scripture and history more than neoliberalism does. The liberal position is characterized by syncretistic contextualization, which involves a dialogical method for pursuing truth. The result of this approach to contextualization is a new syncretistic "gospel."[84]

Hesselgrave, along with Rommen, concludes that contextualizations that are more consistent with Scripture and the historic Christian faith are more authentic than others. They believe that an acceptable contextualization is

---

82. Nicholls, *Contextualization*, 24.

83. Marc Cortez, "Context and Concept: Contextual Theology and the Nature of Theological Discourse," *WTJ* 67 (2005): 85–102 (87).

84. Hesselgrave and Rommen, *Contextualization*, 144–157.

"a direct result of ascertaining the meaning of the biblical text, consciously submitting to its authority, and applying or appropriating that meaning to a given situation. The results of this process may vary in form and intensity, but they will always remain within the scope of meaning prescribed by the biblical text."[85] While Hesselgrave's tripolar taxonomy is helpful, some fear that his contextualization continuum is too simplistic and too neatly categorized.[86] Moreover, his term *syncretistic contextualization* has been questioned by others, noting that it unnecessarily biases the taxonomy in particular directions.[87]

Other taxonomies for contextualization have been proposed throughout the last few decades. For example, Catholic theologian Robert J. Schreiter suggests three broad categories for contextualization approaches based on how each approach relates to its cultural context. According to Schreiter, the three categories are translation models, adaptation models, and contextual models.[88] In 2005, Marc Cortez listed three models according to their correspondence to three levels of biblical discourse: translation, synthetic, and praxis.[89] In 1989, Dean S. Gilliland provided a taxonomic framework that includes six models: anthropological, translation, praxis, adaptation, semiotic, and critical.[90] In his most recent framework, Gilliland drops the semiotic model and adds the synthetic model. Thus Gilliland's current six models are adaptation, anthropological, critical, praxis, synthetic, and translation.[91]

Another taxonomy commonly employed among missiologists is Stephen B. Bevans' six-model taxonomy.[92] Bevans categorizes six different models of contextual theology: translation, anthropological, praxis, synthetic, transcendental, and countercultural.[93] According to Bevans, the translation model,

---

85. Hesselgrave and Rommen, 202.
86. Moreau, *Contextualization*, 109.
87. Cortez, "Context and Concept," 87.
88. Robert J. Schreiter, *Constructing Local Theologies* (Maryknoll, NY: Orbis, 1986), 6–16.
89. Cortez, "Context and Concept," 87–89.
90. Dean S. Gilliland, "Appendix: Contextualization Models," in *The Word Among Us: Contextualizing Theology for Mission Today*, ed. Dean S. Gilliland (Dallas: Word, 1989), 313–317.
91. Dean S. Gilliland, "The Incarnation as Matrix for Appropriate Theologies," in *Appropriate Christianity*, ed. Charles Kraft (Pasadena, CA: William Carey Library, 2005) 493–519.
92. Stephen B. Bevans, *Models of Contextual Theology*, rev. ed. (Maryknoll, NY: Orbis, 2010), 37–137.
93. Bevans, *Models*, 37–137.

which is also called the accommodation or adaptation model, is the most popular and widely used model.[94] In this model Scripture is considered supracultural or supracontextual. Christians using this approach recognize that an essential, supracontextual message of Christianity can be separated from a contextually bound mode of expression. The starting point in this model is always the supracultural, supracontextual essential doctrine. Ultimately, the gospel is the judge of all contexts, and the contextual situation is the vehicle of the message.[95] Another model that considers seriously the message of Christianity as recorded in Scripture and handed down through tradition is the countercultural model, which is also called the prophetic or contrast model. This model emphasizes the radical ambiguity and insufficiency of human cultures. Practitioners of this model believe that the gospel calls into question all cultures. Bevans further indicates that the majority of practitioners of the countercultural model understand culture as contemporary Western culture, the culture from which they come. However, Bevans notes that in this model, Scripture is conceived as a narrative and story, not a list of doctrines or moral principles.[96]

In Bevans' remaining four models, anthropological, praxis, synthetic, and transcendental, Scripture is regarded as culturally conditioned and incomplete.[97] The main concern of the anthropological model, also known as the ethnographic model, is the preservation of a Christian's cultural identity. Practitioners of the anthropological model believe that God's revelation is found within human culture and that the Bible is the product of socially and culturally conditioned religious experiences.[98] The praxis model, also known as the liberation model, perceives God's revelation as "the presence of God in history – in the events of everyday life, in social and economic structures, in situations of oppression, in the experience of the poor and the marginalized."[99] The synthetic, or dialectical, model understands God's revelation as historically circumscribed within the particular contexts in which the Scriptures

---

94. Bevans, 37.
95. Bevans, 40–41.
96. Bevans, 117–124.
97. Bevans, 141–143.
98. Bevans, 54–56.
99. Bevans, 75.

were written.[100] The transcendental, or subjective, model accentuates understanding divine revelation as an event, not as content; divine revelation happens when a person opens himself or herself to reality. Thus revelation is not in the words of Scripture or in the doctrines of tradition.[101]

Bevans considers these six models by nature as not exclusive; therefore, committing oneself to any one model at the exclusion of one or more of the others is unnecessary. Moreover, he believes certain models can function more adequately within certain circumstances. None of these models can claim hegemony. Therefore, the best model of contextualization totally "depends on the context."[102] Bevans' taxonomy is helpful in understanding the relationship between the gospel message and culture.[103] Furthermore, he accurately catalogues the majority of evangelical models under the terms *translation* and *countercultural*.[104]

Many evangelicals rely on biblical congruence as their central criterion for determining the propriety of the contextualization models. Both Nicholls and Hesselgrave apply congruence with Scripture as a boundary marker to separate one type of model from another.[105] As Gilliland points out, all models of contextualization have a commitment to relevance and a focus on real situations in which people live. But he believes that "contextualization must give the highest place to God's word."[106] Contemporary evangelicals believe that ultimately the only viable grounding for good contextualization is Scripture.[107] For example, Osborne thinks biblical revelation "is the final arbiter of all truth and contextualization of necessity must recognize the inviolability of its truths."[108]

Because evangelicals put such emphasis on biblical congruence, Paul Hiebert's approach of contextualization is becoming widely respected among

---

100. Bevans, 91.
101. Bevans, 105.
102. Bevans, 139–140.
103. Olagunju, "Evaluation of Bevans' Models," 37–57 (53).
104. Moreau, *Contextualization*, 44.
105. Moreau, *Contextualization*, 108.
106. Gilliland, "Appendix: Contextualization Models," in *Word Among Us*, 313–317 (313).
107. Moreau, *Contextualization*, 111.
108. Grant R. Osborne, *The Hermeneutical Spiral: A Comprehensive Introduction to Biblical Interpretation* (Downers Grove, IL: InterVarsity Press, 1991), 319.

evangelicals.[109] Based on Jacob Loewen's and John Geertz's experience among the Wanana of Panama, Hiebert developed an approach called "critical contextualization."[110] The process of critical contextualization involves four steps: (1) Exegesis of the culture: The local congregation, led by local church leaders and the missionary, uncritically gather and analyse the traditional beliefs and customs with some questions at hand. The purpose in this stage is to understand the old ways, not to judge them. (2) Exegesis of the Scripture and the hermeneutical bridge: At this point the pastor or missionary leads the congregation in a study of Scripture to identify areas to address. The leaders also need to "translate the biblical message into the cognitive, affective, and evaluative dimensions" of the culture. (3) Critical response: In the third step, the congregants critically evaluate their own past customs in the light of their new biblical understandings and decide how to respond to their new-found truths. (4) New contextualized practices: In the final step, the pastor or missionary helps the congregants arrange the practices they have chosen into a new ritual that expresses the Christian meaning of the event.[111] The strength of critical contextualization involves seriously evaluating both the culture and Scripture and asking the church as a body to participate in the hermeneutical task.[112] Hiebert's method integrates anthropology, theology, and missiology.[113]

This study focuses on contextualizing preaching and therefore will not directly employ the model of critical contextualization, because its remit is wider than this study requires. However, this study will consider three principles in the method of critical contextualization because they are directly germane to our task. The first principle considered is the exegesis of culture. Hiebert believes that old customs should not be rejected or accepted uncritically but should be explicitly examined with regard to their meanings and functions in the society. After this examination, customs can be evaluated in the light of biblical norms.[114] Second, Hiebert stresses that Scripture

---

109. Eunhye Chang, et al., "Paul G. Hiebert and Critical Contextualization," *TRINJ* 30 (2009): 199–207 (201).

110. Paul G. Hiebert, "Critical Contextualization," *IBMR* 11 (1987): 104–112 (109).

111. Hiebert, "Critical Contextualization," 104–112 (109–110).

112. Dean S. Gilliland, "Contextualization Models," in *The Word Among Us*, 313–317 (317).

113. Chang, et al., "Paul G. Hiebert," 201.

114. Hiebert, "Critical Contextualization," 287–296 (290).

should function normatively and correct the culture.[115] After all, as Pete Ward reminds us, the Scripture is "a common source for Christian theology and thinking, whatever the church or cultural environment."[116] Lastly, Hiebert involves local people in evaluating their own culture because they know the meanings of their own customs better than the missionary.[117] This study also draws upon local preachers' strengths in contextualization. As Buswell asserts, "Unquestionably, contextualization must be an emic approach."[118]

2.5 Syncretism

One of the most often recurring discussions on the subject of contextualization is syncretism.[119] As Harvie M. Conn points out, people in Reformed and evangelical circles often raise the concern of syncretism when contextualization is mentioned.[120] John Gration comments that contextualization without a solid biblical mooring can easily lead to syncretism.[121] However, what is syncretism?

In the history of its usage, the concept of syncretism went through various changes in meaning.[122] Levinskaya notes that the word was used by Plutarch, the first-century Greek historian, in his work *On Brotherly Love*. Plutarch applied the term to refer to Cretans who constantly fought one another but stopped fighting and united when threatened by a common enemy. Much later Erasmus used the word in his letter to Melanchthon in 1519. Erasmus spoke

---

115. Chang, et al., "Paul G. Hiebert," 204.

116. Pete Ward, *Introducing Practical Theology: Mission, Ministry, and the Life of the Church* (Grand Rapids, MI: Baker Academic, 2017), 36.

117. Hiebert, "Critical Contextualization," 287–296 (291).

118. Buswell, "Contextualization," 87–111 (98). Please refer to Pike's etic-emic distinctions in chapter 1.

119. Haleblian, "Problem of Contextualization," 96.

120. Conn, "Contextual Theologies," 51–63 (51).

121. John Gration, "Willowbank to Zaire: The Doing of Theology," *Missiology* 12 (1984): 297–309 (306).

122. Andre Droogers, "Syncretism: The Problem of Definition, the Definition of the Problem," in *Dialogue and Syncretism: An Interdisciplinary Approach*, ed. J. D. Gort et al. (Grand Rapids, MI: Eerdmans, 1989), 7–25 (9).

of syncretism in the traditional way that Plutarch did – to come to concord and fight mutual enemies despite differences of opinion.[123]

However, in the seventeenth century, the syncretism became a polemical term with pejorative meaning, referring to the illegitimate reconciliation of opposing theological views.[124] During this period a movement led by George Calixtus of Helmstad called all Protestant churches in Europe to doctrinal reconciliation and mutual access to each other's rituals of communion and baptism. Calixtus's opponents accused him of advancing an entirely unprincipled jumbling together of religions. These debates were known as the "syncretism controversies."[125] Thus the word *syncretism* began to be used negatively from the beginning of the Protestant era. In theological disputes the term referred to a betrayal of principles and an attempt to secure unity at the expense of truth.[126]

In the nineteenth century, scholars began to use the word *syncretism* to define the extensive mixture and even fusion of cults and philosophies in the Hellenistic period. The period is called "Hellenistic" because of the dispersion of Greek language and culture after Alexander the Great's conquests.[127] During the Hellenistic period, a large population within a vast territory interacted with Hellenism, and the process of heterogeneous innovations flourished in Hellenistic religions. Thus the term *syncretism* was used to describe this complex phenomena of heterogeneous innovations in Hellenistic religions. It implies the combination of features from different religions.[128]

Carman indicates that when historians of religion use the word *syncretism*, they usually refer to the Hellenistic era as the prototype for its definition.[129] Yet in spite of reliance on the Hellenistic prototype, historians of religion still have different interpretations of syncretism. For example, G. Van der Leeuw

---

123. Irina A. Levinskaya, "Syncretism – The Term and Phenomenon," *TynBul* 44 (1993): 117–128 (119).

124. Droogers, "Syncretism," 9.

125. Rosalind Shaw and Charles Stewart, "Introduction: Problematizing Syncretism," in *Syncretism/Anti-Syncretism: The Politics of Religious Synthesis*, ed. Charles Stewart and Rosalind Shaw (London: Routledge, 1994), 1–24 (4).

126. Heideman, "Syncretism," 37–49 (38).

127. John B. Carman, "Syncretism: Historical Phenomenon and Theological Judgement," *ANQ* 4 (1964): 30–43 (31).

128. Levinskaya, "Syncretism," 121–122.

129. Carman, "Syncretism," 31.

believes every religion, including Christianity and Islam, is to some extent syncretistic.[130] Leeuw's view of syncretism obviously has had wide influence. This view is reflected in Eric Maroney's recent statement that "all religions are syncretistic in a certain sense. They develop from antecedents and accrue influences from other faiths and add them to their own."[131]

Hendrik Kraemer, a contemporary of Leeuw, has a different view of syncretism. Basically, Kraemer categorizes two kinds of religion: prophetic religions of revelation and naturalist religions of transempirical realisation. Christianity, Islam, and Judaism belong to the group of prophetic religions. Most the other religions, including primitive religions, are considered under the category of naturalist religions.[132] Kraemer believes the prophetic religions "by nature and principle are exclusive, immune to the syncretistic spirit and the syncretistic solution of the problem of ultimate religious truth."[133] While acknowledging that Christianity, Judaism, and Islam throughout history did adopt some extraneous elements, Kraemer refuses to apply the term *syncretism* to these prophetic religions. He says, "It would be more misleading and confusing than elucidating, because their fundamental nature is unsyncretistic."[134] On the other hand, for the naturalist religions, Kraemer thinks syncretism is a necessary and normal trait. He claims that the naturalist religions are fundamentally syncretistic. Thus he objects to the pejorative use of the term *syncretism*. Kraemer emphasizes, "From the standpoint of the naturalist religions, however, it is not correct to speak of syncretism as an illegitimate and unexpected proceeding, because it is just what one should expect to happen."[135] Kraemer's position is in line with some anthropologists who have long recognized syncretism as a distinguishing feature of folk belief.[136]

---

130. G. Van der Leeuw, cited in Carman, "Syncretism," 33.

131. Eric Maroney, *Religious Syncretism* (London: SCM, 2006), 168.

132. Hendrik Kraemer, *The Christian Message in a Non-Christian World* (Grand Rapids, MI: Kregel, 1969), 142–143.

133. Hendrik Kraemer, *Religion and the Christian Faith* (Cambridge: James Clarke, 1956), 397.

134. Kraemer, 397–398.

135. Kraemer, *Christian Message*, 203–204.

136. Clinton E. Arnold, *The Colossian Syncretism: The Interface Between Christianity and Folk Belief at Colossae* (Tubingen: J.C.B. Mohr, 1995), 234–235.

Years later, M. M. Thomas tried to "rescue the word *syncretism* from its bad connotation."[137] Thomas indicates that in the nineteenth and twentieth centuries, European Protestant theologians used the word in a more positive sense. During that period, syncretism referred to "legitimate assimilation by one religion of foreign religious elements without losing its fundamental character."[138] Thus Thomas proposes to redefine the term *syncretism* more neutrally as "covering legitimate, relatively legitimate, and illegitimate mingling of different religious elements – the ultimate principle and goal of legitimacy being left to each religion or ideology."[139]

Today the word *syncretism* has varied meanings, with both positive and negative connotations. Peter Schineller attests, "As used by anthropologists and historians of religion, it is generally used positively. As used by theologians and church leaders, it may be used either positively or negatively. Whether one takes a positive or negative view depends on how one defines syncretism and usually will reflect a conservative or liberal stance."[140] Seeing the word *syncretism* as too ambiguous, open, and subjective, Schineller proposes to abandon it altogether.[141]

Andre Droogers, on the other hand, thinks discarding the term is unwise. He gives several reasons. First, the term is widely used. Second, in Droogers' own words, "Its abandonment is the more improbable when one considers that the number of contacts between believers of different religions increases daily, and with that, the phenomenon referred to by the term 'syncretism,' in all senses of the word."[142] Third, syncretism is an important term in the discussion on interreligious dialogue, regardless of its positive or negative subjective sense. Lastly, those seeking contextualization may use *syncretism* in a positive, proud, and defiant sense, especially in concrete situations in the Majority World.[143]

---

137. M. M. Thomas, "The Absoluteness of Jesus Christ and Christ-centred Syncretism," *ER* 37 (1985): 387–397 (393).

138. Thomas, 393.

139. Thomas, 394.

140. Peter Schineller, "Inculturation and Syncretism: What Is the Real Issue?" *IBMR* 16 (1992): 50–53 (50).

141. Schineller, 52.

142. Droogers, "Syncretism," 7–8.

143. Droogers, 8.

However, Droogers acknowledges that *syncretism* is a tricky term. He thinks the main difficulty is that this term is used both objectively and subjectively. He further explains, "The basic objective meaning refers neutrally and descriptively to the mixing of religions. The subjective meaning includes an evaluation of such intermingling from the point of view of one of the religions involved. As a rule, the mixing of religions is condemned in this evaluation as violating the essence of the belief system."[144]

Although syncretism is a complicated concept, one cannot ignore this issue when dealing with contextualization. Moreau points out that the interconnection between contextualization and syncretism is inevitable since they are both a process of faith and culture.[145] From the beginning of the evangelical deliberations on contextualization, a concern regarding syncretism has been evident in the discussions about theologizing.[146] Back in 1974, at the Lausanne International Congress on World Evangelization, Byang Kato and a study group voiced concern over syncretism. With a negative interpretation, the study group said that syncretism "occurs when critical and basic elements of the gospel are lost in the process of contextualization and are replaced by religious elements from the receiving culture; there is a synthesis with this partial gospel. In some cases syncretism reaches such proportions that a totally new 'gospel' appears."[147]

Kevin J. Vanhoozer reminds us, "If syncretism is a flawed method, its error lies not in mining philosophies and religions for true insights but in assuming that all religions and philosophies are ultimately about the same thing. Even a cursory reading of Scripture shows that the God of Israel had nothing to do with the idols of Canaan."[148] Just as Anderson points out, syncretism in ancient Israel was vehemently denounced by the prophets.[149] Anderson

---

144. Droogers, 7.

145. Moreau, *Contextualization*, 128.

146. Harvie M. Conn, *Eternal Word and Changing Worlds: Theology, Anthropology, and Mission in Trialogue* (Phillipsburg, NJ: P&R, 1984), 176.

147. "The Gospel, Contextualization and Syncretism Report," in *Let the Earth Hear His Voice*, 1224–1228 (1227).

148. Kevin J. Vanhoozer, "One Rule to Rule Them All?," in *Globalizing Theology: Belief and Practice in an Era of World Christianity*, ed. Craig Ott and Harold A. Netland (Grand Rapids, MI: Baker Academic, 2006), 85–126 (103).

149. J. N. D. Anderson, *Christianity and Comparative Religion* (London: Tyndale, 1970), 12.

considers syncretism as an attempt to unite or reconcile diverse religious tenets or practices.[150] He further explains, "Real syncretism is always based on the presupposition that all positive religions are only reflections of a universal original religion and show therefore only gradual differences."[151] According to Eugene S. Heideman, because the term *syncretism* has become negative, "It became necessary in mission contexts to utilize another term, *contextualization*, to provide space for the incorporation into the life and practice of the church elements found in the cultures of Asia, Africa, and indigenous peoples around the world."[152]

2.6 Examples of Contextualization from the New Testament

Norman R. Ericson indicates that the New Testament is indeed a prime example of contextualization. He provides several examples: (1) The decree of the Jerusalem Council declared that Jewish cultic requirements could not be required of Gentile Christians. This decision recognized two different contexts. The first context was the Jewish Christians, and the second context was the mixed community comprised of Jewish Christians and Gentile Christians (Acts 15:1–29). (2) In his letter to the Corinthians, Paul clearly indicated how to deal with contextual behaviour. The meaning of the behaviour determines the acceptability or nonacceptability of cultural forms (1 Cor 8:1–10:22). (3) Paul used society's regulations compatible with Christianity as a persuasive argument (1 Cor 5:1–8). (4) Many of Paul's letters are a direct reflection of the Greco-Roman society. Paul often addressed the society as it is, without demanding external change (Col 3:18–4:1).[153]

Plenty of examples of contextualization are found in the New Testament, especially in Acts and the Epistles.[154] The book of Acts shows clearly that the early Christian missionaries interacted with the religious convictions of their audience when they preached and taught the gospel. Eckhard J. Schnabel

---

150. Anderson, 10.
151. Anderson, 12.
152. Heideman, "Syncretism," 37–49 (39).
153. Norman R. Ericson, "Implications from the New Testament for Contextualization," in *Theology and Mission*, 71–85 (74–79).
154. Osborne, *Hermeneutical Spiral*, 320–321.

mentions the apostle Paul as an example of one who "took into account the scriptural and traditional convictions of the Jews in the synagogue of Pisidian Antiocheia (Acts 13:16–41), the popular superstition of the inhabitants of Lycaonia (Acts 14:8–20), and the natural theology of the Stoic and Epicurean philosophers in Athens (Acts 17:16–34)."[155] Thus Paul, as Sills points out, "is the model missionary who crosses cultural boundaries and contextualizes his unchanging message to the particular contexts of his hearers."[156]

The following section will focus on the accounts of Paul's preaching in Lystra (Acts 14) and Athens (Acts 17). In both cases Paul preached within Gentile contexts.[157] As Dean Flemming indicates, these two sermons are the only ones in Acts directed to pagan Gentiles. Therefore, they are helpful for understanding how the gospel message bridges cultural barriers within the early Christian mission. In both incidents the gospel enters a new cultural and religious world.[158]

2.6.1 Paul's Preaching in Lystra (Acts 14:8–20)

Paul's sermon in Lystra is important because it is the first recorded sermon in Acts preached to an entirely Gentile audience. Moreover, this sermon has a key position at the beginning of the second half of the book of Acts, which describes the movement of the gospel into the Gentile context.[159]

Lystra was a Hellenistic city with a population containing a rich mixture of languages and religious beliefs.[160] Lystrans were often characterized as mostly rustic and uncivilized.[161] However, based on recent research, Schnabel thinks that Lystra was a prosperous city. He argues that the Lystrans speaking

---

155. Eckhard J. Schnabel, *Early Christian Mission*, II (Downers Grove, IL: InterVarsity Press, 2004), 1552.

156. Sills, "Paul and Contextualization," 202.

157. Edouard Ariste Germiquet, "Paul and Barnabas in Lystra (Acts 14:8–20): The Contextualization of the Gospel in a Graeco-Roman City" (unpublished masters thesis, Rhodes University, 1992), 3.

158. Flemming, *Contextualization*, 66.

159. Germiquet, "Paul and Barnabas," 2–3.

160. Germiquet, 97.

161. David G. Peterson, *The Acts of the Apostles*, The Pillar New Testament Commentary (Grand Rapids, MI: Eerdmans, 2009), 406.

Lycaonian (Acts 14:11) does not mean they were rustics; Lystrans were bilingual, speaking their native language as well as Greek.[162]

A man who was lame from birth listened to Paul preach. Paul recognized that the man had come to faith and thus commanded him to stand upright. Immediately the lame man sprang up and began to walk (Acts 14:8–10). The inhabitants of Lystra integrated the miracle into their traditional religiosity and interpreted the miracle as proof of the supernatural character of the missionaries.[163] They assumed that their gods had come to them in human form. The crowds called Barnabas "Zeus" and Paul "Hermes," because Paul was the one who began speaking, and Hermes was the messenger of the gods. Soon the priest of Zeus and the crowd wanted to offer sacrifices to the apostles (Acts 14:11–13). Lystrans believed they must make a great sacrifice to honor the gods, lest judgment fall on the region.[164] Here Paul encountered a spontaneous outpouring of Hellenistic religiosity.[165]

In Acts 14:15–17, Luke summarizes Paul's first address to a purely Gentile audience.[166] David G. Peterson notices that Paul's preaching in Lystra "is not evangelism in the normal NT sense of proclaiming Christ and his saving work." Starting with God as creator of all, Paul employed "the evidence of God's common grace in the sustaining fruitfulness of nature and the pleasures of everyday life as a basis for communication."[167] Germiquet believes even the rhetorical form of the preaching was adapted to the Greek audience. The preaching is structured in a typical Greco-Roman rhetorical form, "whereby the errors are first exposed before the truth can be presented."[168]

Schnabel points out that, in order to adapt to the particular situation, Paul's preaching in Lystra is not christological or kerygmatic as earlier speeches in Acts, but theological, explaining the sovereignty of the one true God. Schnabel further indicates that Paul's explanation of the gospel in Lystra contains four

---

162. Eckhard J. Schnabel, *Acts*, Zondervan Exegetical Commentary on the New Testament (Grand Rapids, MI: Zondervan, 2012), 605.

163. Schnabel, *Early Christian Mission*, 1116.

164. Ben Witherington III, *The Acts of the Apostles: A Socio-Rhetorical Commentary* (Grand Rapids, MI: Eerdmans, 1998), 424–425.

165. Peterson, *Acts of the Apostles*, 407–408.

166. Witherington, *Acts of the Apostles*, 425.

167. Peterson, *Acts of the Apostles*, 411.

168. Germiquet, "Paul and Barnabas," 97.

assertions.[169] The first assertion is a call to turn from worthless idols to the living God and begins negatively before making a positive point. Paul told his Gentile audience to turn away from "worthless things" (μάταια), which includes their gods Zeus and Hermes, the sacrificial bulls, the garland, the procession, the altar of sacrifice, and the temple. In nonbiblical Greek, the term μάταια means "vain and foolish persons" or "empty talks," and would thus be understandable to the polytheists in Lystra. Paul urged them to turn away from their traditional gods, which are useless and powerless, and to turn to the "living God," an expression used in the Old Testament to describe the "one true God."[170]

Paul's second assertion proclaims that God is the sovereign Creator God. This God, who has the power to heal the crippled man, made the heavens, the earth, the sea, and all the animate beings and inanimate objects in the world. The distinction between the Creator God and all creatures is clear. Paul's proclamation provides the opportunity to critique the pantheism of the pagan cosmology.[171]

The third assertion emphasizes "God's forbearance of the nations' behaviour." In past generations, God allowed the nations to walk in their own ways, but He will now no longer tolerate their worship of idols.[172] This final assertion highlights God's goodness as the one who gives rain, fruit, and food. In the context of Lycaonian and Greek traditions, Paul argues that the living God is the one who grants harvest, not their fertility gods.[173] Paul uses the verb ἀγαθοεργέω (do good) to describe God's goodness in action. Darrell L. Bock believes that this assertion is a polemical and contextualized response to the concept of Zeus as καλακάγαθιοσ (who does what is good and fruitful). This word was employed to venerate Zeus and appears in temples at Phrygia and Pisidia.[174] Schnabel expresses a similar view when he comments that "the

---

169. Schnabel, *Acts*, 609–611.
170. Schnabel, 609.
171. Schnabel, 610.
172. Schnabel, 610.
173. Schnabel, 611.
174. Darrell L. Bock, *Acts*, Baker Exegetical Commentary on the New Testament (Grand Rapids, MI: Baker Academic, 2007), 479.

term *agathourgon* in Acts 14:17 is an example of linguistic 'contextualization' by Paul or by Luke."[175]

Dean Flemming asserts that from Paul's preaching in Lystra we see "a groundbreaking translation of the Christian message for a radically new cultural and religious environment."[176] Paul's preaching in Lystra provides a great example of how the early Christian missionaries faithfully proclaimed the gospel without "defusing" their conviction. Although the healing miracle in Lystra caused religious excitement among the Lycaonian population, Paul and Barnabas refused to adapt their convictions or their behaviour to popular piety or to manipulate the seemingly favourable moment.[177]

2.6.2 Paul's Areopagus Address in Athens (Acts 17:16–34)

Schnabel affirms that Paul's sermon before the Areopagus council is a classic example of Paul's interaction with the religious convictions of his listeners.[178] Paul visited Athens on his second missionary journey,[179] which may not have been Paul's intended destination in his original missionary plan. He went to Athens almost by accident. When Paul was preaching in Berea, the Jews in Thessalonica came and agitated the crowds and stirred them up against him (Acts 17:13–15). After the incident Paul was taken to Athens.[180] In Paul's day, Athens was still the cultural capital of the Western world and represented the height of pagan culture.[181] Paul started reasoning in the synagogue with the Jews and with the devout persons, as well as in the market place with those who happened to be present. Before long Paul was brought to the Areopagus (Acts 17:17–21).

Views differ concerning the reason Paul was brought to the Areopagus. The Greek term ἐπιλαμβάνομαι is ambiguous. It can refer to being arrested or being brought somewhere. Derek W. H. Thomas asserts that Paul might

---

175. Schnabel, *Early Christian Mission*, 1118.
176. Flemming, *Contextualization*, 71.
177. Schnabel, *Early Christian Mission*, 1553.
178. Schnabel, 1552.
179. Kenneth O. Gangel, "Paul's Areopagus Speech," *Bsac* 127 (1970): 308–312 (308).
180. Patrick Gray, "Implied Audiences in the Areopagus Narrative," *TynBul* 55 (2004): 205–218 (207).
181. J. Daryl Charles, "Engaging the (Neo) Pagan Mind: Paul's Encounter with Athenian Culture as a Model for Cultural Apologetics (Acts 17:16–34)," *TRINJ* 16 (1995): 47–62 (51).

have been brought to the court of the Areopagus on trial for his ideas, like years before in Socrates' case.[182] Likewise, Joshua W. Jipp believes that Paul was arrested and put on trial before the court of the Areopagus council, the most revered tribunal in the ancient world.[183] Bruce W. Winter, on the other hand, suggests that Paul was taken to the council not for any wrongdoing but simply as a herald of new deities. Winter asserts that the council of Areopagus, in the first century, examined any claims that introduced new deities into Athens.[184] Whatever the case, Paul was officially given an opportunity to explain Christianity to the Gentile audience in the religious court, including representatives of Stoicism, Epicureanism, and Athenian religion.[185] Standing before the Gentile court, Paul delivered his famous speech, which is considered by many to be one of the most brilliant impromptu sermons ever recorded.[186]

In his speech before the council of Areopagus, Paul demonstrates "remarkable rhetorical skill coupled with a precise knowledge of the mental frame of mind of his hearers." Moreover, Paul cleverly deals with the audience's religious and philosophical sensitivity.[187] Schnabel claims that Paul's Areopagus discourse is an excellent example of a "situational sermon" in which Paul presents an exposition of a specific aspect of his teaching before a particular audience.[188] Paul adapted his preaching to his audience by assimilating the ancient Greek view of the universe and its human quest for God with the gospel message. Moreover, he employed a line of reasoning that resembles the reasoning of classical Greek orators and quoted from Greek poets such

---

182. Derek W. H. Thomas, *Acts*, Reformed Expository Commentary (Philipsburg, NJ: P&R, 2011), 501.

183. Joshua W. Jipp, "Paul's Areopagus Speech of Acts 17:16–34 as Both Critique and Propaganda," *JBL* 131 (2012): 567–588 (572–574).

184. Bruce W. Winter, "On Introducing Gods to Athens: An Alternative Reading of Acts 17:28–20," *TynBul* 47 (1996): 71–90 (88–89).

185. Colin J. Hemer, "The Speeches of Acts II: The Areopagus Address," *TynBul* 40 (1989), 239–259 (243).

186. Gangel, "Paul's Areopagus Speech," 308.

187. Gangel, 308.

188. Schnabel, *Early Christian Mission*, 1552.

as Epimenides and Aratus of Soli.[189] Paul's utilization of Greek poets is what missiologists call "redemptive analogies."[190]

Charles summarizes the structure of Paul's Areopagus speech: "It begins with the epistemological assumptions of its hearers, it builds on a common understanding of the cosmos, yet it climaxes in the fullest self-disclose of the Creator – the resurrection of the God-man."[191] It is important to note that while Paul accommodated his terminology to suit the Greek mind, he certainly did not compromise the message of the gospel as he spoke of the resurrection.[192] Flemming points out that the Areopagus speech is one of the most instructive case studies in New Testament contextualization. The recorded discourse demonstrates how Paul transposed the gospel for Greeks with both firmness and flexibility.[193] It is a great example of "a magnificent balance between an 'identificational' approach that proclaims the gospel in culturally relevant forms on the one hand and a 'transformational' approach that resists compromising the gospel's integrity in a pluralistic culture on the other."[194] Colin J. Hemer rightly comments that the Areopagus speech is a classic for intercultural communication.[195]

2.7 Contextualized Preaching

The previous section gives examples of Paul's preaching with great sensitivity to different cultural contexts. This understanding of preaching is one aspect of contextualization. Indeed, Paul's sermons in Lystra and the Areopagus are great examples of contextualized preaching. Paul maintains a good balance between local relevance and faithfulness to the gospel. On one hand, Paul proclaims the gospel in ways the audience can understand. On the other hand, Paul resists compromising the gospel's integrity in a pluralistic world.[196]

---

189. Charles, "Engaging the (Neo) Pagan Mind," 52.
190. Osborne, *Hermeneutical Spiral*, 321.
191. Charles, "Engaging the (Neo) Pagan Mind," 55.
192. Gangel, "Paul's Areopagus Speech," 310.
193. Dean Flemming, "Contextualizing the Gospel in Athens: Paul's Areopagus Address as a Paradigm for Missionary Communication," *Missiology* 30 (2002): 199–214 (199–200).
194. Flemming, 208.
195. Hemer, "Speeches of Acts II," 255.
196. Flemming, *Contextualization*, 86.

Contextualized preaching, by definition, is preaching the gospel in a way that is not only biblically faithful but also culturally relevant. One of the main reasons for ineffective communication in preaching is irrelevancy of the message.[197] Fant asserts, "The word of God is never irrelevant, but my preaching may well be. And it will be, if it does not bear the eternal Word, and if it does not touch the living situation."[198] Robinson warns that sermons will be ineffective unless preachers realise that the listeners live in particular situations. He affirms the importance of exegeting both the Scripture and the congregation.[199] The Word of God and the audience are both essential for preaching.[200]

Effective preachers throughout church history have always adapted their sermons to their audiences in order to make the greatest possible impact. The necessity of relevance in preaching remains from generation to generation.[201] For example, Charles Haddon Spurgeon, D. L. Moody, and William Franklin Graham are all considered relevant preachers in their times.[202]

Preaching must move beyond accurate exposition of the biblical text and relate the message to the audience.[203] According to Cox, "True biblical exposition always keeps the present hearers in view as the Scriptures are interpreted."[204] Cox emphasizes the primacy of the audience, stating, "The speaker who forgets his audience might as well go off by himself and do a crossword puzzle. He is playing a game of oratorical solitaire."[205] A preacher should interpret Scripture deeply mindful of the hearers. Thomas Long attests,

---

197. Stephen Wai Kong, "Evaluating the Effect of Inductive Narrative Sermons Compared to Deductive Didactic Sermons to Increase Memory Retention of Chinese Church Members" (unpublished doctoral thesis, Denver Seminary, 2005), 75.

198. Clyde E. Fant, *Preaching for Today* (San Francisco: Harper & Row, 1987), 82.

199. Haddon W. Robinson, *Biblical Preaching: The Development and Delivery of Expository Messages*, 3rd ed. (Grand Rapids, MI: Baker Academic, 2014), 10–11.

200. Jean-Jacques von Allmen, *Preaching and Congregation* (London: Lutterworth, 1963), 27–28. For von Allmen, the first – Word of God, determines the second.

201. Scott A. Wenig, "Biblical Preaching that Adapts and Contextualizes," in *The Big Idea of Biblical Preaching: Connecting the Bible to People*, eds. Keith Willhite and Scott M. Gibson (Grand Rapids, MI: Baker, 1998), 25–38 (26).

202. John George Gueli, "Increasing Perceived Sermon Relevance through the Identification of Congregational Felt Needs" (unpublished doctoral thesis, Denver Conservative Baptist Seminary, 1993), 39–47.

203. David L. Larsen, *The Anatomy of Preaching* (Grand Rapids, MI: Baker, 1989), 95.

204. James W. Cox, *Preaching* (San Francisco: Harper & Row, 1985), 94.

205. James W. Cox, *Learning to Speak Effectively* (London: Hodder & Stoughton, 1966), 19.

"When preachers go to the Scripture, then, they must take the people with them, since what will be heard there is a word for them."[206] John Stott once said, "Preaching is not exposition only but communication, not just the exegesis of a text but the conveying of a God-given message to living people who need to hear it."[207] He asserts that the task of preachers is to enable God's revealed truth to flow out of the Scriptures into the lives of the men and women of today. For Stott, preaching is like bridge-building between the biblical world and the modern world. In other words, preaching needs to be relevant.[208] However, Stott asserts that "the type of bridge to be built must be determined more by the biblical revelation than by the zeitgeist or spirit of the age."[209]

Preaching, however, cannot be contextualized without giving attention to the culture of the audience. Quicke believes that preachers need to listen within their cultural environments in order to preach clearly and relevantly.[210] Referring to the preaching of Peter and Paul in Acts, Atkins indicates that apostolic preaching is highly culturally sensitive. He highlights the responsiveness of apostolic preaching to cultural context.[211] Atkins also points out the significance of the cultural understanding in preaching. He says, "How preachers regard their cultural context in relation to the gospel determines what and how they preach."[212]

To be faithful in gospel communication, preachers need to remember that the gospel is always proclaimed to people in specific contexts, and culture is an important part of the context.[213] J. L. Moreau aptly attests, "As God in Christ entered concretely into a specific culture at a given time and place, so the

---

206. Thomas G. Long, *The Witness of Preaching*, 2nd ed. (Louisville, KY: Westminster John Knox, 2005), 64.

207. John R. W. Stott, *I Believe in Preaching* (London: Hodder & Stoughton, 1982), 137.

208. Stott, 137–138.

209. Stott, 139.

210. Michael J. Quicke, *360 Degree Preaching: Hearing, Speaking, and Living the Word* (Grand Rapids, MI: Baker Academic, 2003), 161.

211. Martyn D. Atkins, *Preaching in a Cultural Context* (Peterborough: Foundry, 2001), 4.

212. Atkins, 7.

213. Mooyoung Lim, "Preaching and Culture: A Phenomenological Study to Korean American Immigrant Church Pastors' Communication Skills in a Changing Culture," *TRINJ* 33 (2012): 259–271 (260).

message of his revelatory-redemptive act must become incarnate in and for each generation by entering the culture of that generation and redeeming it."[214]

Cathcart insists that preaching, as an action carried out by and among people, cannot be accomplished apart from culture.[215] After conducting research on three effective contemporary American preachers, Cathcart concludes that preachers will be most effective when they actively engage and interact with the voices of culture when they preach.[216] In addition, preachers need to acknowledge the potential cultural oppositions which may be built into the worldview of the audience.[217]

As Tisdale suggests, preachers need to become amateur ethnographers skilled in observing the congregations they serve.[218] Hyunchul Henry Oh considers preaching as an interaction between church and culture. For Oh, the preacher serves and stands between God and the congregation. He believes preachers need to place preaching appropriately and efficiently in the interaction between church and culture.[219]

Contextualized preaching must be handled carefully with an appropriate view of culture. According to Clyde E. Fant, "It is possible to be both over impressed and under impressed with culture. Being over impressed with culture causes the preacher to be dominated by it; being under impressed with culture causes the preacher to ignore it. Where culture has dominated, the ultimate significance of proclamation has been lost; where culture has been ignored, true communication of the message has been lost."[220]

---

214. Jules Laurence Moreau, *Language and Religious Language: A Study in the Dynamics of Translation* (Philadelphia: Westminster, 1961), 194.

215. Rochelle L. Cathcart, "Culture Matters: How Three Effective Preachers – Tim Keller, Rob Bell, Father Pfleger – Engage Culture in the Preaching Event," *TRINJ* 33 (2012): 209–222 (210).

216. Cathcart, 222.

217. David Buttrick, *Homiletic: Moves and Structures* (Philadelphia: Fortress, 1987), 30–31.

218. Leonora Tubbs Tisdale, *Preaching as Local Theology and Folk Art* (Minneapolis: Fortress, 1997), 60.

219. Hyunchul Henry Oh, "Preaching as Interaction between Church and Culture: With Specific Reference to the Korean Church," *AJT* 19 (2005): 92–105 (102).

220. Fant, *Preaching for Today*, 84.

2.8 Contextualization in the Chinese Cultural Context

In reviewing the literature of contextualization in the Chinese context, it is essential to note that the term *indigenization* is still being used among Chinese scholars and pastors, albeit many have adopted the term *contextualization* after 1970s. The Chinese term for indigenization is *ben se hua* 本色化 or *ben tu hua* 本土化, and the term for contextualization is *chu jing hua* 處境化 or *guan lian hua* 關連化. The two terms are used synonymously in some Chinese Christian literature.[221]

According Peter Tze Ming Ng, the idea of localized Christianity in China could be traced back to 1844, when Karl Gutzlaff started the Chinese Union.[222] The wide spread of the indigenization movement calling for a harmonization of Christianity with Chinese culture, nevertheless, began in the 1920s as a response of the Chinese church toward the Anti-Christian Movement (非基督教運動).[223] During this period, Christianity was "placed on the defensive in the face of accusations of hidden agendas and complicity with imperialist exploitation."[224] Feeling the pressures, the Chinese church was forced to find ways to face the challenges from society.[225] In the National Christian Conference held in Shanghai on 2–11 May 1922, the necessity of indigenization was officially recognized.[226] After the conference, the indigenization

---

221. See 李志剛, 基督教與近代中國文化論文集 (*Essays on Christianity and Modern China*) (臺北 [Taipei]: 宇宙光, 1994), 3. See also 段琦, "對中國基督教本色化的兩點思考" (Reflections on Indigenization of Christianity in China), 於中華本色: 近代中國教會史論 (*China's Indigenization: Essays on the History of Christianity in Modern China*), 李金強, 湯紹源, 梁家麟編 (香港 [Hong Kong]: 建道神學院, 2007), 49–63 (62).

222. Peter Tze Ming Ng, *Chinese Christianity: An Interplay between Global and Local Perspectives* (Leiden: Brill, 2012), 68.

223. 莊雅棠, "本土神學的詮釋學輪廓" (Hermeneutics of Local Theology), 於基督生命長成: 現在中國本土基督教神學之發展 (*Growth in Life: 2013 Symposium on Modern Chinese Theology*) (新北市 [New Taipei]: 聖經資源中心, 2014), 39–54 (40).

224. Ryan Dunch, "Christianity and Adaptation to Socialism," in *Chinese Religiosities: Afflictions of Modernity and State Formation*, ed. Mayfair Mei-hui Yang (Berkeley: University of California Press, 2008), 155–178 (157).

225. 楊劍龍, "論非基督教思潮與中國教會本色化運動" (The Anti-Christian Movement and The Chinese Indigenous Church Movement), 於基督教與中國社會文化: 第五屆國際年青學者研討會論文集 (*Studies in Christianity and Chinese Society and Culture: Essays from the Fifth International Young Scholars" Symposium*), 賴品超與吳小新編 (香港 [Hong Kong]: 中文大學出版社, 2014), 25–38 (25).

226. 林榮洪, 風潮中奮起的中國教會 (*Chinese Theology in Construction*) (香港 [Hong Kong]: 天道書樓, 1980), 91–92.

movement in China received support from foreign missionaries as well.[227] More Chinese Christians began to take over the leadership roles in Chinese churches from the missionaries and responded to the need of indigenization.[228]

It is impossible to discuss all the Chinese Christian leaders related to contextualization in Chinese Christianity for almost a century. A few shall be highlighted in this section to show the diversity and complexity. In the early stage of the indigenization movement in China, T. C. Chao (趙紫宸) was considered as one of the key Chinese Christian intellectuals. Chao believed that indigenization of theology is more important than the indigenization of church organization.[229] He insisted that the Chinese church must have its own theology that integrated with the Chinese cultural context.[230] Christianity in China, he asserted, was in need of a philosophy of religion and philosophy of life done by Chinese.[231] Basically, Chao's position was that Christianity would enrich and fulfill traditional Chinese culture.[232] He recognized the problem of humanism in Chinese culture[233] and argued that Christianity can enter into Chinese culture to be its new blood and life.[234] In other words, Chao pointed out the incompleteness of Chinese culture and believed that Christianity can complete it.[235]

---

227. 楊劍龍, 26.

228. 吳國安, 中國基督徒對時代的回應(1919–1926): 以《生命月刊》和《真理周刊》為中心的探討 (*The Contextual Responses of Chinese Christians as Revealved in Life Journal and Truth Weekly 1919–1926*) (香港 [Hong Kong]: 建道神學院, 2000), 2.

229. 許開明, "論趙紫宸先生的脈絡化基督論的神學意義" (The Theological Meaning of T. C. Chao's Christology), 於神學與中國: 紐約神學教育中心暨漢語網絡神學院二十周年紀念文集 (*Theology and China: Essays Celebrating the 20th Anniversary of New York Theological Education Center and Chinese Online School of Theology*), 劉永明編 (香港 [Hong Kong]: 紐約神學教育中心, 2012), 195–237 (223).

230. Baoping Kan, "Theology in the Contemporary Chinese Context," *WW* 17 (1997): 161–167 (162–163).

231. "從今以後, 在中國, 基督教須有一個中國人自作的宗教哲學與人生哲學." See 趙紫宸, "中國民族與基督教" (Chinese and Christianity), 於本色之探: 20世紀中國基督教文化學術論集 (*Indigenization: Essays on Chinese Christianity in 20th Century*), 張西平與卓新平編 (北京 [Beijing]: 中國廣播電視出版社, 1999), 18–33 (33).

232. Wing-hung Lam, "Patterns of Chinese Theology," *OBMR* 4 (1980): 20–24 (22).

233. 林榮洪, 111.

234. Jonathan Chao, "Christianization of Chinese Culture," 於基督教與中國文化更新: 研討會匯報 (Argyle, TX: 大使命中心, 2000), 55–81 (65).

235. 林榮洪與溫偉耀, 基督教與中國文化的相遇 (*Encounter between Christianity and Chinese Culture*) (香港 [Hong Kong]: 香港中文大學崇基學院, 2001), 86.

Another key person in this period was Chih-hsin Wang (王治心), professor at Nanking Theological Seminary.[236] For Wang, the seeds of Christianity in the foreign missionaries' hands were not yet successfully planted into the soil of Chinese culture.[237] He emphasized the possibility of harmonization of Christianity with Confucianism, and tried to support the Chinese moral teachings with biblical truth.[238] Wang's indigenization was an attempt to be loyal to both Christianity and traditional Chinese culture.[239] In one of his articles, Wang even mentioned creating new Chinese Christian festivals for the sake of indigenization. He first listed major Chinese festivals with brief descriptions and then gave suggestions for new indigenous Chinese Christian festivals according to Chinese lunar calendar.[240] Wang's suggestion, although creative, was unfortunately not a practical one.

In the early period, there were other different positions regarding indigenization in the Chinese church. Lei-Chuan Wu (吳雷川), for example, interpreted Christianity from the standpoint of Chinese culture and sought elements from the Christian doctrines that would agree with the teaching of Chinese classics. For Wu, Christianity and Confucianism are merely different expressions of the same truth, the *Dao* 道.[241] On the other hand, the renowned Chinese preacher Ming-Tao Wang (王明道) saw Chinese culture as contaminated by human sinfulness, and Christianity should not to be harmonized with it.[242]

The issue of contextualization continues to be considered as of vital importance for the Chinese church,[243] as it is often linked to the aim of

---

236. Wing-hung Lam, "Patterns of Chinese Theology," 22.

237. "不過我們更希望他們能夠毅然地放手,把這粒種子下種在中國的文化和思想裏" See 王治心, "中國本色教會的討論" (The Discussion on the Indigenous Chinese Church), 於本色之探: 20 世紀中國基督教文化學術論集 (*Indigenization: Essays on the Chinese Christianity in 20ᵗʰ Century*), 張西平與卓新平編 (北京 [Beijing]: 中國廣播電視出版社, 1999), 236–244 (237–238).

238. 林榮洪, 106–108.

239. Wing-hung Lam, "Patterns of Chinese Theology," 22.

240. 王治心, "本色教會應創何種節期適合中國固有的風俗" (Festivals for Indigenous Chinese Church), 於本色之探: 20 世紀中國基督教文化學術論集 (*Indigenization: Essays on the Chinese Christianity in 20ᵗʰ Century*), 張西平與卓新平編 (北京 [Beijing]: 中國廣播電視出版社, 1999), 485–495 (592–495).

241. Wing-hung Lam, "Patterns of Chinese Theology," 21.

242. Wing-hung Lam, 23.

243. Rolv Olsen, "The Wind Blows Wherever It Pleases: A Study of Contextualisation of Christian Worship Services at Tao Fong Shan Christian Center, Hong Kong," *Swedish*

evangelizing.²⁴⁴ For the last few decades, different perspectives on contextualization in Chinese context were offered through varied studies. Arnold M. K. Yeung (楊牧谷, 1945-2002) was one of the key Chinese evangelical scholars who promoted contextual theology in the 1980s.²⁴⁵ For Yeung, a true Christian theology must concern both universality and particularity (context).²⁴⁶ Moreover, Yeung insists that contextualization in the Chinese cultural context should not be limited to dialoguing with Confucianism but should also be concerned with Chinese customs and other issues which the Chinese are dealing with in their culture today.²⁴⁷ His suggestion is a good reminder for the necessity of exploring the study of contextualization on issues such as Chinese festivals.

In-sing Leung (梁燕城), one of the most popular Chinese evangelistic preachers and an influential scholar,²⁴⁸ proposes to use a Chinese way of thinking to solve major theological questions from the Chinese, particularly responding to Confucianism, Taoism, and Buddhism. Leung stresses the importance of doing theological reflections in the context of Chinese culture and calls it *Zhong Hua Shen Xue* (中華神學), instead of indigenization or contextualization.²⁴⁹ Leung also points out that the methodology of Western theology is greatly influenced by Greek culture, thus we must have a biblical theology which has been "dehellenized" (去希臘化) before applying the biblical truth into Chinese culture.²⁵⁰

Well-known Chinese missiologist Enoch Wan (溫以諾) emphasizes a "sino-theology" (中色神學) as a theology with the "colour of Chinese culture"

Missiological Themes 87 (1999): 555-632 (555).

244. 梁家麟, 超前與墮後: 本土釋經與神學研究 (*Far Ahead and Lagging Behind: Studies in Contextual Hermeneutics and Theology*) (香港 [Hong Kong]: 建道神學院, 2003), 147-148.

245. Pan-chui Lai, "Theological Translation and Transmission between China and the West," in *Sino-Christian Theology: A Theological Qua Cultural Movement in Contemporary China*, ed. Pan-chui Lai and Jason Lam (Frankfurt: Peter Lang, 2010), 83-100 (91).

246. 楊牧谷, 復合神學與教會更新 (*Theology of Reconciliation and Church Renewal*) (香港 [Hong Kong]: 種籽出版社, 1987), 44.

247. 楊牧谷, "信徒皆祭司與神學處境化" (The Priesthood of All Believers and Contextual Theology), 於基督教與中國文化更新: 研討會匯報 (*Conference Essays on Christianity and the Renewal of Chinese Culture*), 陳惠文編 (Argyle, TX: 大使命中心, 2000), 128-137 (130).

248. 梁燕城與徐濟時, 119.

249. 梁燕城與徐濟時, XV-XVI.

250. 蔡仁厚,周聯華,與梁燕城,會通與轉化 (*Transcend and Transform*) (臺北 [Taipei]: 宇宙光出版社, 1985), 187.

specifically designed for the Chinese people, in contra-distinction from Western theology.[251] In order to do contextual theology in a Chinese way, Wan suggests employing a Chinese cognitive pattern (shame culture instead of Western guilt culture), Chinese cognitive process (synthetic instead of dialectic), and the Chinese way of interaction (relational and complementary).[252]

Paul Hiebert's approach to critical contextualization is also welcomed by some Chinese researchers. Tsukung Chuang (莊祖鯤), for example, believes that critical contextualization is an appropriate approach for Christians dealing with cultural issues.[253] One of the examples of using critical contextualization in Chinese cultural context is of Yung-Sheng Wen (溫永生), president of Christian Hakka Seminary in Taiwan. Wen applied the critical contextualization approach to examining the issues of ancestor worship and Chinese funerals.[254] In his doctoral dissertation on Chinese folk beliefs and practices, Yeow Beng Mah also adapted Hiebert's four steps of critical contextualization.[255]

One of the recent attempts at contextualization in Chinese cultural context is by Jackson Wu. In his work *One Gospel for All Nations*, Wu presents an example of contextualization using a Chinese cultural perspective. Wu suggests ways that a Chinese worldview could shape a contextualized biblical theology, based on three aspects of Chinese culture, namely face (honor and shame), family, and fortune.[256]

There is some research which has been devoted to the study of contextualization among particular subcultural groups of the Chinese. Paul R. Woods, for example, examines elements of the spiritual and philosophical heritage of Chinese diaspora intellectuals in the West which can be used to contribute

---

251. 溫以諾, 中色神學綱要 (*Sino-Theology: A Survey Study*) (Scarborough: 加拿大恩福協會, 1999), 58.

252. 梁燕城與徐濟時, 中國文化處境的神學反省: 中華福音神學人物研究 (*Theological Reflections in the Context of Chinese Culture: A Study of Christian Scholars toward their Evangelical Theologies*) (Burnaby: Culture Regeneration Research Society, 2012), 178.

253. 莊祖鯤, 宣教與文化 (*Mission and Culture*) (臺北 [Taipei]: 道聲出版社, 2004), 152–158.

254. 溫永生, "敬祖與喪禮處境化模式的建立" (A Design for a Contextualized Model of Christian Ancestor Reverence and Funeral Ritual), 建道學刊 (*Jian Dao*) 22 (2004): 57–98 (75).

255. Yeow Beng Mah, "Critical Contextualization of Chinese Folk Beliefs and Practices: Feng Shui as a Case Study" (unpublished doctoral dissertation, Asbury Theological Seminary, 2004), 8–11.

256. Jackson Wu, *One Gospel for All Nations: A Practical Approach to Biblical Contextualization* (Pasadena: William Carey Library, 2015), 128.

to contextualized Chinese Christian spirituality.[257] Barnabas Roland, on the other hand, identifies appropriate ways to do contextualization among animistic people groups in China's south and southwest regions.[258]

Proposals focusing on contextualization of the Chinese festivals do exist.[259] Betty O. S. Tan, for example, suggests some appropriate ways for Chinese Christians to celebrate the Spring Festival, aiming at applying the Christian truth to the Chinese context.[260] She points out that some Singapore Chinese churches hold a special Chinese New Year dinner for families in order to spread the spirit of Christian love. She believes that the principle of harmony and reconciliation could be emphasized in such functions.[261] Tan also suggests that Chinese Christians relate the house-cleaning practice before the Spring Festival to the Feast of Unleavened Bread in the Old Testament and how Jesus Christ in the New Testament cleanses us from all guilt and shame.[262] Overall Tan's article serves as a good starting point for discussion of contextualization of the Spring Festival. The article, however, mainly focuses on redeeming the cultural forms of the Spring Festival instead of offering insights for contextualized preaching during the festival. Thus its usefulness for a preacher in Chinese context is limited. It is believed that research on contextualized preaching during Chinese festivals is greatly needed. As Andrew Chiu reminds us, the liveliness and effectiveness of preaching always depends on contextualization.[263]

---

257. See Peter R. Woods, "Towards a Contextualized Spirituality for Chinese Diaspora Christians" (unpublished MTh dissertation, Spurgeon's College, 2006).

258. Barnabas Roland, "Communicating the Gospel with Power among China's Animistic Peoples," *ChinaSource Quarterly* 20 (2018): 7–9 (7).

259. 高明發, "節日與信仰: 中國文化與基督教節期的融通芻議" (Festivals and Faith: Comments on Chinese Culture and Christian Festivals), 教牧期刊 *(Pastoral Journal)* 20 (2006): 165–193 (186–191).

260. Betty O. S. Tan, "The Contextualization of the Chinese New Year Festival," *AJT* 15(2001): 115–132 (122–128).

261. Tan, 124.

262. Tan, 125.

263. 丘恩處, 新時代華人神學 (*The New Age Chinese Theology*) (New York: 紐約神學教育中心, 1996), 160.

2.9 Summary

In this chapter some major issues of contextualization, which are specifically related to the concerns of this study, are reviewed. Besides a brief survey on the history of the ecumenical movement and the emergence of contextualization in the twentieth century, the discussed issues also include the definitions of contextualization, the importance of contextualization, the approaches of contextualization, and the concern of syncretism. Examples of contextualization from the New Testament are reviewed as well.

In summary, the literature review reveals that contextualization is both a missiological and theological necessity. In addition, authentic contextualization must be consistent with Scripture and the historic Christian faith. This research recognizes the inviolability of the biblical revelation and agrees with contemporary evangelicals that, ultimately, the only viable grounding for good contextualization is Scripture. Moreover, examples of Paul's contextualized preaching in Acts show that, in the process of contextualization, the exegetical content has to be made relevant without compromising its substance. Faithfulness to the biblical truth is critically important. The review of the literature also illustrates the importance of cultural relevance in preaching. In the last section, discussions on contexualization in the Chinese context are outlined.

In the light of the literature review we have undertaken, I see that an investigation of contextualization is vital for any preacher. Understandings of contextualization and syncretism which I discuss above helped me in my attempts to understand what contextualized preaching is and the challenges related to it. They also remind me to be alert to the dangers of syncretism. My definition of contextualized preaching, therefore, is a preaching that is emphasizing both cultural relevance and faithfulness to the gospel.

CHAPTER 3

Confucianism, Taoism, Buddhism, and Chinese Folk Religion

For more than three millennia, China has been dominated by a strong and influential culture.[1] Hendrik Kraemer considers Chinese civilization as "one of the truly remarkable expressions of the human mind."[2] Ancient China produced a wealth of religious beliefs and practices, including mythological images, symbols, legends, divination arts, elaborate burial and funerary practices, shamanistic and demon-exorcising rites, and schema for understanding the cosmos.[3]

This chapter reviews literature that focuses on the backgrounds and beliefs of Confucianism, Taoism, Buddhism, and Chinese folk religion. The beliefs of each of these religions have significantly influenced the worldview of Chinese people today. Most of the observances of the Chinese festivals practised today are closely related to Confucianism, Taoism, Buddhism, and Chinese folk religion.[4] Understanding the beliefs behind these religions will provide the conceptual basis for studying the Chinese festivals in chapter 5.

---

    1. William A. Dyrness, *Learning about Theology from the Third World* (Grand Rapids, MI: Zondervan, 1990), 135.

    2. Hendrik Kraemer, *The Christian Message in a Non-Christian World* (Grand Rapids, MI: Kregel, 1969), 182.

    3. Judith A. Berling, *A Pilgrim in Chinese Culture: Negotiating Religious Diversity* (Maryknoll, NY: Orbis, 1997), 42–43.

    4. Carol Stepanchuk and Charles Wong, *Mooncakes and Hungry Ghosts: Festivals of China* (San Francisco: China Books and Periodicals, 1991), xi.

3.1 Confucianism

Samuel H. Chao says, "It is almost impossible to know about the Chinese without first knowing Confucianism."[5] Confucianism is considered by many Chinese as "the dominant ideology, a way of life, a system of thought, pervading every aspect of political, social and family affairs."[6] It can truly be said to have molded the Chinese culture in general.[7] Indeed, many governments in Asia today categorize their Chinese population as Confucian.[8]

3.1.1 Texts and Major Tenets of Confucianism

Confucianism, founded by Confucius, was developed during the Spring and Autumn Period of the Eastern Zhou dynasty in China.[9] It was an era that witnessed the flourishing of hundreds of schools of thought as kings and lords employed different experts to give them advice.[10] Confucius is a Latinized form of the Chinese name Kong Fu Zi (孔夫子), or Master Kong.[11] Confucius's given name was Kong Qiu (孔丘), and as an adult he was commonly called Kong Zhong Ni (孔仲尼).[12] Confucius was born in 551 BCE in the small state of Lu, the cultural centre of ancient China.[13] He eventually became recognized as China's greatest sage several centuries after his death.[14]

During the Spring and Autumn Period, common people suffered from exhausting interstate warfare. The barons of different states often warred with

---

5. Samuel H. Chao, "Confucian Chinese and the Gospel: Methodological Considerations," *AJT* 1 (1987):17–36 (19).

6. Chao, 19.

7. Wing-Tsit Chan, *A Source Book in Chinese Philosophy* (Princeton, NJ: Princeton University Press, 1963), 14.

8. Richard Madsen and Elijah Siegler, "The Globalization of Chinese Religions and Traditions," in *Chinese Religious Life*, ed. David A. Palmer, Glenn Shive, and Philip L. Wickeri (New York: Oxford University Press, 2011), 227–240 (235).

9. Xinzhong Yao, *An Introduction to Confucianism* (Cambridge: Cambridge University Press, 2000), 7.

10. David A. Palmer, "Religion in Chinese Social and Political History," in *Chinese Religious Life*, 155–171 (160).

11. Wing-Tsit Chan, *Source Book*, 14.

12. Joseph A. Adler, *Chinese Religious Traditions* (Upper Saddle River, NJ: Prentice Hall, 2002), 31.

13. Ch'u Chai and Winberg Chai, "Confucius," in *The Sacred Books of Confucius and Other Confucian Classics*, trans. and ed. Ch'u Chai and Winberg Chai (New Hyde Park, NY: University Books, 1965), 1–21 (21).

14. D. Howard Smith, *Chinese Religions* (New York: Holt, Rinehart & Winston, 1968), 32.

each other.[15] Regretting that many of the old rituals were no longer practised, Confucius tried to lead the Chinese back to ancient wisdom.[16] He believed that inculcating and following ancient wisdom and virtues would result in "true nobility of character, the greatest happiness and well-being of family and state."[17] Based on ancient Chinese tradition before him, Confucius made the effort to formulate a new philosophy, Confucianism, and propagated it as the path to peace and harmony.[18] He did not intend to establish a mere catalogue of virtues but, instead, to look for a centre, a thread of ancient virtues.[19] The main concern of Confucius was reinstating the timeless Way (*dao* 道) that was revealed and followed by the ancient sages.[20]

Confucius thought that his teachings simply transmitted the traditional wisdom and values of Chinese culture.[21] He referred to himself as a "transmitter" of the ancient past by editing and transmitting the ancient writings and by adding some writings himself.[22] Thus Yao is correct to call Confucianism "a tradition of books."[23] Over time, Confucian texts were combined into variously sized volumes. The "Five Classics" are the basic component of Confucian texts: *The Book of Changes* (*Yi Jing* 易經), *The Book of Poetry* (*Shi Jing* 詩經), *The Book of Documents* (*Shu Jing* 書經 or *Shang Shu* 尚書), *The Book of Rites* (*Li Ji* 禮記), and *The Spring and Autumn Annals* (*Chun Qiu* 春秋).[24] Eventually *The Great Learning* (*Da Xue* 大學), *The Doctrine of the*

---

15. W. E. Soothill, *The Three Religions of China: Lectures Delivered at Oxford* (London: Oxford University Press, 1930), 28–29.

16. Eric Walter Frederick Tomlin, *Great Philosophers of the East* (London: Arrow, 1959), 252.

17. D. Howard Smith, "Confucianism," in *The Encyclopedia of Word Faiths: An Illustrated Survey of the Word's Living Religions*, eds. Peter Bishop and Michael Darton (London: Macdonald, 1987), 273–278 (274).

18. Yao, *Introduction to Confucianism*, 7. It is believed that 孟子 Mencius and 荀子 Hsun Tzu later contributed greatly in the work of building its foundation. See Chai and Chai, "Confucius," 1–21 (1).

19. Heiner Roetz, *Confucian Ethics of the Axial Age: A Reconstruction under the Aspect of the Breakthrough toward Postconventional Thinking* (Albany: State University of New York, 1993), 103.

20. Mario Poceski, *Introducing Chinese Religions* (Oxon: Routledge, 2009), 41. *Dao* is often rendered in English as *Tao*.

21. Conrad Schirokauer, *A Brief History of Chinese Civilization* (Orlando, FL: Harcourt Brace, 1991), 31.

22. Chao, "Confucian Chinese," 19–21.

23. Yao, *Introduction to Confucianism*, 47.

24. Yao, 56–63.

Mean (*Zhong Yong* 中庸), *The Analects* (*Lun Yu* 論語), and *The Book of Mengzi* (*Meng Zi* 孟子) were also included into the key Confucian textbooks as the "Four Books."[25] *The Analects* is particularly important for understanding Confucius and his teachings. This book is a collection of Confucius' statements and conversations between him and his students.[26] In addition to the Five Classics and the Four Books, *The Classic of Filial Piety* (*Xiao Jing* 孝經) and *The Book of Music* (*Yue Jing* 樂經) also hold a prominent position among the Confucian classics.[27] *The Book of Music* was at some point considered as the sixth classic, but it was lost before the Han dynasty.[28] During the Han dynasty, *The Classic of Filial Piety* gained great popularity among the educated class and became an elementary textbook for generations.[29]

The central tenets of Confucianism converged upon the perfection of human conduct in this life. The two principal virtues and fundamental concepts in Confucius's moral teaching are ritual (*li* 禮) and benevolence (*ren* 仁).[30] Ritual (*li*) is extremely important in Confucianism.[31] During the time of Confucius, *li* was a very common word, meaning rites or rituals. Etymologically, the ideogram *li* (禮) symbolizes a sacrificial act.[32] The Chinese character *li* 禮 portrays a sacred 示 ritual vessel 豊, and its original meaning is to arrange ritual vessels to serve gods and pray for good fortune.[33] *Li* refers to a religious rite or ceremony, especially the sacrificial rites directed toward gods and ancestors. Connotations of the term *li* were later extended and developed, including formal behaviour of any kind, from ceremonies to

---

25. According to Xinzhong Yao, the Four Books were officially included during the Song dynasty. From the Yuan dynasty until the beginning of the twentieth century, a majority of Confucian scholars concentrated on the Four Books rather than the Five Classics. See Yao, 63–66.

26. Schirokauer, *Brief History*, 30.

27. Yao, *Introduction to Confucianism*, 67.

28. Yao, 67.

29. *Sacred Books of Confucius*, 325.

30. Poceski, *Introducing Chinese Religions*, 43.

31. Jeaneane Fowler and Merv Fowler, *Chinese Religions: Beliefs and Practices* (Portland, OR: Sussex Academic, 2008), 69.

32. Khiok-Khng Yeo, "Li and Law in the Analects and Galatians: A Chinese Christian Understanding of Ritual and Propriety," *AJT* 19 (2005): 309–332 (315).

33. Yao, *Introduction to Confucianism*, 191.

common patterns of conduct and polite manners of everyday life.[34] *Li* covers seasonal festivals and government functions as well.[35]

For Confucius, benevolence (*ren* 仁) is the perfection of human conduct.[36] As the foundation for cultivating other virtues, *ren* is a supreme virtue in the ethical system of Confucianism.[37] *Ren* is the most frequently discussed virtue by Confucius[38] and is regarded by him as the thread running through all other virtues.[39] *Ren* has been variously translated as humaneness, humanity, love, goodness, benevolence, man-to-man-ness, human-heartedness, and kindness.[40] The word for "benevolence" (*ren* 仁) sounds the same as the word for "human being" (*ren* 人). The etymology of the character *ren* 仁, which contains the elements *(er* 二*)* "two" and (*ren* 人) "human being" stresses correct procedure in human relationships. *Ren* leads to positive efforts for the good of others.[41] Thus *ren* is mainly concerned with human relationships.[42]

Viewing society as hierarchical, Confucius emphasized the importance of the Five Relationships (*wu lun* 五倫): the relationship between father and son, ruler and minister, husband and wife, elder brother and younger brother, and friend and friend. Confucius felt that the reciprocal obligations between people of superior status and people of inferior status were essential. He placed special emphasis on filial piety, the obedience a child owes to a parent.[43]

Confucius also portrayed the gentleman (*jun zi* 君子) as an attainable moral ideal.[44] The term *jun zi* originally referred to someone born into the aristocratic ranks. However, Confucius changed its meaning from nobility by birth to nobility by moral virtue. For Confucius, *jun zi* defined a level of

---

34. Poceski, *Introducing Chinese Religions*, 43.
35. Deborah Sommer, "The Book of Rites," in *Chinese Religion: An Anthology of Sources*, ed. Deborah Sommer (New York: Oxford University Press, 1995), 31.
36. Adler, *Chinese Religious Traditions*, 33.
37. Poceski, *Introducing Chinese Religions*, 44.
38. Rodney L. Taylor, *The Religious Dimensions of Confucianism* (Albany: State University of New York, 1990), 13.
39. Yao, *Introduction to Confucianism*, 213.
40. Yao, 213.
41. Chai and Chai, "Confucius," 1–21 (1).
42. Julia Ching, *Chinese Religions* (Maryknoll, NY: Orbis, 1993), 58.
43. Schirokauer, *Brief History*, 31.
44. Yao, *Introduction to Confucianism*, 25.

moral achievement. Confucius believed that each individual has the capacity to become a gentleman, albeit through diligence and perseverance.[45]

Confucianism flourished during the Han dynasty (206 BC–AD 220). In order to find an alternative to the legalistic principles favored by the previous Qin dynasty (221–206 BC), the Han rulers officially recognized Confucianism as the educational and political doctrine that could stabilise the empire.[46] Since the era of the Han dynasty, the doctrines of Confucianism have never ceased to influence Chinese culture.[47] Although Confucianism was disregarded by the Chinese government after the communist revolution, it has become popular again in mainland China in recent years. The attitude of the Chinese government toward Confucianism is very positive. Thus Anna Sun asserts that the twenty-first century may prove to be the Confucian century for China,[48] affirming that Confucianism remains influential among the Chinese.[49] For many, the cultural identity of modern China is still primarily Confucian.[50] As Khiok-Khng Yeo says, "Even among those Chinese who intentionally want to reject the Confucianist ideal, the Confucian ethic often still plays a significant role in their thinking and way of life."[51]

3.1.2 The Religious Dimensions of Confucianism

The religious dimensions of Confucianism have been debated for many years. Huston Smith indicates that the question of whether Confucianism is a religion or an ethic remains unsettled among the historians.[52] A number

---

45. Taylor, *Religious Dimensions*, 12.

46. Randall L. Nadeau, *Confucianism and Taoism*, Introduction to the World's Major Religions, vol. 2 (Westport, CT: Greenwood, 2006), 17.

47. William Theodore De Bary, Wing-Tsit Chan, and Burton Watson, *Sources of Chinese Tradition* (New York: Columbia University Press, 1960), 15.

48. Anna Sun, *Confucianism as a World Religion: Contested Histories and Contemporary Realities* (Princeton, NJ: Princeton University Press, 2013), 172.

49. Alan W. H. Pang, "A Biblically Foundational, Culturally Appealing, and Contextually Appropriate Discipleship Course for Mainland Chinese People" (Unpublished doctoral thesis, Denver Conservative Baptist Seminary, 1995), 45.

50. Dyrness, *Learning about Theology*, 136.

51. Khiok-Khng Yeo, "Christian Chinese Theology: Theological Ethics of Becoming Human and Holy," in *Global Theology in Evangelical Perspective: Exploring the Contextual Nature of Theology and Mission*, eds. Jeffrey Greenman and Gene L. Green (Downers Grove, IL: IVP Academic, 2012), 102–115 (105–106).

52. Huston Smith, "Chinese Religion in World Perspective," *Dialogue & Alliance* 4 (1990): 4–14 (5).

of attempts have been made to answer this question. Some scholars, both Western and Chinese, maintain that Confucianism is not a religion but, rather, a socio-political ethical system. They see Confucianism primarily as a way of life, based on ethical teaching designed to produce a peaceful, harmonious, and well-ordered society.[53]

Unlike Taoism and Buddhism, Confucianism seems uncommitted to any particular organized religion. However, the religious dimensions of Confucianism should not be ignored. As Elwood claims, "To say that Confucianism is a philosophy or ethic uncommitted to any particular organized religion does not mean that it has no religious content. On the contrary, it is unmistakably a religious philosophy."[54] Indeed, Confucianism is both a religion and a philosophy. Taylor holds a similar position. On one hand, he agrees that Confucianism is an ethical system and humanistic teaching; on the other hand, he insists that Confucianism bears a deep and profound sense of the religious.[55]

In fact, Confucianism incorporated the pre-Confucian religion of ancient China.[56] Confucianism helped maintain the ancient Chinese religion of veneration for ancestors and the worship of a supreme deity named Heaven (*tian* 天).[57] *Tian* is the traditional high god of the ancient Chinese.[58] Confucius himself was a deeply religious man. He had a profound belief in and reverence for Heaven. He also taught the necessity for the meticulous performance of those rituals by which Heaven and the ancestor spirits were worshipped.[59] The sacrifices performed in the ancestral temple were very important to Confucius. In *The Analects* 3:11, Confucius claimed that if anyone understood well the significance of the rites, then that person would be fit to govern the whole land.[60] Because of its emphasis upon the doctrinal as well as the ritual prescriptions for proper behaviour, Confucianism also became known as the

---

53. Smith, "Confucianism," 273.
54. Douglas J. Elwood, "Christian Theology in an Asian Setting: The Gospel and Chinese Intellectual Chinese," *The South East Asia Journal of Theology* 16 (1975), 1–16 (12).
55. Taylor, *Religious Dimensions*, 2.
56. Smith, "Confucianism," 273.
57. Ching, *Chinese Religions*, 60.
58. Taylor, *Religious Dimensions*, 2.
59. Smith, "Confucianism," 275.
60. Smith, *Chinese Religions*, 41.

"Ritual Religion" (*li jiao* 禮教).[61] However, its religious core is found in the relationship of humankind to Heaven.[62] In Confucianism, the human and the divine are not opposed but juxtaposed. Confucianism stresses the unity of humans and Heaven.[63] In fact, harmony and unity between humanity and Heaven is one of the key principles of Confucianism.[64]

Perhaps Yao gives the best summary about the religious elements of Confucianism. He asserts that Confucianism covers not only a wide range of doctrinal deliberations from humanism to spiritualism but also a spiritual concern for human destiny. Confucianism is a kind of humanism that seeks sacredness in an ordinary, yet disciplined, life. By relating the secular to the sacred and the humanistic to the religious, Confucianism demonstrates a unique understanding of the ultimate and transcendent and opens a distinct way to human eternity.[65]

3.2 Taoism

Understanding Taoism, one of the three major religions in Chinese culture, is essential to understanding Chinese civilization.[66] In recent years, scholars like Mario Poceski use the term *Daoism* instead of Taoism. However, the term *Taoism* will be used in this research since the term has been used by most English written books. The term Taoism, however, is ambiguous in Chinese studies. Because of a plurality of Taoist orientations and identities, outlining the origins and basic contour of Taoism is complicated.[67] As Jeaneane and Merv Fowler indicate, "Taoism is the most complicated of the Chinese religions, mainly because it is multifaceted, varied and diffuse, but also because its many strands are themselves complex with origins that are obscure."[68] In reality, Taoism consists of two interrelated strands, one is philosophical Taoism

---

61. Ching, *Chinese Religions*, 60.
62. Taylor, *Religious Dimensions*, 2.
63. Elwood, "Christian Theology in an Asian Setting," 12.
64. Yao, *Introduction to Confucianism*, 45.
65. Yao, *Introduction to Confucianism*, 44–45.
66. Man Kam Leung, "The Study of Religious Taoism in the People's Republic of China (1949–1990): A Bibliographical Survey," *JCR* 19 (1991): 113–126 (113).
67. Poceski, *Introducing Chinese Religions*, 61.
68. Fowler and Fowler, *Chinese Religions*, 92.

(*dao jia* 道家) and the other is religious Taoism (*dao jiao* 道教).[69] Confusion exists in the literature concerning the relationship between philosophical Taoism and religious Taoism.

As Livia Kohn points out, some think that philosophical Taoism and religious Taoism are completely separate entities.[70] These scholars attest that religious Taoism developed in the second century AD had little in common with traditional philosophical Taoism developed in the sixth century BC.[71] However, both philosophical Taoism and religious Taoism overlap; therefore, dividing them into two strands may not be appropriate.[72] Moreover, the canon of religious Taoism contains documents that depend heavily on philosophical Taoism, suggesting a continuation of Taoist philosophy within the framework of religious Taoism.[73] In the following sections, philosophical Taoism will be discussed, followed by religious Taoism.

3.2.1 Philosophical Taoism

The primary emphasis of philosophical Taoism has been natural harmony. Philosophical Taoism calls humankind to return to harmony with nature.[74] Scholars have traditionally believed that Taoism as a philosophy was developed around the sixth century BC and that the first philosopher of the school was Lao Zi (老子).[75] One of the main historical sources containing Lao Zi's biography is the *Historical Annals* (*Shi Ji* 史記), the Chinese history book compiled by Si Ma Qian (司馬遷) during the Han dynasty.[76] According to Si Ma Qian's account, Lao Zi's real name was Li Er (李耳), and he was a contemporary of Confucius. Lao Zi was the imperial court annals archivist, and in

---

69. Fowler and Fowler, 92.

70. Livia Kohn, *Taoist Mystical Philosophy: The Scripture of Western Ascension* (New York: State University of New York Press, 1991), 3.

71. Liu Da, *The Tao and Chinese Culture* (New York: Schocken, 1979), 21.

72. Fowler and Fowler, *Chinese Religions*, 92.

73. Kohn, *Taoist Mystical Philosophy*, 3.

74. Schirokauer, *Brief History*, 43.

75. Livia Kohn, "Laozi: Ancient Philosopher, Master of Immortality, and God," in *Religions of China in Practice*, ed. Donald S. Lopez Jr. (Princeton, NJ: Princeton University Press, 1996), 52–63 (53).

76. Max Kaltenmark, *Lao Tzu and Taoism*, trans. Roger Greaves (Stanford, CA: Stanford University Press, 1969), 6.

old age he departed toward China's western frontier.⁷⁷ Before his withdrawal from the civilized world, it is said that Lao Zi left his book, the *Dao De Jing* (道德經), to the warden of the frontier pass.⁷⁸

Modern scholars do not agree on the historicity of Lao Zi. Some believe that Lao Zi is merely a legendary figure. Some maintain that he is a historical figure but hold different views on when he lived and on certain episodes in his biography.⁷⁹ Holmes Welch asserts that all biographical information about Lao Zi is legendary, most of which may have been incorrectly attached to his name.⁸⁰ Some modern scholars also doubt that Lao Zi is the author of the *Dao De Jing*. Instead they see the *Dao De Jing* as a third century BCE composite, assembled from existing writings or sayings.⁸¹ Today the historicity of Lao Zi and the authorship of the *Dao De Jing* remain in impenetrable obscurity.

What most scholars generally agree on is the significance of the *Dao De Jing*. It is one of the major texts of Taoism⁸² and has been translated far more often than any other Oriental literature.⁸³ The *Dao De Jing* is a small book, approximately five thousand words total and presented in parallel verses and poetic stanzas,⁸⁴ yet its influence upon Chinese culture is unquestionable. Wing-Tsit Chan rightly points out that understanding Chinese philosophy, religion, art, medicine, or even cooking is impossible without a real appreciation of the teaching in the *Dao De Jing*.⁸⁵

Dao De Jing can be read in many different ways, but Kohn believes first and foremost that the *Dao De Jing* is a mystical text in which a certain cosmological interpretation of the universe was presented and an instruction on how to

---

77. Kaltenmark, 7.
78. Soothill, *Three Religions of China*, 46.
79. Kaltenmark, *Lao Tzu and Taoism*, 5.
80. Holmes Welch, *Taoism: The Parting of the Way* (Boston: Beacon, 1965), 3.
81. Mark Csikszentmihalyi and Philip J. Ivanhoe, "Introduction," in *Philosophical Aspects of the Laozi*, ed. Mark Csikszentmihalyi and Philip J. Ivanhoe (Albany: State University of New York, 1999), 1–31 (4–5).
82. Nadeau, *Confucianism and Taoism*, 46.
83. Kaltenmark, *Lao Tzu and Taoism*, 5. Chen believes *Daodejing* has at least forty English translations. See Ellen M. Chen, *The Tao Te Ching: A New Translation with Commentary* (New York: Paragon, 1989), ix.
84. Ching, *Chinese Religions*, 87.
85. Wing-Tsit Chan, *Source Book*, 136–137.

live in perfect harmony with this universe was provided.[86] The *Dao De Jing* is divided into eighty-one short chapters and separated into two parts. The first part primarily deals with the issue of *dao* (道), "the way," while the second part addresses the issue of *de* (德), "virtue."[87] *Dao* is the most important and basic concept of the *Dao De Jing*.[88] The Chinese word *dao* literally means "the road" or "the way."[89] The word *dao* is also a verb, meaning "to speak." Julia Ching indicates that the word *dao* is equivalent to the Greek words λόγος, "the word," and ὁδός, "the way."[90]

Although the concept of *dao* is what has given Taoism its name,[91] other Chinese philosophical schools also make use of the term. For example, Confucius used the term *dao* as the path of the sage kings.[92] However in the *Dao De Jing*, *dao* is described as the organic order underlying and structuring the world.[93] The *Dao De Jing* proclaims that the universe and all creatures and phenomena are generated by the *dao*.[94] Lao Zi believed that all things tangible and all forms and shapes of the universe are derived from the *dao*, which itself is formless and intangible.[95] As Livia Kohn explains, for Lao Zi, "The *dao* is at the root of all existence. It makes the world function, brings all beings to life, and orders the entire universe, ever transforming and changing continuously."[96]

De is another important concept in the *Dao De Jing*. The term *de* appears forty-three times in the *Dao De Jing*. Philip J. Ivanhoe believes the idea of *de* is central to the *Dao De Jing*.[97] *De* is the ideal life for the individual and the

---

86. Livia Kohn, *Early Chinese Mysticism: Philosophy and Soteriology in the Taoist Tradition* (Princeton, NJ: Princeton University Press, 1992), 45.

87. Fowler and Fowler, *Chinese Religions*, 95.

88. Kohn, *Early Chinese Mysticism*, 45.

89. Young Oon Kim, *World Religions Volume 3: Faiths of the Far East* (New York: Golden Gate, 1976), 89.

90. Ching, *Chinese Religions*, 88.

91. Ching, 88.

92. Nadeau, *Confucianism and Taoism*, 48–49.

93. Kohn, *Early Chinese Mysticism*, 45.

94. Palmer, "Religion," 160.

95. Kay Keng Khoo, "The Tao and the Logos: Lao Tzu and the Gospel of John," *IRM* 87 (1998): 77–84 (81).

96. Kohn, *Early Chinese Mysticism*, 46.

97. Philip J. Ivanhoe, "The Concept of De ("Virtue") in the Laozi," in *Religious Philosophical Aspects of the Laozi*, eds. Mark Csikszentmihalyi and Philip J. Ivanhoe (Albany: State University of New York, 1999), 239–257 (239).

ideal order for society. As the way of life, it denotes simplicity, contentment, and letting nature take its own course.[98] In order to accomplish *de*, Lao Zi introduced the idea of *wu wei* (無為). *Wu* (無) means "not," and *wei* (為) means "doing" or "interfering." Watts believes the best explanation of *wu wei* is "don't force it."[99] The key idea of *wu wei* is "naturalness," acting naturally or letting things develop by themselves.[100] Thus Lao Zi asks people to "let things alone."[101] Overall, the *Dao De Jing* exudes a preference for "the negative over the positive, nothing over something, the weak over the strong, the strong over the hard, the yielding over the assertive."[102]

In addition to the *Dao De Jing*, the other major classic of philosophical Taoism is the book *Zhuang Zi* (莊子), which bears the name of its author.[103] Compared to Lao Zi, Zhuang Zi is a more definite figure who lived in 369–286 BC.[104] He is also more poetic and paradoxical than Lao Zi.[105] The book *Zhuang Zi* is written with great gusto and a sense of humour[106] and includes a collection of stories, anecdotes, quips, queries, and conversations. The written style of the book is more fluid than the *Dao De Jing*.[107] The author Zhuang Zi's view of *dao* is similar to Lao Zi's. According to Zhuang Zi, *dao*, as the all-embracing first principle that produces the universe, is eternal. All things in the universe depend upon *dao*.[108] Zhuang Zi also believed that everything in the universe is in a process of change. Nature itself is a process of change. Thus Zhuang Zi's philosophy is the philosophy of change.[109]

---

98. Wing-Tsit Chan, *Source Book*, 136.
99. Alan Watts, *Taoism: Way Beyond Seeking* (Boston: Charles E. Tuttle, 1997), 77.
100. Xiaogan Liu, "An Inquiry into the Core Value of Laozi's Philosophy," in *Religious Philosophical Aspects*, 211–237 (211–212).
101. Tomlin, *Great Philosophers*, 254.
102. Schirokauer, *Brief History*, 43.
103. Nadeau, *Confucianism and Taoism*, 46.
104. T. Patrick Burke, *The Major Religions: An Introduction with Texts* (Cambridge, MA: Blackwell, 1996), 135.
105. Denise Lardner Carmody and John Tully Carmody, *Ways to the Center: An Introduction to World Religions*, 2nd ed. (Belmont, CA: Wadsworth, 1984), 146.
106. Burke, *Major Religions*, 135.
107. Nadeau, *Confucianism and Taoism*, 48.
108. Fung Yu-Lan, *A History of Chinese Philosophy, Volume 1: The Period of the Philosophers*, trans. Derk Bodde (Princeton, NJ: Princeton University Press, 1952), 223.
109. Fung Yu-Lan, 225–226.

Zhuang Zi is "an idealist and a mystic, with all the idealist's hatred of the utilitarian system, and the mystic's contempt for a life of mere external activity."[110] For Zhuang Zi, the way to peace, spiritual ecstasy, and long life is to abandon social conventions and join nature's rhythms. *Dao*, according to Zhuang Zi, eliminates human judgments of good and bad, right and wrong. Zhuang Zi ridiculed those who thought they could tie language directly to thought and clarify all discourse.[111] In the very beginning of his book, Zhuang Zi points out the uselessness of judgments of human being.[112]

The influence of philosophical Taoism on Chinese culture continues to this day. For example, the Taoist sympathy for nature contributed significantly to the Chinese poets and artists who fashioned great nature poetry and fine landscape painting. Philosophical Taoism remains a source of inspiration for contemporary Chinese poets and artists.[113]

3.2.2 Religious Taoism

Religious Taoism is a tradition including not just Taoist philosophical texts but also institutional organizations, rites and ceremonies, myths, a pantheon of terrestrial and celestial deities, and physical and hygienic practices that aim toward immortality.[114] There are different positions concerning the origins of religious Taoism. Some Taoist believers even proclaim that the roots of Taoist teaching can trace back to the Yellow Emperor (Huang Di 黃帝), a legendary emperor of ancient China before recorded history.[115]

Taoism emerged as an organized religion in the second century AD, during the socially turbulent years of the Han dynasty. Zhang Dao Ling (張道陵) began a religious movement known as Five Bushels of Rice Taoism, also known as The Way of the Celestial Masters, in which believers paid an annual tax of five bushels of rice.[116] Zhang Dao Ling claimed that Lao Zi, in a

---

110. Aubrey Moore, "Note on the Philosophy of Chaps. I–vii," in *Chuang Tzu*, 2nd ed., trans. Herbert A. Giles (London: Bernard Quaritch, 1926), xx.
111. Carmody and Carmody, *Ways to the Center*, 146.
112. Moore, "Note on the Philosophy," xix.
113. Schirokauer, *Brief History*, 44.
114. Nadeau, *Confucianism and Taoism*, xxiii.
115. John Blofeld, *Taoism: The Road to Immortality* (Boulder, CO: Shambhala, 1978), 19–20.
116. Fowler and Fowler, *Chinese Religions*, 141.

deified form, appeared to him in a mountain cave in AD 142. In this alleged revelation, Zhang Dao Ling was made the Celestial Master (Tian Shi 天師), with the order to establish true orthodox Taoism.[117] The Five Bushels of Rice Taoism is a hereditary institution. Even today, the prime Celestial Master of Five Bushels of Rice Taoism is believed to be a direct descendant of Zhang Dao Ling.[118] In his new movement, Zhang Dao Ling retained many teachings of philosophical Taoism. The name of Lao Zi (as one of the gods) was often invoked in rituals and in casting magic spells.[119] Lao Zi became one of the gods as "Lord Lao the Most High" (Tai Shang Lao Jun 太上老君) in this new religion.[120] With the mixture of myth, philosophy, and superstition as a base, Zhang Dao Ling soon developed a religious organization that attracted a considerable following.[121] This Taoist religious movement eventually generated many sects and subsects.[122]

In the second century, another, similar Taoist movement known as Way of Great Peace Taoism occurred in eastern China. However, the movement was later destroyed by the Han government when its leaders and members rose in rebellion against the Han.[123] In AD 320, a Taoist called Ge Hong (葛洪) incorporated Chinese traditions of alchemy into Taoism.[124] One of the most influential texts produced by Ge Hong is *The Master Who Embraces Simplicity* (*Bao Pu Zi* 抱樸子), in which he discusses a host of themes central to Taoist practices and techniques employed in the quest for immortality.[125] Ge Hong proclaimed that one could transform into an immortal (*xian* 仙) through a lengthy process of purification and self-cultivation.[126]

From AD 364–370, a Taoist medium called Yang Xi (楊羲) claimed that he received a series of spiritual revelations in the Bucklebent Hills of Mount

---

117. Ching, *Chinese Religions*, 103.

118. Nadeau, *Confucianism and Taoism*, 19. After the Communist takeover of mainland China in 1949, the headquarters of The Way of the Celestial Masters was moved to Taiwan. See Ching, *Chinese Religions*, 104.

119. Liu Da, *Tao and Chinese Culture*, 22.

120. Adler, *Chinese Religious Traditions*, 67.

121. Liu Da, *Tao and Chinese Culture*, 22.

122. Ching, *Chinese Religions*, 112.

123. Fowler and Fowler, *Chinese Religions*, 141–142.

124. Adler, *Chinese Religious Traditions*, 68.

125. Poceski, *Introducing Chinese Religions*, 75.

126. Adler, *Chinese Religious Traditions*, 68.

Mao (Mao Shan 茅山) near Nanjing.[127] According to Yang Xi, the revelations he received were from various deities in the Heaven of Highest Purity (Shang Qing 上清), which was considered to be the highest of the three Taoist heavens. The sect of Taoism which is based on these revelations is called the Shangqing school, or Mao Shan Taoism.[128] The Shang Qing revelations were later collected and edited by Tao Hong Jing (陶宏景) and became the base of the Taoist canon.[129] The teachings of the Shang Qing texts include alchemy instructions, purifying meditation and visualization practices, breathing techniques, and fasting guidelines, as well as gymnastic exercises.[130]

In AD 400, a new corpus of Taoist writings known as the *Ling Bao Scriptures* (靈寶), "Spiritual Treasures," appeared in southern China. These scriptures signify a synthesis of the teachings of the Celestial Masters and the Shang Qing school.[131] The *Ling Bao Scriptures* contain hundreds of instructional manuals concerned with the proper steps, songs, incantations, and symbolic objects associated with religious rituals.[132] The Ling Bao school especially emphasizes merit-giving externalized rituals.[133] During the Tang dynasty (AD 618–907), the Ling Bao public rituals such as dances and chants became extremely popular in society, and many are still performed today.[134]

Since the fifth century, the writings of the Celestial Masters, the Shang Qing school, and the *Ling Bao Scriptures* have been integrated into the Taoist canon,[135] which is a great collection of scriptures, scholastic and exegetical treatises, historical texts, ritual manuals, poetry, and legend.[136] In total, the Taoist canon consists of approximately 1,120 volumes. Most of these volumes are anonymous and are not dated. Some volumes are written in esoteric language.[137]

---

127. Nadeau, *Confucianism and Taoism*, 19.
128. Adler, *Chinese Religious Traditions*, 68. According to Poceski, Maoshan Taoism claimed that its teachings were revealed by deities superior to those of the Celestial Masters. *Introducing Chinese Religions*, 84.
129. Nadeau, *Confucianism and Taoism*, 19–20.
130. Adler, *Chinese Religious Traditions*, 68.
131. Poceski, *Introducing Chinese Religions*, 87–88.
132. Nadeau, *Confucianism and Taoism*, 20–21.
133. Fowler and Fowler, *Chinese Religions*, 143.
134. Adler, *Chinese Religious Traditions*, 69.
135. Adler, *Chinese Religious Traditions*, 69.
136. Poceski, *Introducing Chinese Religions*, 95.
137. Smith, *Chinese Religions*, 98.

By the sixth century, Taoism as a religious movement, with specific rituals, fasts, festivals, and ceremonies, was well established among the Chinese.[138] The Taoist rituals and teachings hold great significance for Chinese life.[139] Many Taoist rituals are still being practised by entire communities in order to attain success and well-being.[140] Taoism today continues to play a major role in Chinese society.[141] As Nadeau points out, "Most Chinese are Taoist to one degree or another, perhaps even unaware of the religious origins of their thinking and habits."[142]

3.3 Buddhism

Beside Confucianism and Taoism, one must understand Buddhism in order to truly comprehend Chinese culture.[143] As one of the three dominant religions, Buddhism is an important factor in Chinese culture. Many consider that at least a quarter to a half of the Chinese people today, in their everyday lives, are still significantly influenced by Buddhism.[144]

3.3.1 The Early Development of Buddhism

Originating from India, Buddhism was founded by Siddhartha whose clan name is Gautama.[145] A number of scholars believe Siddhartha was born approximately 563 BC in Lumbini (Nepal). His father, Shuddhodana, was a king or leader of the people of Shakya. His mother, Mahamaya, died soon after he

---

138. Fowler and Fowler, *Chinese Religions*, 144.
139. Liu Da, *Tao and Chinese Culture*, 154.
140. Adler, *Chinese Religious Traditions*, 69.
141. Chi-Tim Lai, "Daoism in China Today, 1980–2002," in *Religion in China Today: The China Quarterly Special Issues No.3*, ed. Daniel L. Overmyer (Cambridge: Cambridge University Press, 2003), 107.
142. Nadeau, *Confucianism and Taoism*, xxiv.
143. David Hock Tey, *Chinese Culture and the Bible* (Singapore: Here's Life Books, 1988), 16.
144. Alex Smith, "Counting the Buddhist World Fairly," in *Sharing Jesus Holistically with the Buddhist World*, ed. David Lim and Steve Spaulding (Pasadena, CA: William Carey Library, 2005), 1–10 (4).
145. Ralph R. Covell, *Confucius, the Buddha, and Christ: A History of the Gospel in Chinese* (New York: Orbis, 1986), 133.

was born.[146] Legend says that Siddhartha descended from Heaven and entered his mother's womb in the form of an elephant and that she gave birth to him from her side.[147] Siddhartha married at the age of sixteen and fathered a son when he was about twenty-nine.[148] It is said that, after four fateful trips to the outside world from his palace, Siddhartha realized the true facts of the human condition: human beings are subject to sickness, old age, and death. He then decided to leave his home and to live as an ascetic for a few years in order to find the solution to the problem of suffering.[149]

Siddhartha did not find the solution to the problem of suffering through the methods of the ascetics but, rather, through a long meditation under a Bo-tree, which is also called a Bodhi tree. He realised that the solution to human suffering lay in the extinction of the self, the ego. This conception made him the Enlightened One – the Buddha.[150] Buddha has also been called Sakyamuni, meaning "the Sage of the Sakyas."[151] It is important to note that the Buddha never claimed to be God. In fact, he "claimed no inspiration from any god or external power either. He attributed all his realization, attainments and achievements to human endeavour and human intelligence."[152]

The Buddha's teaching is "founded on the understanding that all life in the universe is subject to moral causality, a process that links present actions to future consequences, both in this life and in lives to come."[153] In Buddhism, this natural law of causation is called *karma*.[154] Buddah announced the Four Noble Truths: all life is suffering; all suffering is from desire or craving; if there is no craving, there is no suffering; and if you follow the Eightfold Path, there

---

146. John Snelling, *The Buddhist Handbook: A Complete Guide to Buddhist Schools, Teaching, Practice, and History* (Rochester, VT: Inner Traditions, 1991), 17.

147. Snelling, 18.

148. Snelling, 19.

149. Snelling, 19.

150. Soothill, *Three Religions of China*, 82–83.

151. Soothill, 83.

152. Walpola Sri Rahula, *What the Buddha Taught*, rev. ed. (Bedford: Gordon Fraser, 1967), 1.

153. Todd T. Lewis, "Karma," in *Buddhism: The Illustrated Guide*, ed. Kevin Trainor (London: Duncan Braid, 2001), 60–61 (62).

154. Tulku Thondup, *Joyful Rebirth: A Tibetan Buddhist Guidebook*, ed. Harold Talbott (Boston: Shambhala, 2005), 3.

is no craving, and hence, no suffering.[155] The Buddha continued to explain the Eightfold Path which consists of eight elements: right understanding, right thought, right speech, right action, right livelihood, right effort, right awareness, and right meditation.[156] *Nirvana* is the ultimate goal of the Buddhist path. It is "the state of the utter absence of suffering."[157] It is believed that, upon his death, the Buddha passed into final *nirvana*.[158]

The Buddha believed that everyone has the potentiality of becoming a Buddha.[159] He announced that any person may endeavor to achieve the Buddhist condition of enlightenment by eschewing extremes and following the Middle Way, by transcending the self in everyday life.[160] The Buddha went forth to teach others the path which he believed leads to the cessation of suffering. This teaching, or *Dharma*, became the basis for all his instructions.[161] From these tenets of the Buddha's teaching, which is dedicated primarily to the negation of suffering, Buddhism was developed.[162] The Buddha taught for approximately forty-five years, and he gained a large number of followers.[163] They became monks and nuns and lived by monastic discipline called the *Vinaya*, which mandated a lifestyle of moral self-control and detachment from sensual pleasures.[164] In addition to monks and nuns, the community of Buddha's disciples, which was known as the *sangha*, also included laypeople.[165] The three fundamental pillars of the Buddhist tradition are the Buddha (the teacher), the *dharma* (the Buddha's teachings), and the *sangha* (a community of believers). These three pillars are known as the "Three Jewels" (Chinese:

---

155. George W. Braswell Jr., *Understanding World Religions: Hinduism, Buddhism, Taoism, Confucianism, Judaism, Islam*, rev. ed. (Nashville, TN: Broadman & Holman, 1994), 52–53.

156. Dean C. Halverson, "Buddhism," in *The Compact Guide to World Religions*, ed. Dean C. Halverson (Minneapolis: Bethany House, 1996), 58.

157. Donald S. Lopez, Jr., *Buddhism* (London: Penguin, 2001), 50.

158. Lopez, 50–51.

159. Rahula, *What the Buddha Taught*, 1.

160. Diane Collinson, Kathryn Plant, and Robert Wilkinson, *Fifty Eastern Thinkers* (London: Routledge, 2000), 74.

161. Stephen C. Berkwitz, "The History of Buddhism in Retrospect," in *Buddhism in World Cultures: Comparative Perspectives*, ed. Stephen C. Berkwitz (Santa Barbara, CA: ABC-CLIO), 1–44 (39).

162. Collinson, Plant, and Wilkinson, *Fifty Eastern Thinkers*, 74.

163. Adler, *Chinese Religious Traditions*, 76.

164. Berkwitz, "History of Buddhism," 39.

165. Adler, *Chinese Religious Traditions*, 76.

san bao 三寶) or the "Treasures of Buddhism." One needs to take the "Triple Refuge" to become a Buddhist, which means taking refuge in the Buddha, the dharma, and the sangha.[166]

For a few hundred years after the death of the Buddha, numerous Buddhist sects and schools called *nikayas* were formed. Many of these groups comprised what later critics called "Hinayana Buddhism," which means "the smaller vehicle."[167] The Hinayana traditions are considered by some as the pure, original form of Buddhism.[168] According to Joseph A. Adler, Theravada is the only Hinayana school that still survives today.[169] Thus, some western and eastern scholars use the term Hinayana as a synonym for the Theravada tradition. However, the use of the term Hinayana also poses a problem because of its negative connotation.[170] Eventually, Buddhism in India developed into two main branches: the Theravada in the south and the Mahayana in the north. The Theravada, which means "Teachings of the Elders," took Buddhism to Sri Lanka, Thailand, Myanmar, and Cambodia. The Mahayana, which means "The Larger Vehicle," brought the teachings of Buddhism to Tibet, China, Korea, and Japan.[171]

Even though Theravada Buddhism and Mahayana Buddhism have important similarities, they are different in many ways.[172] One of the major differences entails whether enlightenment is universally accessible. Theravada Buddhism teaches that enlightenment is impossible outside the monastic life and is difficult to attain.[173] In Theravada Buddhism, to be a true and dedicated Buddhist, one must become a monk. Only monks are considered as part of the Buddhist community, the *sangha*.[174] Mahayana Buddhism, however, repre-

---

166. Adler, 78.
167. Berkwitz, "History of Buddhism," 41.
168. Donald S. Lopez, Jr., "Introduction," in *Buddhism in Practice*, ed. Donald S. Lopez Jr. (Princeton, NJ: Princeton University Press, 1995), 6–7.
169. Adler, *Chinese Religious Traditions*, 79.
170. Arvind Sharma, "A Note on the Use of the Word Hinayana in the Teaching of Buddhism," *Eastern Buddhist* 9 (1976): 129–133 (129).
171. Young Oon Kim, *World Religions*, 2.
172. Burke, *Major Religions*, 61.
173. Ching, *Chinese Religions*, 123.
174. Burke, *Major Religions*, 65.

sents an easier Buddhism called the larger vehicle which accommodates more people. One does not have to be a monk or a nun to achieve enlightenment.[175]

Another major difference between Theravada Buddhism and Mahayana Buddhism involves theism. Although both Theravada Buddhism and Mahayana Buddhism acknowledge the existence of gods, Theravada Buddhism believes they are irrelevant to the Buddhist path. Mahayana Buddhism, on the other hand, worships the Buddha and Bodhisattvas, which are Buddhas-to-be.[176] The Mahayanists believe that the Absolute Buddha, who is an inscrutable Supreme Being, has manifested himself in countless ways, especially through the Buddhas, of whom Siddhartha Gautama was one. The Mahayanists also worship the Bodhisattvas as compassionate saviors who refrain from entering *Nirvana*, "the enlightenment," in order to save humanity.[177] Popular Buddhas in Mahayana Buddhism include Sakyamuni, Amitabha, and Vairocana. Popular Bodhisattvas are Manjusri, Avalokitesvara, and Maitreya.[178]

A few centuries after Mahayana Buddhism was established, a third branch of Buddhism, called Vajrayana, which means "Diamond Vehicle," emerged. Vajrayana is also known as Mantrayana, "Secret Mantra Vehicle," Buddhism or Tantric Buddhism. Vajrayana combined Indian tantric methods with Mahayana teachings. The Buddhists today in Tibet belong to Vajrayana Buddhism.[179] According to the Vajrayana perspective, Hinayana (or Theravada), Mahayana, and Vajrayana are the three major stages of the Buddhist path. One first practices the Hinayana, then the Mahayana, and finally the Vajrayana.[180]

3.3.2 Buddhism in China

Buddhism came into China during the Han dynasty, probably in the initial decades of the first century AD.[181] Daisaku Ikeda indicates that even though some merchants and travelers may have brought a knowledge of Buddhism

---

175. Alder, *Chinese Religious Traditions*, 79.
176. Adler, 80.
177. Soothill, *Three Religions of China*, 104–105.
178. Adler, *Chinese Religious Traditions*, 80–81.
179. Snelling, *Buddhist Handbook*, 93.
180. Reginald A. Ray, *Indestructible Truth: The Living Spirituality of Tibetan Buddhism* (Boston: Shambhala, 2000), 80.
181. Covell, *Confucius, the Buddha, and Christ*, 133–136.

into China before the first century AD, the first real period of Buddhist study and propagation in China did not begin until the first and second centuries AD.[182] By the end of the second century, several Buddhist centers were established in China, and Buddhism grew rapidly from then on.[183] One of the key factors that hastened the acculturation of Buddhism in China was the translation of Buddhist literature.[184] The Buddhist scriptures were writings that attributed various teachings to the historical Buddha long after his death. However, the Chinese, with their deeply ingrained confidence in the written word, accepted the Buddhist scriptures as the literal record of the Buddha's preaching career.[185]

From the first to fourth centuries AD, many Buddhist monks and believers, who came from central Asia, became actively involved in translating Buddhist scriptures and commentaries into Chinese.[186] However, due to the language incapability of the translators, these earliest Chinese translations contain a multitude of errors and misunderstandings. Good quality and meaningful Chinese translations of Buddhist scriptures were finally produced by Kumārajīva (Jiu Mo Luo Shen 鳩摩羅什) during the early fifth century. Kumārajīva, a native of Kucha in central Asia, organized a translation bureau and brought the teachings of Mahayana Buddhism into mainstream Chinese thought.[187] Kumārajīva was honored with the title of "National Preceptor" by the Chinese ruler in the north.[188] With the help of many brilliant Chinese monks and some of the best scholars in the country, Kumārajīva produced a large number of readable translations of major Mahayana scriptures and treatises. Most of the texts he translated have remained standard versions throughout the history of Buddhism in East Asia.[189] It is said that the works of Kumārajīva enabled Buddhism to become firmly established in China.[190]

---

182. Daisaku Ikeda, *The Flower of Chinese Buddhism* (New York: Weatherhill, 1986), 9–13.

183. Daniel L. Overmyer, *Religions of China: The World as a Living System* (San Francisco: Harper & Row, 1986), 43.

184. Ching, *Chinese Religions*, 127.

185. Smith, *Chinese Religions*, 124.

186. Ikeda, *Flower of Chinese Buddhism*, 17.

187. Fowler and Fowler, *Chinese Religions*, 115.

188. Ching, *Chinese Religions*, 130.

189. Poceski, *Introducing Chinese Religions*, 122.

190. Smith, *Chinese Religions*, 115.

Kumārajīva, along with Paramārtha (Zhen Di 真諦), Hsuan-tsang (Xuan Zhan 玄奘), and Pu-Kung (Bu Kong 不空), were known as the Four Great Monk-Translators of Buddhist scriptures. They lived from the fifth to eighth centuries.[191] Paramārtha was an Indian scholar monk active during the period of the Six Dynasties.[192] Pu-Kong, also known as Amoghavarja, was a mixed Indian and Sogdian descent.[193] He promoted esoteric Buddhism in eight-century China.[194] Hsuan-tsang, however, is the most well-known in the Chinese world.

During the Tang dynasty (AD 618–907), the number of Chinese Buddhist pilgrims departing for India increased greatly. One of the most famous pilgrims was Hsuan-tsang.[195] Hsuan-tsang was about twenty-six years old when he began his journey.[196] He left China for India in AD 629 and returned to China in AD 645.[197] His adventure story eventually inspired the famous Chinese novel *Journey to the West* (*Xi You Ji* 西游記).[198] Hsuan-tsang brought hundreds of Buddhist texts back to China. He remained twenty years in the capital (present-day Xi'an 西安) and translated the corpus of Mahayana scriptures, treatises, and commentaries. Until his death in AD 664, Hsuan-tsang had completed the translation of seventy-five Buddhist texts.[199] The canon of Chinese Buddhism was completed by the end of Tang dynasty (AD 906).[200] However, Ching indicates that there was never a serious effort to define scriptural authority.[201]

---

191. Ikeda, *Flower of Chinese Buddhism*, 17.

192. Funayama Toru, "The Work of Paramārtha: An Example of Sino-Indian Cross-Cultural Exchange," *JIABS* 31 (2010): 141–183 (141).

193. Zeng Yang, "A Biographical Study on Bukong 不空 (aka. Amoghavajra, 705–774): Networks, Institutions, and Identities" (unpublished doctoral thesis, University of British Columbia, 2018), 23.

194. Yang, 1.

195. Smith, *Chinese Religions*, 122.

196. Hsiang-Kuang Chou, *A History of Chinese Buddhism* (Allahabad: Indo-Chinese Literature, 1955), 252.

197. Smith, *Chinese Religions*, 122.

198. A Chinese novel published in the sixteenth century, attributed to *Wu Cheng En* 吳承恩.

199. Ching, *Chinese Religions*, 131.

200. Ching, 128.

201. Ching, 128.

Over time, different schools of Chinese Buddhism arose. These schools of Chinese Buddhism are primarily doctrinal or exegetical traditions, which usually lack institutional independence or distinct ecclesiastical structures.[202] Although all the Buddhist scriptures were viewed as canonical, different sects emerged under renowned teachers who adopted widely different interpretations of the Buddhist teachings. The extreme diversity of the teachings contained in the Buddhist scriptures also caused the development of the different Buddhist schools in China.[203] Of all the sects of Chinese Buddhism, three schools were particularly important: the Tiantai school (Tian Tai Zong 天臺宗), the Pure Land school (Jing Tu Zong 淨土宗), and the Chan school (Chan Zong 禪宗).[204]

Tiantai, which means "Heavenly Terrace," is the name of the mountain in Hangzhou on the east coast.[205] The Tiantai school was one of the earliest Chinese Buddhist schools in the era of the Sui (AD 581–618) and Tang (AD 618–907) dynasties. In fact, Poceski believes that Tiantai was also the earliest of the so-called New Buddhist schools in China.[206] This school became the most influential Buddhist school during the Tang dynasty.[207] Most scholars consider Zhi Yi (智顗) (AD 538–597) as the founder of the school. However, the Tiantai school was probably established by Zhi Yi's teacher Hui Si (慧思) (AD 515–576). Nevertheless, all agree that Zhi Yi was the first great key figure of the school.[208]

By the sixth century, a great number of Buddhist texts and translations were available in China. However, some Chinese Buddhists struggled with how to make sense of doctrinal contradictions that existed within the vast collection of texts.[209] The Tiantai school addressed these problems by synthesizing many of the different teachings of Buddhism and by melding all

---

202. Poceski, *Introducing Chinese Religions*, 148.
203. Smith, *Chinese Religions*, 124.
204. Young Oon Kim, *World Religions*, 28.
205. Adler, *Chinese Religious Traditions*, 84.
206. Poceski, *Introducing Chinese Religions*, 150.
207. Smith, *Chinese Religions*, 132.
208. Fowler and Fowler, *Chinese Religions*, 119–120. Young Oon Kim (*World Religions*, 28) and Poceski, *Introducing Chinese Religions*, 150) also list Zhi Yi as the founder of the Tiantai school.
209. Adler, *Chinese Religious Traditions*, 85.

the divergent views of the other schools.[210] Zhi Yi created a classification system of the Buddhist scriptures and proclaimed that the Mahayana *Lotus Sutra* (meaning Scripture of the Lotus Blossom), or *Saddharmapundarika Sutra* in Sanskrit, was the Buddha's last and most advanced doctrine.[211] Most Chinese Buddhists consequently began to believe that the *Lotus Sutra* held the core teaching of Buddhism, and they interpreted all other scriptures from its perspective.[212] The *Lotus Sutra* was extremely important for the development of a Buddhist mythology in China, in which the eternal Buddha, represented in countless earthly manifestations, was working out his plan to save all humanity.[213]

A Chinese Buddhist school that was far more popular than the Tiantai school was the Pure Land school. Young Oon Kim believes that before World War II, 60–70 percent of Buddhists belonged to the Pure Land school.[214] Huiyuan is said to be the founder of the school in AD 402.[215] The basic text of the school is the *Pure Land Sutra*. The Pure Land school is named after *Sukhavati*, a Sanskrit word for an ideal Buddhist paradise. Buddha Amitabha (A Mi Tuo Fo 阿彌陀佛), a mythical and much earlier figure than the historical Buddha, is believed to preside over the Pure Land known as the Western Paradise. Working beside Buddha Amitabha is the Bodhisattva Avalokitesvara (Guan Yin Pu Sa 觀音菩薩).[216] According to the teaching of the Pure Land school, whoever believes in Buddha Amitabha, meditates upon him and calls for his aid by repeating his name, will be saved and go to the Western Paradise at death. In paradise they will be surrounded by the Buddha's teachings, which will help them advance toward the final goal of enlightenment.[217] Ching points out that Pure Land Buddhism shows multiple resemblances to Christianity. Karl Barth even called Japanese Pure Land Buddhism, "Japanese Protestantism."[218] Poceski believes that even though depictions of Pure Land

---

210. Fowler and Fowler, *Chinese Religions*, 119.
211. Adler, *Chinese Religious Traditions*, 85.
212. Young Oon Kim, *World Religions*, 29.
213. Smith, *Chinese Religions*, 133.
214. Young Oon Kim, *World Religions*, 30.
215. Smith, *Chinese Religions*, 126.
216. Ching, *Chinese Religions*, 142.
217. Overmyer, *Religions of China*, 44–45.
218. Ching, *Chinese Religions*, 142–143.

appear in some Mahayana scriptures, the teaching focused on the worship of Amitabha, and the quest for rebirth in paradise was a distinct Chinese development.[219]

In addition to offering the masses an easy path of practice, the Pure Land school won converts through its vivid portrayal of hell.[220] Moreover, the teaching of the Pure Land school especially appealed to ordinary people seeking a higher power that responds to their daily needs. In this respect, Avalokitesvara, the always compassionate Bodhisattva, attracts the most devotion.[221] Originally a male figure, Avalokitesvara eventually became transformed into a female in Chinese Buddhism. Thus Avalokitesvara became a Madonna-like figure, a goddess of infinite compassion.[222] By the seventh century the Pure Land school had become the most popular form of Buddhism in China, and it remains the most popular to this very day.[223] Even though some scholars argue that Pure Land Buddhism never developed into an institutionally distinct sect in China, its influence is indisputable.[224] Many Pure Land beliefs and practices, especially the chanting of Amitabha's name, continue to be prominent elements of Chinese Buddhism, as well as Korean and Japanese Buddhism.[225]

The opposite of the Pure Land school, which relies on the "other power" of Amitabha for enlightenment, is the Chan school, which believes that enlightenment is produced by "self-power."[226] The Chan School, also known by its Japanese name, *Zen*, is a meditation discipline aimed at tranquilizing the mind.[227] The character *chan* (禪) comes from *channa*, which is a Chinese transliteration of the Sanskrit word for "meditation," *dhyana*.[228] The Chan

---

219. Poceski, *Introducing Chinese Religions*, 158–159.
220. Young Oon Kim, *World Religions*, 31.
221. Ching, *Chinese Religions*, 142.
222. Young Oon Kim, *World Religions*, 31.
223. Overmyer, *Religions of China*, 45.
224. Poceski, *Introducing Chinese Religions*, 159.
225. Poceski, 160.
226. Poceski, 159.
227. Young Oon Kim, *World Religions*, 31.
228. Adler, *Chinese Religious Traditions*, 85.

school claims that their spiritual ancestry goes back to the historical Buddha via a lineage of patriarchs.[229]

According to tradition, a key figure in Chan Buddhism in China is Bodhidharma (Da Mo 達摩), an itinerant Indian who brought Chan teaching into China sometime during the sixth century. Bodhidharma is known as the first Chinese patriarch of Chinese Chan.[230] Little is known about Bodhidharma. His biography is largely legendary.[231] Legend says that he crossed the Yangzi River on a single reed, that he sat in meditation facing a wall for nine years until his legs atrophied and fell off, that he cut off his eyelids so that he would not fall asleep, and that when his eyelids fell to the ground they sprouted into tea plants.[232] By the seventh and eighth centuries, with charismatic Chan teachers such as Hui Neng (慧能) (638–713) and Ma Zu Dao Yi (馬祖道一) (709–788), the Chan school rose to prominence.[233] Hui Neng, the renowned "sixth patriarch," is credited with the famous *Platform Scripture of Hui Neng* (*Liu Zu Tan Jing* 六祖壇經), the only Chinese Buddhist writing to be honored with the rank of Buddhist sacred scriptures.[234]

The Chan school emphasized quiet meditation as the central practice of Buddhism.[235] For the Chan Buddhists, enlightenment cannot be attained solely by studying Buddhist scriptures because enlightenment is an intuitive experience, not an intellectual one.[236] At the core of Chan belief is that everyone has a Buddha-nature; therefore, anyone can become Buddha. Moreover, the Buddha-mind is everywhere and in everything; therefore, people can practice Chan meditation in monasteries or in their own homes.[237] The Chan school motto is "Become a Buddha yourself by realizing your own inner potential."[238] Howard Smith believes that Chan Buddhism is one of the most distinctive and original products of the Chinese mind.[239]

---

229. Poceski, *Introducing Chinese Religions*, 155.
230. Adler, *Chinese Religious Traditions*, 86.
231. Poceski, *Introducing Chinese Religions*, 155.
232. Adler, *Chinese Religious Traditions*, 86.
233. Poceski, *Introducing Chinese Religions*, 156.
234. Smith, *Chinese Religions*, 131.
235. Overmyer, *Religions of China*, 46.
236. Adler, *Chinese Religious Traditions*, 86.
237. Smith, *Chinese Religions*, 130–131.
238. Overmyer, *Religions of China*, 47.
239. Smith, *Chinese Religions*, 128.

Buddhism continued to expand during the time of the Tang dynasty (AD 618–907) and was supported by all elements of society, including the imperial household, the nobility, the wealthy, and the common people.[240] By the middle of the ninth century, Buddhism had become one of the most prominent religions in China. The AD 845 census revealed a quarter of a million monks and nuns; 4,600 temples; and more than 40,000 lesser shrines in China. The wealth and power of the monastic communities invited envy and provoked persecution from the government.[241] The emperor Wu-tsung ordered the destruction of all Buddhist establishments except for one temple in each of the prefectures and four temples in each of the capital cities. Most of the monks and nuns were forced to return to secular life.[242] The persecution did not last long, and Buddhism quickly rebounded. The next emperor removed the anti-Buddhist policies and was generous to the religion.[243] In the first half of the tenth century, another persecution of Buddhism erupted, and approximately 30,000 temples were closed.[244] Despite occasional outbursts of government persecution, Buddhism continued to attract followers.[245] Eventually, Buddhism was successfully transplanted to China,[246] and made a huge impact on Chinese culture.[247]

3.3.3 Buddhist Influence on the Chinese View of the Afterlife

When Buddhism arrived in ancient China in the first century AD, ancestor veneration was already firmly rooted in ancient Chinese culture.[248] Chinese ancestor worship dates back to the late Neolithic period (3000–2000 BC).[249]

---

240. Chee Beng Tan, "Chinese Religion in Malaysia: A General View," *AFS* 42 (1983): 217–252 (235).
241. Ching, *Chinese Religions*, 136.
242. Smith, *Chinese Religions*, 123–124.
243. Poceski, *Introducing Chinese Religions*, 132.
244. Soothill, *Three Religions of China*, 95.
245. Young Oon Kim, *World Religions*, 27.
246. Covell, *Confucius, the Buddha, and Christ*, 133–136.
247. Ching, *Chinese Religions*, 137.
248. Chiung-Yin Hsu, Margaret O'Connor, Susan Lee, "Understandings of Death and Dying for People of Chinese Origin," *Death Studies* 33 (2009): 153–174 (162).
249. Patricia Buckley Ebrey, *The Cambridge Illustrated History of China* (Cambridge: Cambridge University Press, 1996), 20–21. See also 陳美幸, 節、結、解: 中國教會與祖先崇拜 *(Churches in China and Ancestral Worship)* (臺北 [Taipei]: 大光宣教福音中心, 1993), 9.

According to William Lakos, during the late Neolithic period the Chinese "invested enormous amounts of their energy on tombs, coffins and other artifacts buried with the ancestors."[250] As early as 2400 BC, Chinese ancestor rites had been well developed.[251] Moreover, Constance A. Cook indicates that the practice of ancestor worship "was linked to maintaining a stable political and social hierarchy" in Zhou dynasty.[252] Several scholars believe that Confucius further popularized the practice of ancestor worship in ancient China through his teaching on filial piety.[253] Confucius believed that worshipping ancestors was the highest level of filial piety.[254]

Before the advent of Buddhism in China in the first century, however, the ancient Chinese assumed that after death, human spirits eternally dwell in another dimension. Their cosmology consisted of three dimensions: heaven, the human world, and the underworld.[255] The underworld of the dead was called Yellow Springs (Huang Quan 黃泉).[256] The ancient Chinese claimed that death "was a colourful passage into the timeless present."[257] In fact, they believed that the longer an ancestor was dead, the more powerful that ancestor became.[258] As Holmes Welch asserts, the ancient Chinese "believed that death was permanent: there was no such thing as rebirth."[259] The doctrine of *karma* and reincarnation was brought into Chinese civilization by Buddhism.[260]

---

250. William Lakos, *Chinese Ancestor Worship: A Practice and Ritual Oriented Approach to Understanding Chinese Culture* (Newcastle, UK: Cambridge Scholars, 2010), 13.

251. 麥兆輝著, (*Revering God and Respecting Ancestors*), 20.

252. Constance A. Cook, "Ancestor Worship during the Eastern Zhou," in *Early Chinese Religion, Part One: Shang through Han* (1250 BC–220 AD), eds. John Lagerwey and Marc Kalinowski (Leiden: Brill, 2009), 237–279 (237).

253. Wee Hian Chua, "The Worship of Ancestors," in *Eerdmans' Handbook to the World's Religions*, rev. ed. (Grand Rapids, MI: Eerdmans, 1994), 247.

254. 董芳苑,信仰與習俗 (*Beliefs and Customs*) (臺南 [Tainan]: 人光出版社, 1994), 209.

255. Holmes Welch, *The Practice of Chinese Buddhism: 1900–1950* (Cambridge, MA: Harvard University Press, 1967), 181.

256. Constance A. Cook, *Death in Ancient China: The Tale of One Man's Journey* (Leiden: Brill, 2006), 134.

257. Cook, 151–152.

258. Michael J. Puett, *To Become a God: Cosmology, Sacrifice, and Self-Divinization in Early China* (Cambridge, MA: Harvard University Asia Center, 2002), 47.

259. Welch, *Practice of Chinese Buddhism*, 181.

260. John Kieschnick, "Buddhist Monasticism," in *Early Chinese Religion, Part Two: The Period of Division (220–589 AD)*, eds. John Lagerwey and Marc Kalinowski (Leiden: Brill, 2009), 545–574 (545).

Some believe that this doctrine was introduced to the Chinese "virtually as soon as the religion arrived in China."[261]

In Zhi Qian's 支謙 (AD 220–252) *Fo Shuo Bo Jing Chao* 佛說孛經鈔, the teaching of *karma* and reincarnation is clearly stated. The text states, "Whether a person does good deeds or commits evil, they will follow him like a shadow. A deceased person abandons his body, yet his karmic impulses will not dissipate (人作善惡, 如影隨行. 死者棄身, 其行不亡)."[262] *Fo Shuo Bo Jing Chao* also states, "At death a person's soul will depart; it follows his karmic impulses and goes on to its next birth. Just like the turning wheel of a vehicle, [this process of rebirth] never leaves the ground (人死神去, 隨行往生, 如車輪轉, 不得離地)."[263]

According to Buddhist doctrine, until they reach the stage of *nirvana*, all living creatures "are bound to undergo rebirth and redeath due to their having acted out of ignorance and desire, thereby producing the 'seed' of *karma*."[264] Moreover, it is believed that "as long as one makes and carries this burden of *karma*, rebirth is inevitable."[265] The repetitive cycle of reincarnation is known as *samsara* or "endless wondering."[266] In Buddhism, reincarnation can take many forms and consists of six modes of existence or "realms of beings."[267] The realm into which one is reborn depends on one's *karma*.[268]

The first and highest realm of reincarnation is the domain of gods.[269] To be born as a god (*deva*), one must accumulate very good *karma*.[270] A god lives in one of twenty-six heavens. These heavens, according to Buddhist teaching, are all supremely sublime environments.[271] One of the heavens, for example,

---

261. Yuet-Keung Lo, "Destiny and Retribution in Early Medieval China," in *Philosophy and Religion in Early Medieval China*, ed. Alan K. L. Chan and Yuet-Keung Lo (Albany: State University of New York Press, 2010), 319–356 (337).

262. Lo, 337.

263. Lo, 337.

264. Lewis, "Six Realms of Being," 62–63 (62).

265. Lewis, 62.

266. Damien Keown, *Buddhism: A Brief Insight* (New York: Sterling, 1996), 45–46.

267. Christopher M. Moreman, *Beyond the Threshold: Afterlife Beliefs and Experiences in World Religions* (Lanham, MD: Rowman & Littlefield, 2008), 123.

268. Lewis, "Six Realms of Being," 62.

269. Lopez, *Buddhism*, 23.

270. Lewis, "Six Realms of Being," 62.

271. Lewis, 62.

is described as a "pleasure garden filled with the sound of celestial music, the scent of jasmine, the taste of ambrosia and the touch of beautiful women."[272] Compared to human beings, gods live longer but are not immortal.[273] They are still subject to *karma*. Once their accumulated merit is exhausted, they will be reborn into a lower realm.[274]

The second realm of reincarnation is that of the demigods. A demigod (*ashura*) is less powerful than a god but more powerful than a human being.[275] Even though *ashuras* have some supernatural powers, they are dominated by anger.[276] The third realm of reincarnation is the realm of humanity.[277] Although humans suffer, the world of human beings is considered as the best realm in which to be born because only humans are capable of reaching the stage of *nirvana*.[278]

The other three realms of reincarnation are considered unfortunate realms. They are the realms of animals, ghosts, and hell beings.[279] The realm of animals includes all kinds of animals and sentient creatures, such as insects. The realm of ghosts (*pretas*) is the domain for those frustrated ghostly beings "who inhabit the fringes of the human world due to their strong earthly attachments."[280] *Pretas* are the restless spirits, and the most frequently mentioned *preta* is the hungry ghost. The hungry ghost *pretas* "are born with large stomachs and very small throats, so they suffer with an extreme inability to satisfy their unrelenting thirst and hunger."[281]

The worst realm of reincarnation is the realm of hell beings.[282] Many hells (*naraka*) exist, which are regions of suffering, humiliation, and unspeakable

---

272. Lopez, *Buddhism*, 23.
273. Lopez, 24.
274. Erik Zurcher, "Buddhist Influence on Early Taoism: A Survey of Scriptural Evidence," in *Buddhism: Critical Concepts in Religious Studies, Volume VIII: Buddhism in China, East Asia, and Japan*, ed. Paul Williams (London: Routledge, 2005), 367–419 (395).
275. Lopez, *Buddhism*, 24.
276. Lewis, "Six Realms of Being," 62.
277. Lopez, *Buddhism*, 24.
278. Lewis, "Six Realms of Being," 62.
279. Lopez, *Buddhism*, 24.
280. Peter Harvey, *An Introduction to Buddhism: Teachings, History and Practices* (Cambridge: Cambridge University Press, 1990), 33.
281. Lewis, "Six Realms of Being," 62.
282. Harvey, *Introduction to Buddhism*, 33.

torture.²⁸³ The different types of hells include eight hot hells, eight cold hells, four neighboring hells, and a number of trifling hells.²⁸⁴ Some of the tortures of hells described in Buddhist texts include "being burnt up, cut up, frozen or eaten alive, yet being revived and re-experiencing these torments."²⁸⁵ The levels and forms of suffering in each hell differ, and some are worse than others.²⁸⁶ Eventually, the Buddhist concepts of afterlife and hells merged into the Chinese view of the afterlife.

3.4 Chinese Folk Religion

By definition, folk religion is "the religion of ordinary folk, and it lies to some extent outside the realms of institutional, established beliefs and practices."²⁸⁷ It generally refers to the religion of the common people.²⁸⁸ Sometimes scholars also refer to folk religion as local religion or popular religion. Robert J. Schreiter indicates that a wide variety of terms are used for folk religion. He believes the terms such as *popular religion, folk religion,* and *common religion* all have their specific strengths and weakness. For example, he thinks the term *popular religion* captures a wide range of the concerns, but lacks certain specificity. On the other hand, he thinks term *folk religion* has specificity but carries additional negative overtones.²⁸⁹

In anthropological literature, both terms *Chinese folk religion* and *Chinese popular religion* are commonly in use.²⁹⁰ Many practices of Chinese folk religion are carried out in the midst of everyday life, in families, villages, and city neighborhoods.²⁹¹ In many ways, Chinese folk religion is the integrating

---

283. Zurcher, "Buddhist Influence," 395.
284. Lopez, *Buddhism*, 25.
285. Harvey, *Introduction to Buddhism*, 33–34.
286. Lewis, "Six Realms of Being," 62–63.
287. Fowler and Fowler, *Chinese Religions*, 224.
288. Lukas Tjandra, "Folk Religion among the Chinese in Singapore and Malaysia" (unpublished doctoral dissertation, Fuller Theological Seminary, 1988), 6.
289. Robert J. Schreiter, *Constructing Local Theologies* (Maryknoll, NY: Orbis, 1986), 124–125.
290. Chuck Lowe, *Honouring God and Family: A Christian Response to Idol Food in Chinese Popular Religion* (Bangalore: Theological Book Trust, 2001), 5.
291. Overmyer, *Religions of China*, 51.

factor of Chinese people's corporate lives.[292] Therefore, Chinese folk religion is important for understanding Chinese culture.[293]

As Poceski points out, Chinese folk religion is a religious category created by scholars. Chinese folk religion includes a broad range of prevalent ideas, beliefs, and practices that are not officially part of any of the orthodox beliefs in China, such as Confucianism, Taoism, or Buddhism.[294] Unlike institutional religions, the ideas and values of Chinese folk religion are not based on a single sacred text or set of documents.[295] Instead, Chinese folk religion has emerged from a mixture of local customs, myths, and legends and is informal and heterogeneous.[296] As a dynamic and localized system, Chinese folk religion changes through time and from place to place. Therefore, summarizing Chinese folk religion is challenging.[297]

Syncretism is one of the key features of folk religion.[298] Within the broad context of Chinese religious culture, Chinese folk religion crosses the lines of differentiation between Confucianism, Taoism, and Buddhism[299] and is greatly influenced by these three religions.[300] Most of the beliefs, principles, rites, and deities of Chinese folk religion can be traced to one of the teachings of Confucianism, Taoism, or Buddhism. Elements of each of these three religions are often seamlessly adapted and absorbed into specific paradigms of Chinese folk religion.[301]

The deities of Chinese folk religion are extremely diverse, including scholars of Confucianism, gods and immortals of Taoism, the Buddhas and Bodhisattvas of Buddhism, deified emperors, historical and fictional heroes, nature-spirits, and household gods.[302] Many deities in Chinese folk religion

---

292. Alan Frederick Gates, *Christianity and Animism in Taiwan* (San Francisco: Chinese Materials Center, 1979), 145.

293. David Johnson, "Introduction," in *Ritual and Scripture in Chinese Popular Religion: Five Studies*, ed. David Johnson (Berkeley, CA: IEAS, 1995), vii–xv (vii).

294. Poceski, *Introducing Chinese Religions*, 164.

295. Ching, *Chinese Religions*, 206.

296. Fowler and Fowler, *Chinese Religions*, 224.

297. Adler, *Chinese Religious Traditions*, 113.

298. Poceski, *Introducing Chinese Religions*, 165.

299. Ching, *Chinese Religions*, 206.

300. Tjandra, "Folk Religion," 20–21.

301. Poceski, *Introducing Chinese Religions*, 166–167.

302. Smith, *Chinese Religions*, 172.

are historical personalities believed to have accomplished great deeds for local communities or the nation. The masses admired these heroes then made them folk gods.[303]

One of the most important deities in Chinese folk religion is the Jade Emperor (Yu Huang Da Di 玉皇大帝), the supreme ruler of heaven and earth.[304] The Jade Emperor is originally one of the gods in Taoism. Many believe that he is also the "Lord Heaven" in Confucianism.[305] Another important deity is the Buddha Amitabha, who is incorporated into Chinese folk religion from Buddhism.[306] The kitchen god (the stove god), the earth god, the money god, and the door gods are also very popular deities in Chinese folk religion.[307] The most popular female deities are Bodhisattva Avalokitesvara (Guan Yin Pu Sa 觀音菩薩) of Buddhism and Holy Mother in Heaven (Tian Hou 天后 or Ma Zu 媽祖 in Taiwan).[308]

The divine world in Chinese folk religion reflects the earthly bureaucratic hierarchy on a heavenly scale. Under the Jade Emperor, the high-ranking deities serve in different ministries, while the lower-ranking deities in various localities oversee daily affairs.[309] For the believers of folk religion, different gods have different areas of expertise. Believers often go to the god who will help them the most with a specific difficulty.[310] The highest and most powerful gods are often regarded as too high and too remote to be approached directly. On the other hand, the lower-ranking deities are frequently perceived as the most accessible and responsive to felt needs.[311]

---

303. Wen-hui Tsai, "Historical Personalities in Chinese Folk Religion: A Functional Interpretation," in *Legend, Lore, and Religion in China: Essays in Honor of Wolfram Eberhard on His Seventieth Birthday*, ed. Sarah Allan and Alvin Cohen (San Francisco: Chinese Materials Center, 1979), 23–42 (33–34).
304. Fowler and Fowler, *Chinese Religions*, 230.
305. Ching, *Chinese Religions*, 210.
306. Smith, *Chinese Religions*, 173.
307. Ching, *Chinese Religions*, 210–211.
308. Fowler and Fowler, *Chinese Religions*, 231.
309. Tsai, "Historical Personalities," 33–34.
310. Tik-sang Liu, "A Nameless but Active Religion: An Anthropologist's View of Local Religion in Hong Kong and Macau," in *Religion in China Today*, 67–88 (72).
311. Poceski, *Introducing Chinese Religions*, 172.

The popularity of deities depends on how effectively they respond to the worshippers.[312] Believers hold the gods accountable. If a particular god is perceived as lacking efficacy, worshippers can stop paying respect and offerings to that god. Utilitarian character and pragmatic orientations are the prominent features of Chinese folk religion. The relationship between the deities and the worshippers implies mutual dependency, structured in terms of quid pro quo exchanges between the two groups.[313] In Chinese folk religion, practitioners often do not feel morally obligated to worship any god. They worship mainly because it is a community activity and necessary for maintaining good relations with powerful deities. If a particular god lacks the authority or power to be of any use to them, they transfer their devotion to another god who is more sympathetic and more powerful.[314]

The spiritual world of Chinese folk religion not only includes gods but also ghosts and ancestors.[315] In this tripartite system, gods are equivalent to government bureaucrats, ghosts correlate to beggars, and ancestors are considered as family members.[316] Although practitioners of Chinese folk religion relate to the gods as deities, practitioners may relate to a spirit as either a ghost or an ancestor. Whether a particular spirit is considered a ghost or ancestor depends on the relationship between the practitioner and the spirit. One person's ancestor may be another person's ghost.[317] Ancestors are worshipped only by their descendants, while gods and ghosts are worshipped by a larger community.[318] Ancestor veneration is a moral obligation in a family,[319] and more reverence is given to the gods and the ancestors than to the ghosts.[320] The ghosts are employed as explanations for misfortune.[321]

---

312. Philip C. Baity, "The Ranking of Gods in Chinese Folk Religion," *AFS* 36 (1977): 75–84 (75).

313. Poceski, *Introducing Chinese Religions*, 180–181.

314. Arthur P. Wolf, "Gods, Ghosts, and Ancestors," in *Religion and Ritual in Chinese Society*, ed. Arthur P. Wolf, 131–182 (160).

315. Adler, *Chinese Religious Traditions*, 113.

316. Lowe, *Honouring God*, 3.

317. Wolf, "Gods, Ghosts, and Ancestors," 145–146.

318. Adler, *Chinese Religious Traditions*, 116.

319. Wolf, "Gods, Ghosts, and Ancestors," 160.

320. Poceski, *Introducing Chinese Religions*, 171.

321. David K. Jordan, *Gods, Ghosts, and Ancestors: The Folk Religion of a Taiwanese Village* (Berkeley: University of California Press, 1972), 134.

Ghosts may cause trouble if they have no descendants left or do not receive offerings from their own descendants. Therefore, practitioners must make occasional ritual offerings to ghosts.[322]

Practitioners of folk religion seek help or blessing from a deity by kneeling and offering incense, food, and paper effigies to the deity in the temple. This practice resembles how people showed respect and offered gifts to government officials in the past.[323] At home, lighting candles and burning incense at the family altar and ancestor shrine are major parts of worship.[324]

Divination is a popular practice in Chinese folk religion.[325] For practitioners, divination is an act of communication between humans and the supernatural world.[326] The widespread forms of divination practice include the use of moon blocks and oracle sticks. Moon blocks are two pieces of wood shaped like crescent moons, flat on one side and round on the other.[327] When cast onto the ground, the position of the two pieces of wood indicates the response from the deity.[328] Oracle sticks are a bundle of bamboo sticks held together in a round container. When a request is made to a deity, the petitioner shakes the container until one of the sticks comes out.[329]

The religious beliefs and practices of Chinese folk religion are still widely diffused among ethnic Chinese communities everywhere. This includes mainland China, Taiwan, Hong Kong, Singapore, Southeast Asia, and beyond.[330] Folk religion is particularly practised by hundreds of millions of people in contemporary Southeast China. In some villages, folk religion functions like a second tier of local government, providing services, raising funds, and mobilizing entire communities.[331] In Hong Kong and Macau, folk religion

---

322. Sarah Allan, "Shang Foundations of Modern Chinese Folk Religion," in *Legend, Lore, and Religion*, 1–21 (4).
323. Tik-sang Liu, "Nameless but Active Religion," 71.
324. Fowler and Fowler, *Chinese Religions*, 246.
325. Ching, *Chinese Religions*, 208.
326. Jordan, *Gods, Ghosts, and Ancestors*, 84.
327. Poceski, *Introducing Chinese Religions*, 182.
328. Ching, *Chinese Religions*, 208.
329. Poceski, *Introducing Chinese Religions*, 182.
330. Ching, *Chinese Religions*, 205.
331. Kenneth Dean, "Local Communal Religion in Contemporary South-east China," in *Religion in China Today*, 32–52 (32–33).

activities and people's daily lives are almost inseparable. Folk religion actively organizes local society.³³²

3.5 Summary

In many ways, the various strands of Confucianism, Taoism, Buddhism, and Chinese folk religion intertwine and cooperate. All of them contribute significantly to the lives of the Chinese.³³³ This chapter undertakes a review that focuses on the backgrounds and basic tenets of Confucianism, Taoism, Buddhism, and Chinese folk religion. Although a detailed discussion of these beliefs is beyond the scope of this research, a simple outline of them is provided. The materials in this chapter shape the framework for understanding the Spring Festival, the Qing Ming Festival, and the Hungry Ghost Festival, which are the main research foci of this study.

---

332. Tik-sang Liu, "Nameless but Active Religion," 86.
333. Smith, "Chinese Religion in World Perspective," 4–14 (5).

CHAPTER 4

Research Methods

Chapter 2 reveals that contextualization is both a missiological and theological necessity. The literature review in chapter 3 focuses on the backgrounds and basic tenets of Confucianism, Taoism, Buddhism, and Chinese folk religion. The current chapter presents an overview of the two research methods employed in this study, which are qualitative field research and qualitative interviewing. Both are among the key methods used in social research today.[1] In terms of methodology, these two methods are associated with qualitative research.[2]

Since this research deals with contextualization, qualitative research is believed to be an appropriate research strategy. Broadly speaking, the characteristics of qualitative research are flexibility, spontaneity, and open-endedness. Qualitative research is also less structured than quantitative research.[3] It is a research strategy that "usually emphasizes words rather than quantification in the collection and analysis of data."[4] Alan Bryman indicates that qualitative research is a suitable strategy for research related to worldviews of certain people.[5] Qualitative research, as Jennifer Mason asserts, "has an unrivalled capacity to constitute compelling arguments about how things work in a

---

1. Svend Brinkmann and Steinar Kvale, *InterViews: Learning the Craft of Qualitative Research Interviewing*, 3rd ed. (Thousand Oaks, CA: SAGE, 2014), 14.
2. Alan Bryman, *Social Research Methods*, 5th ed. (Oxford: Oxford University Press, 2016), 377.
3. David Dooley, *Social Research Methods*, 2nd ed. (Englewood Cliffs, NJ: Prentice Hall, 1990), 277.
4. Bryman, *Social Research Methods*, 31–32.
5. Bryman, 36.

particular context."⁶ Bryman also points out that the findings of qualitative research "tend to be oriented to the contextual uniqueness and significance of the aspect of the social world being studied."⁷ Moreover, Mason believes that the findings of well-conducted qualitative research are generalisable because "the qualitative habit of intimately connecting context with explanation means that qualitative research is capable of producing very well-founded cross-contextual generalities."⁸ Qualitative research enables one to engage in a "thick description" of the experience or behaviour rather than a superficial once, and to capture the events under investigation through the eyes and interpretation of its participants. Quantitative, by contrast, tends to broad but superficial data which lacks nuance and depth.

First, this chapter presents an overview of the qualitative field research conducted on three significant Chinese festivals celebrated by the Chinese people in Malaysia. Second, this chapter provides an overview of the qualitative interviews conducted with six Chinese preachers. The aim of this research is to investigate the principles involved in formulating contextualized preaching for the Chinese during the Spring Festival, the Qing Ming Festival, and the Hungry Ghost Festival. Utilizing these two qualitative research methods allowed the opportunity to investigate various, yet complementary, research questions.

4.1 Qualitative Field Research of Three Chinese Festivals

4.1.1 Qualitative Field Research as a Research Method

The first research method employed in this study is qualitative field research, which is a type of observation study.⁹ By definition, the data collection of this research method takes place in the field, a natural setting rather than a controlled setting or lab.¹⁰ According to Earl Babbie, qualitative field research

---

6. Jennifer Mason, *Qualitative Researching*, 2nd ed. (London: SAGE, 2002), 1.
7. Bryman, *Social Research Methods*, 384.
8. Mason, *Qualitative Researching*, 1.
9. Thomas Herzog, *Research Methods in the Social Sciences* (New York: HarperCollins, 1996), 38–41.
10. Leonard Schatzman and Anselm L. Strauss, *Field Research: Strategies for a Natural Sociology* (Englewood Cliffs, NJ: Prentice Hall, 1973), 2.

"enables researchers to observe social life in its natural habitat: to go where the action is and watch."[11] Moreover, qualitative field research is designed to produce qualitative data.[12] It is "a research based on non-quantitative observations made in the field and analyzed in non-statistical ways."[13]

One advantage of qualitative field research is the comprehensiveness of observation. Babbie claims, "By going directly to the social phenomenon under study and observing it as completely as possible, the researcher can develop a deeper and fuller understanding of it."[14] A second advantage of qualitative field research is non-reactivity. The observer does not change the natural setting and minimally disrupts the subjects being studied.[15] A third advantage of field research is ecological validity. Because field research is usually conducted in natural settings, it is "more likely than other methods to produce results that are valid for the so-called real world."[16]

According to Babbie, "Field researchers need not always participate in what they are studying, though they usually will study it directly at the scene of the action."[17] Qualitative field research draws on the direct evidence of the events witnessed firsthand.[18] Therefore, the role of the observer in qualitative field research is essential. The observer has a variety of roles from which to choose, from complete participant to complete non-participating observer.[19] As Bell and Waters assert, the role of the observer, either as a participant or a non-participant, is "to observe and record in as objective a way as possible."[20] In this study, all observations of the festivals were conducted through non-participant observation.

---

11. Earl Babbie, *The Practice of Social Research*, 10th ed. (Belmont, CA: Wadsworth/Thomson Learning, 2004), 281.
12. Babbie, 282.
13. Dooley, *Social Research Methods*, 276.
14. Babbie, *Practice of Social Research*, 282.
15. Dooley, *Social Research Methods*, 277.
16. Herzog, *Research Methods*, 45.
17. Babbie, *Practice of Social Research*, 285.
18. Martyn Denscombe, *The Good Research Guide for Small-Scale Social Research Projects*, 3rd ed. (Maidenhead: Open University Press, 2007), 206.
19. Babbie, *Practice of Social Research*, 285–286.
20. Judith Bell and Stephen Waters, *Doing Your Research Project: A Guide for First-Time Researchers*, 6th ed. (Maidenhead: McGraw-Hill, 2014), 211–214.

Because qualitative field research is involved in observational fieldwork, it could also be considered as a form of ethnographic research in a broad sense. As Barbour says, "In order to be considered as ethnography, there should be at least an element of observational fieldwork."[21] Ethnography, as a term in research methods, literally means a description of peoples or cultures.[22] Generally speaking, ethnography is an approach to research that seeks to describe and explain a particular culture.[23] It was originally associated with social anthropological research.[24] Denscombe asserts that ethnography "has its origin as a research strategy in the works of the early social anthropologists, whose aim was to provide detailed and permanent accounts of the cultures and lives of small, isolated tribes."[25] In earlier times, ethnography is considered as "the branch of anthropology that deals with the systematic description of specific human cultures."[26] In ethnography, a researcher participated in the research setting to varying degrees, from level of complete observer to level of complete participant.[27] Today, however, the term is often used synonymously with *participant observation*.[28] Since the field research of this study is conducted with non-participant observation, the term *qualitative field research* is believed to be more appropriate.

Two main reasons explain why the non-participant observation approach was chosen for this study. First, non-participant observation was implemented in order to minimize the risk of the observer's presence affecting the festival participants. As McNeill and Chapman explain, non-participant observation is an unobtrusive form of observation in which a researcher takes on the role

---

21. Rosaline S. Barbour, *Introducing Qualitative Research: A Student's Guide*, 2nd ed. (London: SAGE, 2014), 155.

22. Denscombe, *Good Research Guide*, 61.

23. James Spradley and David W. McCurdy, *The Cultural Experience: Ethnography in Complex Society* (Prospect Heights, IL: Waveland, 1988), 3.

24. Bryman, *Social Research Methods*, 423.

25. Denscombe, *Good Research Guide*, 61.

26. Pertti J. Pelto, *Applied Ethnography: Guidelines for Field Research* (Walnut Creek, CA: Left Coast), 23.

27. Sharlene Nagy Hesse-Biber and Patricia Leavy, *The Practice of Qualitative Research*, 2nd ed. (Thousand Oaks, CA: SAGE, 2011), 203–204.

28. Robert Sommer and Barbara Sommer, *A Practical Guide to Behavioral Research: Tools and Techniques*, 5th ed. (Oxford: Oxford University Press, 2002), 56.

of a detached onlooker who carries out detailed analyses of social activity.²⁹ Second, not participating in any festival rituals allows the observer to record observations more easily through field notes and audiovisual documentations. Because all the observations were conducted in settings which were totally open to the public, it was assumed that the presence of the observer would not arouse too much suspicion among the ritual participants.

As a researcher, nevertheless, I am aware of the fact that non-participant observation has its limitations. First of all, the method of non-participant observation does limit the observer from experiencing what the ritual participants do. Second, non-participant observation does not allow the researcher to clarify meanings and ask questions in relation to things that are not readily understood.³⁰ Third, this research method is subject to the biases of the researcher, as the researcher may only see what he or she wants to see.³¹ My observations are probably filtered through my own experience and my Christian convictions.

I believe, however, the limitations of non-participant observation can be counteracted with sensitivity. Sensitivity means the ability to carefully observe and respect participants and data.³² It also means not forcing meanings on data. As Juliet Corbin and Anselm Strauss stress, "At all times, the researcher must keep in mind that findings are the result of the interplay between data and what a researcher brings to the analysis, and all interpretations should be considered provisional until supported by additional data or verified with participants."³³ In this research, all the field notes and audiovisual documentations were analysed alongside the review of books and articles related to Chinese festivals and customs. Relevant references were written by authors from Malaysia, Singapore, Hong Kong, Taiwan, and mainland China. I believe these references helped me overcome any predetermined interpretations of the data. Moreover, these resources helped further the understanding of

---

29. Patrick McNeill and Steve Chapman, *Research Methods*, 3rd ed. (London: Routledge, 2006), 92–93.

30. Hesse-Biber and Leavy, *Practice of Qualitative Research*, 204.

31. Edgar J. Elliston, *Introduction to Missiological Research Design* (Pasadena, CA: William Carey Library, 2011), 156.

32. Juliet Corbin and Anselm Strauss, *Basics of Qualitative Research: Techniques and Procedures for Developing Grounded Theory*, 4th ed. (Thousand Oaks, CA: SAGE, 2015), 77.

33. Corbin and Strauss, 78.

each festival, clarifying questions, and noticeably demonstrated the similar practices of the festivals among the Chinese communities worldwide. My personal experience as a Chinese preacher who grew up in a Chinese community in Malaysia can be advantageous to the study as well. As Corbin and Strauss rightly say, "Though experience can blind researchers' perception, it can also enable researchers to understand the significance of some things more quickly. That's because researchers don't have to spend time gaining familiarity with surroundings or events."[34] Moreover, I agree with Edgar J. Elliston that a researcher may avoid most errors in research by a strong sense of integrity and commitment to the central research issue.[35]

The field research consists of field notes and audiovisual documentations recorded with a digital camcorder and a digital camera during each festival observation. As Ronald L. Grimes indicates, audiovisual documentation is important when studying ritual. The recorded materials can be used for note-taking, data gathering, and data analysis.[36] Detailed field notes were composed shortly after each observation.

4.1.2 Selecting Dates and Field Sites of Observations

All field research observations of the Spring Festival, the Qing Ming Festival, and the Hungry Ghost Festival were conducted within the Chinese communities in Malaysia. The Chinese population in Malaysia, to a great extent, has preserved Chinese customs and traditions. Every year the Malaysian Chinese observe many major Chinese festivals.[37] Currently, they celebrate at least six major annual Chinese festivals nationwide. In addition to the Spring Festival, the Qing Ming Festival, and the Hungry Ghost Festival, the Malaysian Chinese also celebrate the Duan Wu Festival, which is also called the Dragon Boat Festival, the Mid-Autumn Festival, and the Winter Solstice

---

34. Corbin and Strauss, 78–79.
35. Elliston, *Introduction*, 196.
36. Ronald L. Grimes, *The Craft of Ritual Studies* (Oxford: Oxford University Press, 2014), 12.
37. 林國興, "新馬華人民間宗教習俗的認識: 回應" (A Response: Understanding of Religious Practices among the Singaporeans and Malaysians), 於福音與新馬華人文化: 研討會報告書 (*A Seminar Report on Gospel and Singapore-Malaysian Chinese Culture*), 週賢正編 (新加坡 [Singapore]: 三一神學院, 1989), 158–160 (158).

Festival.³⁸ The Duan Wu Festival (端午節) occurs on the fifth day of the fifth lunar month. It is considered a Summer festival. On the other hand, the Mid-Autumn Festival (Zhong Qiu Jie 中秋節) is held on the fifteenth day of the eighth lunar month, which is also a night of a full moon. The Mid-Autumn Festival is considered a harvest festival.³⁹

According to the Chinese lunar calendar, the Spring Festival is the first celebration of the year and occurs in February. However, field research for this study began in August 2015. Therefore, the first field observation occurred on 16 August 2015 for the Hungry Ghost Festival. This was followed by field observation of the Spring Festival on 14 February 2016. The Qing Ming Festival involved two field observations: one on 20 March2016 and one on 26 March 2016.

All observations were conducted in public/open settings where the Chinese celebrate the festivals. Compared to non-public/closed settings, access to public settings is relatively easier.⁴⁰ The observation site for the Spring Festival was Thean Hou Temple in Kuala Lumpur. For the Qing Ming Festival, three observation sites were visited: the Kwong Tong Cemetery Columbarium Pagoda, the Gui Yuan Crematorium, and the Petaling Jaya Chinese Cemetery. The observation site for the Hungry Ghost Festival was in a park of a Chinese community, where a large temporary canopy for the festival was erected. The data analysis for the field research observations will be presented in chapter 5. Although the Hungry Ghost Festival was the first festival observed, its analysis report will be presented after the Spring Festival and the Qing Ming Festival, according to the chronological order of the festivals on the Chinese lunar calendar.

4.2 Qualitative Interviews with Chinese Preachers
4.2.1 Qualitative Interviewing as a Research Method
The second research method implemented for this study of contextualized preaching during Chinese festivals is qualitative interviewing with Chinese

---

38. 蘇慶華, 節令、民俗與宗教 *(Festival, Folklore and Religion)* (吉隆坡 [Kuala Lumpur]: 華社資料研究中心, 1994), 2.
39. 程裕禎編, 中國文化攬萃 *(The Collection of Chinese Culture)* (北京 [Beijing]: 學苑出版社, 1989) 322-325. The Winter Solstice Festival always occurs on 22 or 23 December. See 蘇慶華, *Festival, Folklore and Religion*, 13.
40. Bryman, *Social Research Methods*, 425.

preachers. According to Bryman, "The interview is probably the most widely employed method in qualitative research."[41] Simply speaking, an interview is a purposeful conversation with a careful questioning and listening approach.[42] Interviewing is an active process in which the interviewer and interviewee produce knowledge through a conversational relationship.[43]

Denscombe asserts that interviewing is a suitable research method when a researcher needs to gain insights into people's opinions, feelings, emotions, and experiences.[44] Similarly, Daphne M. Keats points out that interviewing is an efficient research method if the researcher wants to explore the reasons and motivations for the attitudes and opinions of people.[45] It permits "a deeper and fuller understanding of the attitudes of a respondent."[46] Because this research investigates Chinese preachers' perceptions and practices regarding contextualized preaching during the Spring Festival, the Qing Ming Festival, and the Hungry Ghost Festival, qualitative interviewing is considered to be an appropriate method.

There are two major types of qualitative interviewing. One is the unstructured interview and the other is the semi-structured interview.[47] In an unstructured interview, the interviewee is allowed "to take the lead to a greater extent."[48] As Bill Gillham explains, "What an unstructured interview does is give responsibility for determining the structure to the interviewee who has to lead the way and tell the story."[49] Although the researcher presumably has a clear purpose in terms of what he or she wants to discover, usually there is no prearranged schedule of questions in an unstructured interview.[50]

---

41. Bryman, *Social Research Methods*, 466.
42. Brinkmann and Kvale, *InterViews*, 5–6.
43. Brinkmann and Kvale, 21.
44. Denscombe, *Good Research Guide*, 174.
45. Daphne M. Keats, *Interviewing: A Practical Guide for Students and Professionals* (Buckingham: Open University Press, 2010), 72.
46. Nancy Jean Vyhmeister and Terry Dwain Robertson, *Your Guide to Writing Quality Research Papers: For Students of Religion and Theology*, 3rd ed. (Grand Rapids, MI: Zondervan, 2014), 41.
47. Bryman, *Social Research Methods*, 468.
48. Sommer and Sommer, *Practical Guide*, 114.
49. Bill Gillham, *Research Interviewing: The Range of Techniques* (Maidenhead: Open University Press, 2005), 45.
50. Gillham, 47.

On the other hand, in a semi-structured interview, the researcher has a list of questions or specific topics to be covered. As Bryman points out, "By and large, all the questions will be asked and a similar wording will be used from interviewee to interviewee."[51] Bill Gillham argues that "the semi-structured interview is the most important way of conducting a research interview because of its flexibility balanced by structure, and the quality of the data so obtained."[52]

4.2.2 Semi-Structured Interviews with Chinese Preachers

In this study, all the interviews were conducted in a semi-structured format that included a prepared schedule of questions to steer the direction of the interview but with sufficient space for the interviewee to shape the ordering and speed of topics covered.[53] Fifteen interview questions were prepared for each interview. The first three questions were general questions. The first question investigated the overall preaching experience of the interviewees. The interviewees were asked to share information about their personal background and experience in preaching ministry. After the first question, the interviewees were asked about the importance of contextualized preaching. The third question probed the interviewees to talk about their overall experience of preaching during the Spring Festival, the Qing Ming Festival, and/or the Hungry Ghost Festival.

After the three general questions, the next twelve questions were specifically related to preaching in the Chinese church during the three Chinese festivals. There were four questions for each festival: the Spring Festival, the Qing Ming Festival, and the Hungry Ghost Festival. With regard to each festival, the interviewees were asked to identify aspects of the festival's religious beliefs, cultural values, and practices in harmony with or contrary to the Christian faith. They were also asked to identify elements of the religious beliefs, cultural values, and practices of each festival that can be used to contextualize preaching the gospel more effectively. Moreover, interviewees were

---

51. Bryman, *Social Research Methods*, 468.
52. Gillham, *Research Interviewing*, 70.
53. Helen Cameron and Catherine Duce, *Researching Practice in Ministry and Mission – A Companion* (London: SCM, 2013), 83.

asked to list Bible passages they believed would be relevant when preaching in church during these festivals and to give an explanation for their choices.

4.2.3 Selection of Interviewees

Because the interview approach in this study is designed to interview experienced and well-known preachers among the Chinese, this approach could be considered what Gillham calls "élite interviewing." As Gillham indicates, élite interviewing is about interviewing people who are especially well-informed about a "particular area of research" or about the context which is being researched.[54] Elites are leaders or experts in a community. Brinkmann and Kvale believe interviews with elites are very productive because "interviews with experts, where the interviewer confronts and also contributes with his or her conceptions of the interview theme, may approximate the intense questioning of a Socratic dialogue, ideally leading to knowledge in the sense of *episteme*."[55]

The purposive sampling method was employed to select the interviewees in this study. Purposive sampling is considered a non-probability form of sampling. As Bryman explains, "The goal of purposive sampling is to sample cases/participants in a strategic way, so that those sampled are relevant to the research questions that are posted."[56] Purposive sampling is also known as judgment or selective sampling. As A. N. Oppenheim indicates, this kind of sampling is typical in the depth interview. Oppenheim claims that this sampling "needs a good spread of respondent characteristics so that we can reasonably hope to have tapped probable respondents of every kind and background."[57] A variety of samples is preferable in purposive sampling.[58] Moreover, as David Silverman indicates, qualitative interview studies tend to be conducted with a small sample size.[59]

Interviewees in this study were selected based on the following criteria. First, to assure the *emic* perspective of this research, the interviewee must be someone who has grown up within Chinese society and can be described

---

54. Gillham, *Research Interviewing*, 54.
55. Brinkmann and Kvale, *InterViews*, 171–172.
56. Bryman, *Social Research Methods*, 408.
57. A. N. Oppenheim, *Questionnaire Design, Interviewing and Attitude Measurement* (London: Continuum, 1992), 68.
58. Bryman, *Social Research Methods*, 408.
59. David Silverman, *Doing Qualitative Research*, 4th ed. (London: SAGE, 2013), 204.

Research Methods

as a custodian of Chinese culture. Second, the interviewee must be well-informed about Chinese customs, particularly related to Chinese festivals. Third, because this study aimed to obtain opinions from experienced preachers, the interviewee must be experienced in preaching among the Chinese for at least ten years.

All six interviewees are theologically evangelical, and their educational backgrounds range from an undergraduate diploma to a PhD. Among the six preachers interviewed, five are male and one is female. Since these were anonymous semi-structured qualitative interviews, the interviewees from Malaysia are identified in this research as Preacher M1, Preacher M2, and Preacher M3. As for the interviewees from Hong Kong, they are identified as Preacher H1, Preacher H2, and Preacher H3.

Preacher M1 has almost forty years of preaching experience in Malaysia. He grew up in a Chinese Taoist family, and his father was a well-known Mao Shan (茅山) Taoist priest. His father remained as a Taoist throughout his life, but Preacher M1 converted to Christianity during his youth. The villagers were fuming when they found out that a Taoist priest's son accepted Christ. Knowing of Preacher M1's baptism, his mother cried and claimed her son was dead to her. Preacher M1 faced many criticisms and finally decided to leave the village. Later, he received his theological training from Malaysia Bible Seminary and was ordained as a pastor. Currently, he is pastoring one of the largest Mandarin-speaking congregations in Malaysia. As a pastor and an evangelist, he is well-known among the Chinese community for his comparative study in Taoism, Confucianism, Buddhism, and Chinese folk religion.

Preacher M2 is a notable preacher and also a well-experienced pastor for almost half a century. Growing up in a traditional Chinese family, his parents dedicated him as a godson to the goddess Bodhisattva Avalokitesvara (Guan Yin Pu Sa 觀音菩薩) and god Guan Di 關帝.[60] Being the only son in the family, his conversion to Christianity had immediately brought upon him great opposition and rejection from his father who was devoted to Chinese folk religion, especially in the issue of ancestral worship. Eventually Preacher M2 brought both of his parents to Christ. He was trained in Singapore Bible

---

60. *Guan Di* 關帝, also known as *Guan Gong* 關公, was a famous general in China's Three Kingdoms period. He was later deified for his courage as a mighty warrior. See 馬國棟和劉志良, 中國民間信仰揭秘 (*Uncovering the Folk Beliefs of China*), 增訂版 (香港 [Hong Kong]: 香港基督徒短期宣教訓練中心暨佈道資源供應中心, 1997), 41.

Seminary and was later ordained in a Baptist church. He pastored one of the largest Cantonese-speaking congregations in Kuala Lumpur before his retirement.

Preacher M3 has more than ten years of preaching experience in Malaysia. She grew up in a Catholic family background, however abandoned her faith during her youth and eventually became involved in mystical practices in Chinese folk religion. Besides worshipping the Chinese deities and ghosts, she studied Chinese astrology and practiced meditation. She was also hired to do fortune telling and Chinese geomancy (Feng Shui 风水).[61] During Chinese New Year, people sought for her help to do folk sorcery practices such as "petty person beating" (*da xiao ren* 打小人).[62] She had been involved in all of these practices for about fifteen years before she accepted Christ. She was then trained in Bible College Malaysia and has been serving as an itinerant preacher among Chinese churches.

Preacher H1 has more than forty years of preaching experience. Before his conversion to Christianity, he used to participate in rituals of Chinese festivals and worshipped Chinese deities. He accepted Christ at a young age when his grandmother and mother accepted Christ. He earned his master of divinity degree from Hong Kong Baptist Theological Seminary and his PhD from Southeastern Baptist Theological Seminary, USA. Preacher H1 has a wide range of experiences in Christian ministries, which includes serving as an editor of a Christian magazine and a seminary lecturer as well as a pastor. Before his retirement, he was a senior pastor for a church with 2,500 attendants in Hong Kong. He is also well respected in his comparison study of Christianity and Chinese religions. Besides translation and writing of some books and booklets related to Chinese tradition and religious philosophy, he has also published over one hundred articles on the related subjects.

---

61. According to Wai Lun Tam, *Feng Shui* represents the Chinese concept of space, literally means "wind-water," and depicts the capturing of chthonic energy of the environment. See Wai Lun Tam, "Communal Worship and Festivals in Chinese Villages," in *Chinese Religious Life*, eds. David A. Palmer, Glenn Shive, and Philip L. Wickeri (New York: Oxford University Press, 2011), 30–49 (32). *Feng Shui* serves the purpose of locating the energy of the environment and the effort to design the environment to harmonize with the forces of nature. See Richard Gunde, *Culture and Customs of China* (Westport, CT: Greenwood, 2002), 144.

62. "Petty person beating" is a folk sorcery practice which functions to give vent to the hatred of someone. Actions of hitting with slippers or other items are used on a paper figure which represents a person to be cursed. See, 馬國棟和劉志良, *(Uncovering the Folk Beliefs)*, 27.

Preacher H2 is a well-known evangelist and writer. Travelling to more than forty countries, he has over four decades of experience in preaching the gospel to Chinese people worldwide. He also has a close relationship with the Chinese churches in Malaysia and has been invited to preach in numerous evangelistic meetings since 1999. When he was sixteen, Preacher H2 was passionate about Buddhist teachings and started to do Zen meditation. After he set his pilgrimage during his college years to India, Nepal, and some other places, he eventually turned to the Lord. Later he obtained his PhD from University of Hawaii, with a specialization in Confucianism. Preacher H2 has published more than thirty books and 1,200 articles on Chinese culture and Christianity, including ninety-eight academic articles in journals. He was the founder and a president of an international organization focusing on building bridges between Chinese culture and Christianity. Besides leading evangelistic meetings worldwide, he has often been invited to give lectures internationally. He has been considered one of the top scholars in the study of Christianity and Chinese philosophy. The government of China has recently invited him to be a committee member of a top level advisory board in religion and cultural matters.

Preacher H3 has about forty years of preaching experience among Chinese. He was born and raised in a traditional Chinese family. Before knowing Christ, he used to follow his family to temples and was made to drink water containing the burned ashes of the incense for the sake of health. He accepted Christ when he was around the age of fifteen. After working for some years, he dedicated himself as a full time minister. Receiving all his theological training in Hong Kong, he graduated from Overseas Theological Seminary and furthered his study in Alliance Bible Seminary and then Bethel Bible Seminary. He was ordained as a pastor in 1986. After pastoring for twenty-two years, he took his early retirement and joined an international Christian social service organization. Currently Preacher H3 is leading an organization focusing on the fostering of Christian discipleship and evangelism. Moreover, he published books on discipleship and spiritual warfare including research on Chinese sorcery and divination.

The interviews were conducted from August to October 2015. The six Chinese preachers were interviewed separately at different locations suitable for interview recording. Three interviews occurred in Malaysia. The other three interviews occurred in Hong Kong during a research trip in September

2015. Before the interviews, each interviewee was required to read and sign a consent form. All interviewees were informed about the topic and the overall purpose of the research. The consent form also informed the interviewees of their right to terminate the interview at any point. Moreover, the interviewees were assured that the presentation of the data analysis of the interviews would be anonymous.[63]

All interviews were audio recorded with an MP3 device. Handwritten notes were also composed during the interviews. Four interviews, including three in Hong Kong and one in Malaysia, were conducted in Cantonese. The other two interviews were conducted in Mandarin. After each interview, the recording was transcribed into Chinese text with computer software. The Chinese texts were then analyzed manually, and the key findings were translated into English. Chapter 6 presents the key findings of the interviews.

---

63. Kvale and Brinkmann give a clear explanation about confidentiality in research. See *InterViews*, 72.

CHAPTER 5

Exploratory Study of the Three Festivals

The current chapter reports the data analysis for the field research observations regarding the Spring Festival, the Qing Ming Festival, and the Hungry Ghost Festival. The field notes and audiovisual documentations were analyzed alongside the review of relevant references. These resources helped further the understanding of the practices and symbols applied in each festival and their implications for understanding the Chinese worldview, including religious beliefs and cultural values.

5.1 Field Research on the Spring Festival

The concept of the New Year holds great symbolic meaning in many cultures.[1] Of all the Chinese festivals, the Spring Festival is the biggest celebration and the most significant one.[2] The Spring Festival celebrates the beginning of the Chinese New Year and emphasizes renewal.[3] The Chinese character for "year" is *nian* 年. Etymologically, *nian* 年 symbolizes the ripening of grains. Therefore, the character for "year" relates to the celebration of harvest.[4]

Because of its long history and rich cultural connotations, the Spring Festival has also been considered the grandest and most exciting festival in

---

1. Laurence G. Thompson, *Chinese Religion: An Introduction,* 4th ed. (Belmont, CA: Wadsworth, 1989), 130.

2. Choon San Wong, *An Illustrated Cycle of Chinese Festivities in Malaysia and Singapore* (Singapore: Jack Chia-MPH, 1987), 57.

3. Richard Gunde, *Culture and Customs of China* (Westport, CT: Greenwood, 2002), 196.

4. 蘇慶華, 節令、民俗與宗教 *(Festival, Folklore and Religion)* (吉隆坡 [Kuala Lumpur]: 華社資料研究中心, 1994), 4–5.

Chinese culture.⁵ The celebration normally lasts fifteen days, beginning the first day and ending the fifteenth day of the Chinese New Year.⁶ In many places, the celebration of the Spring Festival includes an elaborate schedule of events, such as family reunions, feasting, rites of cleansing and renewal, and observances of ancestors and other deities.⁷ Some events during the Chinese New Year are private events that occur exclusively within the family and at home. One of the well-known private events among Chinese is the family reunion dinner held on New Year's Eve. Extra portions of food are prepared so that there will be leftovers, which is a sign of abundance in the coming New Year.⁸ Other events are very public, including noisy celebrations and street entertainment.⁹

On 14 February 2016, which was the seventh day of the Chinese New Year, I observed a Spring Festival celebration in Thean Hou Temple in Kuala Lumpur. The seventh day (初七) of the Chinese New Year is considered the birthday of humankind (*ren ri* 人日). *Ren ri* 人日 is also called *ren qi* 人七 or *ren qing* 人慶. The celebration stresses the value of human beings.¹⁰ In ancient China, no executions (capital punishment) of criminals should occur on the seventh day of the New Year.¹¹

According to the Chinese myth of creation, humankind was created on the seventh day. The goddess Nü Wa 女媧 created one animal each day in the first seven days of creation. She created human beings on the seventh day.¹² The ancient Chinese believed that on the first day chickens were created, on the second day a dog was created, on the third day a boar was created, on

---

5. Liming Wei, *Chinese Festivals* (Cambridge: Cambridge University Press, 2011), 14.

6. Frena Bloomfield, *The Book of Chinese Beliefs: A Journey into the Chinese Inner World* (London: Arrow, 1986), 50.

7. Robert L. Chard, "Rituals and Scriptures of the Stove Cult," in *Ritual and Scripture in Chinese Popular Religion: Five Studies*, ed. David Johnson (Berkeley, CA: IEAS, 1995), 3–54 (3).

8. Daniel Tong, *A Biblical Approach to Chinese Traditions and Beliefs* (Singapore: Genesis, 2012), 28.

9. Carol Stepanchuk and Charles Wong, *Mooncakes and Hungry Ghosts: Festivals of China* (San Francisco: China Books and Periodicals, 1991), 26.

10. 喬繼堂, 細說中國節: 中國傳統節日的起源與內涵 *(The Origin and Connotation of Chinese Traditional Festivals)* (北京 [Beijing]: 九州出版社, 2006), 10.

11. 馬來西亞華人節日風俗 *(Customs of Malaysian Chinese Festivals)*, 賴觀福, 孟沙, 與鍾澤才編 (吉隆坡 [Kuala Lumpur]: 馬來西亞中華大會堂, 1997), 17.

12. 李秀娥, 臺灣民俗節慶: 歲時節俗的民俗意涵與祭祀文化 *(Festivals and Customs of Taiwan: Connotations of Customs During Seasonal Festivals and Sacrificial Culture)* (臺中 [Taichung]: 晨星出版有限公司, 2004), 78.

the fourth day a sheep was created, on the fifth day a cow was created, and on the sixth day a horse was created.[13]

The Thean Hou Temple is a six-tiered Chinese temple dedicated to the goddess Tian Hou (天后). The goddess Tian Hou is one of the most popular goddesses in Hong Kong and Taiwan (Tian Hou is called Ma Zu 媽祖 in Taiwan). She is a patron goddess for fishermen and sailors.[14] Many Chinese believe that *Tian Hou* is very powerful. She can provide prosperity, protection, and healing. The childless pray to her for the birth of a son.[15] During the Spring Festival, the Thean Hou Temple is one of the most popular destinations in Kuala Lumpur for the Spring Festival's temple fairs. The temple fair is a popular activity during the Spring Festival. During the Spring Festival, many people go to local temple fairs for ritual praying and shopping. The temple fair originated in ancient festival seasons when people offered sacrifices to the village god. It gradually changed into a marketplace.[16]

One volunteer helped me with video recording, and we arrived at the temple fair of the Thean Hou Temple at 12:00 p.m. We encountered heavy traffic going up the hill where Thean Hou Temple is located. Many handicraft stalls and food stalls for the Spring Festival's temple fair were set up along the pathway to the temple. Key findings from the Spring Festival field research are presented below.

5.1.1 Finding 1: Chinese Legends and Chinese Zodiac Remain Part of the Atmosphere of the Spring Festival

According to the legends of ancient China, a ferocious beast called Nian 年 ("year") lived in a mountain and slept for an entire year. Nian awoke only at the end of the year and would come out from the mountain to attack the people and their livestock.[17] Another version of Nian's legend states that it

---

13. 中國風俗 (*Customs in China*), 楊秀編 (蘇州 [Suzhou]: 古吳軒出版社, 2010), 31.

14. 周樹佳, 香港諸神: 起源、廟宇與崇拜 (*Deities in Hong Kong: Origin, Temples and Veneration of Deities*) (香港 [Hong Kong]: 中華書局, 2009), 49.

15. Manchao Cheng, *The Origin of Chinese Deities* (Beijing: Foreign Languages Press, 1995), 104.

16. Ren Qiliang et al., "Folk Customs: Folk Temple Fair," in *Common Knowledge about Chinese Culture*, ed. Ren Qiliang et al., rev. ed. (Xi'an: Shaanxi Normal University General Publishing, 2015), 55–56 (55).

17. 中國節日的故事 (*Stories about China's Festivals*), 陳淑英編 (臺北 [Taipei]: 將門文物出版有限公司, 1997), 15.

was living in a deep sea and came to the land every year to attack people.[18] Eventually the villagers discovered that the beast had three weaknesses: Nian was intimidated by noise, disliked sunshine, and was frightened by the colour red. Therefore at the end of the year, the people would successfully chase away the beast by painting the doors of their homes red and by setting off hundreds of firecrackers.[19]

The celebration of the Spring Festival today is obviously still closely associated with the legend. The colour red is predominant during the Spring Festival. Thousands of Chinese red lanterns were hanging everywhere in the Thean Hou Temple (see figure 5.1.1 and figure 5.1.2). Two pots of tangerine plants, which were wrapped with red cloth, were placed before the staircase leading to the entrance of the main building (see figure 5.1.3). In the Chinese culture, the tangerine is symbolic of fortune.[20] The tangerine plants were decorated with red packets (*hong bao* 紅包, see figure 5.1.4). During the Spring Festival, the Chinese give children and younger relatives red packets filled with money to wish them good luck.[21] In ancient China, this practice was called *ya chong qian* 壓祟錢 (today it is called *ya sui qian* 壓歲錢). According to another Chinese legend, Chong 祟 was a white-faced demon with black hands and would come to hurt children on New Year's Eve. The ancient Chinese believed that the money would chase away the demon and protect the children.[22]

Spring couplets written on red paper were pasted on each side of the front doors of the temple (see figure 5.1.5). Spring couplets, or *chun lian* 春聯, are auspicious couplets normally composed of a pair of poetry lines vertically pasted on both sides of the front door of houses to welcome blessing.[23] The couplets may convey wishes of happiness, longevity, wealth, or good harvest.[24] Some believe that the custom of hanging spring couplets on the doors began

---

18. 喬繼堂, 細說中國節: 中國傳統節日的起源與內涵, 276.
19. Stepanchuk and Wong, *Mooncakes*, 14.
20. Wong, *Illustrated Cycle*, 87.
21. Xiang Wei, *Chinese Customs* (New York: Better Link, 2008), 23.
22. 洪丕謨, 福祿: 民俗文化趣談 (*A Discussion on Custom and Culture*) (香港 [Hong Kong]: 萬里書店, 2006), 51.
23. David Hock Tey, *Chinese Culture and the Bible* (Singapore: Here's Life Books, 1988), 122–123.
24. Vivien Sung, *Five-Fold Happiness: Chinese Concepts of Luck, Prosperity, Longevity, Happiness, and Wealth* (San Francisco: Chronicle Books, 2002), 43.

as early as the Spring and Autumn Period (770–746 BC).²⁵ Spring couplets were originally called peach wood charms (*tao fu* 桃符), which were boards made of peach wood, painted with charm inscriptions or pictures of gods. The images which were painted on the two panels of the charms as exorcists were two door gods Shen Tu 神荼 and Yu Lei 鬱壘. They were hung on the doors allegedly to ward off evil spirits.²⁶ The word *chun lian* was first used in the Ming dynasty (AD 1364–1644). Emperor Zhu Yuan Zhang 朱元璋 once issued a decree on the eve of the Spring Festival ordering every family to put couplets on their doors. Since then the custom became more widespread.²⁷ According to Hsieh and Chou, the spring couplets are considered as a type of expressive culture, in which people express their wishes and frustrations.²⁸

The items for sale in the stalls revealed the influence of the legend of Nian as well. Auspicious red decorative items and red pinwheels were sold in the stalls (see figure 5.1.6). A pinwheel is a toy fan and spins when the wind blows. Many buy pinwheels at the temple fair to pray for blessings.²⁹ Firecrackers were also for sale in the stalls (see figure 5.1.7). Chinese firecrackers are typically made of gunpowder wrapped in multilayered paper.³⁰ The ancient Chinese believed that firecrackers could chase away demons and monsters. This belief is also related to another Chinese legend. According to the legend, a one-foot-long monster called Shan Xiao 山魈 lived in a mountain in the far west. Shan Xiao looked like a human being but had only one leg. It liked to come down from the mountain at the end of the year. Whoever encountered Shan Xiao would contract a high fever and die in pain. The only device that could chase away Shan Xiao was the firecracker.³¹

---

25. Nailu Jin, "When Did Shi'er Shengxiao (The Twelve Animals of Chinese Zodiac) Come into Being?," in *A Hundred Questions on the Chinese Culture*, ed. Nailu Jin (Beijing: Beijing Language and Culture University Press, 2005), 143–144 (144).

26. Jiann Hsieh and Ying-Hsiung Chou, "Public Aspirations in the New Year Couplets: A Comparative Study Between the People's Republic and Taiwan," *AFS* 40 (1981): 125–149 (125).

27. Nailu Jin, "When Did Shi'er Shengxiao," 144.

28. Hsieh and Chou, "Public Aspirations," 125–126.

29. Ren Qiliang et al., "Folk Customs," 56.

30. Xiang Wei, *Chinese Customs*, 20.

31. 節俗 *(Festivals and Customs)*, 鴻宇編 (香港 [Hong Kong]: 漢榮書局有限公司, 2006), 12–13.

Figure 5.1.1: Thousands of Red Chinese Lanterns Hanging Everywhere

Figure 5.1.2: Red Chinese Lanterns outside the Main Prayer Hall

Exploratory Study of the Three Festivals   145

Figure 5.1.3: Two Pots of Tangerine Plants Wrapped with Red Cloth

Figure 5.1.4: Tangerine Plant Decorated with Red Packets

Figure 5.1.5: Couplets Written on Red Paper

Figure 5.1.6: Red Decorative Items, Pinwheels, and Toys

Figure 5.1.7: Firecrackers for Sale

The celebration of the Spring Festival is also closely related to the Chinese zodiac. The Chinese use the twelve zodiac animals to label each year in a sequence of twelve years.[32] According to traditional Chinese astrology, five cycles of twelve years completes a cycle of sixty years. A sixty-year cycle forms the basis of the Chinese calendar. It is generally agreed that the Chinese zodiac gained popularity in the first century AD in China, when the lunar calendar was officially adopted during the Han dynasty.[33] The zodiac animal cycle begins with the rat, followed by the ox, tiger, rabbit, dragon, snake, horse, sheep, monkey, rooster, dog, and boar.[34] According to the Chinese calendar, 2016 was the year of the monkey. Therefore, decorative monkey figures were hanging on the trees along the roadside to the temple (see figure 5.1.8 and figure 5.1.9). The Monkey King god was very popular this year. The Monkey King is also called Sun Wu Kong 孫悟空 or Qi Tian Da Shen 齊天大聖 (meaning "the great sage equaling heaven"). Originally, the Monkey King was a fictional hero of the Chinese novel *Journey to the West*. In the novel, he protects Hsuan-tsang during his famous pilgrim to India. Monkey King is well-known for

---

32. Stepanchuk and Wong, *Mooncakes*, 27.
33. Nailu Jin, "When Did Shi'er Shengxiao," 144.
34. Wolfram Eberhard, *Chinese Festivals* (New York: Henry Schuman, 1952), 54.

vanquishing demons.³⁵ Monkey King decorations were also for sale in the stalls (see figure 5.1.10). Outside the main building of the Thean Hou Temple is a Chinese zodiac park that displays twelve statues of the zodiac animals. During the Spring Festival, the monkey statue was popular with the visitors for photographing (see figure 5.1.11).

Figure 5.1.8: Decorative Monkey Figures on the Trees

Figure 5.1.9: Decorative Monkey Figures on the Trees

---

35. Cheng, *Origin of Chinese Deities*, 164.

Exploratory Study of the Three Festivals 149

Figure 5.1.10: Decorative Monkey King Items for Sale

Figure 5.1.11: The Monkey Statue is Popular with the Visitors

5.1.2 Finding 2: Seeking Good Fortune Is Emphasized during the Spring Festival

The stalls during the Spring Festival's temple fair sold a variety of auspicious items. These items included Buddha statues and Buddha lockets from a Siamese temple and Chinese lucky charms with taglines that promised protection, peace, warding off evil, and turning misfortunes to blessings (see figure 5.1.12). Lucky wood carvings were also sold in stalls along the road (see figure 5.1.13). On the ground floor inside the temple building were more stalls selling lucky charms and chanting beads (see figure 5.1.14). The stalls inside the temple were also selling Chinese gourd charms (see figure 5.1.15). In Taoist tradition, the gourd is considered a weapon of gods and has magical power.[36] In one of the Chinese myths, a big gourd saved a couple from a great flood, and they became ancestors of the human race.[37] People could also buy a set of items symbolizing Chinese New Year blessings (*xin chun fu pin* 新春福品) from the temple for the price of RM68 (about £11). "Sixty-eight" in Chinese sounds like continual prosperity *lu fa* 路發 (see figure 5.1.16).

Figure 5.1.12: Buddha Statues, Buddha Lockets, and Chinese Lucky Charms for Sale

---

36. 高明强, *神秘的圖騰* (江蘇 [Jiangsu]: 江蘇人民出版社, 1989), 250.
37. 高明强, *(The Mysterious Totem)*, 238–245.

Figure 5.1.13: Lucky Wood Carvings and Wooden Chanting Beads

Figure 5.1.14: Lucky Charms and Chanting Beads for Sale

Figure 5.1.15: Chinese Gourd Charms for Sale

Figure 5.1.16: Sets of Items Symbolizing Chinese New Year Blessings

There was one stall outside the temple offering fortune telling (see figure 5.1.17). Many go to fortune tellers during the Spring Festival when the year begins in order to know the future and to obtain good luck. *Ming* 命 and *yun* 運 are the two basic ideas of the Chinese concept of fate. *Ming* means "fate" or "destiny," and it is predestinated and cannot be changed. *Yun* means "fortune" or "luck." It is predictable and also changeable with proper guidance.[38] People visit fortune tellers to interpret their horoscope which is based on the year, month, date, and time of birth.[39] Chinese tradition has a broad scope of divination methods. Besides horoscopes, divination methods such as physiognomy, divination boards, the manipulation of personal names, feng shui 風水 are also very common.[40] During the temple fair, the fortune teller provided the traditional Chinese fortune-telling services, such as palm reading and face reading. The cost ranged from RM30 (£5) to RM180 (£30), depending on the service.

Fortune telling through oracle sticks (Chinese fortune sticks) was available inside the prayer hall of the temple. Using oracle sticks for divination has a long history in China. Historical records reveal the practice of oracle sticks during the Five dynasties (AD 907–960).[41] Inside the prayer hall, four big containers of oracle sticks were found. People would pick up a bundle of oracle sticks and drop the bundle on the container to discover the sole stick that represented his or her luck. Fortunes were then revealed by matching the number on the stick with the number on the drawers of the container. Each drawer contained a slip of paper with a fortune written on it. A fortune telling paper was retrieved from the drawer that corresponded with the number on the oracle stick (see figure 5.1.18).

---

38. 呂一中, 江湖一點訣: 法術、預言、算命之研究 (*A Study of Spells, Prophecies and Fortune-telling*) (臺北 [Taipei]: 校園書房, 2007), 131.

39. Jean DeBernardi, *The Way that Lives in the Heart: Chinese Popular Religion and Spirit Mediums in Penang, Malaysia* (Stanford, CA: Stanford University Press, 2006), 63.

40. Lisa Raphals, "Fate, Fortune, Change, and Luck in Chinese and Greek: A Comparative Semantic History," *Philosophy East and West* 53 (2003): 537–574 (553).

41. 王世禎, 迷信在中國 (*Superstition in China*) (臺北 [Taipei]: 星光出版社, 1981), 2.

Figure 5.1.17: Fortune Telling

Figure 5.1.18: Container of Oracle Sticks in the Prayer Hall

During the Spring Festival, the Thean Hou Temple erects a bridge to enable those who want to change their luck and overcome their bad fortune by crossing over it. The bridge was called Zhuan Yun Qiao 轉運橋 (see figure 5.1.19). In the middle of the bridge devotees could receive blessings for a change of luck. Buddhist monks from Sri Lanka were hired to perform the ceremonies of blessing (see figure 5.1.20). In addition, lotus wishing candles were available for the public to make New Year wishes. Most temples provide wishing candles for the public to make wishes during the Spring Festival. In fact, both Buddhism and Taoism encourage the practice of wishing candles.[42] With a donation of RM8 (about £1.25), people could light a wishing candle and make a wish, hoping to receive blessings of peace, health, luck, joy, and wisdom (see figure 5.1.21.)

Figure 5.1.19: A Bridge to Enable Those Who Want to Change Their Luck

---

42. 李秀娥, *(Festivals and Customs of Taiwan)*, 60.

Figure 5.1.20: Buddhist Monks Performing the Ceremonies of Blessings

Figure 5.1.21: Lotus Wishing Candles

5.1.3 Finding 3: Asking Deities for a Blessing Is Important during the Spring Festival

The main purpose for visiting the Thean Hou Temple during the Spring Festival is to worship gods and goddesses (see figure 5.1.22). Inside the prayer hall were altars for three goddesses. The main altar in the center is dedicated to the goddess Tian Hou (see figure 5.1.23). On the right of the main altar was the altar to the Buddhist goddess Bodhisattva Avalokitesvara[43] (Guan Yin Pu Sa 觀音菩薩, see figure 5.1.24). On the left of the main altar was the altar to the goddess Shui Wei Sheng Niang 水尾聖娘 (see figure 5.1.25). Shui Wei Sheng Niang is more popular among the Chinese Hainanese diaspora and is often worshipped with the goddess Tian Hou.[44]

Figure 5.1.22: People Worshipping Deities

---

43. According to tradition, Bodhisattva Avalokitesvara was originally a male-figure god in India but later became a female-figure goddess in China. See 周樹佳, *(Deities in Hong Kong)*, 88.

44. Kim Hong Tan, *The Chinese in Penang: A Pictorial History* (Penang: Areca, 2007), 56.

Figure 5.1.23: Tian Hou

Figure 5.1.24: Bodhisattva Avalokitesvara

Exploratory Study of the Three Festivals

Figure 5.1.25: Shui Wei Sheng Niang

In addition to the three main altars for the goddesses inside the prayer hall, the temple also included temporary altars outside the prayer hall during the Spring Festival. The three altars on the left of the prayer hall were dedicated to Bodhisattva Avalokitesvara, Wen Chang Di Jun (文昌帝君), and the god of wealth. The statue of Bodhisattva Avalokitesvara outside the prayer hall was much smaller compared to the one inside (see figure 5.1.26). However, the smaller statue of Bodhisattva Avalokitesvara was still very popular among the visitors. The Chinese believe that Bodhisattva Avalokitesvara dispenses her favours liberally without need for recompense and can save people in times of danger.[45] Next to Bodhisattva Avalokitesvara was the altar of Wen Chang Di Jun, a god of wisdom. According to Chinese tradition, Wen Chang Di Jun is a star god represented by a constellation of six stars near the Big Dipper.[46] The Chinese believe that Wen Chang Di Jun is in charge of giving blessings to people who are involved in any form of academics. He is always popular

---

45. Jonathan Chamberlain, *Chinese Gods* (Petaling Jaya: Pelanduk, 1987), 72.
46. 金良年, 民間諸神 *(The Deities of the Folk)* (上海 [Shanghai]: 三聯書店, 1991), 52

among students and scholars. Many Chinese parents bring their children to worship Wen Chang Di Jun at the beginning of the school year.[47] From the altar, devotees could receive a set of Wen Chang Di Jun's Chinese calligraphy set for a donation of RM8 (about £1.25). The Chinese believe that this calligraphy set is able to encourage students and bless them with diligence and perseverance in their academic achievements (see figure 5.1.27). Next to Wen Chang Di Jun was the altar of the god of wealth (Cai Shen 財神 in Chinese). The god of wealth is very popular among the Chinese, especially during the Spring Festival. Several deities of wealth are venerated by the Chinese.[48] In front of the altar was a large golden container in the shape of a Chinese ingot containing many small golden Chinese ingots. These ingots were available for devotees to take home for a donation of RM8 (£1.25). The Chinese believe that these ingots bring blessings of wealth and fortune (see figure 5.1.28).

Figure 5.1.26: Smaller Statue of Bodhisattva Avalokitesvara

---

47. 周樹佳, *(Deities in Hong Kong)*, 51–52

48. 陳潤棠, 破迷, 鬪邪, 趕鬼, 第二集: 東南亞華人民間宗教 *(Against Superstition, Witchcraft and Demon Possession)*, 第四版 (香港 [Hong Kong]: 基道書樓, 2005), 69.

Figure 5.1.27: Wen Chang Di Jun

Figure 5.1.28: God of Wealth

The additional altars on the right of the prayer hall were temporary altars dedicated to the god of marriage (Yue Xia Lao Ren 月下老人) and the Medicine Buddha (Yao Shi Ru Lai 药师如来 or Bhaisajyaguru). Yue Xia Lao Ren literally means "an old man under the moon." He is a matchmaking deity in charge of marriages.[49] People, especially couples, could receive a red thread from the altar for the god of marriage and tie the red thread on the blossom flower plant in front of the altar (see figure 5.1.29). The Chinese believe that tying a red thread on this plant brings blessings of love.

Next to the god of marriage was the Medicine Buddha. According to Buddhist tradition, the Medicine Buddha is a Buddha with great power to heal and can bless people with longevity.[50] From the altar of the Medicine Buddha, devotees could purchase a bottle of "healing water" for a donation of RM8 (£1.25; see figure 5.1.30). The Chinese believe that giving a donation is an act of kindness that also brings blessings. Donation boxes were common around the altars and temple halls. Typical donation amounts, such as the number "eight" in RM8, sound like the Chinese words for "prosperity" and "wealth."

Figure 5.1.29: God of Marriage

---

49. 周樹佳, *(Deities in Hong Kong)*, 218.
50. 周樹佳, *(Deities in Hong Kong)*, 82.

Figure 5.1.30: Medicine Buddha with Healing Water

5.1.4 Finding 4: The Lion Dance Is Still Prevalent during the Spring Festival

The lion dance (*wu shi* 舞獅) is an important custom during the Spring Festival. Some believe that the lion dance originated from the legend of Nian. Thus it is possible that the lion in the dance represents the beast Nian.[51] Some scholars believe that the lion dance evolved from the Chinese dragon dance (*wu long* 舞龍).[52] The dragon is very important in Chinese culture. The Chinese believe that they are "descendants of the dragon" (*long de chuan ren* 龍的傳人).[53] Ancient Chinese practised the dragon dance to pray for rain. Eventually the lion dance became another form of the dragon dance.[54]

---

51. 吳宗文, 傳統與信仰續編 *(Traditions and Faith)* (香港 [Hong Kong]: 基督教卓越使團, 2004), 100.

52. 張君, 神秘的節俗: 傳統節日禮俗、禁忌研究 *(Mystery of Festivals: Research on Traditional Festival Etiquettes and Taboos)* (廣西 [Guangxi]: 廣西人民出版社, 1994), 73–77.

53. 廉正明, 龍的文化 *(The Dragon Culture)* (香港 [Hong Kong]: 明窗出版社, 1999), 2.

54. 張君, 神秘的節俗, *(Mystery of Festivals)*, 73–77.

The two main types of the Chinese lion dance are the northern (*bei shi* 北獅) and southern (*nan shi* 南獅) styles. The lion in the northern-style dance looks like a real animal compared to the lion in the southern-style dance.[55] According to traditional Chinese belief, the lion dance not only chases away evil spirits but also brings blessings to the people. The Chinese view lions as symbols of peace, royalty, righteousness, and bravery.[56] However, lions are not native to China. According to the Chinese historical records, lions were first presented to Emperor Wu (Han Wu Di 漢武帝) by emissaries from ancient Afghanistan and ancient Iran during the Han dynasty.[57] Due to the influence of Buddhism, lions have their own favour and respect from the Chinese. This is because in some Buddhist manuscripts, Buddha is referred to as "a lion among human beings."[58] Scholars believe that lion dances in China began during the Wei, Jin, and Northern and Southern dynasties (AD 220–581) and became popular folk art during the Tang dynasty (AD 618–907).[59]

On the day of the field research, two lions performed a lion dance from 2:00 p.m. to 3:00 p.m. (see figure 5.1.31). Each lion consisted of two people. One person was the head of the lion, and one person was the tail. A single horn on the lion's head and the design of the lion's body revealed that this dance was a Chinese southern-style lion dance. The dance was accompanied by the music of drums, cymbals, and gongs (see figure 5.1.32).

---

55. Nailu Jin, "Why Do People Perform Lion and Dragon Dances on Days of Jubilation?," in *Hundred Questions*, 145–147 (146–147).

56. 馬來西亞華人農曆新年 (*Lunar New Year of Malaysian Chinese*), 林嘉瓊等編 (吉隆坡 [Kuala Lumpur]: 馬來西亞國家博物館, 1983), 13.

57. Nailu Jin, "Why Do People Perform," 146–147.

58. Nailu Jin, "There Are Always a Pair of Stone Lions before Some Big Architectures in China. What Does This Imply?," in *Hundred Questions*, 156–157 (157).

59. Nailu Jin, "Why Do People Perform," 146–147.

Figure 5.1.31: Lion Dance

Figure 5.1.32: Lion Dance Band

Figure 5.1.33: The Lion Gave Out Candy to Children

Figure 5.1.34: The Public Taking Pictures with the Lion

The two lions started dancing at the entrance of the temple and paraded into the prayer hall to pay respect to the goddess Tian Hou and then to the other deities. After the worship ceremony, the lions walked around the temple and gave mandarin oranges and candy to the visitors and the children (see figure 5.1.33). The Chinese believe that whoever receives the mandarin oranges or candy from the lion will receive great blessings. In return, some people gave red packets and even cash to the lions by putting red packets or cash into the mouth of the lion. Many children walked to the lions and touched their fur. Occasionally the lions would stand still and let the public take pictures or even selfies with them (see figure 5.1.34).

5.2 Field Research on the Qing Ming Festival

The Qing Ming Festival is considered the second most important festival in Chinese culture.[60] For the Chinese, the Qing Ming Festival is a period of time for visiting gravesides to worship ancestors and to honor deceased family members.[61] In China, the practice of ancestor veneration has existed since ancient times.[62] During the Tang dynasty (AD 618–907), the government made the Qing Ming Festival an official day of tomb sweeping. By the time of the Song dynasty (AD 960–1279), the Qing Ming Festival had become a nationwide festival in which people were required to sweep the tombs of their ancestors.[63] Today, the Qing Ming Festival is one of the most popular Chinese festivals. This festival is particularly important to Chinese families. According to a Chinese saying, those who do not worship their ancestors during Qing Ming will turn into a pig or a dog when they die (清明不祭祖, 死了變豬狗).[64]

The Qing Ming Festival falls on the fourth or fifth of April and is the only traditional Chinese festival based on the solar calendar.[65] However, many Chinese families visit and clean the graves of their ancestors a few weeks prior to or after the official day of the Qing Ming Festival in order to avoid heavy traffic around the cemeteries.[66] Therefore, the period of celebration of the Qing Ming Festival could be six weeks long. The Qing Ming Festival is still widely observed among the Chinese communities in Malaysia.[67]

---

60. Thompson, *Chinese Religion*, 132. Similarly, Smith points out that the Qing Ming Festival, next to the Spring Festival, is the most popular of the annual festivals in Hong Kong. See Henry Newton Smith, "Chinese Ancestor Practices and Christianity: Toward a Viable Contextualization of Christian Ethics in a Hong Kong Setting" (unpublished doctoral dissertation, Southwestern Baptist Theological Seminary, 1987), 27.

61. In many ancient societies as well as modern ones, rituals honoring ancestors are an exceedingly important part of life. See Richard Taylor, *Death and the Afterlife: A Cultural Encyclopedia* (Santa Barbara, CA: ABC-CLIO, 2000), 9.

62. Leon Comber, *Chinese Ancestor Worship in Malaysia* (Singapore: Donald Moore, 1956), 1.

63. 鄭金明, 世界節日的故事 *(Tales of World Wide Festivals)* (臺中 [Taichung]: 好讀出版, 2006), 96–97.

64. 節俗, 鴻宇編, 65.

65. Gunde, *Culture and Customs*, 202.

66. 李秀娥, *(Festivals and Customs of Taiwan)*, 120. In Taiwan on the day of the Qing Ming Festival, severe traffic congestion is expected in many cities as well as on highways. 鄭金明, *(Tales of World)*, 98.

67. Wong, *Illustrated Cycle*, 134.

With a volunteer to help video recording, field research on the Qing Ming Festival was conducted on two occasions during March 2016. The first field research was conducted the afternoon of 20 March at the Kwong Tong Cemetery Columbarium Pagoda of Kuala Lumpur. The second field research was conducted the morning of 26 March at the Gui Yuan Crematorium and the Petaling Jaya Chinese Cemetery, which are next to each other. Key findings from field research of the Qing Ming Festival are presented below.

5.2.1 Finding 1: The Chinese Worship Their Deceased Ancestors during the Qing Ming Festival, but the Practices are Slightly Different Depending on the Setting

In the field research of this study during the Qing Ming Festival, people worshipped their deceased family members either at the Petaling Jaya Chinese Cemetery (see figure 5.2.1), the Gui Yuan Crematorium (see figure 5.2.2), or the Kwong Tong Cemetery Pagoda Columbarium (see figure 5.2.3). However, due to the differences in setting, the practice of worship was slightly different among these three locations.

Figure 5.2.1: People Observing the Qing Ming Festival at the Petaling Jaya Chinese Cemetery

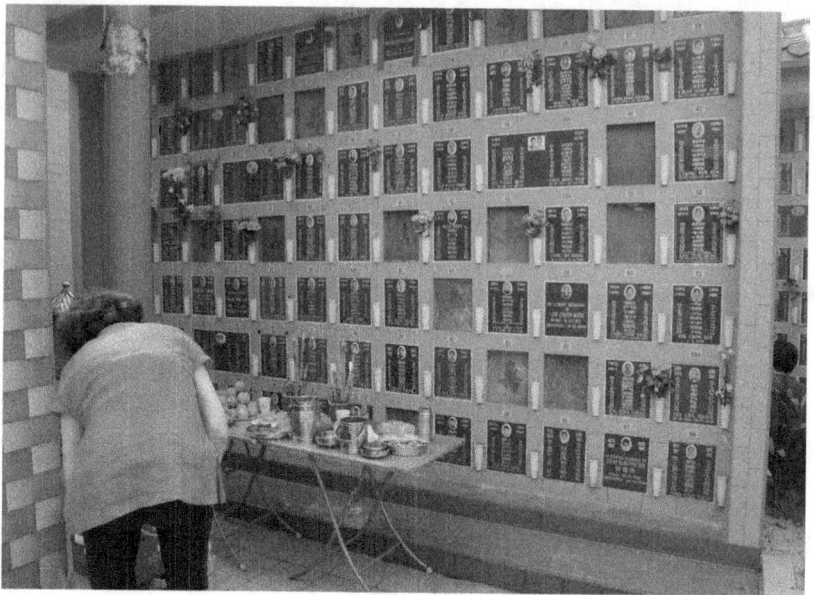

Figure 5.2.2: People Observing the Qing Ming Festival at the Gui Yuan Crematorium

Figure 5.2.3: People Observing the Qing Ming Festival at the Kwong Tong Cemetery Pagoda Columbarium

Ancestor worship at the Petaling Jaya Chinese Cemetery

The Chinese have traditionally preferred the practice of interment, in which their deceased family members are buried in a cemetery. Daniel Tong believes that the Chinese preference for interment is due to the belief that the soul of the deceased resides in the tomb.[68] However, it is important to note that the ancient Chinese had at least two models of thought concerning the afterlife. As Jue Guo explains, one model suggests that the tomb is the final destination for the deceased. The other model proposes that the tomb is not the final residence but a transit-station for the deceased.[69]

The Petaling Jaya Chinese Cemetery is a burial ground for deceased Chinese people. Most of the tombs in the Petaling Jaya Chinese Cemetery are turtle-back tombs (see figure 5.2.4). The turtle-back tomb, *mu gui* 墓龜 in Chinese, is very common. The deceased is buried behind the tombstone. The inscription on the tombstone contains a fair amount of detail about the individual, including the name, dates of birth and death, and other information.[70] The shape of the Chinese turtle-back tomb resembles a tortoise shell. In Chinese culture, the tortoise "is an emblem of longevity, strength, and endurance."[71] It also "symbolises the universe. Its dome-shaped back represents the vault of heaven, whilst its flat belly is the earth floating on the waters."[72] According to Chinese mythology, the goddess Nü Wa 女媧 used the legs of a turtle as four poles to prop up the sky.[73]

Before worshipping the deceased, people clean the compound of the tombs and uproot the weeds in the vicinity. This process is called *pei mu* 培墓.[74] Some families even repainted the tomb of their deceased (see figure 5.2.5)

---

68. Tong, *Biblical Approach*, 95–96.

69. Jue Guo, "Concepts of Death and the Afterlife Reflected in Newly Discovered Tomb Objects and Texts from Han China," in *Mortality in Traditional Chinese Thought*, eds. Amy Olberding and Philip J. Ivanhoe (Albany, NY: SUNY, 2011), 85–116 (88–93).

70. 董芳苑, 探討臺灣民間信仰 *(Exploration of Folk Beliefs in Taiwan)* (臺北 [Taipei]: 常民文化出版, 1996), 233–234.

71. Charles Alfred Speed Williams, *Chinese Symbolism and Art Motifs: A Comprehensive Handbook on Symbolism in Chinese Art through the Ages*, 4th ed. (Rutland, VT: Tuttle, 2012), 382.

72. Valentine Rodolphe Burckhardt, *Chinese Creeds and Customs* (London: Kegan Paul, 2006), 126.

73. Sarah Allan, *The Shape of the Turtle: Myth, Art, and Cosmos in Early China* (Albany: State University of New York Press, 1991), 104.

74. 史慧玲, 傳統習俗事典 *(The Tradition Handbook)* (香港 [Hong Kong]: 文化會社有限公司, 2014), 63.

or the inscription on the tombstone (see figure 5.2.6). After the tombs were tidied, people started to sacrifice to the deceased by lighting joss sticks and candles, offering food and drink, and burning the joss papers and paper effigies[75] on the ground in front of the tombstones (see figure 5.2.7). For each tomb that had been cleaned and worshipped, joss papers with small stones were put on top of the tombstone, indicating the worship process was complete (see figure 5.2.8). This practice is called *gua zhi* 挂纸 or *ya mu zhi* 壓墓紙.[76]

Figure 5.2.4: Turtle-Back Tomb Style

---

75. As Xiang Wei indicates, today in mainland China burning joss paper is restricted to only rural areas. See Xiang Wei, *Chinese Customs*, 70. For example, Beijing has prohibited the burning of joss paper since 1995. See Gunde, *Culture and Customs*, 204.

76. 李秀娥, *(Festivals and Customs of Taiwan)*, 123.

Exploratory Study of the Three Festivals 173

Figure 5.2.5: People Repainting the Tombstone

Figure 5.2.6: People Repainting an Inscription on a Tombstone

Figure 5.2.7: Sacrificing in Front of the Tombstone

Figure 5.2.8: Joss Papers on Top of the Tombstone

Ancestor worship at the Gui Yuan Crematorium and the Kwong Tong Cemetery Columbarium Pagoda

Cremation has a long history in China. Since the Tang dynasty, the practice of cremation – the burning of the dead bodies – has become a popular alternative to Chinese traditional burial.[77] In the last few decades, due to the shortage of land, cremation has gradually become a common practice among the Chinese in Singapore, Hong Kong, and cities of mainland China. Today, it is also a very common method in Malaysia.

Both the Kwong Tong Cemetery Pagoda Columbarium and the Gui Yuan Crematorium are places that house the cinerary urns containing cremated remains for the Chinese. Worshipping the deceased at these two places differed from the worship at the Petaling Jaya Chinese Cemetery as tomb repairing was not needed. Both the Gui Yuan Crematorium and the Kwong Tong Cemetery Columbarium Pagoda were well maintained.

At the Gui Yuan Crematorium, urns were placed in six tiers in a block. A columbarium block could house forty-two urns, and a bigger block could house up to eighty-four urns (see figure 5.2.9). A table was erected as an altar in front of a columbarium block where the urn of a deceased family member was placed. Candles, joss sticks, and food were placed on top of the table for worship use (see figure 5.2.10). However, if people wanted to burn joss papers, they had to bring the joss papers to a centralized furnace instead of burning them in front of the columbarium (see figure 5.2.11).

The Kwong Tong Cemetery Columbarium Pagoda had designated a centralized place outside the pagoda for worship use. Facing the pagoda, people could worship their deceased only from the outside. More than one hundred tables were set up as an altar. Many red joss stick censers were placed on top of the tables (see figure 5.2.12). People were free to choose any table with a censer to worship their deceased family members. Lit candles and joss sticks were put onto the censers. Food and drink were also placed on the table for worshipping the deceased (see figure 5.2.13). The Kwong Tong Cemetery Columbarium Pagoda also prepared several centralized joss paper furnaces for people to burn joss papers (see figure 5.2.14).

---

77. Christina Han, "Cremation and Body Burning in Five Dynasties China," *Journal of Chinese Studies* 55 (2012): 1–22 (1).

Figure 5.2.9: Urns in a Columbarium Block

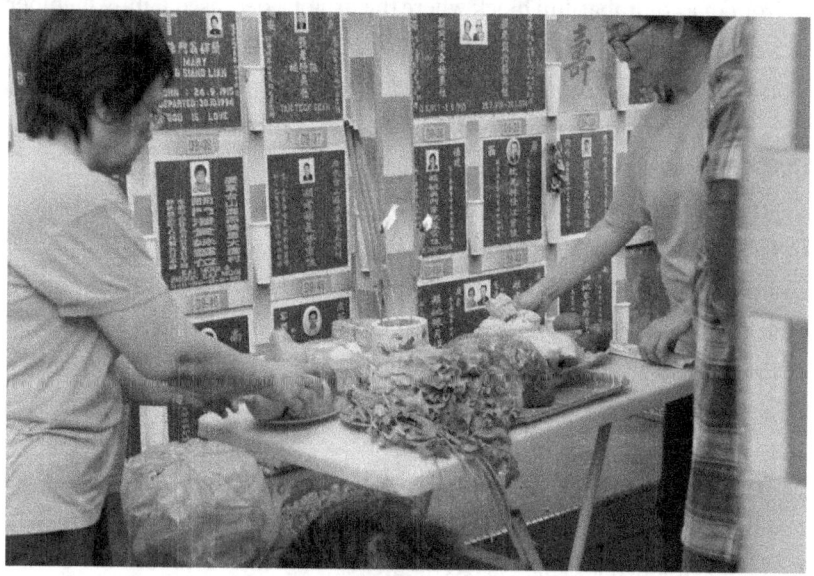

Figure 5.2.10: Altar in Front of a Columbarium Block

Exploratory Study of the Three Festivals 177

Figure 5.2.11: A Centralized Burning Furnace

Figure 5.2.12: A Centralized Worship Place outside the Pagoda

Figure 5.2.13: Candles, Joss Sticks, Food, and Drink on the Altar

Figure 5.2.14: Joss Paper Furnace at Pagoda

5.2.2 Finding 2: The Chinese Believe That the Needs of a Deceased Family Member Are Similar to the Needs of a Living Person

The Chinese believe that the needs of the deceased resemble the needs of the living.[78] Therefore, food is an essential element in ancestral worship during the Qing Ming Festival. According to Chinese custom, food offered to ancestors is usually cooked food. The Chinese term for cooked food is *shu shi* 熟食. The Chinese character *shu* 熟 could also mean "know well" or "acquaintance." Thus the offering of cooked food to the ancestors is an indication of a close relationship.[79] On the other hand, raw food will only be offered to gods and ghosts who are not family members. The Chinese character for "raw" is *sheng* 生. The character *sheng* also means "unacquainted." The offering of raw food is an indication of full respect but not acquaintance.[80]

A variety of cooked food was offered to the deceased. One family offered roasted pork, steamed buns, and fruits to their ancestor (see figure 5.2.15). Another family offered even more kinds of food, including sticky rice dumplings, glutinous pastries, cupcakes, fruits, roasted pork, and steamed chicken (see figure 5.2.16). Some families offered food with chopsticks and spoons provided (see figure 5.2.17). Other families opted for vegetarian food such as fried soybean curd, rice noodles, and soy-based fish curry (see figure 5.2.18). Almost all the food offered was accompanied with Chinese tea or rice wine (see figure 5.2.19).

---

78. Gunde, *Culture and Customs*, 202.
79. 李亦園, 信仰與文化 *(Belief and Culture)* (臺北 [Taipei]: 巨流圖書公司, 1983), 129.
80. 李亦園, *(Belief and Culture)*, 128.

Figure 5.2.15: Roasted Pork, Steamed Buns, and Fruits Offered to the Deceased

Figure 5.2.16: Sticky Rice Dumplings and Other Foods Offered to the Deceased

Exploratory Study of the Three Festivals 181

Figure 5.2.17: Food with Chopsticks and Spoons Provided

Figure 5.2.18: Vegetarian Food Offered to the Deceased

Figure 5.2.19: Chinese Tea and Rice Wine Offered to the Deceased

Joss papers, also known as "hell bank notes," are another important element in ancestral worship (see figure 5.2.20). The Chinese started to make joss papers as hell bank notes during the Tang dynasty (AD 618–907). The idea of joss paper was influenced by both Taoism and Buddhism.[81] Today there are many types of joss papers. Some types of joss papers are for worshipping gods and goddesses; some are for worshipping ancestors and ghosts.[82] Scholars

---

81. 蕭登福, 道教與民俗 *(Taoism and Folklore)* (臺北 [Taipei]: 文津出版社, 2002), 73–108.

82. 李秀娥, *(Festivals and Customs of Taiwan)*, 40–48.

also refer to joss paper as paper offering, spirit paper, bamboo ceremonial paper, ceremonial paper, or clothing paper.[83] Joss paper is printed with various marks made into burning offering. There are three main categories of joss paper: gold, silver, and copper.[84] According to Chinese tradition, joss paper, also called *wang sheng qian* 往生錢 or *guang ming qian* 光明錢, is a hell bank note that can be used in the underworld.[85] The underworld (*ming shi* 冥世 in Chinese) is like the human world, where there are some rich and some poor people.[86] By sending hell bank notes to the underworld, the Chinese are hoping to make their deceased family members rich and have the ability to buy whatever they need in the underworld. The joss paper box, which looks like a treasure chest, was also a popular item during the Qing Ming Festival (see figure 5.2.21). Many families were burning joss paper boxes as offerings for their deceased family members.

At the Petaling Jaya Chinese Cemetery (a burial ground cemetery), people were also strewing, instead of burning, coloured joss papers all over the graves of their ancestors (see figure 5.2.22). The people primarily used five different colours of paper – blue, red, yellow, white, and green. These five colours of paper are called *wu se zhi* 五色紙.[87] Joss papers are scattered over the graves to show that family members have visited the grave.

The Chinese also offer other daily supplies to the deceased. The Chinese believe that a deceased person, like a living one, is in need of clothing, food, and housing as well as transportation. In Chinese, these four basic needs are called *yi shi zhu xing* 衣食住行.[88] In one case, a paper double-story house (as a place of shelter to live in) and a paper Toyota Vellfire van (as a vehicle for the deceased to drive) were offered. In addition, pair of paper servants (a male and a female) were burned as an offering in front of the tomb (see figure 5.2.23). The Chinese believe that their ancestors need servants to take care of

---

83. Janet Lee Scott, *For Gods, Ghosts, and Ancestors: The Chinese Tradition of Paper Offerings* (Hong Kong: Hong Kong University Press, 2007), 22.

84. 曾景來, 臺灣的迷信與陋習 (*Superstitions and Customs in Taiwan*) (臺北 [Taipei]: 武陵出版公司, 1994), 161–181.

85. See 鄭金明, (*Tales of World*), 97–98.

86. 郭春梅與張慶捷, 世俗迷信與中國社會 (*Superstitious Beliefs and Society of China*) (北京 [Beijing]: 宗教文化出版社, 2001), 263.

87. 李秀娥, (*Festivals and Customs of Taiwan*), 44–46.

88. 萬建中, 圖文中國民俗: 喪俗 (*A Pictorial Illustration of the Customs in China: Bereavement*) (北京 [Beijing]: 中國旅游出版社, 2004), 118.

them. One family even offered a paper shopping mall with McDonald's and other stores printed on it (see figure 5.2.24).

Figure 5.2.20: Bags of Joss Paper

Figure 5.2.21: Joss Paper Box

Figure 5.2.22: Coloured Joss Papers on the Grave

Figure 5.2.23: A Paper Double-Storey House, a Paper Van, and a Pair of Paper Servants

Figure 5.2.24: A Paper Shopping Mall, Joss Paper Boxes, and Joss Papers

5.2.3 Finding 3: The Chinese Believe that the Deceased Still Need Protection and Help from Deities

At the Petaling Jaya Chinese Cemetery, a small shrine was set up beside each tomb. These shrines were built for the god Hou Tu (后土). Hou Tu is considered as a guardian deity for the interred place. He is an earth god and is usually called Tu Di Gong. Tu Di Gong 土地公 is also called She Gong 社公 or Fu De Zheng Shen 福德正神. The shrine of the earth god is usually small compared to other deities. The Chinese believe that the earth god is only an official who administers a small local area, and his power is narrow. However, he is considered a very friendly god.[89] Ancient China was an agricultural country. Therefore the earth god or god of land is always popular among the Chinese.[90]

When people were worshipping their ancestors, they would worship Hou Tu as well. A smaller portion of food, cups of libation, and a pair of lit candles

---

89. 金良年, *(The Deities of the Folk)*, 43–45.
90. 馬國棟和劉志良, *(Uncovering the Folk Beliefs)*, 25. According to 林金一, the earth god is indeed the most common and widely worshipped god in Taiwan. See 林金一, "土地公在臺灣" (Earth God in Taiwan), 於臺灣民間宗教信仰 *(Folk Religion in Taiwan)*, 董芳苑編 (臺北 [Taipei]: 長青文化事業股份有限公司, 1981), 415–425 (415).

and joss sticks were offered to Hou Tu (see figure 5.2.25). The Chinese seem to believe that the deceased and the tombs still need protection from this god of land. A temple to Hou Tu was in the compound of the Gui Yuan Crematorium (see figure 5.2.26). In addition to worshipping their deceased family members, people also worshipped Hou Tu with joss sticks and fruits in the temple.

At the Kwong Tong Cemetery Columbarium Pagoda, some Chinese were also worshipping the Ksitigarbha Bodhisattva, a Buddhist deity of the hell realm. Originally, Kritigarbha was an earth god in Indian religion. Later he was adopted into Buddhism and became a very popular earth god of Buddhism in China.[91] He is called Di Zang Wang 地藏王 in Chinese (see figure 5.2.27).[92] Di Zang Wang is known as "the savior par excellence of the dead, especially of those undergoing torments in hell because of their wicked way."[93]

Figure 5.2.25: Hou Tu Shrine

---

91. 龔天民, 諸佛、菩薩與鬼神真相 (*A Study of Buddhas, Bodhisattvas, Gods, and Ghosts*) (臺北 [Taipei]: 道聲, 1997), 15.

92. 周樹佳, *(Deities in Hong Kong)*, 90–91.

93. Zhiru Ng, *The Making of Savior Bodhisattva: Dizang in Medieval China* (Honolulu: University of Hawaii Press, 2007), 3.

Figure 5.2.26: Hou Tu Temple

Figure 5.2.27: Ksitigarbha Bodhisattva (Di Zang Wang 地藏王)

5.3 Field Research on the Hungry Ghost Festival

The Chinese have been worshipping ghosts for a few thousand years. Records show that the ancient Chinese in the Zhou dynasty already had an official ceremony for ghost worship.⁹⁴ The ancient Chinese believed that in order to prevent ghosts from turning to evil and hurting people, they must be worshipped properly – "鬼有所歸,乃不為厲."⁹⁵ Today, the Hungry Ghost Festival is one of the oldest remaining Chinese festivals and is celebrated every year during the seventh lunar month. According to the tradition, the gates of hell are opened on the first day of the seventh lunar month to allow the hungry ghosts to roam the earth for one month.⁹⁶ *Di yu* 地獄, the Chinese term for hell, is literally "earth prison."⁹⁷ During the Hungry Ghost Festival, ghosts are believed to be temporarily let out from the underworld prison.

Taoists call the Hungry Ghost Festival the Zhong Yuan Jie (中元節), while Chinese Buddhists celebrate it as the Yu Lan Pen Jie (盂蘭盆節).⁹⁸ Scholars do not agree on the origin of the Hungry Ghost Festival. Some believe that the festival originated from Taoism and was later adapted into Buddhism.⁹⁹ Others maintain that the major beliefs of the festival originated from Buddhism.¹⁰⁰ The Buddhist origins of the Festival can be traced back to the story of Mu Lian (目蓮), who saved his mother from hell. In the story, Mu Lian's mother was sent to hell as a hungry ghost after she died. With the help from Buddha and many good deeds, Mu Lian finally saved his mother from suffering.¹⁰¹ This story, which emphasizes filial piety of a son, is fairly well-known among the Chinese. Daniel L. Overmyer further points out that the

---

94. 呂理政, 傳統信仰與現代社會 *(Traditional Beliefs and Modern Society)* (臺北 [Taipei]: 稻香出版社, 1992), 98–99.

95. 張鶴泉, 周代祭祀研究 *(Research on Sacrificial Practices of Zhou Dynasty)* (臺北 [Taipei]: 文津出版社, 1992), 46–48.

96. Tong, *Biblical Approach*, 47.

97. Anne Swann Goodrich, *Chinese Hell: The Peking Temple of Eighteen Hells and Chinese Conceptions of Hell* (St. Augustin: Monumenta Serica, 1981), 67.

98. 喬繼堂, 中國歲時禮俗 *(Seasonal Etiquette in China)* (天津 [Tianjin]: 天津人民出版社, 1992), 217.

99. 中國民間節日文化辭典 *(Cultural Dictionary of China's Festivals)*, 莫福山編 (北京 [Beijing]: 中國勞動出版社, 1992), 412–413. For a detailed discussion, see 蕭登福, 道教與佛教 *(Taoism and Buddhism)* (臺北 [Taipei]: 東大圖書股份有限公司, 1995), 231–320.

100. 韓盈和王土然, 節令風俗 *(Festival Customs)* (上海 [Shanghai]: 上海古籍出版社, 1998), 67–73.

101. 徐福全, 臺灣民間祭祀禮儀 *(Taiwan Folk Sacrificial Etiquette)* (新竹 [Hsinchu]: 臺灣省立新竹社會教育館, 1996), 186–187.

festival is influenced by Buddhist ideas of purgatory and rebirth.[102] Moreover, David K. Jordan argues that the idea of hungry ghosts derives originally from Hindu *preta*.[103] In reality, both Taoist and Buddhist elements are mixed in the Hungry Ghost Festival today.[104]

Most Chinese communities in Malaysia celebrate the Hungry Ghost Festival during the seventh lunar month. The celebration can be held on different days of the month, which vary in different communities.[105] Data collection for the Hungry Ghost Festival field research was conducted the night of 16 August 2015, which is 3 July on the lunar calendar. The duration of the celebration was 13–17 August, five nights in district SS2, one of the most established commercial hubs in the state of Selangor. The organizer of the celebration, Persatuan Perayaan Poh Toh SS2,[106] built a large temporary canopy inside a SS2 community park. The SS2 park was in the heart of the commercial area of the SS2 town centre, thus the canopy was surrounded by commercial shops, restaurants, offices, a bank, and a police station. The canopy was approximately 220 feet long, 36 feet wide, and 20 feet high. The canopy cover was blue on the outside and red on the inside (see figure 5.3.1). The canopy consisted of three sections: a gods-worshipping section, a ghost-worshipping section, and a ghost-entertainment performance section (see figure 5.3.2). Key findings from the SS2 Hungry Ghost Festival field research are presented below.

---

102. Daniel L. Overmyer, *Religions of China: The World as a Living System* (San Francisco: Harper & Row, 1986), 65–66.

103. David K. Jordan, *Gods, Ghosts, and Ancestors: The Folk Religion of a Taiwanese Village* (Berkeley: University of California Press, 1972), 34.

104. As Teiser indicates, the mixture of the Taoist and Buddhist elements in the Hungry Ghost Festival happened as early as the Tang dynasty. See Stephen F. Teiser, *The Ghost Festival in Medieval China* (Princeton, NJ: Princeton University Press, 1988), 35.

105. 王琛發, 馬來西亞華人民間節日研究 (*A Study of Festivals among Malaysian Chinese*) (士拉央 [Selayang]: 藝品多媒體傳播中心, 2001), 103.

106. Persatuan Perayaan Poh Toh SS2 is an officially registered organization in Malaysia.

Exploratory Study of the Three Festivals   191

Figure 5.3.1: The Canopy of the Hungry Ghost Festival in the SS2 Park

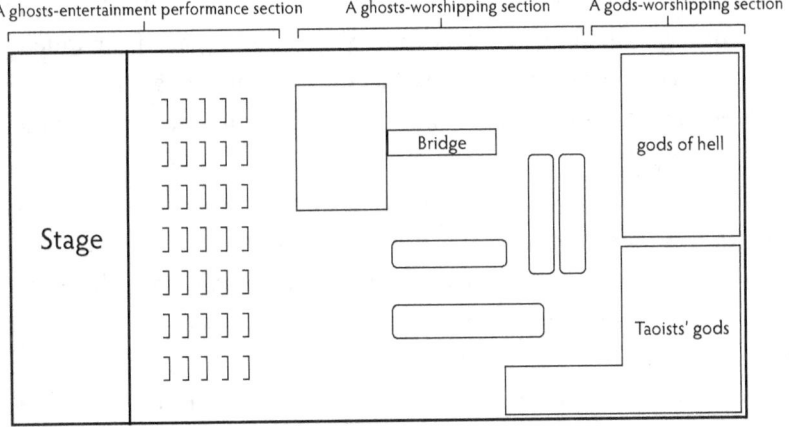

Figure 5.3.2: Layout of the Canopy

5.3.1 Finding 1: The Chinese Believe Ghosts Are the Spirits of Deceased Persons

The Hungry Ghost Festival reveals the concept of ghosts in the Chinese culture. The Chinese believe that existence continues after death. A ghost is commonly considered a spirit of a person who has died. A spirit, like a living person, has many needs. The Chinese believe that the needs of a ghost are similar to the needs of a living person.

As Stuart E. Thompson rightly attests, "Food is intrinsic to most Chinese ritual activity."[107] In the case of the Hungry Ghost Festival, food appears to be the most important element. According to a Chinese saying, food is the first human necessity (民以食為天). Therefore, the Chinese believe that food is very important to a ghost as well. The food offered to the hungry ghosts was noticeably plentiful, which is understandable since the Chinese were worshipping ghosts who are very hungry. The food prepared for the hungry ghosts was primarily the daily food of the Chinese.

The ghost-worshipping section was in the middle section of the festival canopy. Within this section, several long tables displayed plenty of food items. The first two long tables were placed very close to the gods-worshipping section. One long table was slightly lower than the other. The lower long table offered various items of food such as one box of crab, three roasted chickens, approximately twenty-six whole poached chickens, two trays of pan-fried fish, a big tray of fruits, and an assortment of Chinese-style cakes and pastries. Most of these Chinese-style cakes and pastries were made from different types of grains. The Chinese believe that different kinds of grains, generally referred to as the "five grains" (*wu gu* 五谷), and fruits are all important in worshipping.[108]

The second long table, which was higher, stood beside two red wooden racks. One whole raw pig and one whole raw goat were tied separately to the red wooden racks as key sacrifices in the festival. Sacrificing a whole pig or a whole goat is considered a "big animal sacrifice" (*da sheng* 大牲). In some Chinese festivals, a whole cow is also sacrificed as one of the "three big animal sacrifices" (*da san sheng* 大三牲).[109] On top of this long table were seven roasted suckling pigs, a large joss stick censer,[110] big and small red candles,

---

107. Stuart E. Thompson, "Death, Food, and Fertility," in *Death Ritual in Late Imperial and Modern China*, eds. James L. Watson and Evelyn S. Rawski (Berkeley: University of California Press, 1988), 71–108 (71).

108. 林云和聶達, 祭拜趣談 (*Discussions about Venerations of Deities*) (上海 [Shanghai]: 上海古籍出版社, 2005), 31–32

109. 董芳苑, 探討臺灣民間信仰 (*Exploration of Folk Beliefs*), 169.

110. The Chinese started to use joss stick censers to worship gods during the Han dynasty. See 巫美梅和劉銳宏, 拜祀衣紙扎作與香港民間風俗 (*Paper Effigies and Customs in Hong Kong*) (香港 [Hong Kong]: 中華文教交流服務中心, 2011), 54.

fruits, and candy. Joss sticks were placed on each food item mentioned above as a ritual of worship (see figure 5.3.3).

Figure 5.3.3: One Whole Raw Pig and One Whole Raw Goat on Red Wooden Racks and Other Foods

Another table was placed closest to the edge of the canopy. This table held five cone-shaped "mountains" (*shan* 山) that displayed various foods. One mountain was fully ornamented with green vegetables, the second with coloured-icing sugar biscuits, the third with steamed buns, the fourth with uncooked rice, and the fifth with raw rice vermicelli (see figure 5.3.4). All five mountains of food were apparently for vegetarians. Displaying food in a mountain shape probably symbolises extreme abundance, according to one Chinese saying, "Pile up like a mountain (堆積如山)."[111]

---

111. Sometimes the Hungry Ghost Festival in Hong Kong includes a mountain ornamented with bacon. See 陳守仁, 神功戲在香港: 粵劇、潮劇及福佬劇 (*The Chinese Operas of Hong Kong's Hungry Ghost Festival*) (香港 [Hong Kong]: 三聯書店, 1996), 17.

Figure 5.3.4: A Table with Five Cone-Shaped Mountains

Figure 5.3.5: The Main Ghost-Worshipping Altar with the "Bridge"

In addition to food, the ghost worshippers also offered hell bank notes, paper clothes, paper housing, paper transportation, and other daily supplies to the hungry ghosts. The largest and tallest structure in the ghost-worshipping section was the main ghost-worshipping altar located in the middle of the canopy. The altar was built attached to a piece of cloth forming a slope, which was called the "bridge." Lit candles lined the two sides of the bridge. The candles were lit on stacks of joss paper, which are also known as hell bank notes. The Chinese believe that a ghost, like a living person, needs a great sum of money in order to have a better life. The Chinese also believe that a ghost needs money to bribe the judges and guards of hell, just as living people bribe judges in the world today. On the floor at the bottom slope of the bridge, items such as hell bank notes, hell coins, poker cards, paper opium sets with matches, lipsticks, paper shoes, and paper hats were offered as well (see figure 5.3.5).

The ghost-worshipping section also provided housing for the hungry ghosts. A large paper four-storey apartment was offered to the hungry ghosts during the festival. On top of the paper four-storey apartment was a sign with the Chinese words *shi nong gong shang* (仕農工商), which translates as "scholars, peasants, workers, and business people." This sign was an invitation to all ghosts from different backgrounds. A table was set before the paper four-storey apartment. This table offered food such as fish, chicken, fruits, red beans, soya beans, peanuts, green beans, kidney beans, and twelve boxes of rice with meats and vegetables. Besides foods, candles, joss sticks, and joss papers were also offered (see figure 5.3.6).

Figure 5.3.6: A Paper Four-Storey Apartment

Figure 5.3.7: A Paper Taxi and a Paper Bus

Figure 5.3.8: A Paper Boat

To meet the transportation needs of the hungry ghosts, the worshippers offered a paper taxi and a paper bus (see figure 5.3.7). The back of the taxi displayed the model of the car: Benz E300.¹¹² This taxi contained many hell bank notes as well as a paper doll "taxi driver." In addition to the taxi and the bus, a fifteen-foot-long paper boat was offered to the hungry ghosts as well (see figure 5.3.8). Inside this boat were also many large stacks of "hell bank notes."

In addition to food, clothing, housing, and transportation, the Chinese believe that providing entertainment to the hungry ghosts during the festival is also important. In his discussion of sacrificial ritual in ancient China, Roel Sterckx attests that sacrificial events "were multimedia events that offered multiple avenues of sensory contact with the spirit world: olfaction, taste, sound, visual display, and movement."¹¹³ Ancient Chinese tradition incorporates dancing and singing as worship rituals. Eventually, Chinese opera became very important in gods and ghosts worship. One of the most traditional and popular operas performed in the Hungry Ghost Festival is the drama of Mu Lian 目蓮 saving his mother from purgatory.¹¹⁴ In Hong Kong, various Chinese operas are performed during the Hungry Ghost Festival.¹¹⁵

In Malaysia, however, modern songs and dances were performed during the festival, and traditional Chinese operas are often substituted with popular songs, modern stage lighting, and a professional sound system. Artists who perform in the ghost-entertainment event are professional and usually perform in various neighborhoods throughout the seventh lunar month. In this case, the live ghost entertainment during the Hungry Ghost Festival at SS2 park was performed by three female and two male artists who wore elaborate clothes. The show incorporated a professional sound system that played high volumes and songs in various Chinese dialects, such as Mandarin, Hokkien, and Cantonese songs, and English love songs (see figure 5.3.9). The reason for the high volume is to attract hungry ghosts nearby to attend.

---

112. Benz E300 is an expensive car in Malaysia.

113. Roel Sterckx, *Food, Sacrifice, and Sagehood in Early China* (Cambridge: Cambridge University Press, 2011), 107.

114. 馬書田, 冥間鬼神 *(Deities in the Underworld)* (臺北 [Taipei]: 風格司藝術創作坊, 2012), 34–40.

115. 陳守仁, *(The Chinese Operas)*, 19.

Figure 5.3.9: Nightly Live Performance for Hungry Ghosts Entertainment

Food and beverages were placed on the first row of seats. The first row consisted of priority seats reserved for the ghosts to watch the performance. Behind the first row sat approximately fifty people, including adults and young children, watching the performance. Others stood along the street and watched the performance from a distance. Most of the songs performed were popular songs from the 1970s and 80s.

5.3.2 Finding 2: The Chinese Worship the Ghosts Due to Fear

The main function of the Hungry Ghost Festival is to worship the hungry ghosts who come out from hell. The ghost worshippers do not appear to trust or love the hungry ghosts. Instead, they worship the ghosts in a fearful manner. As Fung-Wan Tong points out, the Chinese worship the hungry ghosts mainly because of fear. The Chinese consider all sickness, suffering, and local disasters as coming from the ghosts.[116] The Chinese believe that inviting powerful gods to the festival is important so that they will oversee the ghosts from hell. Otherwise the festival may become chaotic and bring

---

116. 董芳苑, 探討臺灣民間信仰 (*Exploration of Folk Beliefs*), 264.

disaster. Therefore, many deities were worshipped during the Hungry Ghost Festival (see figure 5.3.10).

Figure 5.3.10: A Chinese Devotee Performing Prayers to the Deities

Among all the deities worshipped in the Hungry Ghost Festival canopy, a paper sculpture of Da Shi Wang (大仕王) was the highlight (see figure 5.3.11). Da Shi Wang has many different names: Da Shi Ye (大士爺), Mian Ran Da Shi (面燃大士), Pu Du Gong (普渡公), and others. Da Shi Wang is considered the king of ghosts (Gui Wang 鬼王). The Chinese believe that during the Hungry Ghost Festival, Da Shi Wang is in charge of keeping all the hungry ghosts in order. At the end of the celebration, the paper sculpture of Da Shi Wang is burned.[117]

The height of the paper sculpture of Da Shi Wang was approximately eighteen feet and was the biggest deity sculpture in the canopy. According to Buddhist tradition, Da Shi Wang is one of the emanations of the Bodhisattva Avalokitesvara (Guan Yin Pu Sa 觀音菩薩).[118] Bodhisattva Avalokitesvara, also known as the goddess of mercy, is believed to have many different

---

117. 史慧玲, *(The Tradition Handbook)*, 123.

118. 馬國棟和劉志良, *(Uncovering the Folk Beliefs)*, 128. See also 王琛發, *(A Study of Festivals among Malaysian Chinese)*, 107. Bodhisattva Avalokitesvara is one of the most

emanations. Da Shi Wang is one of her most dreadful emanations. At the Hungry Ghost Festival, the statue of Da Shi Wang portrayed a blue face with sharp horns on the head and ferocious snarls on the face with a long red tongue sticking out from the mouth. The ghost worshippers believe that Bodhisattva Avalokitesvara in this male emanation serves as the king of ghosts and has great power over all the ghosts. The goddess of mercy needs to turn herself into a dreadful emanation as Da Shi Wang when dealing with these dangerous and vengeful hungry ghosts. Paper sculptures of the golden boy (Jin Tong 金童) and the jade girl (Yu Nü 玉女) stood before the Da Shi Wang's legs (see figure 5.3.11). The golden boy stood to the Da Shi Wang's left, and the jade girl stood to the right. In Buddhism, the golden boy is also known as Shan Cai Tong Zi (善財童子), and the jade girl is known as Long Nü (龍女). According to the Buddhist tradition, both the golden boy and the jade girl always accompany Bodhisattva Avalokitesvara. Both Jin Tong and Yu Nü are attendants of Bodhisattva Avalokitesvara. According to Buddhist tradition, Jin Tong was from a very wealthy family. Yu Nü, on the other hand, is the dragon king's daughter and extremely smart.[119]

Four gods of hell also accompanied the Da Shi Wang (see figure 5.3.12): the horse-face hell guard, the ox-head hell guard, the white hell patrol, and the black hell patrol. These gods are believed to be hell guards and hell patrols who are called to duty to ensure safety during the festival. The horse-face hell guard (Ma Mian 馬面) and the white hell patrol (Bai Wu Chang 白無常) stood on the Da Shi Wang's left side. The ox-head hell guard (Niu Tou 牛頭) and the black hell patrol (Hei Wu Chang 黑無常) stood on the Da Shi Wang's right side. In Buddhist teaching, the horse-face hell guard and the ox-head hell guard are the guardians of the underworld.[120] The paper sculpture of the horse-face hell guard held a long spear, while the ox-head hell guard held a big fork in his hand. According to tradition, the ox-head hell guard uses the iron fork to put ghosts into hot oil to be burned.[121]

---

popular deities in Chinese culture. 馬書田, 華夏諸神 (Deities of China) (北京 [Beijing]: 北京燕山出版社, 1990), 452. See also 金良年, (The Deities of the Folk), 77–79.

119. 馬書田, 華夏諸神 (Deities of China), 470–475.

120. 易夫, 冥界諸神 (Deities of the Underworld) (北京 [Beijing]: 大眾文藝出版社, 1999), 231–241. See also 馬書田, 冥間鬼神, 131–133.

121. 易夫, (Deities of the Underworld), 237.

Figure 5.3.11: Da Shi Wang, the Golden Boy, and the Jade Girl

The white hell patrol and the black hell patrol are the two gods of hell who are in charge of escorting the spirits of the dead. Whether the white and black hell patrols originate from Buddhism or Taoism remains debatable. Today these gods are popular in Chinese Buddhism, Taoism, and Chinese folk religion.[122] Both sculptures had tongues sticking out from their mouths. The black hell patrol was portrayed as a fierce-looking man with a dark complexion, wearing a black traditional robe and a tall black hat bearing a Chinese verse *yi jian da ji* (一見大吉), which means "becoming lucky upon encountering me." His left hand held a square sign with the words "rewarding the goods and punishing the evils" (*shang shan fa e* 賞善罰惡), and his right hand held a smoke pipe. The white hell patrol was portrayed as a more approachable man with a fair complexion. He wore a white traditional robe and a tall white

---

122. 易夫, *(Deities of the Underworld)*, 239–243. See also 馬書田, 華夏諸神 *(Deities of China)*, 284–286.

hat bearing a Chinese verse *yi jian fa cai* (一見發財), which means "become rich upon encountering me." He held a feather-like stick in his right hand and a hand-held fan in his left hand.

Figure 5.3.12: Hell Guards and Hell Patrols in Front of Da Shi Wang

To further tighten up the "spiritual security," the worshippers also worshipped other deities during the festival. In the Taoist gods-worshipping area, a statue of the Taoist deity Fa Zhu Gong (法主公) was placed in the centre. The pantheon of Taoist deities tends to mirror the bureaucracy of ancient imperial China. Under the Jade Emperor (Yu Huang Da Di 玉皇大帝) was a ministry of administration and a ministry of military. Fa Zhu Gong 法主公 is one of the deities in the ministry of military.[123] According to the Taoist tradition, Fa Zhu Gong is a powerful god who can suppress ghosts and evil spirits.[124]

The statue of Fa Zhu Gong (法主公) portrayed a man with a dark complexion, wide stern eyes, and a long beard. The statue wore a black cloak and a traditional Chinese army general suit, and under both feet were golden wheels. Thirteen banners with portraits of Taoist deities formed a half circle

---

123. 董芳苑, 探討臺灣民間信仰 (*Exploration of Folk Beliefs*), 178–182.

124. 窪德忠著, 蕭坤華譯, 道教諸神 (*The Taoist Deities*) (成都 [Chengdu]: 四川人民出版社, 1989), 221–223.

around the altar of Fa Zhu Gong. Individual altars stood in front of the thirteen banners. Each altar contained plates of fruits and a spiral joss stick between two candles and two cups (see figure 5.3.13).

Figure 5.3.13: Taoist Deity Fa Zhu Gong and Thirteen Banners

Among the thirteen banners, the middle three are considered most important and were placed higher than the other banners. The Chinese words written on the top of the three main banners, from left to right, were Dou Shuai Gong (兜率宮), Yu Xu Gong (玉虛宮), and Bi You Gong (碧游宮). Under the word Dou Shuai Gong (兜率宮) was a portrait of Lao Zi (also known as Tai Shang Lao Jun 太上老君 in religious Taoism). Under Yu Xu Gong (玉虛宮) was a portrait of Yuan Shi Tian Zun (元始天尊), and under Bi You Gong (碧游宮) was a portrait of Ling Bao Tian Zun (靈寶天尊). These three deities are known as the Three Pure Ones (San Qing 三清) or the Taoist trinity. They are the three highest gods in the Taoist pantheon.[125]

---

125. For more discussion about the Three Pure Ones, see John Blofeld, *Taoism: The Road to Immortality* (Boulder, CO: Shambhala, 1978), 95. See also 汪桂平與郭清執," 道教信仰與傳統文化" (Taoist Belief and Traditional Culture), 於中國道教基礎知識 *(Basic Knowledge about Taoism in China)*, 王卡編 (北京 [Beijing]: 宗教文化出版社, 2006), 325–396 (325–327); and 潛明茲, 中國神源 *(The Origin of Chinese Deities)* (重慶 [Chongqing]: 重慶出版社, 1999), 303–305.

According to many Taoist scriptures, approximately four hundred and thirty gods appear in the Taoist pantheon of deities. The Three Pure Ones are the highest among them. Even the Jade Emperor is under these three deities.[126] A banner on the left side of the three main banners conveyed the Chinese word Wu Dang Shan (武當山). Wu Dang Shan (武當山), or mount Wu Dang, is considered the number one sacred mountain in Taoism from the Ming dynasty.[127] A banner on the right side of the main three banners bore the Chinese word Long Hu Shan (龍虎山). Long Hu Shan (龍虎山) are also recognized as sacred mountains of Taoism. According to Taoist tradition, Zhang Dao Ling, the founder of religious Taoism, practised his meditation in Long Hu Shan (龍虎山) before he established the religion.[128]

Fa Zhu Gong is not a high-ranking god in the pantheon of Taoist deities. Compared to the Three Pure Ones, who are the supreme council of the Taoist world, Fa Zhu Gong is a low-ranking general or policeman. Nevertheless, Fa Zhu Gong was placed in a key position during the festival because the ghost worshippers believe that Fa Zhu Gong is a powerful deity who can contain the hungry ghosts. Thus Fa Zhu Gong was serving as an officer on duty during the ceremony.

To ensure a safe and proper festival and to prevent chaos from the hungry ghosts, a professional Taoist priest was hired to lead a special chanting ceremony during the festival. Taoist priests or Buddhist monks are the key persons during the celebration of the Hungry Ghost Festival. They serve as redeemers to the hungry ghosts who come to eat the food and listen to their chants.[129] At 7:30 p.m. each night, the Taoist priest began to lead the ceremony. The priest wore a Taoist black cap and a golden-threaded red cloak with black edges (see figure 5.3.14). Consecration Taoist prayers were led by the priest, accompanied by a religious procession: a Chinese suona[130] player, a hand-drum player, and a Chinese gong player. The Taoist priest chanted to

---

126. 盧建業編, 宗教世界 (*A World of Religion*) (香港 [Hong Kong]: 中華書局, 1992), 104.

127. 史孝進和劉仲宇, 道教風俗談 (*Taoist Customs*) (上海 [Shanghai]: 上海辭書出版社, 2003), 269–277.

128. 史孝進和劉仲宇, (*Taoist Customs*), 298–304.

129. 林富士, 孤魂與鬼雄的世界: 北臺灣的厲鬼信仰 (*Lonely Souls and the Ghostly World: The Malicious Ghost Belief of Northern Taiwan*) (臺北 [Taipei]: 臺北縣立文化中心, 1995), 178–179.

130. Suona is a Chinese woodwind musical instrument.

the rhythms and constantly rang the bell in his hand to keep the entire group of hungry ghosts in order the whole night.

Figure 5.3.14: A Taoist Priest Leading a Chanting Ceremony

5.3.3 Finding 3: The Chinese Believe the Hungry Ghost Festival Is the Time of Charitable Giving to Both the Hungry Ghosts and the Needy in Society

Although foods in the Hungry Ghost Festival were offered to the hungry ghosts or gods, some food items were also served as donations to the needy after the festival. One long table offered food donated by various families. The food on this table was labeled with the name of the family who donated a particular food item. Approximately fifty extra-large packs of rice were on this table. During the Hungry Ghost Festival, Chinese families offered rice to the hungry ghosts and later freely distributed the rice to the poor. This rice is called Rice of Peace (*ping an mi* 平安米).[131] In addition to the packs of rice, other foods were also donated. These food items were stored in plastic bags, plastic buckets, and plastic containers and included oil, sugar, salt, cookies, instant noodles, and instant mix beverages such as tea, coffee, and a chocolate

---

131. 史慧玲, *(The Tradition Handbook)*, 123.

beverage. Festival flags and joss sticks were placed among these food items (see figure 5.3.15).

Figure 5.3.15: Rice of Peace and Other Foods

Inside the festival canopy, a large yellow chart board was displayed with information about the organizer of the celebration, the expenses, and charity donations (see figure 5.3.16). The costs of all festival items were listed clearly with the names of the sponsors. The chart board also revealed information about charity donations. For example, people donated RM2,000 (about £380), RM500 (about £100), or RM288 (about £55) to education foundations. Some people donated RM2,000 or RM100 (about £20) to a dialysis center, and some donated RM500 to a disability service center. However, most donations were spent on the cost of the festival itself. For example, the cost of the paper statue of the Da Shi Wang was RM3,888 (about £750), the cost of the paper bus was RM 2,188 (about £420), and the cost of a raw pig was RM1,088 (about £210). The entertainment performance cost was RM3,388 (about £652) per night, and the Taoist priest's service charge was RM3,188 (about £613) per night. The total cost for the priest's services for five nights totaled RM15,940 (about £3065).

Exploratory Study of the Three Festivals   207

Figure 5.3.16: A Chart Board with Donation Information

5.3.4 Finding 4: Its Utilitarian Character Is One of the Prominent Features of the Hungry Ghost Festival

By participating in the Hungry Ghost Festival, the worshippers hoped to obtain blessings from the gods and the ghosts. The gods worshipped during this festival also included the three Taoist star gods Fu, Lu, and Shou (Fu Lu Shou San Xing 福祿壽三星) (see figure 5.3.17). Fu is known as the star of Prosperity (Fu Xing 福星); Lu is the star of Status (Lu Xing 祿星); and Shou is the star of Longevity (Shou Xing 壽星). The star of Prosperity wore a colourful hat and robe; the star of Status wore a black hat and a colourful robe with green and blue stripes; and the star of Longevity appeared to be an old man holding a golden staff. In Taoism, the star of Prosperity refers to the planet Jupiter, and it is a god who brings good luck. The star of Status is a star of good career and influence. The star of Longevity is a star which controls life spans of mortals.[132] These three gods are considered the most popular group of gods in Chinese society because the Chinese believe that these three gods bring all kinds of blessings.[133] A statue of the god of wealth was also present during the festival (see figure 5.3.18).[134]

---

132. 林云和聶達, *(Discussions about Venerations)*, 91–98.

133. 馬書田, 中國人的神靈世界 *(Spiritual World of the People in China)* (北京 [Beijing]: 北京燕山出版社, 1990), 2–11.

134. The god of wealth is one of the most popular gods in Chinese culture, because the Chinese believe that he can bring great wealth to people. See 馬書田, 華夏諸神 *(Deities of*

Figure 5.3.17: The Three Taoist Star Gods

Figure 5.3.18: The God of Wealth

China), 310. Accordingly, the beliefs regarding the god of wealth have been popular among the Chinese since the Ming dynasty. See 余喆編, 神鬼世界 *(The Spiritual World)* (香港 [Hong Kong]: 中華書局, 1992), 88–89.

Seeking prosperity was the emphasis during the Hungry Ghost Festival. One of the largest joss paper sculptures inside the canopy was a paper golden pineapple. In Chinese culture, a pineapple means "prosperity and great wealth to come." The golden pineapple was made from gold joss paper folded into ingots and stacked into an elaborate pineapple shape (see figure 5.3.19).

Figure 5.3.19: The Joss Paper Pineapple

Chinese superstition about numbers was also revealed in this field research. The paper taxi and paper bus indicated the longing for prosperity. The number plate of the paper taxi was "OK 1688." The number 1688 resembles the sound of the Chinese word that means "unlimited prosperity." Affixed on the paper bus was a tax sticker with the expiration date 14 July 2128. The number 2128 sounds like the Chinese word "very easy to get prosperity."[135] Even the first song of the ghost-entertainment performance was a Hokkien song about prosperity. Throughout the performance, the artists repeated great

---

135. Chinese superstition about numbers is well known. For example, Cantonese people like the number three, which sounds like the word "life," the number nine, which sounds like the word "long time," and the number eight, which sounds like the word "prosperity." See 曾文星編, 華人的心理與治療 *(Psychology and Therapy for the Chinese)* (臺北 [Taipei]: 桂冠圖書股份有限公司, 1996), 81–82.

blessings to the audience. Obviously, receiving blessings is an expectation during the Hungry Ghost Festival.

5.4 Summary

This chapter explores the field research findings of the three festivals. There are four findings from the Spring Festival. The first finding explores the Chinese legends and Chinese zodiac and shows that they remain part of the atmosphere of the Spring Festival. The second finding discusses the emphasis on seeking good fortune during the Spring Festival. The third finding ascertains that asking deities for blessings is important during the Spring Festival. The fourth finding shows that the lion dance is still prevalent during Spring Festival.

There are three findings from the field research on the Qing Ming festival. The first finding observes the Chinese worshipping their deceased ancestors during the Qing Ming Festival, but the practices are slightly different depending on the setting. The second finding further elaborates on the Chinese belief that the needs of a deceased family member are similar to the needs of a living person. The third finding identifies that the Chinese believe the deceased still need protection and help from deities.

Four findings are discussed in the field research on the Hungry Ghost Festival. The first finding is that the Chinese believe ghosts are the spirits of deceased persons. The second finding reveals that the Chinese worship the ghosts due to fear. The third finding indicates that the Chinese believe the Hungry Ghost Festival is the time of charitable giving to both the hungry ghosts and the needy in society. The fourth finding discloses its utilitarian character as one of the prominent features of the Hungry Ghost Festival.

CHAPTER 6

Chinese Preachers' Perceptions and Practices of Contextualized Preaching at Three Chinese Festivals

This chapter reports the key findings gleaned from interviews with six Chinese preachers regarding their perceptions and practices of contextualized preaching during the three Chinese festivals discussed in this study: the Spring Festival, the Qing Ming Festival, and the Hungry Ghost Festival. The interview transcripts have been translated and analysed in order to discern common themes and concepts regarding contextualized preaching among the Chinese during the three Chinese festivals. The analysis of the interviews identifies variations and similarities in six preachers' perceptions and practices regarding how and what to preach during these festivals. The six interviewees in this chapter are anonymous and are presented as Preachers M1, M2, M3, H1, H2, and H3. Preachers M1, M2, and M3 are preachers from Malaysia, while preachers H1, H2, and H3 are preachers from Hong Kong. All are preachers in urban contexts. The key findings from the analysis of the interviews are presented below.

6.1 The Chinese Preachers Agree That Contextualized Preaching Is Important

All six preachers stated or gave the impression that contextualized preaching is important among the Chinese. Preacher H2 underscored a great need for contextualized preaching in Chinese churches. He believes that Chinese

Christians must understand the Bible through the lens of Chinese culture. Preacher H2 noted that, in ancient times, Christianity went through a process of contextualization in Western culture. Therefore, Christian theology in the West today is greatly influenced by Greek and Roman culture. However, Preacher H2 argued, "If we understand Christianity through only the Western point of view, we would not be able to respond properly to the questions the Chinese ask about Christianity." He believes contextualized preaching among the Chinese means providing biblical answers to the questions raised within Chinese culture.

Moreover, Preacher H2 insisted that preachers must show respect for the Chinese culture when preaching to the Chinese. He believes that preachers should have a favourable attitude toward the Chinese culture. He explained, "Chinese people place a strong emphasis on respecting others. If they do not feel like you are respecting them, they will not listen to you." When encountering Chinese culture as a preacher, he suggested, "Always begin with positive comments about the culture. We must try to look for the positive sides of the culture before we criticize the negative sides of the culture and introduce the Christian truth."

Preacher H3 believes that contextualized preaching could effectively help Chinese believers to understand biblical teachings because contextualization allows people to understand biblical truth via the perspective of their own cultures. He explained, "The message of the gospel needs to be understood by the Chinese within their culture." Furthermore, he mentioned that contextualization allows Christians to distinguish between cultural conditional practices and the unchanging truth of the Bible.

Preacher M1 affirmed the value of contextualization in preaching and asserted that preachers should not neglect contextualization. He warned that Chinese preachers should never lose their racial identity as Chinese. Preacher M1 further acknowledged that the Chinese often regard Christianity as a Western religion and consider Christian converts as no longer truly Chinese. He believes that if preachers assure Chinese non-Christians that we did not abandon the Chinese culture after becoming a Christian, they will be more open to listen to us.

Both Preachers M2 and M3 also agreed that contextualized preaching is important. Preacher M3 believes that contextualized preaching enables the audience to relate easily with the preaching content. According to Preacher

M3, "Contextualized preaching helps the listeners understand what is being preached." Likewise, Preacher M2 underlined the importance of contextualization in preaching the gospel to the Chinese. He claimed, "When Chinese preachers preach, they must be sensitive to Chinese traditions and customs." Moreover, he mentioned that the Chinese concept of *ying jing* 應景, which means "according to seasons," is very important when preaching to the Chinese. Therefore, Preacher M2 believes that Chinese preachers must preach according to the seasons of the Chinese calendar.

Preacher H1 asserted that contextualizing one's preaching is a biblical mandate. He explained, for example, that Jesus's exhortation in Matthew 24:45–46 is a good reminder for preachers to be relevant and to supply spiritual food to their congregation according to the seasons of the culture.[1] Preacher H1 claimed that the concept of "proper time" is key in this passage. Good preachers must know what to preach during certain seasons. According to Preacher H1, "Contextualized preaching, both theologically and practically, is time-relevant preaching." He believes that his contextualized preaching in the church is one of the main reasons his church has grown from a few hundred to approximately two thousand members.

6.2 Regarding the Spring Festival

6.2.1 The Chinese Preachers Generally Agreed that the Celebration of the Spring Festival Is Compatible with the Christian Faith

Preacher M2 asserted that the Chinese church should celebrate the Spring Festival because it is the most important festival in the Chinese culture and everyone celebrates it. According to Preacher M2, it is good for the Chinese church to have a special worship service on the first day of the Spring Festival. He shared, "I have pastored two Chinese churches. One church had only one special service on the first day of January, while the other church celebrated not only the first day of January but also the first day of the lunar New Year. I like to celebrate the first day of the Chinese New Year in church because

---

1. "Who then is the faithful and sensible slave whom his master put in charge of his household to give them their food at the proper time? Blessed is that slave whom his master finds so doing when he comes" (Matt 24:45–46).

what better place to give thanks to God for the Chinese New Year and to wish one another a happy New Year? I think celebrating the Chinese New Year in church is a good practice."

Although Preacher H1's church does not necessarily have a special worship service on the first day of the Spring Festival, it does have a special Sunday service during the Spring Festival, which lasts for at least fifteen days. Preacher H1 described this service, saying, "During the first Sunday service of the Spring Festival, I wear traditional Chinese clothing when I preach." Moreover, he believes that his congregation always looks forward to hearing his message on the first Sunday of the Chinese New Year. And he mentioned that "the congregation expects to receive God's special instruction for the coming New Year."

Preacher H3 also encouraged Chinese Christians to celebrate the Spring Festival, noting that "some churches in Hong Kong have a special worship service on the first day of the Spring Festival." He continued, "I think celebrating the Spring Festival in church is a very good practice. We should worship God on the first day of the Chinese New Year." According to Preacher H3, "The Spring Festival is also a good time for ministers to visit their church members. Church members feel honored by their minister's visit during the Spring Festival. I also encourage other church members to visit one another during the Spring Festival. It is a good time for fellowship."

Furthermore, Preacher H3 believes that Chinese Christians should try their best to respect the customs of the Spring Festival. One example he mentioned is the distribution of red packets to children.[2] He acknowledged, "I know some Christians do not distribute red packets because they think it is against the Christian faith. Some distribute red packets with gospel tracts inside instead of money. However, I think we should follow a tradition." According to Preacher H3, we should respect the custom of distributing red packets with money inside because the practice symbolises blessings to the children. Moreover, he claimed, "The Hong Kong Chinese Christian Churches Union was never against the practice of distributing red packets. They even produce red packets with Bible verses on them for Chinese Christians to distribute."

---

2. At the Spring Festival, red packets with money gifts are given to the children to wish them good luck. See section 5.1.1.

Regarding other customs during the Spring Festival, some of the interviewees confessed that they try to deal with them as positively as they can. For example, Preacher H1 sometimes talks about the Chinese zodiac during the Spring Festival. He said, "I do not believe in the Chinese zodiac, and I do not talk about the Chinese zodiac in the traditional Chinese way. I only use the animal of that particular year as a metaphor, as a starting point for my sermon preaching. I then preach about that particular animal from a biblical point of view, and I mention any spiritual lesson we can learn from that." Preacher H3 shared a similar experience: "The belief of the Chinese zodiac is deeply rooted in Chinese culture. Therefore, I sometimes talk about the Chinese zodiac during the Spring Festival. For example, in the year of the sheep, I employed sheep as a metaphor in my sermons, and I preached about how people are lost sheep."

Preacher H2 said that even the spring couplets[3] can serve as a metaphor when preaching to the Chinese: "The spring couplets are written on red paper, and the Chinese like to paste the spring couplets on the door panels. The original meaning of the practice is to protect the household from any harm. Using the spring couplets as a metaphor allows us to preach about the Passover account in the book of Exodus." Preacher H2 believes that a correlation exists between the spring couplets pasted on the door panels and the blood of a slaughtered sheep sprinkled on the doorposts. He noted, "On the night of the Passover, the blood of the slaughtered sheep protected the Israelites from the plague of death." Preacher H2 claimed that the connection between the spring couplets and the blood of the Passover lamb can eventually open the door to preaching about Jesus's blood as the power of redemption. Furthermore, Preacher H2 also suggested referring to the lion dance as a metaphor in preaching: "The lion in the lion dance is not a symbol of a lion but of a beast called *Nian*. *Nian* represents the ultimate enemy of mankind. It is a life destroyer. The Chinese use the colour red and firecrackers to chase away the beast. However, only the blood of Jesus Christ, which is also red, can defeat the ultimate enemy."

---

3. See section 5.1.1, about the spring couplets.

6.2.2 Some Beliefs and Practices Associated with the Spring Festival Are Contrary to the Christian Faith

Although all six preachers believe that the celebration of the Spring Festival, in general, is compatible with Christianity, they also believe that some beliefs and practices associated with the festival are contrary to the Christian faith. Preacher M3 first referred to ancestral worship on the eve of the Chinese New Year, namely the Spring Festival. Traditionally, before the family sits down to eat the reunion dinner on the eve of the Chinese New Year, they must first worship their ancestors by setting out foods on a table before the ancestral altar.[4] Preacher M3 attested that ancestral worship is unacceptable, and Preacher H1 also maintained that ancestral worship is one of the most controversial practices in the Chinese culture during the Spring Festival.

In addition to ancestral worship, Preacher H1 emphasized the problem of Chinese deity worship during the Spring Festival and mentioned sending off the kitchen god to heaven. Sending off the kitchen god takes place either on the twenty-third or twenty-fourth day of the twelfth lunar month, depending on the area. The day is also called "Small New Year's Eve" (*guo xiao nian* 過小年 in Chinese) and usually marks the beginning of the Spring Festival period.[5] According to Chinese tradition, the kitchen god, who is also called the stove god or the hearth god, reports to the celestial authorities at the end of the lunar year.[6] Preacher H1 explained, "In ancient times, the kitchen was the main place where Chinese family members ate and talked with one another. The Chinese believe that the kitchen god keeps a record of every family's good deeds and bad deeds for the whole year and reports to the Jade Emperor."[7] The Chinese offer many foods to the kitchen god in order to entreat him to conceal the bad deeds he has seen and to report only their good deeds. The foods offered to the kitchen god include alcoholic beverages, sticky candy, and other Chinese foods. Sticky candy is offered to sweeten the kitchen god's mood and to glue his jaws shut so that he will be silent in the presence of the

---

4. Chuck Lowe, *Honouring God and Family: A Christian Response to Idol Food in Chinese Popular Religion* (Bangalore: Theological Book Trust, 2001), 20.

5. Robert L. Chard, "Rituals and Scriptures of the Stove Cult," in *Ritual and Scripture in Chinese Popular Religion: Five Studies*, ed. David Johnson (Berkeley, CA: IEAS, 1995), 16.

6. John Lagerwey, *Taoist Ritual in Chinese Society and History* (New York: Macmillan, 1987), 19.

7. The Jade Emperor is considered the supreme ruler of heaven and earth.

Jade Emperor.⁸ Alcoholic beverages are offered to make the kitchen god too drunk to give a bad report.⁹

Preacher M3 mentioned two practices during the Spring Festival that are contrary to the Christian faith. The first practice is Jie Cai Shen 接財神, which welcomes the god of wealth on the eve of the Chinese New Year.¹⁰ Preacher M3 explained, "The Chinese believe that the god of wealth comes from different directions each year, so they are busy figuring out which way the god of wealth will come." Moreover, she pointed out that even the identity of the god of wealth is confusing. In fact, the Chinese worship many deities as gods of wealth. According to Chinese tradition, these deities include Bi Gan 比干, Cai Bo Xing Jun 財帛星君, Zhao Gong Yuan Shuai 趙公元帥, Guan Gong 關公, and many others.¹¹

Preacher M3 also shared her personal experience, stating, "Before I became a Christian, I ushered in the god of wealth every year. But ushering in the god of wealth never made me rich." She mentioned the worship of the deity Tai Sui 太歲 during the Spring Festival. Tai Sui is one of the most highly feared deities in Chinese beliefs. The Chinese people believe that Tai Sui is in charge of blessing and cursing and of even the weather for the whole year.¹² Preacher M3 further explained, "The belief of Tai Sui also closely relates to the Chinese zodiac. Every year the Chinese need to figure out, through Chinese astrology, which deity is the Tai Sui of the current year and make an offering to the Tai Sui." According to a cycle of sixty years, sixty deities take turns being Tai Sui. The Chinese worship the Tai Sui of the year during the Spring Festival in order to obtain blessings from the deity and to prevent misfortune.¹³ The Chinese believe that an offended Tai Sui will cause great

---

8. Chard, "Rituals and Scriptures," 17.

9. See 洪丕謨, *(A Discussion on Custom and Culture)*, 46.

10. In ancient China, people erected a wooden statue of the god of wealth and worshipped it after the reunion dinner on New Year's Eve. See Nailu Jin, "There Were Some Folk Festive Activities Like Song Zao-wang (Seeing off the God of the Hearth) and Ying Caishen (Welcoming the God of Wealth) during the Spring Festival in the Past. Were There Any Stories about These Two Gods?," in *A Hundred Questions on the Chinese Culture*, ed. Nailu Jin (Beijing: Beijing Language and Culture University Press, 2005), 133–136 (135).

11. 洪丕謨, *(A Discussion on Custom and Culture)*, 72.

12. 李秀娥, *(Festivals and Customs of Taiwan)*, 62–63.

13. A Chinese cycle of sixty years is also called *liu shi hua jia* 六十花甲, or Sexagenary. See 史慧玲, *(The Tradition Handbook)*, 82.

misfortunes. According to one Chinese saying, "Who dares to touch the head of the Tai Sui?" (誰敢在太歲頭上動土).[14]

Preacher H3 highlighted that, during the Spring Festival, some people will seek fortune telling through oracle sticks, face reading, or palmistry. He believes that all of these practices are prohibited in the Bible. Moreover, the interviewees considered many Chinese New Year taboos to be superstitutions. For example, Preacher M3 attested, "It is a taboo to sweep the floor or to wash one's hair on the first day of the Chinese New Year because it is believed that these actions will sweep away or wash away good luck and wealth." She affirmed that these kinds of taboos are contradictory to the Christian faith. Preacher M2 felt the same way and said, "How can we leave the dirt on the floor and not sweep it away? This taboo is just superstition."

6.2.3 The Concept of Renewal Could Be Used as a Cultural Contact Point[15] for Contextualized Preaching during the Spring Festival

Preacher M3 noted that looking forward to renewal is the key element in the Spring Festival. She explained, "In the celebration of the Chinese New Year, the Chinese always hope for a better new year." Preacher H3 agreed, "One of the most important concepts of the Spring Festival is discarding the old and welcoming the new." The Chinese are eager to get rid of the failures or bad habits of the past years and to have a new beginning.

Preacher H1 described this concept of renewal in more detail. According to Preacher H1, one way to summarize the celebration of the Spring Festival is saying goodbye to one year and looking forward to another year. He claimed that many customs and activities of the Spring Festival symbolise the idea of renewal. Some religious activities, such as sending off the kitchen god to heaven and welcoming the god of wealth, all reflect the desire for renewal. Renewal in the Spring Festival means "settling all unfinished business and having new opportunities," declared Preacher H1. Moreover, he believes this

---

14. 汪桂平與郭清執,"道教信仰與傳統文化," (Taoist Belief and Traditional Culture), 343.

15. "Contact point" or "a point of contact" is an element that provides an intelligible basis for communication. See Eugene A. Nida, *Message and Mission: The Communication of the Christian Faith*, rev. ed. (Pasadena, CA: William Carey Library, 1990), 18.

concept of renewal is in harmony with the doctrine of new creation in the Christian faith.

Thus, during the Spring Festival, Preacher H1 likes to preach sermons that help people to review the past and look forward to future prospects. He asserted, "No matter how hard last year was, we can start fresh for the new year. A new year brings forth new possibilities." Furthermore, he mentioned that passages which talk about the new creation, such as 2 Corinthians 5:17, are suitable to preach to the Chinese during the Spring Festival.

The church in which Preacher M2 formerly pastored always has a special worship service on the first day of the Spring Festival. He recalled, "Renewal was the theme I preached most often at those special Chinese New Year services." He would also remind the members of the congregation to clean up their inner being every New Year in addition to cleaning up their homes. Similarly, Preacher M1 mentioned that he preached many sermons related to renewal during the time of the Spring Festival. He shared, "I preached on topics such as new beginnings, renewal of strength, and forging a new heart."

Preacher H2 believes that saying goodbye to the past can also be emphasized during the Spring Festival. He noted, "On the twenty-eighth day of the twelfth lunar month, the Chinese clean the whole house." Chinese families clean the whole house on the twenty-eighth day of the twelfth lunar month hoping to chase away misfortunes and to prevent disasters (年廿八洗邋遢 – cleaning on the twenty-eighth day).[16] He then explained, "By sweeping away the dust, we want to get rid of past issues." The Chinese character for "dust" is *chen* 塵. In Chinese, the word "dust" is a homophone for the word "old" (*chen jiu* 陳舊). According to Preacher H2, this concept can be applied as a contact point to preach to the Chinese during the Spring Festival. He underlined the need to teach people to think how to clean spiritually. The main point of the message should be clear: We need God to cleanse our soul, and we need to repent from our sins.

Preacher H2, moreover, indicated that the twelfth lunar month is called *La Yue* 臘月. He explained, "*La Yue* 臘月 means the month of changing from old to new."[17] He suggested that from the term *La Yue*, pastors can preach

---

16. 史慧玲, *(The Tradition Handbook)*, 51.

17. The Chinese also have a custom to eat a special soup, which is called *la ba zhou* 臘八粥, on the eighth day of the twelfth lunar month. The *la ba zhou* is a sweet gruel made

about regeneration because regeneration is also about transition from an old life to a new life. This suggestion is indeed useful for preaching during the Spring Festival. However, it should be noted that the Chinese word *la* 臘 had multiple meanings in ancient times. Zhang Liang 張亮 of the Jin dynasty said that the word *la* 臘 means transition from old to new (臘者接也, 祭宜在新故交接也). On the other hand, historian Ying Shao 應劭 of the Han dynasty said *la* 臘 means hunting. Ancient Chinese people went hunting in the twelfth lunar month in order to offer an animal sacrifice to their ancestors and gods for the harvest festival (臘者獵也, 因獵取野獸, 以祭祖先).[18] In view of the fact that *La Yue* is celebrated at the end of the year, the celebration seems to put the emphasis on transition from old to new, even though in ancient times the celebration might include hunting and offering sacrifices to ancestors. Nevertheless, caution must be exercised when referring to the *La Yue* 臘月.

6.2.4 The Concept of Reunion Could Be Used as a Cultural Contact Point for Contextualized Preaching during the Spring Festival

Chinese New Year's Eve, or *Chu Xi* 除夕 in Chinese, is a time for a reunion dinner.[19] It is a very important occasion celebrated by the entire family and a few chosen friends.[20] On that night, the whole family gathers together for a big dinner, which is a symbol of unity.[21] Preacher M3 emphasized the importance of the reunion dinner to the Chinese on New Year's Eve. She asserted that employing the concept of reunion as a cultural contact point is suitable for preaching during the Spring Festival because the concept of reunion is in harmony with the doctrine of reconciliation. "The reunion dinner is a

---

of whole grains of rice or other cereals, with admixtures of walnuts, pine seeds, persimmons, chestnuts, and other fruits. See Wolfram Eberhard, *Chinese Festivals* (New York: Henry Schuman, 1952), 10.

18. 齊治平, 節令的故事 *(The Tale of Festivals)* (香港 [Hong Kong]: 大方文化事業公司, 1979), 276.

19. Ren Qiliang et al., "Folk Customs: Traditional Festivals," in *Common Knowledge about Chinese Culture*, ed. Ren Qiliang et al., rev. ed. (Xi'an: Shaanxi Normal University General Publishing, 2015), 38.

20. Lawrence G. Thompson, "The Festival Year," in *The Chinese Way in Religion*, eds. Jordan Paper and Lawrence G. Thompson, 2nd ed. (Belmont, CA: Wadsworth, 1998), 187.

21. 齊治平, *(The Tale of Festivals)*, 28.

reminder for the Chinese to be reunited with family members every year," she explained. "In a similar way, God wants to be reunited with His children." She further suggested, "At the Spring Festival the Chinese will think of family because it is a season of going home. Therefore, we can ask the Chinese to think of their Creator and heavenly home."

Likewise, Preacher H2 mentioned that the reunion dinner on New Year's Eve is about children coming home to have dinner with their parents. Therefore, New Year's Eve is all about family relationships. In addition, he pointed out that family relationships are an essential factor in Chinese culture, stating, "When I preach the gospel to the Chinese, I always talk about family relationships in heaven." He further explained, "Our heavenly Father is longing for His children to come home and be reunited with Him."

The New Year's Eve reunion dinner is a feast with many traditional Chinese foods.[22] Preacher H2 attested that the concept of the reunion dinner can be applied to explain effectively the eschatological hopes of the gospel. He declared, "At the end, God will prepare a lavish banquet for His children." Preacher H2 believes this banquet is a supreme reunion dinner in heaven. At this banquet our heavenly Father, the Lord of the universe, will have dinner with us.

6.2.5 Suitable Biblical Passages for Preaching during the Spring Festival

During the interviews, the interviewees were asked to give examples of biblical passages or themes on which they often base their preaching during the Spring Festival. Preacher H1 refered to the crossing of the Jordan River in the book of Joshua[23] to talk about renewal and moving toward a new life. He expounded, "The crossing of the Jordan happened on the tenth day of the first month of the Jewish New Year. First, this crossing was a new period of time. Second, after crossing the river, the Israelites became a new people. Third, they entered a new place. Therefore, based on this biblical passage, I explain how Christians move towards the eternal new life."

Preacher H1 also preaches the eight beatitudes of Jesus during the Spring Festival.[24] He noted, "The Chinese like to talk about five blessings, *wu fu* 五福.

---

22. 齊治平, *(The Tale of Festivals)*, 28.
23. Josh 3:1–4:24.
24. Matt 5:1–12.

The five blessings are longevity (*chang shou* 長壽), wealth (*fu you* 富有), health and composure (*an kang* 安康), love of virtue (*mei de* 美德), and peaceful death (*shan zhong* 善終).[25] However, all five of these blessings refer to the material life." Preacher H1 preaches sermons based on the eight beatitudes of Jesus and explains that the blessings of Jesus are eternal and spiritual.

Preacher H2, referring to the reunion dinner of the Chinese New Year's Eve, preaches on the parable of the prodigal son[26] to explain God's love toward his children and God's longing to be reunited with them. Because the Spring Festival is also about a new beginning, Preacher H2 said he also preaches about the creation account in the book of Genesis.[27] Similarly, during the Spring Festival, Preacher H3 refers to Genesis chapter 1 and 2 to preach about a new beginning. He also refers to the eight beatitudes of Jesus to preach about the real blessings of life. Occasionally, he preaches from the book of Joshua or Psalm 1 to explain the blessings of God.

Preacher M3, on the other hand, relies on Exodus 20:12 to talk about filial piety and family relationships.[28] She also refers to Joshua 24:15 to show the importance of family.[29] Bible passages from which Preacher M1 preaches during the Spring Festival are mostly related to regeneration or new life in Christ. For example, he refers to John 3:1–16 and 2 Corinthians 5:17.[30] He also likes to preach the book of Ecclesiastes, especially the first three chapters and chapter twelve, during the Spring Festival. "I like to preach about times and seasons during the Chinese New Year," he said.

At the Spring Festival, Preacher M2 focuses his messages on knowing more about God's nature, the promises of God, and the love of God. The biblical passages from which he preaches include Exodus 34:6–8, Deuteronomy 8:1–20, and 11:8–16. He also refers to Romans 8:38–39 to preach about God's unfailing love.

---

25. 洪丕謨, *(A Discussion on Custom and Culture)*, 12.
26. Luke 15:11–32.
27. Gen 1:1–2:25.
28. "Honor your father and your mother, that your days may be prolonged in the land which the Lord your God gives you" (Exod 20:12).
29. "But as for me and my house, we will serve the Lord" (Josh 24:15).
30. "Therefore if anyone is in Christ, *he is* a new creature; the old things passed away; behold, new things have come" (2 Cor 5:17).

6.3 Regarding the Qing Ming Festival

6.3.1 It Is Permissible to Celebrate the Qing Ming Festival with the Practice of Tomb Sweeping but not with the Practice of Ancestral Worship

According to Preacher M1, it is acceptable for Christians to celebrate the Qing Ming Festival through the practice of tomb sweeping. However, he asserted that tomb sweeping is different from ancestral worship and that Christians should never participate in ancestral worship. Preacher M1 avowed, "Christians can remember and honor their ancestors by going to their tombs and cleaning them during the Qing Ming Festival, but Christians should never worship their ancestors."

Similarly, Preacher M3 said that a Christian can participate in tomb sweeping as a family member but should never join in any ritual of ancestral worship. She insisted, "We should not buy any sacrificial or worship items for ancestral worship." Instead, Preacher M3 always treats her entire family for lunch after the tomb cleaning ritual during the Qing Ming Festival. Participating in this ritual allows her to show her family members that, even though she participated in the Qing Ming Festival as a part of the family, she did not worship the ancestors.

Preacher H3 also claimed that Christians should never participate in ancestral worship during the Qing Ming Festival. However, he affirmed that a Chinese Christian must participate in tomb sweeping as a family member. Preacher H3 suggested cleaning the weeds around the tomb and the tomb itself in order to show respect for one's ancestors. He also recommended presenting flowers in front of the tomb as a sign of respect.

According to Preacher H1, the key problem during the Qing Ming Festival is the incorrect worldview. He attested, "The Chinese have a superstitious worldview. They assume deceased persons have the same daily needs in hell as they did in the living world." This incorrect worldview has led the Chinese to believe that a deceased person in hell needs all the daily things they had in life. Preacher H1 reported that people in Hong Kong burn all kinds of paper effigies to their ancestors, noting, "Some people burn paper iPads, paper Calvin Klein underwear, paper foot massagers, and even paper bird cages." Burning these paper objects means, in Chinese traditional worldview, they are being conveyed to the ancestors in another world. He even mentioned that some Chinese Christians today are still influenced by this incorrect worldview. For example, he shared about a Christian from his own church whose non-Christian mother had passed away. This Christian asked if he could burn a blanket to his deceased mother. He told Preacher H1 that his deceased mother came to him in a dream and asked for a blanket, because it was very cold in hell. Preacher H1 had to tell this brother that this kind of worldview is incorrect.

Preacher H2 explained that the Chinese believe their ancestors become ghosts when they pass away and that we are supposed to feed the deceased ancestors through incense burning. He indicated that the practice of burning incense for deceased ancestors is absolutely contrary to the Christian faith. Moreover, he insisted it is important to inform the Chinese that incense burning for ancestral worship was not even practised in ancient China. He clarified, "Burning incense for the deceased did not originate from ancient China but from Indian Buddhism. In ancient China, incense was never used for worship. According to the book of *Zhou Li* 周禮, incense burning was used for bug repellent and room fragrances in ancient China." According to Preacher H2, the Chinese started to burn incense for the deceased only after Buddhism was introduced into China.

Preacher M1 claimed that Chinese ancestral worship is illogical. He explained, "The Chinese believe in the reincarnation of the six realms. A monk might tell you that your deceased father reincarnated into an animal after death. So what is the point of sending stuffs to hell for your father every year since he is an animal now?" He asserted that contradiction lies within the Chinese traditional worldview. He said, "If you believe in the reincarnation of the six realms, this traditional way of ancestral worship makes no sense." Preacher M1 argued that, based on the Buddhist understanding, none of the six realms of reincarnation can receive anything from ancestral worship. No matter which realm deceased people go to, it is useless to burn anything to them. Hence, even according to the traditional belief of the reincarnation of the six realms, ancestral worship is meaningless.[31]

---

31. Moreman points out the paradox in Chinese belief: "On the one hand, the dead are thought to reside in the funeral tablet until they eventually merge into the ancestral community, while on the other hand, the Buddhist notion of rebirth insists upon the reincarnation of each individual." See Christopher M. Moreman, *Beyond the Threshold: Afterlife Beliefs and Experiences in World Religions* (Lanham, MD: Rowman & Littlefield, 2008), 155.

Preacher M3 affirmed a similar point regarding ancestral worship. She said, "The Chinese believe in life after death and also believe in reincarnation, but there is one problem. When you go to the Qing Ming Festival to worship an ancestor, how can you be sure the ancestor is still around to receive anything? The ancestor might have already reincarnated into someone or something else." She thinks it is important to help the Chinese understand that reincarnation and ancestral worship is a contradiction.

6.3.2 The Emphasis on Filial Piety Could Be Used as a Cultural Contact Point for Contextualized Preaching during the Qing Ming Festival

Preacher M1 indicated that the key cultural value of the Qing Ming Festival is the idea of filial piety, which comes from Confucianism.[32] He explained, "According to a Chinese saying, when one drinks water, one must not forget from where it comes (*yin shui si yuan* 飲水思源). We received many good things from our parents, and we should not forget about that." Furthermore, Preacher M1 believes that the main principle of filial piety is to love one's parents, declaring, "Filial piety is all about love."

Therefore, Preacher M1 affirmed that preaching about loving and honoring parents is appropriate during the Qing Ming Festival. Quoting from Matthew 22:36–40, Preacher M1 believes that loving God and loving neighbor demonstrates true filial piety.[33] "I love God. God gave me my parents, so I love my parents too," he explicated. He also referred to Exodus 20:12, where God commands us to honor our parents, noting, "The Bible emphasizes honoring your parents while they are still alive. Love them, respect them, care for them, and honor them."

---

32. Filial piety is very important in Confucian culture. Reverence and glorification of one's ancestors is one's greatest duty and greatest honor. See Xinzhong Yao, *An Introduction to Confucianism* (Cambridge: Cambridge University Press, 2000), 199. It is believed that "Confucian teachings stress moral cultivation rather than the observance of ritual as the basis of filial piety." See *The Sacred Books of Confucius and Other Confucian Classics*, trans. and ed. Ch'u Chai and Winberg Chai (New Hyde Park, NY: University Books, 1965), 325.

33. "And He said to him, 'You shall love the Lord your God with all your heart, and with all your soul, and with all your mind.' This is the great and foremost commandment. The second is like it, 'You shall love your neighbor as yourself.' On these two commandments depend the whole Law and the Prophets" (Matt 22:37–39).

Preacher H1 also preaches about filial piety during the season of the Qing Ming Festival. Based on Exodus 20:12 and the teaching of Paul in Ephesians 6:1–3, he preaches about honoring and caring for parents while they are still alive. Preacher H1 preaches also from 1 Timothy 5:4,[34] where Paul commands people to practice piety in their own family. Preacher H1 indicated that his teaching on filial piety focuses on how people should care for and honor their parents while their parents are still alive, not when their parents are dead. He explained, "According to a Taiwanese idiom, it is better to give one bean to our parents while they are still alive than to give them a pig's head when they pass away (*zai sheng yi li dou, ka ying si le bai zhu tou* 在生一粒豆，卡贏死了拜豬頭). While our parents are still alive, we should take care of them. When they pass away, they are not able to receive anything from us, even a pig's head."

Preacher M2 said that *xiao qin jing lao* 孝親敬老, a Chinese term for filial piety and respecting elders, is one of the recurring themes in his sermons during the Qing Ming Festival. He argued that the Bible teaches us to respect and care for our parents as well as our elders. According to Preacher M2, "Being a Christian does not mean that you should forget all your ancestors. We treasure our deceased parents and grandparents in our heart. We just do not worship them anymore."

6.3.3 The Resurrection of Jesus Christ Is a Suitable Topic for Contextualized Preaching during the Qing Ming Festival

Preacher H1 pointed out that the date of the Qing Ming Festival is usually close to the date of Easter. Therefore, he believes that pastors should preach about the death and resurrection of Christ during the Qing Ming Festival. Preacher H1 asserted, "The purpose of the Qing Ming Festival is to remember deceased ancestors, while the purpose of Easter is to remember the hope of the resurrection." Moreover, he argued that, since the date of Easter is also close to the date of the Jewish Passover, sermons during the Qing Ming Festival should also include the redemptive works of God, such as the Exodus account.

---

34. "But if any widow has children or grandchildren, they must first learn to practice piety in regard to their own family and to make some return to their parents; for this is acceptable in the sight of God."

Preacher M2 also often preaches about the resurrection of Christ during the time of the Qing Ming Festival. He declared, "Since the Qing Ming Festival is so close to Easter day, I preach about life and resurrection and mainly emphasize the hope brought forth by the resurrection of Christ." Likewise, Preacher H3 believes that the close proximity between the date of the Qing Ming Festival and the date of Easter creates good opportunity for evangelistic preaching. He claimed, "Easter is one of the most important dates on the church calendar. Because the Qing Ming Festival is close to the date of Easter, we can preach Easter sermons during the Qing Ming Festival."

When asked about the messages he preaches during the Qing Ming Festival, Preacher H2 answered, "I preach about the empty tomb of Jesus Christ. When people participate in tomb sweeping, they believe something is inside the tomb. They worry that whatever is inside the tomb will come out to ask for food. That is why they want to feed the deceased. However, there is no life in the tomb." Preacher H2 also noted that the celebration of the Qing Ming Festival is partly motivated by the fear of death. This fear indicates that the Chinese worry about death and the afterlife. Therefore, Preacher H2 emphasized that preaching Christ's resurrection during the Qing Ming Festival is very important because "the resurrection of Jesus Christ proves that He can overcome the problem of death." Moreover, Preacher H2 asserts that preaching about the resurrection of Jesus would help the Chinese to understand there is no reincarnation, stating, "Since we can receive eternal life from Christ, there is no need for reincarnation."

6.4 Regarding the Hungry Ghost Festival

6.4.1 The Celebration of the Hungry Ghost Festival Is Incompatible with the Christian Faith

All six interviewees consider the celebration of the Hungry Ghost Festival unacceptable. Preacher M2 disapproves of any Christian's participation in the Hungry Ghost Festival. He asserted, "If you are Christian, you would not participate in it," because he argued that the beliefs of the Hungry Ghost Festival are unbiblical. Preacher M2 explained, "The Bible never talks about opening the gates of hell or feeding hungry ghosts." Likewise, Preacher H1 insisted that no Christian should participate in the celebration of the Hungry Ghost Festival. He believes that this festival originates from religious myths, which are all superstitious. According to Preacher H1, "The superstitious worldview of the Hungry Ghost Festival is completely contrary to the Christian faith."

Preacher M1 insisted that many beliefs of the Hungry Ghost Festival are not only unbiblical but also illogical. He expounded, "According to Buddhism, hell is a prison which locks in the ghosts. People become ghosts because they were bad people who did bad things in life. Therefore, how can a prison allow bad people to come out to hurt others for a month every year? There is no such prison in this world."

Preacher M3 believes that the celebration of the Hungry Ghost Festival is, in fact, satanic. She said, "The Hungry Ghost Festival is a deception from Satan. Hungry ghosts are demonic spirits wandering around. When people worship these hungry ghosts, they are worshipping Satan and the demons, who are all fallen angels."

Preacher H3 also insisted that Christians should not participate in the Hungry Ghost Festival. He attested that many Christians are fearful during the month of the Hungry Ghost Festival and that the festival creates too much fear in people, including Christians. Preacher H3 shared, "In the community where I live, the ceremony of worshipping the hungry ghosts lasts for one week. During that particular week, the atmosphere of the community is filled with fear."

6.4.2 Preaching about Salvation from God during the Month of the Hungry Ghost Festival Is Appropriate

Although Preacher M3 discourages Chinese Christians from celebrating the Hungry Ghost Festival, she believes that the month of the Hungry Ghost Festival is a good season to preach an evangelistic message to the Chinese. At the Hungry Ghost Festival many churches invite her to preach an evangelistic message. Furthermore, Preacher M3 pointed out that the Chinese are fearful during the month of the Hungry Ghost Festival. She explained, "They believe many bad things will happen during that month, so they are fearful. Therefore, I usually preach about the peace that comes from Jesus Christ."

Preacher H1 thinks that the celebration of the Hungry Ghost Festival is contrary to Christian faith, and he believes that the message of salvation should be preached during the month of the Hungry Ghost Festival. He mentioned, "After all, the Hungry Ghost Festival is also called Pu Du 普渡, which means universal salvation for all beings. In a sense, people are longing for salvation." Similarly Preacher H2 noted that, according to the Buddhist tradition, the Hungry Ghost Festival is a festival about salvation for the ghosts in hell (*chao du di yu wang ling* 超渡地獄亡靈). According to Preacher H2, "People observe the Hungry Ghost Festival because they hope to bring salvation to the underworld. They also hope that by celebrating this festival they will also receive salvation when they pass away and become ghosts." Chinese believe that they are making merit by participating in the Hungry Ghost Festival.[35] However, it should be noted that the concept of salvation in the Hungry Ghost Festival (or Pu Du) is different from the idea of salvation in Christianity. The salvation in the Hungry Ghost Festival is mainly about helping the hungry ghosts to a better rebirth.[36]

6.4.3 Preaching the Biblical Truth about Ghosts Is Important during the Hungry Ghost Festival

Preacher H3 insisted that the concept of ghosts in Chinese tradition is completely unbiblical. He claimed, "The Chinese have too many misunderstandings about ghosts."[37] He mentioned three points when preaching about ghosts. First, ghosts are not deceased persons. Second, ghosts are not fictional creatures but real beings. Third, ghosts are nothing like Chinese mythological creatures, such as fox demons and snake demons, in the ghost stories.

Preacher H2 pointed out that the Chinese understanding of ghosts is very different from the Christian understanding of ghosts. He explained, "According to Christian faith, a ghost is not a soul of a deceased person but an evil spirit in a spiritual realm. Christians do not believe a person will turn into a ghost after death." Preacher H2 clarified the Chinese misunderstanding of ghosts by beginning with a comparison between Halloween and the Hungry Ghost Festival, followed by an explanation of the biblical view of the spiritual realm. He shared, "Some people have told me that they saw their

---

35. 董芳苑, "就臺灣民間信仰之認識論基督教的場合化," 41.

36. Peter Harvey, *An Introduction to Buddhism: Teachings, History and Practices* (Cambridge: Cambridge University Press, 1990), 195

37. There are various points of view about ghosts in the Chinese culture. One view claims that ghosts are deceased people who live in the world of the shades, a ghostly sphere. Ghosts can interpenetrate the world of the living in time and space. The Chinese believe that ghosts can live comfortably and peacefully if they are well provided for by their descendants with food offerings, clothing, housing, and, above all, money. See Jordan, *Gods, Ghosts, and Ancestors*, 32–33.

deceased family members come back home. I explained to them that these were evil spirits and not really their deceased family members."

Preacher H1 acknowledged that Chinese people's superstitious beliefs about ghosts are overwhelming. They believe the deceased can come back to this world to disturb us. Therefore, he thinks it is important to preach passages such as Jesus's parable of the rich man and Lazarus in Luke 16:19–31. Through this parable, Jesus teaches that the dead souls in the underworld can never come back to the living world. For those who believe they see dead souls, Preacher H1 insisted it is important to teach them that this belief is a deception. He avowed, "I preach about Satan, and I explain that, because Satan is a deceiver, he deceives people."

Preacher M1 also believes it is important to help people understand what ghosts are and what they do. According to Preacher M1, "These ghosts, which are the fallen angels, are against God. Their job is to confuse us, to tempt us to sin, and to destroy us." On the other hand, he believes it is crucial to inform people that believers of Christ have the power to overcome the fallen angels. He proclaimed, "Christians should not be afraid of the fallen angels. We must understand the power of Christ. We have the blood of Christ and the power of the Holy Spirit. We can even cast out demons."

6.5 Summary

This chapter reports key findings from the analysis of the interviews among six Chinese preachers regarding contextualized preaching during the Spring Festival, the Qing Ming Festival, and the Hungry Ghost Festival. The analysis reveals the importance of contextualized preaching among the Chinese churches. The analysis also highlights that some of the beliefs and practices associated with the Spring Festival, the Qing Ming Festival, and the Hungry Ghost Festival are contrary to the Christian faith. Among the three festivals, the Hungry Ghost Festival seems to be the most controversial. For effective contextualized preaching during the three festivals, some cultural contact points, suitable preaching topics, and biblical passages are also revealed in the findings.

CHAPTER 7

Theological Reflections of the Cult of the Dead and the Spiritual Realm

People who live in different cultures ask different theological questions.[1] Contextualized preaching among the Chinese involves preaching the biblical truth with an emphasis on answering relevant theological questions within the Chinese culture. This study reveals that veneration of the dead is a common practice during the Spring Festival, the Qing Ming Festival, and the Hungry Ghost Festival. Moreover, this study also demonstrates that within the Chinese culture is the common belief that ghosts communicate with the living.

Consequently, some critical questions must be answered: What is the cult of the dead? How should Christians deal with the cult of the dead? What is the biblical view of the afterlife? What are demons, and who is Satan in the Bible? Are demons in the Bible the same as ghosts in the Chinese culture? What is the origin of demons and Satan? What should Christians do about Satan and demons? The current chapter, drawing on theological resources, attempts to explicitly deal with the critical questions identified by this study. It will consider theological reflections on the cult of the dead and the spiritual realm.

---

1. Paul G. Hiebert, *Anthropological Insights for Missionaries* (Grand Rapids, MI: Baker, 2004), 210.

7.1 Theological Reflections on the Cult of the Dead

The Chinese worship their ancestors during the Spring Festival and during the Qing Ming Festival, and they make sacrifices to unrelated deceased people during the Hungry Ghost Festival. The worship rituals of these festivals signify that the cult of the dead in Chinese culture is not limited only to ancestral veneration. Distinguishing the ancestor cult from the cult of the dead, Schmidt explains, "The ancestor cult comprises beliefs and practices directed toward dead predecessors. The cult of the dead is directed toward the dead in general while the ancestor cult is a lineage cult."[2] Generally speaking, the ancestor cult is considered a subclass of the cult of the dead.[3]

In most cultures, however, the cult of the dead is family oriented.[4] People practice the cult of the dead in order to keep deceased family members active in current family life. According to Hallote, in the cult of the dead, "no one ever disappeared from the community – their roles just shifted slightly after they died."[5] Korean people, for example, offer their ancestors food and drink on New Year's Day, the lunar Autumn Festival, and the Death-day Festival. In Korean mortuary rituals, commemorated ancestors are treated almost like living elders.[6] In Japan, ancestors are venerated with daily offerings.[7] Although many African customs are changing, the African belief that the dead still live continues. People in many parts of Africa still believe it is important to obey the deceased by appeasing them and fellowshipping with them through food and drink.[8] In traditional Africa, death was a passage into a different type of existence. Where this inherited tradition remains embedded in African life people believe that departed ancestors are still interested in the living and should be treated as vital members of the family. In some tribes, ancestors

---

2. Brain B. Schmidt, *Israel's Beneficent Dead: Ancestor Cult and Necromancy in Ancient Israelite Religion and Tradition* (Tübingen: J. C. B. Mohr, 1994), 6–7.

3. Richard S. Hess, *Israelite Religions: An Archaeological and Biblical Survey* (Grand Rapids, MI: Baker Academic, 2007), 327–329.

4. Rachel S. Hallote, *Death, Burial, and Afterlife in the Biblical World: How the Israelites and Their Neighbors Treated the Dead* (Chicago: Ivan R. Dee, 2001), 54–55.

5. Hallote, 12.

6. Taek Joo Woo, "The *Marzeah* Institution and Rites for the Dead: A Comparative and Systemic Study with Special Attention to the Eight-Century Prophets' Setting" (unpublished doctoral dissertation, University of California, 1998), 91.

7. George W. Braswell, Jr., *Understanding World Religions: Hinduism, Buddhism, Taoism, Confucianism, Judaism, Islam*, rev. ed. (Nashville, TN: Broadman & Holman, 1994), 66.

8. Richard J. Gehman, *Who Are the Living-Dead?* (Nairobi: Evangel, 1999), 1.

must be included in major life events. Offerings, sacrifices, and libations are given to the ancestors.[9] People in Mexico today invite the dead to come home for a few hours to join the living in a feast on the days of the dead, such as All Saints Day and All Souls Day.[10] Thus, it is obvious that the cult of the dead is still popular today among many nations' cultures.

From a historical point of view, the cult of the dead is indeed one of the earliest forms of religion. It has been part of human history for a long time. Excavated oracles on bones and tortoise shells demonstrate ancient Chinese practices of the cult of the dead during the Shang dynasty, late second millennium BC.[11] Accordingly, various forms of the cult of the dead also appeared in many ancient civilizations.

7.1.1 The Cult of the Dead in the Ancient Near East

Hallote attests that the cult of the dead was one of the most active domestic cults in ancient Israel and its surrounding nations.[12] For the ancient Egyptians, death was the gateway to eternity.[13] Protecting all physical and spiritual components (*ba, akh,* and *ka*) of their bodies from any harm in the afterlife was essential to the ancient Egyptians.[14] To ensure enjoyment of the afterlife for the deceased, the Egyptians preserved the corpse through mummification and buried it with a set of funerary equipments. In some cases of the royal cult, a steady flow of offerings was also provided to the deceased.[15] The ancient Egyptians regularly visited the tombs and made offerings to their dead.

---

9. A. Scott Moreau, *The World of the Spirits: A Biblical Study in the African Context* (Nairobi: Evangel, 1990), 105.

10. Victor De Waal, "Death's Rituals," in *Beyond Death: Theological and Philosophical Reflections on Life After Death,* eds. Dan Cohn-Sherbok and Christopher Lewis (New York: St. Martin's, 1995), 95–103 (95). *Coco,* which received the 2018 Oscar for best animated feature, centers its story on the Day of the Dead in Mexico.

11. Anna Seidel, "Chinese Concepts of the Soul and the Afterlife," in *Death, Afterlife, and the Soul,* ed. Lawrence E. Sullivan (New York: Macmillan, 1989), 183–188 (183). See Section 3.3.3, 176–177.

12. Hallote, *Death, Burial, and Afterlife,* 54.

13. Margaret Bunson, *A Dictionary of Ancient Egypt* (Oxford: Oxford University Press, 1991), 86.

14. Leonard H. Lesko, "Death and the Afterlife in Ancient Egyptian Thought," in *Civilizations of the Ancient Near East* III, ed. Jack M. Sasson (New York: Charles Scribner's Sons, 1995), 1763–1774 (1774).

15. Ian Shaw and Paul Nicholson, *British Museum Dictionary of Ancient Egypt* (London: British Museum Press, 1995), 104.

Meals for the dead were also present on feast days for celebrations.[16] At their yearly festival of *heb nefer en inet* (the beautiful feast of the valley), the ancient Egyptians visited the tombs of their deceased relatives and sought renewal for the deceased.[17]

In Mesopotamia, the bones of the dead were well cared for because Mesopotamians believed that the deceased continued to live and to reunite with the family group. Mettinger attests that "the Akkadian term for 'corpse' was *salamtu*, from a root semantically related to the notion of completeness and integrity."[18] As Cohen explains, "Death did not end the deceased's membership in his family, nor did death absolve the living from responsibilities to the dead."[19] Mesopotamians believed that if the ghosts of the deceased had not received the proper burial rites or their share of the funerary offerings, they would return to the earth and might haunt the living.[20]

Toorn has noted that offerings to the dead were a daily ritual in ancient Babylonia. In Old Babylonian times, a bowl of fine flour and water were offered to the ancestors on a daily basis. The technical term for this daily veneration of ancestors is *kispu ginu*, which means "regular funerary offering."[21] A full meal was offered to the ancestors at the end of each month, and all living family members were expected to participate.[22] The rites were usually carried out during the last days of the waning moon. People believed that this was the last moment to appease the dead spirits. Without the moonlight, the malevolent spirits would perform their evil in the world of the living.[23] At this monthly celebration, the deceased were summoned to join in a meal

---

16. Henri Frankfort, *Ancient Egyptian Religion: An Interpretation* (New York: Harper Torchbooks, 1961), 93.

17. Richard H. Wilkinson, *The Complete Temples of Ancient Egypt* (London: Thames & Hudson, 2000), 95–96.

18. Tryggve N. D. Mettinger, *The Riddle of Resurrection: Dying and Rising Gods in the Ancient Near East* (Stockholm: Almqvist & Wiksell International, 2001), 45.

19. Mark E. Cohen, *The Cultic Calendars of the Ancient Near East* (Bethesda, MD: CDL, 1993), 454.

20. Karen Rhea Nemet-Nejat, *Daily Life in Ancient Mesopotamia* (Peabody, MA: Hendrickson, 1998), 205.

21. Karel van der Toorn, *Family Religion in Babylonia, Syria and Israel: Continuity and Change in the Forms of Religious Life* (Leiden: Brill, 1996), 49.

22. van der Toorn, 49–50.

23. Cohen, *Cultic Calendars*, 455.

with the living.[24] At the Mesopotamian city Nippur, the *ne-IZI-gar* festival (the festival for the dead) occurred approximately the eleventh and twelfth days of the fifth month (July/August). During the *ne-IZI-gar* festival, each household would prepare a ceremonial meal for the spirits of the dead. Fires and torches were set up to lead the spirits of the deceased back to the world of the living for a brief stay.[25]

Before we look at the issue of the cult of the dead in ancient Israel, we must first discuss the cult of the dead in ancient Ugarit and Canaan. Some scholars emphasize that the Ugaritic texts, particularly, contribute insights into the religious conditions in ancient Israel.[26] Although some often refer to these texts to discuss Canaanite religion,[27] in the strictest sense, Ugaritic texts are not Canaanite texts.[28] Ugarit was a small ancient nation state situated at the northeastern coast of the Mediterranean that ceased to exist early in the twelfth century BC. On the other hand, Canaan designates "a geographical area occupied over time by a variety of different states, located on the southeastern coast of the Mediterranean."[29] However, the fact that Ugarit shares some general linguistic and cultural characteristics with Canaan is undeniable.[30]

Based on his analysis of Ugaritic texts and archaeological evidence, Theodore J. Lewis concludes that an elaborate cult of the dead existed in ancient Ugarit.[31] In ancient Ugaritic society, people usually lived alongside the tombs of their ancestors and hoped to maintain permanent communication

---

24. Mettinger, *Riddle of Resurrection*, 45.

25. Cohen, *Cultic Calendars*, 456–457.

26. Mark S. Smith, "Recent Study of Israelite Religion in Light of the Ugaritic Texts," in *Ugarit at Seventy-Five*, ed. K. Lawson Younger Jr. (Winona Lake, IN: Eisenbrauns, 2007), 1–25 (1).

27. G. del Olmo Lete, *Canaanite Religion: According to the Liturgical Texts of Ugarit* (Winona Lake, IN: Eisenbrauns, 2004), 3–7.

28. Mark S. Smith, "Myth and Mythmaking in Canaan and Ancient Israel," in *Civilizations of the Ancient Near East*, III, ed. Jack M. Sasson (New York: Charles Scribner's Sons, 1995), 2031–2041 (2031).

29. Peter C. Craigie, "Ugarit, Canaan, and Israel," *TynBul* 34 (1983): 145–167 (145–146).

30. Craigie, 153.

31. Theodore J. Lewis, *Cults of the Dead in Ancient Israel and Ugarit* (Atlanta: Scholars, 1989), 97.

with the dead. Family tombs were built beneath their homes.[32] Ancestor veneration was a major concern in the household, and the responsibility usually fell on the oldest son to worship the ancestors.[33] According to Lewis, the ritual of ancestor worship took place at night and had a twofold function. The first function was to present the dead ancestors with essential services such as libations and offerings. The second function was to obtain favours or blessings from the dead for those living in the present life.[34]

Texts and archaeological remains also demonstrate that ancestor worship was an important aspect of Canaanite religion.[35] Literary evidence indicates that the practices of venerating, feeding, appeasing, and honoring the deceased were common in Canaan.[36] Hallote believes that some form of the Canaanite cult of the dead survived from the Bronze Age Canaanite period into the Israelite period and beyond.[37] Bloch-Smith is one of several scholars who insists that the cult of the dead existed throughout ancient Israel, even though the official religion of Israel opposed this popular pagan practice. Her conclusion is based on evidence from archaeological findings. Bloch-Smith believes that vessels found in ancient Israelite burial sites, including bowls, lamps, jars, chalices, cooking pots, and wine decanters, were intended for the dead.[38] However, some question the validity of this interpretation of the archaeological evidence. Philip Johnston, for example, emphasizes that neither archaeological nor textual evidence concerning ancient Judahite burials suggests continued sustenance of the dead in ancient Israel.[39] Similarly, Brian B. Schmidt argues that ancient Israelite observation of ancestor veneration

---

32. Paolo Xella, "Death and the Afterlife in Canaanite and Hebrew Thought," in *Civilizations of the Ancient Near East* III, ed. Jack M. Sasson (New York: Charles Scribner's Sons, 1995), 2059–2070 (2061).

33. Marvin H. Pope, "The Cult of the Dead at Ugarit," in *Ugarit in Retrospect*, ed. Gordon Douglas Young (Winona Lake, IN: Eisenbrauns, 1981), 159–179 (159).

34. Lewis, *Cults of the Dead*, 95.

35. Beth Alpert Nakhai, "Canaanite Religion," in *Near Eastern Archaeology: A Reader*, ed. Suzanne Richard (Winona Lake, IN: Eisenbrauns, 2003), 343–348 (347).

36. Alan F. Segal, *Life after Death: A History of the Afterlife in the Religions of the West* (New York: Doubleday, 2004), 115.

37. Hallote, *Death, Burial, and Afterlife*, 54–55.

38. Elizabeth Bloch-Smith, *Judahite Burial Practices and Beliefs about the Dead* (Sheffield: JSOT, 1992), 148–151.

39. Philip S. Johnston, "The Underworld and the Dead in the Old Testament," *TynBul* 45 (1994): 415–419 (417).

cannot be deduced from the existing archaeological evidence, thus he concludes that the ancestor cult was not practised in early Israel.[40]

Regarding the archaeological evidence, Hess asserts, "Given the diversity of evidence in religious expression, it is not possible to conclude that there was an absolute distinction in this practice and that no Israelites would have been involved in these food and drink rituals associated with the dead."[41] Hess further indicates that, based on the fact that some tombs did not have the same archaeological evidence, this practice of feeding the dead was a family and personal activity, not a state-enforced one.[42] Therefore, it is possible to conclude that some forms of the cult of the dead did exist in ancient Israel, though not on a large scale. Nevertheless, the evidence for the popularity of this cult remains to be established.[43]

7.1.2 The Cult of the Dead in the Ancient Greco-Roman World

Klauck attests that veneration of the dead was popular in the ancient Greco-Roman world. Among the Greeks, feeding the dead took place on the third, the seventh or ninth, and the thirtieth day after the day of burial.[44] Referring to the writings of Homer, Hesiod, Plato, and Plutarch, as well as Greek tragedy and comedy, Peter G. Bolt concludes that ancient Greco-Romans believed that a deceased person could turn into a ghost or demon.[45] As Kramer explains, ancient Greeks believed in the immortality of the soul. A deceased person, whose soul is free from worldly stains, can forever associate with the gods. However, if a deceased person's soul was polluted and impure, it would wander among tombs and graves.[46] Visiting the tombs of deceased relatives

---

40. Schmidt, *Israel's Beneficent Dead*, 274–276.
41. Hess, *Israelite Religions*, 329.
42. Hess, 329.
43. Hess, 329.
44. Hans-Josef Klauck, *The Religious Context of Early Christianity: A Guide to Graeco-Roman Religions*, trans. Brian McNeil (Edinburgh: T&T Clark), 76–77.
45. Peter G. Bolt, "Jesus, the Daimons and the Dead," in *The Unseen World: Christian Reflections on Angels, Demons and the Heavenly Realm*, ed. Anthony N. S. Lane (Grand Rapids, MI: Paternoster and Baker, 1996), 75–102 (75–79).
46. Kenneth Kramer, *The Sacred Art of Dying: How World Religions Understand Death* (New York: Paulist, 1988), 117. Nilsson has noted that during the Mycenaean age of the ancient Greeks, "weapons and jewels, food and fire-pan were placed in the grave of the dead man, so that he might continue life in the same way as in the past." See Martin Nilsson, *A History of*

and offering a tomb feast to them was very important in the ancient Greek world. In the celebrations of the cult of the dead, food, drinks, gifts, and items of ritual significance were brought to the tomb. The ancient Greeks also decorated the tomb with a sash or ribbon.[47]

Recent studies suggest that the cult of the dead in Greek culture traces back to the era of Mycenaean Greece.[48] Mycenae flourished from 1700–1200 BC, during the Middle and Late Bronze Age.[49] Chrysanthi Gallou, in his recent study of cultic action in Mycenaean Greece, concludes that these ancient Greeks established official sites for the cult of the dead and performed sacral acts in order to invoke the presence of the ancestral spirits among the living. Through sacred ritual offerings, the Mycenaeans tried to communicate with the dead and to gain the benevolence of the ancestors in order to ensure the well-being of the living community.[50]

Similarly, ancient Romans believed that the deceased continued to exist as disembodied spirits and needed food and clothes. Ancient Roman tombs usually have holes or pipes through which food and drink could be poured into the grave. Food was offered on significant occasions, such as the birth and death dates of the deceased.[51] As for the Romans, sacrifices for the dead were offered on the day of burial, the ninth day after the burial, and each year on the birthday of the deceased.[52] The imperial cult of ancient Rome was also closely related with the cult of the dead. During the late Roman Republic, posthumous deification was the normal practice for Roman rulers. As Cole explains, "The conceptually cognate idea of a posthumous status-transition to immortality and divinity has roots in the Roman cult of the dead and ideas

---

Greek Religion, trans. F. J. Fielden (Oxford: Clarendon, 1949), 101. Nilsson believes that the Greek hero cult arose from the cult of the dead. See Nilsson, 103.

47. Garland provides a detailed description of the cult of the dead among the Athenians of the classical Greek period. See Robert Garland, *The Greek Way of Death* (Ithaca, NY: Cornell University Press, 1985), 104–120.

48. Chrysanthi Gallou, *The Mycenaean Cult of the Dead* (Oxford: Archaeopress, 2005), 132.

49. Eric H. Cline, "Mycenae," in *The Oxford Encyclopedia of Ancient Greece and Rome*, vol. V, ed. Michael Gagarin (Oxford: Oxford University Press, 2010), 22–23 (22).

50. Gallou, *Mycenaean Cult*, 132.

51. Chuck Lowe, *Honouring God and Family: A Christian Response to Idol Food in Chinese Popular Religion* (Bangalore: Theological Book Trust, 2001), 91.

52. Klauck, *Religious Context*, 76–77.

about the survival of souls."⁵³ According to Cole, Cicero at one point even proposed to deify his deceased daughter Tullia, who died in 45 BC.⁵⁴

In summary, the cult of the dead existed in various forms in the Old Testament and New Testament worlds. As Nida points out, widespread ancestor cult worship was active during the early church era. The evidence includes many tomb inscriptions "requesting the prayers of the dead for the living."⁵⁵ Nida believes this cult eventually led to "saint worship."⁵⁶ Today, the cult of the dead remains a challenge to Christianity in many cultures.⁵⁷ In the history of Christian missions, the Chinese rites controversy is perhaps the most well-known conflict concerning the cult of the dead.

7.1.3 Christianity and Chinese Ancestor Worship

Siu Fai Mak believes that the initial encounter between Christianity and the practice of Chinese ancestor veneration should be traced back to the Nestorian missionary movement in China during the Tang dynasty (AD 618–907).⁵⁸ Similarly, Yamamoto Sumiko also refers to Nestorianism during the Tang dynasty as the starting point of Christianity's initial encounter with ancestor worship in China.⁵⁹ However, as Mak points out, no records indicate that Nestorian missionaries had raised any objections against the practice of Chinese ancestor worship.⁶⁰ According to Sumiko, "It seems that Nestorianism was willing to compromise with Chinese culture, including the beliefs and practices of ancestor worship."⁶¹ Nestorian Christianity remained in China for approximately two and a half centuries and eventually

---

53. Spencer Cole, *Cicero and the Rise of Deification at Rome* (Cambridge: Cambridge University Press, 2013), 197. Although in Caesar's case, he was declared a god while still alive.

54. Cole, 1.

55. Eugene A. Nida, *Message and Mission: The Communication of the Christian Faith*, rev. ed. (Pasadena, CA: William Carey Library, 1990), 132.

56. Nida, 132.

57. Henry Newton Smith, "Chinese Ancestor Practice and Christianity: Toward a Viable Contextualization of Christian Ethics in a Hong Kong Setting," (unpublished doctoral dissertation, Southwestern Baptist Theological Seminary, 1987), 1.

58. 麥兆輝, (*Revering God and Respecting Ancestors*), 90.

59. Yamamato Sumiko, *History of Protestantism in China* (Tokyo: Institute of Eastern Culture, 2000), 369.

60. 麥兆輝, (*Revering God and Respecting Ancestors*), 104.

61. Sumiko, *History of Protestantism*, 373.

ceased to exist there.⁶² The Chinese rites controversy arose during the later missionary movements.

Catholic missionaries and the Chinese rites controversy

Francis Xavier was the first Jesuit missionary who attempted to enter China to convert the Chinese to Christianity in 1552. However, he died of fever that same year in Shangchuang, an island ten kilometers off the mainland.⁶³ Xavier never realized his mission goals for China, but he did turn Jesuit mission attention to the "Middle Kingdom." Moreover, his missionary policy of accommodation – requiring missionaries to become an integral part of a particular civilization – greatly influenced later missionaries, including Matteo Ricci, or Li Ma Dou (利瑪竇) as the Chinese called him.⁶⁴

Ricci arrived in Macao on 8 August 1582. His first assignment was to prepare a short descriptive account of China's people, customs, institutions, and government. In the booklet of his descriptive account, Ricci advocated that the Chinese civilization must be respected and admired.⁶⁵ At the end of 1594, Ricci had translated the *Four Books of Confucianism* into Latin with commentaries.⁶⁶ Studying the classics of Confucianism helped Ricci integrate with Chinese society and earned him the respect of Confucian literati.⁶⁷ Under Ricci, many Confucians converted to the Catholic faith, including Xu Guang Qi (徐光啟), Li Zhi Zao (李之藻), and Yang Ting Yun (楊廷筠). These three Confucian Catholic converts were known as the pillars of the Catholic Church in China.⁶⁸ Xu Guang Qi later became one of the grand secretaries of the Grand Secretariat. He also helped arrange Ricci's trip to Peking to meet Emperor Wan Li (萬歷皇帝) of the Ming dynasty in 1601.⁶⁹ After moving

---

62. Kenneth Scott Latourette, *A History of Christian Missions in China* (Taipei: Cheng-Wen, 1975), 57.

63. Ambrose Ih-Ren Mong, "The Legacy of Matteo Ricci and His Companions," *Missiology* 43 (2015): 385–397 (386).

64. John D. Young, *East-West Synthesis: Matteo Ricci and Confucianism* (Hong Kong: University of Hong Kong, 1980), 7–8.

65. Young, 14.

66. Mong, "Legacy of Matteo Ricci," 390.

67. Mong, 390.

68. Khiok-Khng Yeo, "Paul's Theological Ethic and the Chinese Morality of Ren Ren," in *Cross-Cultural Paul: Journeys to Others, Journeys to Ourselves*, eds. Charles H. Cosgrove, Herold Weiss, and Khiok-Khng Yeo (Grand Rapids, MI: Eerdmans, 2005), 104–140 (110).

69. Young, *East-West Synthesis*, 19.

to Peking, Ricci never left the Forbidden City for the rest of his life. With an incredible reputation among the Chinese, Ricci died in 1610.[70]

As Minamiki points out, Ricci's attitude and policy on the veneration of Confucius and ancestors later induced the Chinese rites controversy.[71] For Ricci, the key factor in interpreting the veneration rites of Confucius and ancestors was the intention of the participants. He gave permission to the Chinese converts to venerate ancestors as long as they sought merely to honor them.[72] Following Ricci's policy, some Jesuit missionaries believed that veneration of Confucius and ancestors was not an act of worship but an act of honoring and remembering.[73] However, in some respects, Ricci and his followers had underestimated the religious dimensions of the ancestral rites.[74] Ricci's approach to the rites was also inconsistent. For example, Ricci believed that food offerings were not intended to supply the needs of the dead but that offerings of clothing were intended to supply the needs of the dead.[75]

On the other hand, some Jesuit fathers and most Dominicans and Franciscans held that ancestral veneration was an act of idolatry and that allowing ancestral veneration was the same as condoning pagan elements in Christianity.[76] In 1643, Friar Morales, a Dominican, expressed his criticism of the Chinese rites as superstitious to Pope Innocent X.[77] In 1693, Charles Maigrot, Vicar Apostolic of Fukien and member of the Paris Foreign Mission Society, published a booklet against ancestral veneration.[78] In 1740, Pope Clement XI issued a decree prohibiting the rites.[79] These actions eventually led to the imperial expulsion of Catholic missionaries from China. Moreover, an imperial edict to ban Christianity was issued.[80]

---

70. Young, 21.
71. George Minamiki, *The Chinese Rites Controversy from Its Beginning to Modern Times* (Chicago: Loyola University Press, 1985), 15.
72. Lowe, *Honouring God and Family*, 40–41.
73. Khiok-Khng Yeo, "Paul's Theological Ethic," 111.
74. Lowe, *Honouring God and Family*, 40.
75. Lowe, 41.
76. Khiok-Khng Yeo, "Paul's Theological Ethic," 111–112.
77. Lowe, *Honouring God and Family*, 38.
78. Khiok-Khng Yeo, "Paul's Theological Ethic," 112.
79. Khiok-Khng Yeo, 112.
80. Lung-Kwong Lo, "The Nature of the Issue of Ancestral Worship among Chinese Christians," *StudWorldChr* 9 (2003), 30–42 (31). In 1939, Pope Pius XII reversed his position on the rites controversy, authorizing Christians to observe ancestral veneration.

Protestantism and Chinese ancestor worship

The controversy of ancestor worship erupted again when the Protestant missionary movement entered China in the nineteenth century.[81] The issue of ancestral veneration was discussed at three Protestant missionary conferences held in Shanghai. The first conference occurred in 1877. Most participants at this conference were against ancestral veneration. Matthew Yates, for example, presented an article entitled "Ancestral Worship" and argued that it "is the principal religion of the Chinese."[82] To Yates, ancestral worship was the direct worship of the dead. He also believed that the Chinese worship their ancestors "to avert the calamities which the spirits of the departed are supposed to be able to inflict upon the living, as a punishment for inattention to their necessities."[83] A proposal to develop Christian rites in order to replace ancestral worship was suggested.

In the General Conference of Protestant Missionaries of China in 1890, the issue of ancestral worship was debated again.[84] During the conference, William Martin's essay, "The Worship of Ancestors – A Plea for Toleration," was presented. Martin suggested that missionaries refrain from any interference with the Chinese ancestor worship.[85] Henry Blodget, on the other hand, considered the rites irremediably cultic.[86] Blodget insisted that there must be "in Christians a complete separation from ancestral worship in all its forms."[87] The issue of ancestral worship aroused heated debates among the conference participants.[88] At the end of the conference, the majority of the participants rejected Martin's suggestion of toleration.[89] Hudson Taylor, one of the key

---

81. Lowe, *Honouring God and Family*, 47. As Sumiko points out, "The history of Protestantism in China began with the arrival of Robert Morrison in 1807." See Sumiko, *History of Protestantism*, 13.

82. Matthew Yates, "Ancestral Worship," in *Records of the General Conference of the Protestant Missionaries of China Held at Shanghai, May 10–24, 1877* (Taipei: Cheng Wen, 1973), 367–387 (368).

83. Yates, 370.

84. Lo, "Nature of the Issue," 32.

85. William Martin, "The Worship of Ancestors – A Plea for Toleration," in *Records of the General Conference of the Protestant Missionaries of China Held at Shanghai, May 7–20, 1890* (Shanghai: American Presbyterian Mission Press, 1890), 619–631 (631).

86. Lowe, *Honouring God and Family*, 50.

87. Henry Blodget, "The Attitude of Christianity toward Ancestral Worship," in *Records of the General Conference*, 631–654 (654).

88. 麥兆輝, (*Revering God and Respecting Ancestors*), 104.

89. 麥兆輝, (*Revering God and Respecting Ancestors*), 104.

leaders among the missionaries, concluded that Chinese ancestral veneration was unacceptable in the church. He said, "Ancestral worship is idolatry from beginning to end, the whole of it and everything connected with it."[90]

During the China Centenary Missionary Conference in 1907, the subject of ancestor worship surfaced again for discussion. James Jackson, representing a committee of thirteen, presented a paper entitled "Ancestral Worship" during the conference. This paper considered the problem of ancestor worship as "one of the greatest obstacles to the progress of Christianity" in China.[91] As Jackson explained, the paper was "endeavoring to find some relief for the present distress, in removing all unnecessary stumbling-blocks, while at the same time securing the purity of the Church."[92]

Jackson indicated that ancestor worship was incompatible with Christian faith. He pointed out, "Whether ancestral worship is in all forms and under all circumstances idolatrous or not, it is undoubtedly a rival to the worship of the one supreme God."[93] On the other hand, Jackson asserted that affection and filial piety are both important motives in Chinese ancestor worship. Even though Jackson believed that the fear of ghosts was also an important element in ancestor worship, he believed the root of ancestor worship was filial piety and affection toward the deceased family members.[94] Furthermore, Jackson advocated a more sympathetic and constructive approach toward Chinese ancestor worship. He believed that the way to solve the problem of ancestor worship was by "substituting something better."[95] During the Chinese indigenous church movement from 1919 to 1927, Chinese Protestant leaders explored Christian adaptation to Chinese social customs and tried to Christianize traditional Chinese festivals, including the Qing Ming Festival.[96]

---

90. "Discussion: Ancestral Worship," in *Records of the General Conference*, 699–702 (701).

91. James Jackson, "Ancestral Worship," in *China Centenary Missionary Conference, Held at Shanghai, April 25 to May 8, 1907* (Shanghai: Centenary Conference Committee, 1907), 215–246 (215–216).

92. Jackson, 216.

93. Jackson, 232.

94. Jackson, 219–220.

95. Jackson, 239.

96. Jonathan Tien-En Chao, "The Chinese Indigenous Church Movement, 1917–1927: A Protestant Response to the Anti-Christian Movements in Modern China" (unpublished doctoral dissertation, University of Pennsylvania, 1986), 263–266.

The dispute over the issue of ancestor worship continues today. In particular the discussion of ancestor worship has attracted renewed interest in the last few decades.[97] Many contemporary Chinese Christian leaders have adopted the substitution approach suggested by James Jackson, whereby traditional ancestor worship was replaced by something more acceptable in Christianity. Stephen Liaw, for instance, encourages Chinese Christians to celebrate the Qing Ming Festival with a Christian memorial service at their ancestors' graves as a substitute for offering sacrifices to the ancestors.[98]

Some believe that ancestor worship is permissible for Chinese Christians. Lung-Kwong Lo insists viewing the problem of ancestral worship from the perspective of the culture instead of religion.[99] He further advocates allowing Chinese Christians to continue their practice of ancestral worship "in order to avoid their falling off from Christianity."[100] In 1985, Henry Smith conducted a survey with 163 Hong Kong residents concerning the practices of ancestor veneration in contemporary Hong Kong. Smith concludes that ancestor worship is a social custom, not a religious ritual. He believes that the Hong Kong Chinese, in their practice of ancestor veneration, are motivated mainly by filial concern or social pressure.[101] He further suggests that "the churches need not feel the compulsion to oppose all ancestor-related practices."[102] However, both Lo and Smith seem to neglect the religious elements of ancestor worship. Ka Lun Leung, on the other hand, reminds us that Chinese ancestor worship contains both religious and non-religious functions. He emphasizes that neither religious nor non-religious functions should be ignored when dealing with the issue of ancestor worship.[103]

---

97. 廖元威,"從基督教倫理和禮儀看祭祖問題" (Christian Ethics and Etiquette View of Ancestral Worship), 於歷史文化與詮釋學·中原大學宗教學術研討會論文集(二) (*History, Culture and Hermeneutics: The Religion Symposium of Chung Yuan Christian University*), 林治平編 (臺北 [Taipei]: 宇宙光, 2001), 191–211 (192–193).

98. Stephen Liaw, "Ancestor Worship in Taiwan and Evangelism of the Chinese," in *Christian Alternatives to Ancestor Practices*, ed. Bong Rin Ro (Taichung: Asia Theological Association, 1985), 181–193 (193).

99. Lo, "Nature of the Issue," 39.

100. Lo, 38.

101. Henry N. Smith, "Ancestor Practices in Contemporary Hong Kong: Religious Ritual or Social Custom?," *AJT* 3 (1989): 31–45 (43).

102. Smith, 44.

103. 邢福增與梁家麟, 中國祭祖問題 (*Chinese Ancestor Worship*) (香港 [Hong Kong]: 建道神學院, 1997), 198.

Concerning the problem of ancestor worship, Mak's suggestion is certainly helpful. He believes identifying the different elements of ancestor worship is important. Moreover, he suggests that the obviously superstitious and religious elements must be abolished.[104] The field research of this study did find religious elements, such as burning paper effigies and offering food, in the practice of ancestral veneration. In fact, many of these religious elements were present in both the Qing Ming Festival and the Hungry Ghost Festival. As John Marcos Yeh points out, the rituals of Chinese ancestor worship are not much different from the rituals of hungry ghost worship.[105] The religious elements in these two festivals, such as burning paper effigies and offering food to the dead, reflect the Chinese traditional worldview of the afterlife. These elements are related to the cult of the dead. Thus Chung-Man Ng is right when he suggests abandoning the practices of paper effigies and offering food to the dead.[106]

This brief review of the history of the Chinese rites controversy from the seventeenth century until the present day reveals that ancestral worship remains one of the most important practical issues in the Chinese church.[107] According to the results of the interviews conducted for this study, all six interviewees do not condone the practice of ancestor worship. They also point out that the worldview behind the practice of ancestor worship, which is the same worldview behind the cult of the dead, is incorrect. Therefore, a discussion of the biblical worldview concerning the afterlife is essential in the Chinese church. For contextualized preaching to be effective among the Chinese, who in many ways are still greatly influenced by the cult of the dead, the issue of the afterlife must be considered within a Christian theological framework.

---

104. 麥兆輝, *(Revering God and Respecting Ancestors)*, 224–230.
105. 葉明翰, 祭祖與輪迴 *(Worship of Ancestors and Reincarnation)* (臺北 [Taipei]: 大光傳播, 1999), 196.
106. 吳宗文, "祭祖儀節及用品之處置等問題" (Issues of Ancestral Rituals and Ceremonial Products), 基督教週報 *(Christian Weekly)* 2230 (2007): 4.
107. 邢福增與梁家麟, *(Chinese Ancestor Worship)*, 3–5.

7.1.4 Theological Reflections on the Issue of the Afterlife

The afterlife is regarded by some as "the greatest challenge to all religious and philosophical viewpoints."[108] N. T. Wright attests, "From Plato to Hegel and beyond, some of the greatest philosophers declared that what you think about death, and life beyond it, is the key to thinking seriously about everything else."[109] Nevertheless, beliefs about death and what lies beyond are extraordinarily varied. The cyclic notion of birth, death, and rebirth is the key concept in Hinduism and Buddhism,[110] while the Western modern secular perspective views death as the "total extinction of life."[111] However, various beliefs about reincarnation, the cult of the dead, and the idea that the deceased are absorbed into the natural world are becoming popular in the Western world today.[112] Those who claim to be agnostic say that knowing anything about the afterlife is impossible.[113]

The afterlife is also one of the most important theological issues of Christianity. Indeed, belief in the afterlife is indispensable in Christianity.[114] However, differing views on the afterlife are evident even among Christians. D. A. Carson indicates that "the manner in which Christians have thought about life after death, or about the world to come, has varied considerably from century to century and from place to place."[115] Concerning the issue of life beyond death, agreement still eludes the church today.[116]

---

108. Bobby Bose, *Reincarnation, Oblivion, or Heaven: A Christian Exploration* (Carlisle: Langham, 2016), 48.

109. N. T. Wright, *Surprised by Hope: Rethinking Heaven, the Resurrection, and the Mission of the Church* (New York: HarperCollins, 2008), 6.

110. Bose, *Reincarnation*, 11.

111. Bose, 45.

112. Wright, *Surprised by Hope*, 9–12.

113. Marcus Borg, "Is Christianity about Heaven?," *WW* 31 (2011): 5–12 (9).

114. Terence Penelhum, "Christianity," in *Life after Death in World Religions*, ed. Harold Coward (Maryknoll, NY: Orbis, 1997), 31–47 (41).

115. D. A. Carson, "Preface," in *Coming Home: Essays on the New Heaven and New Earth*, eds. D. A. Carson and Jeff Robinson Sr. (Wheaton, IL: Crossway, 2017), 9–11 (9).

116. N. T. Wright, "Heaven Is Not Our Home: The Bodily Resurrection Is the Good News of the Gospel – and Thus Our Social and Political Mandate," *Christianity Today* 52 (2008): 36–39 (36).

The Old Testament view of the afterlife

Both Old and New Testaments teach about the afterlife. Overall, as Robin L. Routledge explains, "Death in the Old Testament is viewed as inevitable and natural."[117] In the Old Testament, the most frequently used Hebrew word for the underworld is שְׁאוֹל (*sheol* in most English versions). *Sheol* occurs sixty-six times[118] and always refers to the place where the soul or spirit of a deceased person goes.[119] William B. Nelson Jr. asserts, "Through much of the Old Testament period, it was believed that all went one place, whether human or animal (Ps. 49:12, 14, 20), whether righteous or wicked (Ecc. 9:2–3)."[120] Moreover, "Sheol is thought to open its mouth wide but never to be satisfied (Isa. 5:14; Hab. 2:5)."[121]

The etymology of the term *sheol* is vague.[122] The description of *sheol* is also not clearly stated in the Old Testament.[123] The Old Testament seems to envision a universe that includes heaven, earth, and *sheol*. *Sheol* (LXX "Hades") is where everyone goes after life.[124] As Ralph L. Smith explains, "It is clear from the way the word is used in the Old Testament that *sheol* was located in the depths of the earth."[125] He indicates that the terms "go down" or "brought down" are applied to the term *sheol* twenty times in the Old Testament.[126] *Sheol* was "below the surface of the earth (Ezek. 31:15, 17; Ps. 86:13), a place of dust (Job 17:16), darkness (Job 10:21), silence (Ps. 94:17), and forgetfulness

---

117. Robin L. Routledge, "Death and Afterlife in the Old Testament," *Journal of European Baptist Studies* 9 (2008): 22–39 (22).

118. Philip S. Johnston, *Shades of Sheol: Death and Afterlife in the Old Testament* (Downers Grove, IL: InterVarsity Press, 2002), 70.

119. Robert A. Morey, *Death and the Afterlife* (Minneapolis: Bethany House, 1984), 72.

120. William B. Nelson Jr., "Sheol: Old Testament," in *Baker Theological Dictionary of the Bible*, ed. Walter A. Elwell (Grand Rapids, MI: Baker, 2000), 735.

121. Philip S. Johnston, "Afterlife," in *Dictionary of the Old Testament: Prophets*, ed. J. Gordon (Downers Grove, IL: InterVarsity Press, 2012), 1–5 (1).

122. Bruce Milne, *The Message of Heaven and Hell: Grace and Destiny* (Leicester: InterVarsity Press, 2002), 27.

123. Morey, *Death and the Afterlife*, 77.

124. Jaime Clark-Soles, "The Afterlife: Considering Heaven and Hell," *Word & World* 31 (2011): 65–74 (65).

125. Ralph L. Smith, *Old Testament Theology: Its History, Method, and Message* (Nashville, TN: Broadman & Holman, 1993), 382.

126. Ralph L. Smith, "Hell," in *HolBD*, ed. Trent C. Butler (Nashville, TN: Holman Bible, 1991), 631–632 (632).

(Ps. 88:12)."[127] In summary, the ancient Israelites perceived *sheol* as a new dimension of reality with its own kind of insubstantial existence. The deceased are cut off from the living once they enter *sheol*.[128] However, *sheol* is never beyond divine sovereignty. God can reach to *sheol* to execute his judgment.[129]

Some scholars suggest that there are three phases of the ancient Israelite belief about the afterlife.[130] In the first phase, the ancient Israelites believed that little or no hope existed beyond death. In the second phase, the ancient Israelites believed that there was hope for life or joy after death. In the third phase, the ancient Israelites affirmed the idea of bodily resurrection after "life after death."[131] Philip S. Johnston, nevertheless, asserts that the afterlife is never a major theme in the Old Testament. He concludes, "Israelite faith concerned a living relationship with Yahweh in the present, not speculation about the future."[132] Peter Toon also attests that the Old Testament "contains little clear and explicit teaching about heaven and hell in terms of human destiny."[133]

The New Testament view of the afterlife

God's revelation of what happens beyond death is more fully revealed in the New Testament.[134] Trent C. Butler asserts, "The New Testament represents a wide advance over the Old Testament's hints, clues, and implications about the afterlife."[135] Christianity's principal basis for faith concerning the afterlife

---

127. D. K. Innes, "Sheol," in *The Illustrated Bible Dictionary* (Leicester: Inter-Varsity Press, 1980), 1435–1436 (1436).

128. Morey, *Death and the Afterlife*, 79. See also Eccl 9:10.

129. David Powys, *"Hell": A Hard Look at a Hard Question: The Fate of the Unrighteous in New Testament Thought* (Carlisle: Paternoster, 1997), 84. See also Amos 9:2.

130. N. T. Wright is obviously willing to accept this theory of three phases of afterlife belief in ancient Israel. See N. T. Wright, *The Resurrection of the Son of God* (London: SPCK, 2003), 86.

131. Wright, 86.

132. Johnston, *Shades of Sheol*, 70.

133. Peter Toon, *Heaven and Hell: A Biblical and Theological Overview* (Nashville, TN: Thomas Nelson, 1986), III.

134. Bose, *Reincarnation*, 218.

135. Trent C. Butler, *Luke*, Holman New Testament Commentary, ed. Max Anders (Nashville, TN: Holman Reference, 2000), 273.

is found in the New Testament.[136] The unique message of hope after death is revealed to God's people as Jesus promises eternal life for his followers.[137]

Christ's resurrection is the key to the New Testament's teaching about the afterlife. His resurrection is considered "the cornerstone of the entire New Testament."[138] Jesus's resurrection is indeed the basis for the Christian's hope in the face of death.[139] As Paul Badham notes, "Christianity came into being as a religion of salvation, offering to mankind the hope of an eternal destiny beyond the grave."[140] C. F. Evans argues, "To a greater extent than it is anything else, Christianity – at least the Christianity of the New Testament – is a religion of resurrection."[141] The messages recorded in the gospels are clear: Salvation for human beings has been accomplished by the cross, and the resurrection of Jesus defeated death ultimately.[142]

Therefore, Wright stresses that the starting point for all Christian thinking about the topic of the afterlife "must be Jesus' own resurrection."[143] Indeed, Christ's resurrection foreshadows the coming resurrection of the dead.[144] For Christian believers, the resurrection of Jesus Christ is the basis for their hope in their own forthcoming resurrection and future immortality.[145] The apostle Paul indicates that the foundation of the belief in the resurrection of the believers is the resurrection of Jesus Christ (1 Cor 15:1–11).[146] Moreover,

---

136. Harold L. Creager, "The Biblical View of Life after Death," *LQ* 17 (1965): 111–121 (116).

137. Bose, *Reincarnation*, 241.

138. George Eldon Ladd, *I Believe in the Resurrection of Jesus* (London: Hodder & Stoughton, 1975), 43.

139. Millard J. Erickson, *Christian Theology*, 2nd ed. (Grand Rapids, MI: Baker, 2001), 1200.

140. Paul Badham, "The Christian Hope Today," in *Death and Immortality in the Religions of the World*, eds. Paul Badham and Linda Badham (New York: Paragon, 1987), 37–50 (37).

141. Christopher Francis Evans, *Resurrection and the New Testament* (London: SCM, 1970), 1.

142. Donald A. Hagner, "Gospel, Kingdom, and Resurrection in the Synoptic Gospels," in *Life in the Face of Death: The Resurrection Message of the New Testament*, ed. Richard N. Longenecker (Grand Rapids, MI: Eerdmans, 1998), 99–121 (120).

143. Wright, *Surprised by Hope*, 28.

144. Hagner, "Gospel, Kingdom, and Resurrection," 99.

145. Murray J. Harris, "Resurrection and Immortality in the Pauline Corpus," in *Life in the Face of Death: The Resurrection Message of the New Testament*, ed. Richard N. Longenecker (Grand Rapids, MI: Eerdmans, 1998), 147–170 (147).

146. Harris says that 1 Corinthians 15 is the classic passage that deals with the theme of resurrection. See Murray J. Harris, *Raised Immortal: Resurrection and Immortality in the New Testament* (Grand Rapids, MI: Eerdmans, 1985), 114.

Paul explains that in the coming resurrection, all believers shall rise with a "heavenly body" in the likeness of the risen Christ (1 Cor 15:44–49).[147] The resurrected body will be imperishable, glorious, powerful, and free of sinful propensities.[148] In some theological writings, this stage in which believers receive a resurrected body is also called *glorification*.[149] Glorification refers to the final step in the application of Christ's work of redemption to Christian believers, in which believers' bodies "are entirely set free from the effects of the fall and brought to the state of perfection for which God created them."[150]

The final bodily resurrection of believers will "take place within the context of God's victorious transformation of the whole cosmos."[151] The bodily resurrection will happen on the new earth, when both heaven and earth are transformed into a new creation.[152] In this last stage, the old heaven and the old earth will be replaced by the new heaven and the new earth.[153] The final destiny of the Christian believers is to serve God eternally in a newly created cosmos, not some dematerialized spiritual existence.[154]

In light of this eschatological understanding, contemporary evangelicals such as N. T. Wright and J. Richard Middleton attempt to redirect believers today to what New Testament Christians believed about the final destination of believers. Wright argues, "The ultimate destination is not going to heaven when you die but being bodily raised into the transformed, glorious likeness of Jesus Christ."[155] Similarly, Middleton asserts that the term "heaven" is never used in Scripture as the eternal destiny of believers.[156] Wright seems more willing to use the term "heaven" (or "paradise") to designate the intermediate state in which departed Christians "are held firmly within the conscious love

---

147. Xavier Leon-Dufour, *Life and Death in The New Testament: The Teachings of Jesus and Paul*, trans. Terrence Prendergast (San Francisco: Harper & Row, 1986), 203.

148. Harris, *Raised Immortal*, 124.

149. Wayne Grudem, *Systematic Theology: An Introduction to Biblical Doctrine* (Leicester: Inter-Varsity Press, 1994), 828.

150. Grudem, 828.

151. Wright, *Surprised by Hope*, 101.

152. Wright, 159.

153. Wright, 105.

154. Derek Tidball, *The Voices of the New Testament: A Conversational Approach to the Message of Good News* (Leicester: Inter-Varsity Press, 2016), 249–250.

155. Wright, *Surprised by Hope*, 168.

156. J. Richard Middleton, *A New Heaven and a New Earth: Reclaiming Biblical Eschatology* (Grand Rapids, MI: Baker Academic, 2014), 237.

of God and the conscious presence of Jesus Christ" while they await the day of bodily resurrection.[157] According to Wright, "Resurrection isn't life after death; it is life *after* life after death."[158] Moreover, Wright believes that heaven and earth are two different dimensions of space and time. Heaven is a parallel world to our earthly world.[159]

Wright's argument is helpful for understanding biblical eschatology by differentiating between the intermediate stage following death and the resurrected life. Wright's argument also reminds us to apply the term *heaven* more cautiously. After all, as Michael F. Bird explains, "The immediate postmortem experience of heaven is eschatologically intermediate; that is, it is a glorious interlude, not the final destination."[160] On the other hand, one must remember the reasons why the afterlife of believers is traditionally called *heaven*.[161] Johnston lists some of these reasons in his article in the *New Dictionary of Biblical Theology*. Johnston notes, "God dwells in heaven, so those who live with him after death will be in heaven."[162] Although resurrected believers will live on a new earth in the final stage of the afterlife, this new earth will be a heavenly renewed earth. Wright also acknowledges that "it is heaven that comes to earth."[163] Johnston points out that another convincing reason is found in Philippians 3:20 where the apostle Paul "asserts believers' heavenly citizenship."[164]

In his historical survey of prominent preachers throughout church history, David L. Larsen emphasizes that many preachers gave great attention to the themes of heaven or hell in their preaching.[165] Referring to the "prince of preachers," Charles Haddon Spurgeon, Larsen notes that "the themes of

---

157. Wright, *Surprised by Hope*, 171–172.
158. Wright, 169.
159. Wright, 115.
160. Michael F. Bird, *Evangelical Theology: A Biblical and Systematic Introduction* (Grand Rapids, MI: Zondervan, 2013), 328.
161. Philip S. Johnston, "Heaven," in *NDBT*, ed. T. Desmond Alexander et al. (Leicester: Inter-Varsity Press, 2000), 540–542 (541).
162. Johnston, 541.
163. Wright, *Surprised by Hope*, 104.
164. Johnston, "Heaven," 541.
165. David L. Larsen, "Heaven and Hell in the Preaching of the Gospel," *TRINJ* 22 (2001): 237–258.

heaven or hell were often addressed" in his preaching.[166] Larsen concludes that heaven and hell are central tenets in gospel preaching[167] and that "classical orthodoxy has always insisted that a double destiny for humankind calls for a choice by everyone."[168] Many of Jesus's parables illustrate the truth of these two distinct human destinies. Examples include the parable of the wheat and the weeds (Matt 13:24–30, 36–43) and the parable of the sheep and the goats (Matt 25:31–45).[169] The two options for human destiny are heaven or hell.[170] All human beings are destined for either the eternal blessedness of the heavenly renewed earth or the torment of hell.[171]

For the last few decades, considerable debate over the doctrine of hell has erupted among evangelicals. Although evangelicals have taken a variety of positions over this doctrine, two main positions concerning the doctrine of hell are prominent in the evangelical world today. The first position holds that the torment in hell is eternal. The other position, known as annihilationism, holds that the suffering in hell will eventually end, and the damned will simply cease to exist.[172] Discussing this debate is beyond the scope of this study. Nevertheless, it is important to note that neither positions doubt the existence of hell or that hell is a place of torment. The Bible clearly teaches about "the existence of hell as a dreadful and horrendous state and place where there was a complete absence of any gracious relationship with God."[173]

---

166. Larsen, 254.
167. Larsen, 257.
168. Larsen, 238.
169. Milne, *Message of Heaven and Hell*, 112–129.
170. Terence Nichols, *Death and Afterlife: A Theological Introduction* (Grand Rapids, MI: Brazos, 2010), 177. In modern theology, the doctrine of hell is considered by many as *odium theologium* and dismissed as an embarrassing artefact from ancient times. For a detailed discussion, see R. Albert Mohler Jr., "Modern Theology: The Disappearance of Hell," in *Hell Under Fire: Modern Scholarship Reinvents Eternal Punishment*, eds. Christopher W. Morgan and Robert A. Peterson (Grand Rapids, MI: Zondervan, 2004), 15–41 (16).
171. Harry Buis, "Hell," in *The Zondervan Encyclopedia of the Bible*, vol. 3, ed. Merrill C. Tenney (Grand Rapids, MI: Zondervan, 2009), 116–120 (119).
172. Andy Saville, "Reconciliationism – A Forgotten Evangelical Doctrine of Hell," *EvQ* 79 (2007): 35–51 (35).
173. Toon, *Heaven and Hell*, 105.

The Cult of the Dead and the Spiritual Realm 253

Two biblical passages critical for responding to the Chinese conception of the afterlife: Luke 16:19–31 and 1 Samuel 28:3–25

One of the interviewees in this study suggests preaching on Luke 16:19–31, the parable of Lazarus and the rich man, as a biblical response to the traditional Chinese concept of the afterlife. An important point of this passage, which may be particularly useful for contextualized preaching to the Chinese, is that the dead rich man cannot go back to the world of the living and warn his brothers. The dead rich man in this parable is powerless. Moreover, this parable reveals that a great chasm separates two human destinies, and it was impossible to bridge the gulf. As Trites points out, "God had pronounced judgment on the destinies of the two men; it was final and irreversible."[174] In this parable, both the rich man and Lazarus died. Nevertheless, they entered into two different human destinies. Lazarus was in the place of comfort with Abraham, while the rich man was "in torment."[175] This parable also reflects a belief that "the dead are already experiencing torment or bliss."[176] The afterlife description in this parable has had a profound impact on many Christian thinkers throughout history.[177]

A number of scholars, however, are hesitant to incorporate the teaching of Luke 16:19–31 into a doctrinal system of heaven and hell. Their main concern is that this passage is a parable, a story Jesus told.[178] Thus, we must first deal with the genre of this passage. Is Luke 16:19–31 a parable? David Gooding insists that this passage is not a parable. He argues that parables are based on actual realities and activities in this world, not the ultimate realities such as heaven and hell.[179] However, many modern commentators have not hesitated to interpret this passage as a parable. Robert H. Stein, for example, argues that Luke intended this passage to be read as a parable.[180] I. Howard

---

174. Allison A. Trites, *The Gospel of Luke*, Cornerstone Biblical Commentary (Carol Stream, IL: Tyndale s, 2006), 231.

175. Trites, 230–231.

176. Johnston, "Death and Resurrection," 443–447 (445).

177. Outi Lehtipuu, *The Afterlife Imagery in Luke's Story of the Rich Man and Lazarus* (Leiden: Brill, 2007), 3.

178. Butler, *Luke*, 273.

179. David Gooding, *According to Luke: A New Exposition of the Third Gospel* (Leicester: Inter-Varsity Press, 1987), 277.

180. Robert H. Stein, *Luke*, The New American Commentary (Nashville, TN: Broadman, 1992), 422.

Marshall understands Luke 16:19–31 as a parable that Jesus conveyed to the Pharisees.[181] The parable, as Stephen I. Wright indicates, "is set as a warning to the Pharisees about the dangers of the love of money."[182] It seems acceptable, therefore, to regard Luke 16:19–31 as a parable of Jesus. Moreover, this parable is unique in two ways. First, it is the only parable in which a character is named. Second, this is the only parable in which Jesus focused on the afterlife rather than everyday reality.[183]

If Luke 16:19–31 is indeed a parable, can we use this passage as a reference to preach about the reality of the afterlife? N. T. Wright, for example, thinks this parable has nothing to do with the description of the afterlife.[184] Stein, on the other hand, asserts that the description of hell in this parable portrays the reality of hell's horror, even though the description is not a literal portrayal of hell. Hell is horrible because "even licking water from a fingertip would bring some welcome relief."[185] The picture of unquenchable fire and burning heat helps the reader understand the pain and torment of hell.[186] This parable clearly illustrates that "hell is a place of torment, and heaven a place for the messianic feast."[187] Darrell L. Bock regards the descriptions in this parable as "graphic portrayals of the afterlife."[188]

---

181. I. Howard Marshall, *The Gospel of Luke: A Commentary on the Greek Text*, The New International Greek Testament Commentary (Exeter: Paternoster, 1978), 632. The view is shared by Bovon and Edwards. See François Bovon, *Luke 2: A Commentary on the Gospel of Luke 9:51–19:27*, trans. Donald S. Deer (Minneapolis: Fortress, 2013), 473. See also James R. Edwards, *The Gospel according to Luke*, The Pillar New Testament Commentary (Nottingham: Apollos, 2015), 466.

182. Stephen I. Wright, "Parables on Poverty and Riches (Luke 1:13–21; 16:1–13; 16:19–31)," in *The Challenge of Jesus' Parables*, ed. Richard N. Longenecker (Grand Rapids, MI: Eerdmans, 2000), 217–239 (230).

183. Klyne Snodgrass, *Stories with Intent: A Comprehensive Guide to the Parables of Jesus* (Grand Rapids, MI: Eerdmans, 2008), 419.

184. N. T. Wright, *Jesus and the Victory of God: Christian Origins and the Question of God* (Minneapolis: Fortress, 1996), 255.

185. Stein, *Luke*, 425.

186. *Luke*, Reformation Commentary on Scripture, ed. Beth Kreitzer (Downers Grove, IL: IVP Academic, 2015), 326.

187. Arthur A. Just Jr., *Luke 9:51–24:53*, Concordia Commentary: A Theological Exposition of Sacred Scripture (Saint Louis, MO: Concordia, 1997), 634.

188. Darrell L. Bock, *Luke, vol. II: 9:51–24:53*, Baker Exegetical Commentary on the New Testament (Grand Rapids, MI: Baker, 1996), 1363.

According to "the rule of end stress" for parable interpretation, nonetheless, the most important part of the parable is the end of the parable.[189] The conclusion of the parable of Lazarus and the rich man implies that the focus of the parable is on the rich man's family would not believe even if people return from the dead. In addition, as guidelines for interpretation, we should remember that details in parables "should not be allegorized and parables should not be pushed beyond their purpose."[190] Therefore, the parable of Lazarus and the rich man should not be interpreted as a literal description of hell.

On the other hand, with caution, some implications may be drawn from this parable. According to the description of this parable, there is no "hungry ghost" way back into the world of the living. In fact, there is no communication between the world of the dead and the world of the living. The dead rich man was in torment, but no food or water could be sent to him from the world of the living. The dead rich man is also incapable of bringing any blessing or harm to the living. These implications from the parable could be useful for contextualized preaching to the Chinese.

The interviewees in this study also emphasize that the dead souls in the underworld can never come back to the living world. Furthermore, they assert that any encounter with a ghost is really an encounter with a demon, not a soul of a deceased person. An encounter with what appears to be the soul of a deceased person is a deception from Satan. In light of this understanding, a particular passage in the Bible, 1 Samuel 28:3–25, should be examined.

The narrative of Saul and the woman who practices necromancy[191] at Endor (1 Sam 28) is a controversial passage. Norman L. Geisler and Thomas Howe list it as one of the challenging passages in the Bible.[192] For centuries, this passage has been interpreted in various ways among rabbinic and

---

189. Klyne R. Snodgrass, "Parable," in *DJG*, eds. Joel B. Green, Scot McKnight, I. Howard Marshall (Downers Grove, IL: InterVarsity Press, 1992), 591–601 (599).

190. Snodgrass, 598.

191. As Miranda Vroon-van Vugt explains, necromancy is "a claimed form of magic involving communication with the deceased – either by summoning their spirit as apparition or raising them bodily – for the purpose of divination, imparting the means to foretell future events or discover hidden knowledge." See Miranda Vroon-van Vugt, *Dead Man Walking in Endor: Narrative Mental Spaces and Conceptual Blending in 1 Samuel 28* (Ridderkerk: Ridderprint BV, 2013), 190.

192. Norman L. Geisler and Thomas Howe, *The Big Book of Bible Difficulties: Clear and Concise Answers from Genesis to Revelation* (Grand Rapids, MI: Baker, 1992), 167–168.

Christian exegetes.[193] One main interpretive question pertains to the identity of the man who spoke to King Saul after being brought back from the dead by the necromancer of Endor. Was this Samuel's postmortem appearance, a demon impersonating Samuel,[194] or Saul's imagination?[195]

Some commentators insist that Samuel himself did not appear at Endor. As Smelik points out, historically, many authoritative commentators argued that the necromancy at Endor was completely delusive. Tertullian, Gregory of Nyssa, and Jerome are among these commentators.[196] These earlier commentators argued that the woman only claimed to conjure up Samuel or even a demon posed as Samuel to deceive Saul.[197] Martin Luther took a similar approach. He believed that the spirit "skillfully spoke all the words of Samuel and added more to them."[198] This kind of reading of the text obviously influenced a number of Bible commentators and leaders in the Chinese church. Timothy S. K. Dzao, for example, implies that the appearance of Samuel in this necromancy is likely a deception from Satan.[199] Similarly, Lukas Tjandra argues that Satan was posing as Samuel to accuse and threaten Saul.[200]

However, some contemporary commentators suggest that the figure summoned by the necromancer was truly postmortem Samuel. David G. Firth, for example, believes that Samuel's ghost was raised by the woman through necromancy. Firth asserts that the Old Testament only condemns necromancy but "never questions its possible effectiveness."[201] Esther J. Hamori indicates

---

193. K. A. D. Smelik, "The Witch of Endor: 1 Samuel 28 in Rabbinic and Christian Exegesis till 800 AD," *VC* 33 (1979): 160–179 (160).

194. Greenvillen J. R. Kent, "'Call Up Samuel': Who Appeared to the Witch at En-Dor (1 Samuel 28:3–25)," *Andrews University Seminary Studies* 52 (2014): 141–160 (141).

195. Fred Blumenthal, "The Ghost of Samuel: Real or Imaginary?," *JBQ* 41 (2013): 104–106 (105).

196. Smelik, "The Witch of Endor," 165–166.

197. Stephen B. Chapman, *1 Samuel as Christian Scripture: A Theological Commentary* (Grand Rapids, MI: Eerdmans, 2016), 201.

198. Martin Luther, *1–2 Samuel, 1–2 Kings, 1–2 Chronicles: Old Testament V, Reformation Commentary on Scripture*, eds. Derek Cooper and Martin Lohrmann (Downers Grove: IVP Academic, 2016), 128.

199. 趙世光, 撒母耳記上下 *(1 & 2 Samuel)* (香港 [Hong Kong]: 靈糧出版社, 1970), 125–126.

200. 陳潤棠, 破迷, 闢邪, 趕鬼 *(Against Superstition, Witchcraft and Demon Possession)* 第十一版 (新山 [Johor Bharu]: 人人書樓, 2008), 125–127.

201. David G. Firth, *1 & 2 Samuel*, Apollos Old Testament Commentary (Leicester: Inter-Varsity Press, 2009), 292.

that Samuel's ghost was conjured through the meditation of the necromancer, even though Samuel did not want to be summoned.[202] Reading the passage literally, Robert B. Chisholm Jr. concludes that Samuel really appeared and prophesied to Saul. Chisholm attests that Samuel was summoned from the dead by the necromancer, although somehow the necromancer was surprised by Samuel's appearance.[203] This literal understanding of the text seems to imply the effectiveness of necromancy.[204]

An alternative reading of this passage, therefore, has been suggested by other modern commentators. These commentators accept the possibility of postmortem Samuel's appearance but question the authenticity of the necromancy.[205] They insist that Samuel's conjured appearance was an act of God instead of the result of witchcraft.[206] These commentators point out that the necromancer was taken by surprise when Samuel appeared, implying she did not expect Samuel to appear. David F. Payne, for example, claims that God "chose to bring Samuel back from the dead on this one special occasion."[207] Walter C. Kaiser Jr. also attests that "God allowed Samuel's spirit to appear to give Saul one more warning about the evil of his ways."[208] Accordingly, this is the most prevalent view and is supported by the most orthodox commentators.[209]

---

202. Esther J. Hamori, "The Prophet and the Necromancer: Women's Divination for Kings," *JBL* 132 (2013): 827–843 (834).

203. Robert B. Chisholm Jr., *1 & 2 Samuel*, Teach the Text Commentary Series (Grand Rapids, MI: Baker, 2013), 183–185. Chisholm offers two possible explanations for the medium's surprise. The first explanation is that "the conjured spirit does not normally appear, but simply speaks." The second explanation is that "a conjured spirit does not typically arrive accompanied by 'gods.'"

204. Francesca Aran Murphy, *1 Samuel*, Brazos Theological Commentary on the Bible (Grand Rapids, MI: Brazos, 2010), 269.

205. Joyce G. Baldwin, *1 and 2 Samuel: An Introduction and Commentary*, Tyndale Old Testament Commentaries (Leicester: Inter-Varsity Press, 1988), 159.

206. Gleason L. Archer, *Encyclopedia of Bible Difficulties* (Grand Rapids, MI: Regency Reference Library, 1992), 181.

207. David F. Payne, *I & II Samuel*, The Daily Study Bible Series (Louisville, KY: Westminster John Knox, 1982), 145.

208. Walter C. Kaiser Jr., *More Hard Sayings of the Old Testament* (Downers Grove, IL: InterVarsity Press, 1992), 165.

209. Walter C. Kaiser Jr. et al., *Hard Sayings of the Bible* (Downers Grove, IL: IVP Academic, 1996), 217.

Mary J. Evans asserts that this account in Endor is indeed "shrouded in mystery."[210] The details in this passage remain difficult to interpret. There are no clear-cut answers to the questions concerning the identity of the summoned figure and who brought about the appearance.[211] For the purpose of this study, however, a few theological concerns must be highlighted. First, the proper way to approach this challenging passage is to pay attention to its main message and not to be diverted by the vague details. The main message of this pericope, according to Robert Vannoy, asserts that the Lord had left Saul and become his enemy (1 Sam 28:16) after Saul had failed to execute the Lord's anger against the Amalekites (28:18).[212] Second, due to the ambiguity of this passage, this account of Saul and the necromancer should never be referenced as a proof text to argue that the dead can be summoned to the living world by any religious ritual or necromancy. Third, and most importantly, a believer should never be drawn into the realm of necromancy.[213] Divination is firmly prohibited by Deuteronomic law.[214] In fact, the Bible sternly condemns all forms of witchcraft and necromancy (Exod 22:18; Lev 20:6, 27; Deut 18:9–12; Isa 8:19).[215] Believers should have nothing to do with necromancy. Ramesh Khatry claims, "Those who do so, like King Saul who consulted the witch (medium) of Endor, bring disaster on themselves."[216]

In conclusion, almost no indication exists that the biblical writers believed deceased persons could influence the living. Moreover, the Bible nowhere suggests that the spirits who afflict the living are deceased persons.[217] Belief in ghosts and the possibility of contact with the dead, as Wright accurately attests, does not correspond with Christian orthodoxy.[218] Any form of the cult

---

210. Mary J. Evans, *The Message of Samuel*, The Bible Speaks Today (Leicester: Inter-Varsity Press, 2004), 154.

211. J. Robert Vannoy, *1-2 Samuel*, Cornerstone Biblical Commentary (Carol Stream, IL: Tyndale, 2009), 243.

212. Vannoy, 244.

213. Vannoy, 243.

214. Ralph W. Klein, *1 Samuel*, Word Biblical Commentary (Waco, TX: Word, 1983), 271.

215. Geisler and Howe, *Big Book of Bible Difficulties*, 167.

216. Ramesh Khatry, "Witchcraft and Demons," in *South Asia Bible Commentary: A One-Volume Commentary on the Whole Bible*, ed. Brian Wintle (Rajasthan: Open Door, 2015), 371 (371).

217. Keith Ferdinando, *The Triumph of Christ in African Perspective: A Study of Demonology and Redemption in the African Context* (Carlisle: Paternoster, 1999), 388.

218. Wright, *Surprised by Hope*, 12.

of the dead should be excluded from the Christian church. On the other hand, the Bible in many ways does acknowledge the existence of evil spirits and the spiritual realm. This raises other critical questions: What are the evil spirits, and what are the nature and activities of the spiritual realm? In the following sections, these issues will be discussed in detail within a biblical framework.

7.2 Theological Reflections on the Spiritual Realm
7.2.1 The Reality of the Evil Spiritual Powers

The concept of evil has existed in various cultures from the very beginning of history.[219] Today there are diverse approaches to the reality of evils spirits. One is simply to deny the existence of the devil and demons. Since the Age of Enlightenment, radical skepticism, which has dominated the Western worldview, has rejected the supernatural.[220] In his 1982 article "The Flaw of the Excluded Middle," Paul Hiebert indicates that dualism has had a great impact on the Western worldview. According to Hiebert, the Western worldview allows only two tiers of reality – the upper tier of the invisible world and the lower tier of the visible world. Therefore, the Western worldview tends to exclude the middle tier, which is comprised of the spirits and invisible powers of this world.[221] In many ways, spirits, demons, and Satan have become unmentionable topics and are excluded from the dominant materialistic worldview.[222]

The existence of the devil and demons has been considered as merely a myth by some. Rudolf Bultmann, a German theologian, argues, "It is impossible to use electric light and the wireless and to avail ourselves of modern medical and surgical discoveries, and at the same time to believe in the New Testament world of spirits and miracles."[223] Because the laws of nature had

---

219. Jeffrey Burton Russell, *The Devil: Perceptions of Evil from Antiquity to Primitive Christianity* (London: Cornell University Press, 1977), 58–64.

220. Jeffrey Burton Russell, *The Prince of Darkness: Radical Evil and the Power of Good in History* (London: Thames & Hudson, 1989), 206–219.

221. Paul G. Hiebert, "The Flaw of the Excluded Middle," *Missiology* 10 (1982): 35–47 (40–45).

222. Walter Wink, *Unmasking the Powers: The Invisible Forces that Determine Human Existence* (Philadelphia: Fortress, 1986), 1.

223. Rudolf Bultmann, et al., *Kerygma and Myth: A Theological Debate*, ed. Hans Werner Bartsch, rev. ed. (New York: Harper & Row, 1961), 5.

been discovered, Bultmann claimed that "we can no longer believe in spirits, whether good or evil."²²⁴ In the 1940s, Bultmann pleaded for demythologizing the New Testament.²²⁵ Similarly, Alfred Edersheim considers demons and Satan only as mythological conceptions originating from Persian culture. He attests that the concept of demons "is the outcome of Eastern or of prurient imagination, of national conceit, of ignorant superstition, and of foreign, especially Persian, elements."²²⁶ A serious flaw in this approach is inconsistency. These theologians continue to accept belief in God while rejecting belief in the devil's existence. However, as Michael Green says, "The existence of a devil is a necessary part of consistent theism."²²⁷ A biblical worldview includes the theme of conflict with the power of evil. Understanding Satan and his principalities and powers is important to our understanding of the power of God.²²⁸ A believer in Jesus Christ must agree with what Jesus believes. Jesus himself clearly believes in the external existence of the devil and was aware of a personal conflict with such evil.²²⁹ Belief in the existence of evil spirits is a central theme in the New Testament; a rejection of this belief jeopardizes the teaching of the New Testament.²³⁰

Another theological approach toward the reality of evil spirits is to depersonalize demons. Paul Tillich is one theologian who takes this approach. Tillich denies the external reality of Satan and demons. Tillich believes that evil is part of the social forces and structures of this world rather than personal beings. Furthermore, he asserts that these structures of evil "rule individual souls, nations, and even nature."²³¹ Trevor Ling also takes a similar existential approach toward the reality of Satan. Ling argues that, according to the New

---

224. Bultmann, 4.

225. Bultmann "is known to most people solely by a lecture he gave in 1941 on 'New Testament and Mythology,' which announced his program of demythologizing." See David W. Congdon, *Rudolf Bultmann: A Companion to His Theology* (Eugene, OR: Cascade, 2015), 101.

226. Alfred Edersheim, *The Life and Times of Jesus The Messiah*, vol. 2, New American ed. (Grand Rapids, MI: Eerdmans, 1962), 748.

227. Michael Green, *I Believe in Satan's Downfall* (London: Hodder & Stoughton, 1981), 31.

228. Clinton E. Arnold, *Three Crucial Questions about Spiritual Warfare* (Grand Rapids, MI: Baker, 2001), 30.

229. Nigel Goring Wright, *The Theology of the Dark Side: Putting the Power of Evil in Its Place* (Carlisle: Paternoster, 2003), 21.

230. Wright, 22.

231. Paul Tillich, *Systematic Theology: Three Volumes in One*, vol. 2 (New York: Harper & Row, 1967), 27.

Testament writers, Satan is the spirit of a society alienated from God, "rather than an individual local spirit-being."[232] Ling insists that Satan is merely the personification of evil forces. Ling further argues that "personification of a hostile evil force should not necessarily be taken to imply real personality."[233]

An alternative approach is that of depersonalizing Satan and demons, as advocated by Walter Wink. Wink considers spiritual powers neither as personal beings nor as personifications of evil.[234] He considers the spiritual powers "as the inner aspect of material or tangible manifestations of power."[235] Thus the powers do not have a separate spiritual existence. To Wink, the "principalities and powers" are the gestalt of an institution, state, or system. Moreover, Satan is "the actual power that congeals around collective idolatry, injustice, or inhumanity."[236] Wink believes that Satan is not a person or a being but an archetypal reality or a profound experience of uncanny power in a human being.[237] Moreover, Wink categorizes two classes of the demonic, which are the "inner demons" and "outer demons." The inner demons are personal psychological struggles, while the outer demons are the demonic powers influencing a society or an institution.[238]

Even though Wink's approach is helpful for highlighting the evil influences of Satan and demons on human beings and societies through institutions, there are major faults in his approach to evil powers. First of all, Wink's approach does not seem to be compatible with the biblical view of demonic powers. The apostle Paul never equated demonic powers with structural societal evil.[239] On the contrary, Paul thinks Satan is a real enemy with schemes against Christian believers (Eph 6:11). Second, "Wink's approach makes it dangerously easy for him to demonize political viewpoints with which he

---

232. Trevor Ling, *The Significance of Satan: New Testament Demonology and Its Contemporary Relevance* (London: SPCK, 1961), 84.

233. Ling, 24.

234. Walter Wink cited in Duana A. Garrett, *Angels and the New Spirituality* (Nashville, TN: Broadman & Holman, 1995), 206.

235. Walter Wink, *Naming the Powers: The Language of Power in the New Testament* (Philadelphia: Fortress, 1984), 103–104.

236. Wink, 104–105.

237. Wink, *Unmasking the Powers*, 25.

238. Wink, 41–68.

239. Gregory A. Boyd, *God at War: The Bible and Spiritual Conflict* (Downers Grove, IL: InterVarsity Press, 1997), 276.

disagrees."[240] Moreover, Wink frequently retranslates the New Testament words to fit his own understanding of evil powers.[241]

The third approach toward the reality of evil spirits that accepts the biblical doctrine asserts that demons and a personal devil exist. The Bible reveals the devil and his demons primarily as spiritual beings, which are typically invisible to the natural eye.[242] Although invisible, they are real beings.[243] Richard H. Bell argues that the devil and demons have personalities and can be disembodied spirits, which is contrary to Wink's argument that the spiritual has to be integrated with the physical.[244]

The devil presented in the Bible is never an abstraction but a personal, supernatural being that is intelligent and powerful.[245] As Arnold explains, "The devil is an intelligent, powerful spirit-being that is thoroughly evil and is directly involved in perpetrating evil in the lives of individuals as well as on a much larger scale."[246] In the Bible, the devil is "frequently associated with human suffering and death."[247]

Although what is said about Satan is often vague, and although the concept of Satan was not well developed in the Old Testament,[248] the whole biblical tradition is impregnated with his presence.[249] Traditional Jewish and Christian commentators agree that the devil is the one who harnessed the serpent and

---

240. Garrett, *Angels and the New Spirituality*, 210.

241. Garrett, 211–212.

242. Merrill F. Unger, *Demons in the World Today: A Study of Occultism in the Light of God's Word* (Wheaton, IL: Tyndale, 1971), 22–24. Unger mainly refers to Matt 8:16; Luke 10:17–20; Eph 6:12; and Rev 16:14.

243. Lewis Sperry Chafer, *Chafer Systematic Theology*, vol. 2 (Dallas: Dallas Seminary Press, 1980), 35.

244. Richard H. Bell, *Deliver Us from Evil: Interpreting the Redemption from the Power of Satan in New Testament Theology* (Tübingen: Mohr Siebeck, 2007), 344–351.

245. Arnold, *Three Crucial Questions*, 35.

246. Arnold, 35.

247. David Raymond Smith, *Hand This Man over to Satan: Curse, Exclusion and Salvation in 1 Corinthians 5* (London: T&T Clark, 2008), 159.

248. Sydney H. T. Page, *Powers of Evil: A Biblical Study of Satan and Demons* (Grand Rapids, MI: Baker, 1995), 11. As Oldridge says, "The Devil is an elusive figure in the Old Testament." See Darren Oldridge, *The Devil: A Very Short Introduction* (Oxford: Oxford University Press, 2012), 21.

249. Maurice Garcon and Jean Vinchon, *The Devil: An Historical Critical and Medical Study*, trans. Stephen Haden Guest (London: Victor Gollancz, 1929), 21.

acted through it in Genesis 3.[250] Satan in the Old Testament "is portrayed both as a general adversary and as a legal accuser who tests the faithfulness of God's people."[251] He is a living being who causes suffering and death.[252]

The English word *Satan* is a transliteration of the Hebrew word שטן (*satan*), which means "adversary" or "opponent."[253] The Septuagint translates שטן with the Greek word διάβολος, from which the English word "devil" is derived.[254] In the Old Testament, the Hebrew term often refers to a role rather than a particular being. In five instances, שטן refers to human beings and denotes the role of adversary or accuser.[255] Nevertheless, at some point the term שטן became personified into a personal being – Satan. This being is mentioned eighteen times in three books in the Old Testament: Job 1–2; Zechariah 3:1–2; and 1 Chronicles 21:1.[256] In the book of Job, Satan appears as a member of the heavenly council.[257] In Zechariah 3:1–2, Satan stands in the heavenly court as the accuser of the high priest.[258] In 1 Chronicles 21:1,

---

250. Larry Richards, *Every Good and Evil Angel in the Bible* (Nashville, TN: Thomas Nelson, 1998), 5. Today, however, scholars such as Gerhard von Rad, Brevard Childs, and Paul Ricoeur believe that the snake should not be identified as Satan in any way. Noll disagrees with these scholars and insists that the snake is no mere creature of dust nor a simply latent human aspiration. For his argument see Stephen F. Noll, *Angels of Light, Powers of Darkness: Thinking Biblically About Angels, Satan and Principalities* (Downers Grove, IL: InterVarsity Press, 1998), 96–102.

251. G. H. Twelftree, "Spiritual Powers," in *NDBT*, 796–802 (797).

252. Oldridge, *The Devil*, 2. Russell points out that certain civilizations, such as Egypt, Mesopotamia, Canaan, and Greece, were closely connected to the historical background of the Judeo-Christian concept of the devil. See Russell, *The Prince of Darkness*, 12. Torre and Hernandez believe that the concept of personified evil was well developed in ancient Egypt long before Judaism's unique concept of Satan was developed. See Miguel A. De La Torre and Albert Hernandez, *The Quest for the Historical Satan* (Minneapolis: Fortress, 2011), 56. However, Russell's explanation is more convincing. He says, "All Egyptian deities are manifestations of the whole cosmos and so reflect both the constructive and the destructive aspects of cosmic harmony." Therefore, "no Egyptian deity ever became the principle of evil." See Russell, *The Prince of Darkness*, 13.

253. Page, *Powers of Evil*, 23.

254. Philip C. Almond, *The Devil: A New Biography* (Ithaca, NY: Cornell University Press, 2014), 23. The Latin form of the word *satan* is *diabolos*.

255. Almond, 16.

256. Torre and Hernandez, *Quest for the Historical Satan*, 57. Torre and Hernandez explain that in the books of Zechariah and Job, the definite article appears with the word "satan," literally "the satan." They believe the definite article in Hebrew can sometimes introduce proper names. Therefore they insist these two books in some ways still personify "the Satan."

257. Bell, *Deliver Us from Evil*, 10. Although Satan appears in the heavenly council, this does not mean he occupies an approved position in the council. See Noll, *Angels of Light*, 103.

258. Almond, *The Devil*, 18.

Satan acts as a tempter. He incited King David to sin against God by taking a census of the people. In each of these three books, the word *Satan* refers to a celestial being.²⁵⁹

Arnold attests that all the New Testament writers, as well as their contemporaries in the first century, believed in the actual existence of evil spirits.²⁶⁰ Moreover, much that was written in the New Testament about Satan may be traced to similar ideas about Satan offered in the Old Testament.²⁶¹ As Joan O'Grady indicates, "The Jewish people, who listened to the first Christian teaching, were clearly accustomed to think that there existed an evil spirit who opposed God and man, and was Lord over innumerable lesser devils."²⁶² However, compared to the Old Testament, the New Testament refers to Satan significantly more often,²⁶³ and he plays a more prominent role.²⁶⁴ Kristen Nielsen says, "No one who reads the New Testament can be in any doubt that the devil is referred to here with the greatest seriousness."²⁶⁵

The New Testament refers to Satan with the Greek words σατανᾶς (*satanas*, thirty-six times) and διάβολος (*diabolos*, thirty-seven times).²⁶⁶ In the New Testament, σατανᾶς "had become the direct proper name of the anti-divine

---

259. Page, *Powers of Evil*, 24.

260. Clinton E. Arnold, *Powers of Darkness: A Thoughtful, Biblical Look at an Urgent Challenge Facing the Church* (Leicester: Inter-Varsity Press, 1992), 176.

261. Ferdinando, *Triumph of Christ*, 134.

262. Joan O'Grady, *The Prince of Darkness: The Devil in History, Religion and the Human Psyche* (Shaftesbury: Element, 1989), 14.

263. Anthony Finlay, *Demons: The Devil, Possession and Exorcism* (London: Blandford, 1999), 12. Page believes that the difference between the Testaments is because the Jews' interest in demonology increased significantly during the intertestamental period. See Page, *Powers of Evil*, 87. Indeed, an abundance of literature pertaining to Satan became available during second commonwealth Judaism. See Samuel Y. Chang, "A Comparison of the Diabologies of Tertullian and Origen" (unpublished master thesis, Wheaton College, 1996), 11. Gokey writes a good overview chapter about these extra-biblical Judaism writings concerning the theories of Satan and evil spirits. See Francis X. Gokey, *The Terminology for the Devil and Evil Spirits in the Apostolic Fathers* (Washington, DC: Catholic University of America Press, 1961), 10–24.

264. T. J. Wray and Gregory Mobley, *The Birth of Satan: Tracing the Devil's Biblical Roots* (New York: Palgrave MacMillan, 2005), 113.

265. Kirsten Nielsen, *Satan – The Prodigal Son?: A Family Problem in the Bible* (Sheffield: Sheffield Academic Press, 1998), 21.

266. Bell, *Deliver Us from Evil*, 10. Four words in the New Testament Greek are rendered in English versions as Satan or devil: *diabolos, satanas, daimon*, and *daimonion*, which is derived from *daimon*. See W. M'Donald, *Spiritualism: Identical with Ancient Sorcery, New Testament Demonology, and Modern Witchcraft* (New York: Carlton & Porter, 1866), 54–60.

power."²⁶⁷ He is presented as a figure that has power to control the world.²⁶⁸ In the New Testament worldview, the world lies under the devil's power.²⁶⁹ The New Testament also teaches that Satan is the master of sorcery and idolatry. As accuser, tempter, liar, murderer, and prince of the world, Satan is the principal adversary of Jesus Christ.²⁷⁰ As Page points out, however, the central message of the New Testament is the salvific work of Christ and the defeat of Satan.²⁷¹

Satan is also in control of the abode of demons.²⁷² Demons, like the devil, are real beings as well. As James W. Boyd attests, "the very existence of demons, as well as their activities, is an elaboration and extension of the pervasive and threatening spiritual power which is identified as satanic."²⁷³ Overall there are not many references to demons in the Old Testament. The Hebrew term שֵׁד (plural שֵׁדִים) for demons only appears twice in the Old Testament (Deut 32:17; Ps 106:37).²⁷⁴ Demons are also depicted as evil spirits who are used to bring God's judgment (Judg 9:22-24; 1 Sam 16:14).²⁷⁵

In the New Testament, the term δαιμόνιον (*daimonion*) is a commonly used word to designate demons.²⁷⁶ Other New Testament terms for demons include *spirits, evil spirits, unclean spirits, spirit of an unclean demon, rulers, authorities,* and *powers.* All of these terms are used interchangeably.²⁷⁷ Demons are understood to have "personal identity, intelligence, will and

---

267. Eckhard J. Schnabel, *Mark: An Introduction and Commentary*, Tyndale New Testament Commentary (Downers Grove, IL: IVP Academic, 2017), 47.

268. Wright, *Theology of the Dark Side*, 19.

269. Russell, *Prince of Darkness*, 44.

270. Walter Sundberg, "Satan the Enemy," *WW* 28 (2008): 29–37 (30).

271. Page, *Powers of Evil*, 87.

272. Clinton E. Arnold, *Ephesians: Power and Magic – The Concept of Power in Ephesians in Light of Its Historical Setting* (Cambridge: Cambridge University Press, 1989), 60.

273. James W. Boyd, *Satan and Mara: Christian and Buddhist Symbols of Evil* (Leiden: Brill, 1975), 51.

274. A. Scott Moreau, "Demon," in *Baker Theological Dictionary of the Bible*, ed. Walter A. Elwell (Grand Rapids, MI: Baker, 1996), 163–165 (163).

275. A. Scott Moreau, "Demon, Demonization," in *Evangelical Dictionary of World Missions*, ed. Scott Moreau (Grand Rapids, MI: Baker, 2000), 267–268 (267).

276. Michael J. Gruenthaner, "The Demonology of the Old Testament," *CBQ* 6 (1944): 6–27 (6).

277. "Demon," in *Mounce's Complete Expository Dictionary of Old and New Testament Words*, ed. William D. Mounce (Grand Rapids, MI: Zondervan, 2006), 167.

self-consciousness."[278] In the gospels, demons are portrayed as an army of evil spiritual powers that fight against Jesus and the kingdom of God.[279]

In Ephesians 6:12, Paul declares, "For our struggle is not against flesh and blood, but against the rulers, against the powers, against the worldly forces of this darkness, against the spiritual forces of wickedness in the heavenly places." In the Greek New Testament, the word for "rulers" is ἀρχαί, and the word for "powers" is ἐξουσίαι. The Greek word ἀρχαί is translated as "principalities" in the King James Version. Today, the phrase "principalities and powers" is widely used by modern authors to translate the meaning of ἀρχαί and ἐξουσίαι.[280]

Scholars have disputed what the Pauline phrase "principalities (rulers) and powers" refers to.[281] Some deny that principalities and powers are transcendent personal beings. In line with his view on Satan and demons, mentioned above, Wink contends that principalities and powers denote both visible (human authorities or institutions) and invisible (spiritual entities) reality. According to Wink, "the Powers are the simultaneity of two aspects in a single entity."[282]

A contrary view argues that principalities and powers are real spiritual beings. In this regard, Clinton E. Arnold's *Ephesians: Power and Magic* is very persuasive. Arnold understands the teaching of "powers" in Ephesians in light of the religious background of western Asia Minor in the first century AD. He concludes that the writer of Ephesians does not demythologize the powers. Instead, the writer "reflects the prevailing Jewish and Hellenistic view of a belief in the reality of evil spirit-beings."[283] In his later commen-

---

278. Keith Ferdinando, "Screwtape Revisited: Demonology Western, African, and Biblical," in *The Unseen World*, 103–132 (120).

279. Twelftree, "Spiritual Powers," 798.

280. Page, *Powers of Evil*, 240.

281. C. Peter Wagner, *Warfare Prayer: Strategies for Combating the Rulers of Darkness* (Tunbridge Wells: Monarch, 1992), 94–95. Today, the issue of "principalities and powers" continues to be a controversial topic. At the 2014 Conference of the Center for Catholic and Evangelical Theology, questions about "principalities and powers" were the main themes in the theological discussion among Catholic and evangelical theologians. See *Life Amid the Principalities: Identifying, Understanding, and Engaging Created, Fallen, and Disarmed Powers Today*, ed. Michael Root and James J. Buckley (Eugene, OR: Cascade, 2016).

282. Walter Wink, "Demons and DMins: The Church's Response to the Demonic," *RevExp* 89 (1992): 503–513 (504).

283. Arnold, *Ephesians: Power and Magic*, 69.

tary on Ephesians, Arnold reemphasized this view. Arnold believes that both the terms ἀρχαί and ἐξουσίαι, are "Paul's most common expressions for demonic spirits."[284] Furthermore, Arnold argues that Paul's third expression, κοσμοκράτορες ("world forces" or "world powers") in Ephesians 6:12, is interchangeable with expressions such as "demons" and "spirits" in folk Judaism and may also be an expression for demonic spirits behind pagan gods.[285] Thus Arnold believes that in 6:12, Paul alludes to an important truth about spiritual realities. As Arnold explains, "The opposition is not one powerful supernatural, but a whole range of spiritual forces of varying rank, authority, and capabilities."[286] All these evil powers are purposely set against the believer and carry out the schemes of the devil.[287]

The evil powers are also mentioned in Colossians 1:16 and 2:15. According to Colossians 1:16, both visible and invisible realities have been created through Jesus Christ.[288] The spiritual world is a part of the creation of God, same as the material world.[289] Peter T. O'Brien further argues that the four terms *thrones, dominions, principalities*, and *authorities* in Colossians 1:16 describe four classes of angelic powers.[290] Similarly, Douglas J. Moo believes that all four titles likely refer to spiritual beings.[291] In his recent commentary on Colossians, Scot McKnight rightly emphasizes that the evil powers in Colossians 1:16 and 2:15 are supernatural beings rather than structures.[292] According to McKnight, the evil powers are "real demonic beings who seek to destroy God's will for our world."[293] Furthermore, Arnold asserts that in the Pauline corpus both ἀρχαί ("powers") and ἐξουσίαι ("authorities") are

---

284. Clinton Arnold, *Ephesians*, Zondervan Exegetical Commentary on the New Testament (Grand Rapids, MI: Zondervan, 2010), 447.

285. Arnold, 448.

286. Arnold, 447.

287. Boyd, *God at War*, 274–275.

288. Wright, *Theology of the Dark Side*, 64.

289. Thomas A. Noble, "The Spirit World: A Theological Approach," in *The Unseen World*, 185–223 (193).

290. Peter T. O'Brien, *Colossians, Philemon*, Word Biblical Commentary (Dallas: Word, 1982), 46.

291. Douglas J. Moo, *The Letters to the Colossians and to Philemon*, The Pillar New Testament Commentary (Nottingham: Apollos, 2008), 122.

292. Scot McKnight, *The Letter to the Colossians*, New International Commentary on the New Testament (Grand Rapids, MI: Eerdmans, 2018), 253.

293. McKnight, 257.

consistently portrayed as evil beings who are hostile to the purposes of God.[294] In summary, a more literal assessment of the biblical material argues that Satan and demons are spiritual beings that have their own independent existence. They are not mere projections of abstract notions.

7.2.2 The Difference between the Concepts of Ghosts and Demons

Due to the fact that belief in ghosts plays an important role in Chinese culture, the fundamental differences between the concepts of demons and ghosts in the Bible must be illuminated. In the Chinese language, the most common word for ghost is *gui* 鬼. The Chinese word *gui* 鬼 in oracle bone script (*jia gu wen* 甲古文) is a symbol of a mask covering a face. This symbol of covering a face conveys that a person has passed away.[295] A person becomes a ghost (*gui*) after dying and goes on to live in the underworld. In Chinese, the word *gui* 鬼 ("ghost") is pronounced similarly to the word *gui* 歸 ("to return home").[296] According to ancient Chinese teaching, *gui* 鬼 is the place to which a human returns (*ren suo gui wei gui* 人所歸為鬼).[297] However, *gui* 鬼 ("ghost") is also used to signify demons. Thus, in most Chinese translations of the Bible, both the terms *demons* and *ghosts* are translated as *gui* 鬼. Additionally, the Greek term διάβολος ("devil") is usually translated as *mo gui* 魔鬼. This can be confusing to the Chinese, especially to those who believe ghosts are souls of the dead.

The usage of the word *ghost* in English translations of the Bible is another matter. In some older English translations of the Bible, the word *ghost* appears in more than one hundred verses.[298] For example, the word *ghost* is found 109 times in the King James Version (1611). However, in most of the later English translations of the Bible, the word *ghost* rarely appears. In the New King James

---

294. Clinton E. Arnold, *The Colossian Syncretism: The Interface Between Christianity and Folk Belief at Colossae* (Tubingen: J.C.B. Mohr, 1995), 255.

295. 楊牧谷, 魔惑眾生: 魔鬼學研究 *(Study in Demonology)* (香港 [Hong Kong]: 卓越出版社,1995), 61.

296. The two words are pronounced with different tones. In Mandarin, for example, *gui* 鬼 is pronounced with the third tone while *gui* 歸 is pronounced with the first tone.

297. Constance A. Cook, *Death in Ancient China: The Tale of One Man's Journey* (Leiden: Brill, 2006), 19–20. The ancient graph for the word *tu* 土 depicted a mound on top of a horizontal line.

298. John W. Martens, "Holy Ghost Story," *America* 211 (2014): 37 (37).

Version (1982) and the New American Standard Version (1995), the word *ghost* appears only twice: once in the Gospel of Matthew (14:26) and again in the Gospel of Mark (6:49). *Ghost* appears in these two verses in reference to Jesus's walking on the water. In the New English Translation as well as the New International Version (2011), *ghost* occurs only four times. In addition to Matthew 14:26 and Mark 6:49, *ghost* also appears in Luke 24:37 and 24:39 in reference to Jesus's post-resurrection appearances. In many current English translations, the word *spirit* is used as an alternative for the word *ghost*.

One of the main factors why the usage of ghost has changed in Bible translation, according to Martens, is because the meanings of words change over time.[299] In the older English translations, such as the King James Version or the Douay-Rheims, the term *Holy Ghost* is used to translate the Greek phrase ἅγιος πνεῦμα.[300] Apparently one hundred years ago the word *ghost* (old English *gast*) had multiple meanings.[301] Today, the meaning of the English word *ghost* has changed. According to the Oxford Advanced Learner's Dictionary, ghost means "the spirit of a dead person that a living person believes they can see or hear."[302] Therefore the current translations tend to render ἅγιος πνεῦμα as "Holy Spirit" instead of "Holy Ghost."[303]

As mentioned earlier, the New Testament contains only two incidents in which some current English translations employ the word *ghost*. The first incident is Jesus miraculous walking on water.[304] The gospel writers report the fearful responses of the disciples toward Jesus's miraculous deed. In the dark, the disciples did not recognize the figure as Jesus.[305] Both Matthew and Mark report that the disciples assumed they saw a ghost. The Greek term in Matthew and Mark is φάντασμα, which is translated as "ghost" in some

---

299. Martens, 37.

300. Martens, 37.

301. *The Concise Oxford Dictionary of English Etymology*, ed. T. F. Hoad (Oxford: Oxford University Press, 2003) 643, in Oxford Reference, http://www.oxfordreference.com/view/10.1093/acref/9780192830982.001.0001/acref-9780192830982-e-6428?rskey=dtgrv5&result=6429.

302. *Oxford Advanced Learner's Dictionary of Current English*, 6th ed., ed. Sally Wehmeier, (Oxford: Oxford University Press, 2000).

303. Martens, "Holy Ghost Story," 37.

304. The pericope of Jesus walking on the water is recorded in the Gospels of Matthew, Mark, and John. See Orville E. Daniel, *A Harmony of the Four Gospels: The New International Version*, 2nd ed. (Grand Rapids, MI: Baker, 1996), 91–92.

305. Ezra Gould, *Gospel According to St. Mark*, Critical and Exegetical Commentary (Edinburgh: T&T Clark, 1982), 122.

modern English translations of the Bible.[306] This Greek word is found only in Matthew 14:26 and Mark 6:49.[307] Neither Matthew nor Mark give any further explanation of the term. According to James R. Edwards, in classical Greek, Φάντασμα "means the appearance of a spirit or apparition, hence a ghost."[308] As R. T. France explains, in both Jewish and pagan literatures, the word Φάντασμα signifies a disembodied ghost. When the disciples saw what they perceived to be Jesus's physically impossible action on the lake, they obviously assumed they were seeing a ghost.[309]

In some current English translations of the New Testament, the other incident in which the word *ghost* occurs is Jesus's post-resurrection appearance. For example, in the NIV and NLT, the Greek word πνεῦμα in Luke 24:37 and 24:39 is rendered as "ghost." According to Luke, Jesus's appearance frightened the disciples because they possibly thought they were seeing a disembodied spirit coming back from the dead.[310] However, as Daniel A. Smith points out, "πνεῦμα was not a word typically used in classical or Hellenistic Greek for a postmortem apparition."[311] Thus it is arguable that it is right to translate πνεῦμα in Luke 24:37 and 24:39 as "ghost," in light of the meaning of the word *ghost* in contemporary English. Even if the word *ghost* is a proper translation of the word πνεῦμα in Luke 24:37 and 24:39, this does not mean that the writer of the Gospel of Luke believes in ghosts coming back to the living world. The writer simply describes the responses of the disciples. As David Daube points out, ancient Jewish legends speak of deceased saints who return on special missions. Thus the disciples, who may have been influenced by these ancient Jewish legends, possibly viewed Jesus as a spirit in the interim condition.[312]

---

306. For example, the NKJV, NASB, NIV, NLT, etc. However some versions, such as the KJV (1611), translate the word as "spirit."

307. Robert H. Stein, *Mark*, Baker Exegetical Commentary on the New Testament (Grand Rapids, MI: Baker Academic, 2008), 325.

308. James R. Edwards, *The Gospel According to Mark*, The Pillar New Testament Commentary (Grand Rapids, MI: Eerdmans, 2002), 200.

309. R. T. France, *The Gospel of Mark: A Commentary on the Greek Text*, The New International Greek Testament Commentary (Grand Rapids, MI: Eerdmans, 2002), 272.

310. Bock, *Luke, vol. II: 9:51–24:53*, 1932.

311. Daniel A. Smith, "Seeing a Pneuma (tic Body): The Apologetic Interests of Luke 24:36–43," *CBQ* 72 (2010): 752–772 (755).

312. David Daube, "On Acts 23: Sadducees and Angels," *JBL* 109 (1990): 493–497 (495–496).

Ghosts, spirits of the dead, are not the same as demons in the Bible. The word *demon* comes from the Greek term δαίμων (*daimon*).[313] The principal meaning of δαίμων in ancient Greek changed over different periods of time.[314] During the Homeric period (also known as the Greek Dark Age), the term δαίμων (*daimon*) commonly referred to a god/goddess or divine power (distinct from θεός, which designated a god in person).[315] The Greek word δαίμων also referred to an individual's destiny or fate.[316] After the Homeric period, however, the Greeks started to apply the term δαίμων to the souls of the dead as well.[317] Plato, for example, identified δαίμων as the soul of a dead person and believed that a δαίμων served as a mediator between gods and men.[318] These δαίμων were generally considered semi-divine beings inferior to the gods.[319] Therefore, during the Homeric period of ancient Greece, the terms *demons* and *ghosts* were likely interchangeable. Demons were often understood as the spirits or souls of dead human beings.[320]

During the two hundred years before the time of Jesus (the intertestamental period), angels, spirits, and demons were popular topics in Jewish literature.[321] Jews in this period generally believed that the world was full of demons that were able to bring calamity, sickness, and misfortune.[322] Many Jews throughout the Mediterranean world also practiced magic for protection from evil spirits.[323] Some scholars, such as Peter G. Bolt, argue that the concept of demons as ghosts was common in Hellenistic-Jewish literature, alongside

---

313. Peter G. Bolt, "Towards a Biblical Theology of the Defeat of the Evil Powers," in *Christ's Victory Over Evil: Biblical Theology and Pastoral Ministry*, ed. Peter G. Bolt (Nottingham: Apollos, 2009), 35–81 (49).

314. Merrill F. Unger, *Biblical Demonology: A Study of Spiritual Forces at Work Today* (Grand Rapids, MI: Kregel Publications, 1994), 56–58.

315. R. K. Harrison, "Demon," in *The Zondervan Encyclopedia of the Bible*, vol. 2, ed. Merrill C. Tenney (Grand Rapids, MI: Zondervan, 2009), 95–105 (95).

316. *The Brill Dictionary of Ancient Greek*, ed. Franco Montanari (Leiden: Brill, 2015), 450.

317. *Brill Dictionary of Ancient Greek*, 450.

318. Harrison, "Demon," 95.

319. LSJ, 9th ed. with Revised Supplement, ed. H. G. Liddell, R. Scott, H. S. Jones (Oxford: Clarendon, 1996), 366.

320. Jason Robert Combs, "Ghost on the Water?: Understanding an Absurdity in Mark 6:49–50," *JBL* 127 (2008): 345–358 (349).

321. Arnold, *Powers of Darkness*, 64.

322. Harrison, "Demon," 102.

323. Arnold, *Powers of Darkness*, 71–72.

Greco-Roman literature and Greek magical resources.[324] Bolt further argues that the readers of the gospel exorcism accounts also assumed the connection between demons and ghosts.[325] However, the level of popularity among the Jews regarding the connection between demons and ghosts is questionable. One of the most prominent themes in Jewish literature during the last two centuries BC, as Arnold indicates, was the belief that demons were the offspring of angels and human beings.[326] This belief maintains that "the sons of God" in Genesis 6:2 were angels (also known as "watchers") who had sexual intercourse with mortal women, who then gave birth to demons. According to Jewish literature from this time period, demons corrupt humankind in one way or another until the day of judgment.[327]

For the Jews in the intertestamental period, δαίμων (daimon) and δαιμόνιον (daimonion)[328] also had a negative connotation that referred to malevolent spirits in league with the devil.[329] In the context of the Septuagint and the New Testament, daimon and daimonion denote evil spirits who are Satan's active agents.[330] Overall, the New Testament writers had a different understanding of demons than the ancient Greek writers did. Reviewing the differences between the concept of demons in earlier Greek literature and in the New Testament writings, Eric Sorensen clarifies that the New Testament "does not equate demons with the spirits of the dead."[331] In this regard, the trend in the modern English translations of the Bible certainly sheds light on the issue. No current English translation of the Bible employs the word *ghost* to translate δαιμόνιον (or the plural form δαιμόνια). It is possible that translators consider

---

324. Bolt, "Jesus, the Daimons and the Dead," 75–96.
325. Bolt, 96.
326. Arnold, *Powers of Darkness*, 65.
327. Kelley Coblentz Bautch, "The Fall and Fate of Renegade Angels: The Intersection of Watchers Traditions and the Book of Revelation," in *The Fallen Angels Traditions: Second Temple Developments and Reception History*, eds. Angela Kim Harkins, Kelley Coblentz Bautch, and John C. Endres, S.J. (Washington, DC: Catholic Biblical Association of America, 2014), 69–93 (72).
328. Δαιμόνιον is a derivative form of δαίμων. See "Demon, Demoniac," in *Expository Dictionary of Bible Words: Word Studies for Key English Bible Words*, ed. Stephen D. Renn (Peabody, MA: Hendrickson, 2005), 262–263 (263).
329. G. J. Riley, "Demon," in *DDD*, ed. Karel van der Toorn, Bob Becking, and Pieter W. van der Horst, 2nd extensively revised ed. (Leiden: Brill, 1999), 235–240 (238).
330. Unger, *Biblical Demonology*, 55–58.
331. Eric Sorensen, *Possession and Exorcism in the New Testament and Early Christianity* (Tübingen: Mohr Siebeck, 2002), 121.

the word *ghost* as an inappropriate translation of δαιμόνιον. Therefore, today most English translations of the Bible render the term δαιμόνιον as "demon," not "ghost." This observable fact helps to confirm that the term for *demon* in the Bible is not what the word *ghost* means today in English.

Understanding the differences between the concepts of demons and ghosts in the Bible leads to another discussion: What are the ghosts that the Chinese worship in the Hungry Ghost Festival? At least four of the interviewees (M1, M3, H1, and H2) from this study explicitly stressed that the Hungry Ghost Festival is satanic. In their views, there is a close connection between ghost worship and demonic activity. These interviewees insisted that when people worship hungry ghosts, they are in fact worshipping Satan and the demons, instead of the souls of the dead. Any sacrifice offered to ghosts is indeed offered to demons. They view the Hungry Ghost Festival as a form of worship of demons and stressed that the Bible forbids believers to make sacrifices to demons or Satan.

In fact, many Chinese evangelicals hold a similar view. Ka Lun Leung in his commentary on the 1 Corinthians, for example, points out that ghosts as well as pagan gods are just different emanations of evil spirits.[332] Vincent Cheung, likewise, states that any form of idol worship is a worship of demons, and Satan is active in such worship.[333] In 1 Corinthians 8:1–6, Paul argues that all things sacrificed to idols are not to God, because there is no God but One, the Father. Later in 1 Corinthians 10:20, Paul clearly indicates that demons were the actual recipients of the sacrificed meat.[334] According to Paul, a spiritual reality lies behind pagan religious meals.[335] These demons who receive the sacrificed meat are real and exert formidable power to defile and destroy humans.[336] Furthermore, Paul warns that believers should never participate with demons.[337]

---

332. 梁家麟, 今日歌林多教會: 歌林多前書注釋 (*Today Corinthian Church: A Commentary on the First Corinthians*) (香港 [Hong Kong]: 天道書樓, 1992), 229.

333. 張永信, 歌林多前書注釋 (*Commentary on 1 Corinthians*) (香港 [Hong Kong]: 宣道出版社, 1997), 291–292.

334. Arnold, *Powers of Darkness*, 95.

335. Roy E. Ciampa and Brian S. Rosner, *The First Letter to the Corinthians*, The Pillar New Testament Commentary (Nottingham: Apollos, 2010), 479.

336. David E. Garland, *1 Corinthians*, Baker Exegetical Commentary on the New Testament (Grand Rapids, MI: Baker Academic, 2003), 480.

337. Ciampa and Rosner, *First Letter to the Corinthians*, 482.

7.2.3 The Origin of Evil Spiritual Powers

All six Chinese preachers who were interviewed in this study, moreover, regard Satan and his demons as fallen angelic creatures. This understanding of fallen angels is also in agreement with many evangelical theologians. Lewis Sperry Chafer, for instance, asserts that demons are unholy angels and that Satan is the chief of these fallen angels.[338] Wayne Grudem, in his *Systematic Theology*, clearly defines demons as "evil angels who sinned against God and who now continually work evil in the world."[339] Others, such as Millard J. Erickson[340] and James Montgomery Boice,[341] also discuss demons, Satan, and angels simultaneously, incorporating these discussions into the same chapter of their systematic theologies. Concerning the origin of demons, Erickson claims that demons were created by God and were once good angels.[342] Unger believes that this view on the origin of demons is "the best supported and the most clearly authenticated explanation."[343] Contemporary Chinese evangelical scholars such as David Hock Tey also believe that Satan is the fallen angel.[344]

Scholars have proposed a number of theories surrounding the origin of evil spiritual powers. One theory which is commonly assumed, as previously mentioned, maintains that demons are offspring of fallen angels and mortal women. This theory was popular in Judaism during the Greco-Roman period. Another theory argues that demons are the disembodied spirits of a pre-Adamite race of beings.[345] G. H. Pember, for example, believes that a pre-Adamite race existed on earth "before the ruin described in the second verse of Genesis," and that demons are the disembodied spirits of this race.[346] According to Pember's theory, the creation account in Genesis 1 records six days of restoration.[347]

---

338. Lewis Sperry Chafer, *Satan: His Motives and Methods* (Grand Rapids, MI: Kregel, 1990), 33.

339. Grudem, *Systematic Theology*, 412.

340. Erickson, *Christian Theology*, 457–475.

341. James Montgomery Boice, *Foundations of the Christian Faith* (Leicester: Inter-Varsity Press, 1986), 167–175.

342. Erickson, *Christian Theology*, 472.

343. Unger, *Biblical Demonology*, 52.

344. 鄭國治, 如何趕鬼 (*How to Perform an Exorcism*) (Johor Bahru: 人人書樓, 1998), 83.

345. Unger, *Biblical Demonology*, 42–45.

346. G. H. Pember, *Earth's Earliest Ages* (Grand Rapids, MI: Kregel, 1975), 58–59.

347. Pember, 63.

On the other hand, the Bible has little to say about the origin of evil spiritual powers. In fact, direct biblical references to Satan are also rare.[348] Regarding to the fall of Satan, three primary biblical passages mentioned by the interviewees included Isaiah 14:4–21, Ezekiel 28:11–19, and Luke 10:18. Apparently these preachers preach on the issues of ghosts and the origins of evil spirit power based on the aforementioned passages. Proper exegesis, nevertheless, is essential to the preaching of these passages since they have been interpreted in various ways.

Isaiah 14:4–21

Isaiah 14:4–21 is considered one of the finest Hebrew poems.[349] However, this passage has been challenging to be interpreted as many interpretations have been proposed. Traditionally, the king of Babylon in Isaiah 14 has been interpreted as referring to Satan. Early theologians such as Origen of Alexandria, Augustine of Hippo, and John Cassian believe that Isaiah 14:4–21 discloses the fall and fate of Satan.[350] The Hebrew phrase הֵילֵל בֶּן־שָׁחַר (*helel ben shachar*) in Isaiah 14:12 is interpreted as a reference to Satan. The translators of the Septuagint rendered the word הֵילֵל as ἑωσφόρος (*heosphoros*), and the Latin Vulgate translates הֵילֵל as *Lucifer*. Both the Greek term ἑωσφόρος and the Latin term *Lucifer* mean "light carrier" or "shining one."[351] Eventually the Latin term *Lucifer* became a name for Satan in Christian tradition.[352]

These early theologians' understanding of Isaiah 14 has impacted more than a few contemporary scholars. Wayne Grudem, for example, argues that Isaiah 14 is a reference to the fall of Satan and believes that this text also describes Satan's sin.[353] Kent Philpott also points out that Isaiah 14 indeed gives a

---

348. Wray and Mobley, *Birth of Satan*, 1.

349. John N. Oswalt, *The Book of Isaiah: Chapters 1–39* (Grand Rapids, MI: Eerdmans, 1986), 315.

350. "Isaiah 14," in *Isaiah: Interpreted by Early Christian and Medieval Commentators*, trans. and eds. Robert Louis Wilken, Angela Russell Christman, and Michael J. Hollerich (Grand Rapids, MI: Eerdmans, 2007), 168–181 (175–177).

351. Robert L. Alden, "Lucifer, Who or What?," *Bulletin of the Evangelical Theological Society* 11 (1968): 35–39 (35).

352. Marvin E. Tate, "Satan in the Old Testament," *RevExp* 89 (1992): 461–474 (467).

353. Grudem, *Systematic Theology*, 413.

very reasonable explanation of the origin of Satan and demons. Kent Philpott believes that Satan's downfall happened "at some time in the distant past."[354]

While acknowledging that Isaiah 14 refers to Satan, some view Isaiah 14:12–14 as a prophecy of Satan's defeat instead of a history of Satan's fall. This interpretative approach to Isaiah was popular in Second Temple Judaism. As Edwards indicates, "Second Temple Judaism widely interpreted Isaiah 14 with reference to the final, precipitous fall of Satan and his demons."[355] This approach is adopted by some contemporary scholars. Chafer, for instance, believes that Isaiah's vision predicts the future judgment upon Satan. He insists that Satan is still currently in heaven.[356] Similarly, McKenna also asserts that the fate of Satan in the apocalyptic context is revealed in the prophecy of Isaiah 14. The king of Babylon symbolizes Satan as the person of evil and iniquity. In Isaiah's prophecy, the downfall of Satan is irredeemable.[357] Denny Y. C. Ma, a renowned Chinese evangelical scholar, also holds a similar view. Ma believes that the message in Isaiah 14 was addressed to the evil one behind the king of Babylon, prophesying his final defeat at the end time.[358]

A number of scholars, however, oppose interpreting Isaiah 14 as a reference to Satan. Henry A. Kelly, for instance, criticizes Origen for misinterpreting Isaiah 14.[359] Robert L. Alden also asserts that identifying Lucifer with Satan is a mistake,[360] because he believes that Lucifer in Isaiah 14 is referring to the king of Babylon.[361] Some biblical scholars try to link the word הֵילֵל in Isaiah 14:12 to various mythological backgrounds. Possible mythological backgrounds include Greek, Ugaritic, Old South Arabian, Mesopotamian, and others.[362] Some suggest that הֵילֵל refers to the planet Venus, which was "some-

---

354. Kent Philpott, *A Manual of Demonology and the Occult* (Grand Rapids, MI: Zondervan, 1973), 74–75.

355. Edwards, *Gospel According to Luke*, 311.

356. Chafer, *Satan: His Motives and Methods*, 18.

357. David L. McKenna, *Isaiah 1–39*, The Communicator's Commentary (Dallas: Word, 1993), 176–181.

358. Denny Y. C. Ma 馬有藻, 神必救贖: 以賽亞書詮釋 *(The Glory of Redemption – A Commentary on the Book of Isaiah)* (臺北 [Taipei]: 天恩出版社, 2005), 59–62.

359. Henry Ansgar Kelly, *Satan: A Biography* (Cambridge: Cambridge University Press, 2006), 191–202.

360. Alden, "Lucifer, Who or What?," 35.

361. Alden, 39.

362. Robert H. O'Connell, "Isaiah XIV 4B–23: Ironic Reversal Through Concentric Structure and Mythic Allusion," *VT* 38 (1988): 406–418 (416–418).

The Cult of the Dead and the Spiritual Realm

times used to represent a divinity in ancient Near Eastern religion."³⁶³ Others draw parallels between הֵילֵל and deities in Babylonian-Assyrian or Canaanite mythology.³⁶⁴ However, no compelling evidence supports such theories. As Alden points out, "We have no evidence of a story from the ancient Near East dealing with the rebellion of a younger god against a chief god."³⁶⁵

On the other hand, some believe that Isaiah 14 merely speaks about the end of a tyrannical reign.³⁶⁶ Various explanations for the king of Babylon in Isaiah 14 have been proposed.³⁶⁷ Some explanations point to the human rulers of Babylon.³⁶⁸ John Calvin seems to hold this position.³⁶⁹ Brevard S. Childs asserts that Isaiah 14:4b-21 is a taunt song "against the king of Babylon."³⁷⁰ John H. Hayes and Stuart A. Irvine identify the king of Babylon in this passage as Tiglath-pileser.³⁷¹ Others suggest Neo-Assyrian rulers. For example, Seth Erlandsson argues that the tyranny described in Isaiah 14:4b-21 fits many Assyrian kings but no neo-Babylonian king.³⁷² Others suggest this king is Assyrian King Sargon II.³⁷³ Some argue that the precise identification of the ruler in this passage is difficult to verify and points to a proud but fallen

---

363. Gary V. Smith, *Isaiah 1-39*, The New American Commentary (Nashville, TN: B&H, 2007), 315.

364. Brevard S. Childs, *Isaiah: A Commentary* (Louisville, KY: Westminster John Knox, 2001), 126.

365. Alden, "Lucifer, Who or What?," 37.

366. Edward J. Young, *The Book of Isaiah, Volume I: Chapters I-XVIII*, The New International Commentary on the Old Testament (Grand Rapids, MI: Eerdmans, 1965), 441.

367. Noam Mizrahi, "The Textual History and Literary Background of Isa 14, 4," *ZAW* 125 (2013): 433-447 (433).

368. Bryan E. Beyer, *Encountering the Book of Isaiah: A Historical and Theological Survey* (Grand Rapids, MI: Baker Academic, 2007), 101.

369. John Calvin, *Commentary on the Book of the Prophet Isaiah, vol. 1*, trans. William Pringle (Grand Rapids, MI: Baker, 1999), 442.

370. Childs, *Isaiah*, 123.

371. John H. Hayes and Stuart A. Irvine, *Isaiah the Eighth-Century Prophet: His Times and His Preaching* (Nashville, TN: Abingdon, 1987), 227. Grogan, however, points out that most commentators believe "that only one king is in view." See Geoffrey W. Grogan, "Isaiah," in *The Expositor's Bible Commentary: Proverbs-Isaiah, vol.6*, rev. ed., eds. Tremper Longman III and David E. Garland (Grand Rapids, MI: Zondervan, 2008), 433-863 (563).

372. Seth Erlandsson, "The Burden of Babylon. A Study of Isaiah 13:2-14:23," *Springfielder* 38 (1974):1-12 (8).

373. Mizrahi, "Textual History," 433.

Mesopotamian despot.[374] Marvin E. Tate suggests that the tyrant in Isaiah 14 is archetypical for tyrants in human history.[375]

Ezekiel 28:11–19

Interpretations of Ezekiel 28:11–19 vary over a broad spectrum. Hector M. Patmore notes "a certain ambiguity in the text concerning the person to whom the lament is addressed."[376] According to traditional Christian interpretation, especially the church fathers, this passage refers to Satan. As Patmore indicates, "The most persistent interpretation offered by the church fathers is that Ezekiel 28 describes the fall of Satan."[377] Jerome, for example, believed that Ezekiel's words in this passage are addressed to the devil.[378] Several contemporary commentators and theologians still hold a similar interpretation. Lamar Eugene Cooper, for example, points out that the characteristics of the figure in Ezekiel 28:12–19 match the descriptions of Satan in other biblical texts.[379] Referring to Ezekiel 28, Michael Green also attests, "The devil was one of God's creatures – a spirit of great ability, who became consumed by pride, rebelled, lost his position, and set up in opposition an implacable hatred against God, the source of his existence."[380]

In rabbinical traditions from ancient times, however, the figure of Ezekiel 28:11–19 was linked to the narrative of Adam in Genesis.[381] Some contemporary scholars hold a similar view. Norman C. Habel, for example, believes that this passage is a lamentation for the fall of Adam. According to Habel, the ruler of Tyre in Ezekiel 28:1–10 and the king of Tyre in Ezekiel 28:11–19 refer to two different people. Habel asserts that Ezekiel 28:1–10 is a prophetic oracle against the earthly ruler of Tyre, while Ezekiel 28:11–19 refers to the

---

374. O'Connell, "Isaiah XIV 4B–23," 418.

375. Tate, "Satan in the Old Testament," 468.

376. Hector M. Patmore, *Adam, Satan, and the King of Tyre: The Interpretation of Ezekiel 28:11–19 in Late Antiquity* (Leiden: Brill, 2012), 3.

377. Patmore, 41.

378. Jerome, "Ezekiel 28:11–19: The Fall of Satan," in *Ezekiel, Daniel: Ancient Christian Commentary on Scripture, Old Testament XIII*, eds. Kenneth Stevenson and Michael Glerup (Downers Grove, IL: InterVarsity Press, 2008), 93–97 (96).

379. Lamar Eugene Cooper Sr., *Ezekiel*, The New American Commentary (Nashville, TN: B&H, 1994), 266–268.

380. Michael Green, *Exposing the Prince of Darkness* (Ann Arbor, MI: Servant, 1991), 34.

381. Patmore, *Adam, Satan, and the King of Tyre*, 16–17.

fall of the first man in Eden.³⁸² Daphna Arbel, based on her understanding of the Genesis Rabbah tradition, even suggests that Ezekiel 28:11–19 applies to the fall of Eve, the first woman in Eden.³⁸³

Linking Ezekiel 28 to Genesis 1–3, however, is not without difficulties. Patmore's summary is helpful for us to understand the differences between Ezekiel 28:11–19 and the account of the fall in Genesis. First, no woman or serpent is mentioned in Ezekiel 28:11–19. Second, the events in Ezekiel 28 took place on the holy mountain, but Genesis 1–3 mentions no mountain. Third, "Ezekiel's lament condemns the figure to complete and immediate annihilation, whereas Adam is banished from the garden to a life of hard toil."³⁸⁴ Moreover, the cause for this figure's loss of favor and exalted position is also very different from the cause for Adam and Eve's loss of position in the Garden of Eden after the fall.³⁸⁵

Some modern scholars, on the other hand, believe that Ezekiel 28:11–19 literally concerns only the land of Tyre and its ruler. For example, Daniel I. Block insists that מֶלֶךְ (*melek*) in the book of Ezekiel always refers to an earthly king.³⁸⁶ Douglas Stuart asserts that the prophecy against Tyre's king in Ezekiel 28 refers mainly to Ittobaal II (also spelled as Ethbaal II), the ruler of Tyre in Ezekiel's day.³⁸⁷ Leslie C. Allen seems to agree with Stuart, believing that the judgment oracle was targeted to Ittobaal II, who was overconfident in his power, wealth, and impregnable island city.³⁸⁸ Christopher J. H. Wright, holding a similar view, indicates that Ezekiel employs the creation narrative as a metaphorical way to portray "the great height from which the king of Tyre would fall."³⁸⁹ Analyzing Ezekiel 26:1–28:19 as a whole literary unit that

---

382. Norman C. Habel, "Ezekiel 28 and the Fall of the First Man," *CTM* 38 (1967): 516–524 (517).

383. Daphna Arbel, "Questions about Eve's Iniquity, Beauty, and Fall: The 'Primal Figure' in Ezekiel 28:11–19 and Genesis Rabbah Traditions of Eve," *JBL* 124 (2005): 641–655 (654–655).

384. Patmore, *Adam, Satan, and the King of Tyre*, 6.

385. Cooper, *Ezekiel*, 267.

386. Daniel I. Block, *The Book of Ezekiel: Chapters 25–48*, The New International Commentary on the Old Testament (Grand Rapids, MI: Eerdmans, 1998), 103.

387. Douglas Stuart, *Ezekiel*, The Communicator's Commentary (Dallas: Word, 1989), 268–274.

388. Leslie C. Allen, *Ezekiel 20–48*, Word Biblical Commentary (Dallas: Word, 1990), 93.

389. Christopher J. H. Wright, *The Message of Ezekiel: A New Heart and a New Spirit*, The Bible Speaks Today (Leicester: Inter-Varsity Press, 2001), 244. Ralph W. Klein believes that the reason for using the creation and fall motifs is to convey the fall of Tyre's king as a repetition of

includes a funeral dirge and judgment oracle, Greg Schmidt Goering also concludes that the judgment oracle is against Tyre and its king as a *fait accompli*.[390]

Obviously the lament in Ezekiel 28:11–19 is primarily addressed to a ruler of Tyre. However, it is possible that the text "also speaks about someone else."[391] It is worth noting that the imagery with which the figure is described in Ezekiel 28 does not fit any earthly monarch.[392] The king of Tyre in Ezekiel 28:11–19 is described as a "seal of perfection," "full of wisdom," and "perfect in beauty" (v.12). Moreover, verse 14 notes that this figure was once an anointed guardian cherub who walked among the fiery stones. As Lamar Eugene Cooper asserts, "Such descriptions make it unlikely that a strictly human creature is in view."[393] No earthly ruler could completely fit into such descriptions. The full meaning of Ezekiel 28 requires more research. The ambiguity of the text should be considered when interpreting its intended meaning. Moreover, since the devil is not explicitly mentioned in the text, we need to be careful before applying the text to the rebellion and fall of Satan.

In both Isaiah 14 and Ezekiel 28, the direct reference seems to be essentially to earthly monarchs. Any reference to Satan can only be cited indirectly. Uncertainty remains in the interpretation of both texts. Thus Nigel Wright helpfully reminds us that "we need to be cautious before grounding a doctrine of the fall of angels on uncertain exegesis."[394] According to the interviewees, another biblical passage considered as referring to the fall of Satan is Luke 10:18.

Luke 10:18

Compared to the Old Testament, the concept of Satan is treated in more detail in the New Testament.[395] Satan is broadly topical in the New Testament.[396]

---

the story of a primeval human being. See Ralph W. Klein, *Ezekiel: The Prophet and His Message* (Columbia: University of South Carolina, 1988), 132.

390. Greg Schmidt Goering, "Proleptic Fulfillment of the Prophetic Word: Ezekiel's Dirges over Tyre and Its Ruler," *JSOT* 36 (2012): 483–505 (505).

391. Patmore, *Adam, Satan, and the King of Tyre*, 3.

392. Patmore, 3.

393. Cooper, *Ezekiel*, 266–267.

394. Wright, *Theology of the Dark Side*, 63.

395. Brian Anthony Bompiani, "The Development of the Concept of Satan" (unpublished MA thesis, Trinity Evangelical Divinity School, 2004), 6.

396. Thomas J. Farrar and Guy J. Williams, "Talk of the Devil: Unpacking the Language of New Testament Satanology," *JSNT* 39 (2016): 72–96 (90).

According to Thomas J. Farrar and Guy J. Williams, there are about 137 references to Satan in the New Testament.[397] Of all the New Testament verses that mention Satan, Luke 10:18 is considered one of the most enigmatic.[398] Scholars debate whether Jesus is reporting a vision or making a metaphorical statement.[399]

George Eldon Ladd, along with several others, believes that Jesus's words in Luke 10:18 are "metaphorical language."[400] I. Howard Marshall argues that Jesus's statement in Luke 10:18 must be understood symbolically,[401] believing that Jesus is emphasizing the importance of the exorcism of demons. According to Marshall, Jesus makes clear that exorcisms are a sign of Satan's eschatological defeat.[402] Likewise, Robert H. Stein asserts that Luke 10:18 refers symbolically to the mission of the disciples as they cast out demons.[403] Clinton E. Arnold also insists that Luke 10:18 is not an ecstatic vision of Jesus. According to Arnold, Jesus's statement indicates that the disciples' clash with Satan's kingdom met "with victory over Satan's power and influence."[404] As David Lyle Jeffrey explains, Jesus reveals that the apostolic ministry has effected "a severe blow to the power of the adversary."[405]

Others, however, refuse to view Jesus's statement in Luke 10:18 as a metaphor. For example, Torsten Löfstedt believes that Luke intended this verse to be understood as a vision report. He makes a convincing argument, pointing out that vision writing is important in Luke's writings, both in Acts and

---

397. Thomas J. Farrar and Guy J. Williams, "Diabolical Data: A Critical Inventory of New Testament Satanology," *JSNT* 39 (2016): 40–71 (61).

398. Simon Gathercole, "Jesus' Eschatological Vision of the Fall of Satan: Luke 10,18 Reconsidered," *ZNW* 94 (2003): 143–163 (143–144).

399. Torsten Löfstedt, "Satan's Fall and the Mission of the Seventy-Two," *SEÅ* 76 (2011): 95–114 (97). Darrell L. Bock even argues, "There is no way to be certain if this was a vision or simply a remark." See Bock, *Luke, vol. II: 9:51–24:53*, 1006.

400. George Eldon Ladd, *A Theology of the New Testament*, rev. ed., ed. Donald A. Hagner (Grand Rapids, MI: Eerdmans, 1993), 64.

401. Marshall, *Gospel of Luke*, 428.

402. Marshall, 429.

403. Stein, *Luke*, 309. Joseph A. Fitzmyer also holds a similar view with Stein. See Joseph A. Fitzmyer, *The Gospel According to Luke*, The Anchor Bible (Garden City, NY: Doubleday, 1983), 860.

404. Arnold, *Three Crucial Questions*, 83. Likewise, Page believes that Jesus speaks figuratively to highlight Satan's decisive defeat. See Page, *Powers of Evil*, 110–111.

405. David Lyle Jeffrey, *Luke*, Brazos Theological Commentary on the Bible (Grand Rapids, MI: Brazos, 2012), 147.

his gospel. The vision reports in Acts include the visions of Stephen (Acts 7:55–56), Paul (Acts 9:3–7; 16:9; 22:17–21; 26:12–18), Ananias (Acts 9:10–16), Cornelius (Acts 10:3–6), and Peter (Acts 10:9–16). The vision reports in the gospel include Zechariah's vision (Luke 1:11–20), the shepherds' vison (Luke 2:9–15), and the vision of Jacob's mother, Johanna, and Mary of Magdala (Luke 24:4–7). Moreover, Löfstedt argues that the verb form of "watching" in Luke 10:18 offers evidence that interpreting Jesus's statement as a vision report is correct.[406] Likewise, Michael Bird believes that the vision report option is "to be preferred," over the symbolic metaphor option. His arguments include the presence of other visionary descriptions from Jesus's ministry (baptism and temptation stories) in the New Testament and Jesus's understanding of a literal Satan, demons, and spiritual battle.[407]

If Jesus's statement in Luke 10:18 is to be accepted as a vision report, when did Satan's downfall happen, or when is it supposed to take place?[408] Scholars hold diverse views concerning this issue. Simon Gathercole lists three principal interpretative options.[409] The first option interprets Luke 10:18 as Jesus having a vision "of a primeval past event."[410] Frederick Cornwallis Conybeare also argues for this position. He believes that Satan's original fall was common knowledge during Jesus's time.[411] Gathercole points out that the primeval view is related to the writings of Tertullian, Origen, Jerome, and Jewish literature.[412] However, within this position are several proposals regarding when Satan's fall takes place. One option envisages the prehistoric fall of Satan happening before the creation of the human race. As Walter C. Kaiser and others point out, this view was popularized by John Milton's *Paradise Lost*.[413] Another op-

---

406. Löfstedt, "Satan's Fall," 97–99.

407. Michael F. Bird, "Mission as an Apocalyptic Event: Reflections on Luke 10:18 and Mark 13:10," *EvQ* 76 (2004): 117–134 (122).

408. Lenski argues that Satan is a spiritual being and that his fall occurred in the supernatural world where no time exists. See R. C. H. Lenski, *The Interpretation of St. Luke's Gospel*, Commentary on the New Testament (Peabody, MA: Hendrickson, 1961), 581. However, not many scholars support this view.

409. Gathercole, "Jesus' Eschatological Vision," 144.

410. Gathercole, 144.

411. Frederick Cornwallis Conybeare, "The Demonology of the New Testament," *JQR* 8 (1896): 576–608 (577–578).

412. Gathercole, "Jesus' Eschatological Vision," 145–148.

413. Walter C. Kaiser Jr., et al., *Hard Sayings of the Bible*, 465. Apparently, John Milton's *Paradise Lost* relied on sources of earlier writers, "stretching all the way back to earliest

tion envisages the primeval fall of Satan happening simultaneously with the creation events of Genesis 1–2, either on the second day of creation or the sixth day of creation.[414] According to Gathercole, another alternative position envisages the fall of Satan as the descent of the Nephilim in Genesis 6.[415]

The second principal interpretative option understands Jesus's vision in Luke 10:18 as a vision "of an event in the recent past," prior to or simultaneous with the vision.[416] N. T. Wright, for example, believes that Luke 10:18 refers to Jesus having a vision while he was praying. Jesus tells his disciples that he saw Satan's defeat correspond to the earthly victories won by the seventy (or seventy-two), echoing the prophetic visions of Isaiah 14:4–24 and Ezekiel 28:1–19.[417] James R. Edwards also assumes that Satan's downfall happened over a period of time during the mission of the seventy.[418] Likewise, Ed Murphy indicates that in the spiritual realm, Jesus sees Satan's downfall, which is directly connected to the ministry of the disciples.[419] While acknowledging Satan's downfall as a long process which started at the time of his rebellion and will only be completed at the final judgment, Philip Graham Ryken asserts that Jesus's vision of Satan's downfall in Luke 10:18 refers to something more immediate and more directly connected to the ministry of the disciples.[420]

The third principal interpretive option understands Jesus's vision in Luke 10:18 as "a vision of a future event,"[421] either at the cross or at Jesus's second advent. For example, Susan R. Garrett believes that Jesus is prophesying his death and resurrection, which would cause Satan to fall.[422] Similarly, Peter G.

Apocryphal and Pseudepigraphical sources." See Gary A. Anderson, "The Exaltation of Adam and the Fall of Satan," *Journal of Jewish Thought and Philosophy* 6 (1997): 105–134 (105).

414. Gathercole, "Jesus' Eschatological Vision," 147–148.

415. Gathercole, 148.

416. Gathercole, 144.

417. N. T. Wright, *Luke for Everyone* (London: SPCK, 2001), 125. Bruce Larson holds a similar view. See Bruce Larson, *Luke*, The Communicator's Commentary (Waco, TX: Word, 1983), 182.

418. Edwards, *Gospel According to Luke*, 312.

419. Ed Murphy, *The Handbook for Spiritual Warfare*, rev. and updated ed. (Nashville, TN: Thomas Nelson, 2003), 36.

420. Philip Graham Ryken, *Luke*, vol. 1, Reformed Expository Commentary (Phillipsburg, NJ: P&R, 2009), 524–525.

421. Gathercole, "Jesus' Eschatological Vision," 144.

422. Susan R. Garrett, *The Demise of the Devil: Magic and the Demonic in Luke's Writings* (Minneapolis: Fortress, 1989), 58.

Bolt insists that Luke 10:17–20 is not teaching about a primeval fall of Satan but Satan's defeat by means of the cross.[423] However, some believe that the vision only refers to Jesus's *parousia*. As John T. Carroll argues, "Jesus' vision of Satan's fall, then, must be a prophetic vision of the future, final defeat of Satan."[424] Likewise, Chafer insists that Luke 10:18 is Jesus's prophetic utterance about God's final judgments against Satan.[425]

Apparently, no consensus exists for the explanation of Luke 10:18. It is important to note that the Bible does not present a clear picture of the origin of Satan and demons. The obscurity surrounding the biblical texts regarding the origin of evil spirits should not be ignored. However, as Nigel Wright indicates, there are still "theological reasons for moving towards the concept of an angelic fall."[426]

7.2.4 Christ's Supremacy and Spiritual Warfare

What should believers do about evil spirits, fallen angels? Two biblical teachings are relevant when preaching to the Chinese during the Hungry Ghost Festival. The first teaching relates to the supremacy of Christ over evil powers (Col 1:15–20; 2:8–15). The second teaching concerns the believers' spiritual warfare (Eph 6:10–20).

First, believers must understand that, by the power of Christ, they can overcome evil spirits. Fear of ghosts is common among the Chinese, especially during the Hungry Ghost Festival. This study finds that the Chinese worship the ghosts mainly because of fear. Therefore, one of the interviewees in this study emphasizes that preaching about Christ's supremacy over demonic powers is essential. We should not fear evil spirits because Christ has defeated them.

Paul's teachings in Colossians 1:15–20 and 2:8–15 are helpful when preaching to the Chinese during the Hungry Ghost Festival. The sovereignty of the Creator with respect to the powers is clearly pictured in Colossians 1:15–20.[427] This passage, as Moo has stated, is "one of the christological high

---

423. Bolt, "Towards a Biblical Theology," 63.
424. John T. Carroll, *Luke: A Commentary*, The New Testament Library (Louisville, KY: Westminster John Knox, 2012), 239.
425. Chafer, *Satan: His Motives and Methods*, 20.
426. Wright, *Theology of the Dark Side*, 63.
427. Arnold, *Powers of Darkness*, 100.

points of the New Testament."[428] There are two stanzas in Colossians 1:15–20, and both refer to the supremacy of Christ. The first stanza (1:15–17) depicts Christ as Lord of creation. The second stanza (1:18–20) portrays Christ as Lord of the new creation.[429] In 1:16, Paul proclaims that the entire creation, including the spiritual realm, is linked to Christ's destiny.[430] Thompson claims, "Christ's unique agency in creation and redemption elevates him above all the principalities and powers."[431] All angelic powers, from the highest to the lowest, are subject to Jesus Christ.[432] It is clear in Colossians 1:16 that the evil spirits are "utterly unable to rival Christ in any way."[433]

Paul's teaching in Colossians 2:8–15 is also important to our understanding of Christ's supremacy. In this passage, the identity of Christ and the significance of the cross are emphasized.[434] The metaphor of "the head" in 2:10 highlights the supremacy and authority of Christ over every ruler and authority.[435] Moreover, Paul indicates in 2:15 that the demonic spiritual powers were disarmed by the power of the cross.[436] Arnold asserts, "Nowhere else in the New Testament is Christ's victory over the powers of darkness given fuller expression than in Colossians 2:15."[437] The death and resurrection of Christ, once and for all, disarmed the evil powers which are against himself and the church.[438] Christ's power, victory, and love will now chart the destiny of believers; they are no longer subject to the rule and supremacy of darkness.[439]

On the other hand, believers must learn to stand against the spiritual forces of evil through spiritual warfare. As Nigel Wright asserts, "The fact that on

---

428. Moo, *Letters*, 107.
429. Richard R. Melick, Jr., *Philippians, Colossians, Philemon*, The New American Commentary (Nashville, TN: Broadman, 1991), 214.
430. Robert W. Wall, *Colossians & Philemon*, The IVP New Testament Commentary Series (Downers Grove, IL: InterVarsity Press, 1993), 68.
431. Marianne Meye Thompson, *Colossians and Philemon*, The Two Horizons New Testament Commentary (Grand Rapids, MI: Eerdmans, 2005), 34.
432. O'Brien, *Colossians, Philemon*, 47.
433. Moo, *Letters*, 123.
434. Thompson, *Colossians and Philemon*, 52.
435. David W. Pao, *Colossians & Philemon*, Zondervan Exegetical Commentary on the New Testament (Grand Rapids, MI: Zondervan, 2012), 163.
436. Pao, 172.
437. Arnold, *Powers of Darkness*, 104.
438. Arnold, 104.
439. Thompson, *Colossians and Philemon*, 60.

the cross evil was overcome does not mean that the conflict with the powers of darkness does not continue."[440] By definition, spiritual warfare is "warfare in the realm of the spirit involving the heavenly army and the Church (as its earthly force) and the Satanic army and evil men (as their earthly agents and force)."[441] Even though the term *spiritual warfare* is not specifically mentioned in the Bible, the concept of spiritual warfare is not new to Christianity.[442] The notion of spiritual warfare, for example, is mentioned in 2 Corinthians 10:4 and Ephesians 6:11. Dean Sherman believes that God emphasizes spiritual warfare throughout history.[443] Spiritual warfare is obviously an important theme in Jesus's message of the kingdom of God. Arnold attests, "From the very beginning of his public ministry, Jesus both spoke of and demonstrated the nature of the conflict with the opposing kingdom."[444]

Today, scholars take different approaches to the issue of spiritual warfare. Some reinterpret spiritual realities as "mythical projections of psychological, sociological, political, economic, and medical phenomena."[445] This view emphasizes resisting oppressive political and social economic powers in society. However, as Peter Aiken rightly argues, this approach is not compatible with biblical teaching.[446]

Rejecting the interpretation that the spiritual powers being opposed are human institutions, in the 1960s it became popular in some circles to see spiritual warfare as essentially deliverance from demons.[447] This approach was widely adopted in charismatic circles. Indeed, the rise and spread of Pentecostalism and the Charismatic Movement have brought renewed interest in the topic of spiritual warfare.[448] In this view, the spiritual battle focuses

---

440. Wright, *Theology of the Dark Side*, 66.

441. Ezekiel A. Ajibade, "The Kingdom of God and Spiritual Warfare," *Ogbomoso Journal of Theology* 12 (2007): 107–116 (108).

442. Graham Russell Smith, "The Church Militant: A Study of 'Spiritual Warfare' in the Anglican Charismatic Renewal" (unpublished doctoral dissertation, University of Birmingham, 2011), 32.

443. Dean Sherman, *Spiritual Warfare for Every Christian* (Seattle: Frontline, 1990), 20.

444. Arnold, *Three Crucial Questions*, 20.

445. David Powlison, *Power Encounters: Reclaiming Spiritual Warfare* (Grand Rapids, MI: Baker, 1995), 27.

446. Peter Aiken, "Should Reformed Believers Engage in Spiritual Warfare?" *PRJ* 7 (2015): 245–255 (245).

447. Powlison, *Power Encounters*, 27.

448. Smith, "The Church Militant," 3–4.

on the unseen world of demons and evil spirits.[449] Powlison uses the term "ekballistic mode of ministry – EMM" to label this approach. According to Powlison, "Ekballistic comes from the Greek word *ekballo*, which means to cast out."[450] This new approach to spiritual warfare assumes that demons of sin can reside within the human heart and can even take over the heart to a greater or lesser extent. Just as computer viruses attack a computer hard disk, demons penetrate the defence of the human personality to blind understanding and enslave the will. Thus, spiritual warfare is about casting out the demons that indwell a person's heart and mind.[451] It should be noted that "early Christian literature is full of references to the power of Christians to expel demons in the name of Christ."[452] Exorcism, one of the manifestations of spiritual warfare, was considered an official ministry in many churches during the post-Apostolic era.[453]

According to the traditional Christian view, however, spiritual warfare is "focused on the reality of needing to stand firm on the truth of God's Word in a world where Satan seeks to tempt, distract, discourage, and dissuade believers from living a life of holiness."[454] This view is referred to as the "classic Christian mode of spiritual warfare."[455] This classical view recognizes the demonic influence upon humans and emphasizes resisting sin and worldly temptation.[456] Walter Sundberg indicates that early Christians considered spiritual warfare as the crucible "in which their faith and witness were put to test."[457]

Paul's teaching in Ephesians 6:10–20 is essential for understanding spiritual warfare. The passage is "a general summary which views the entire Christian life under the figure of warfare, or a series of battles to be fought

---

449. Aiken, "Should Reformed Believers," 246.
450. Powlison, *Power Encounters*, 28.
451. Powlison, 27–30.
452. Everett Ferguson, *Demonology of the Early Christian World* (New York: E. Mellen, 1984), 129–130.
453. Nam Shin Park, "Hermeneutic and Spiritual Warfare," *Did* 22 (2011): 85–103 (88).
454. Aiken, "Should Reformed Believers," 246.
455. Powlison, *Power Encounters*, 27.
456. Aiken, "Should Reformed Believers," 245.
457. Sundberg, "Satan the Enemy," 31.

against a deadly enemy."[458] This passage is the most detailed description of the nature of spiritual warfare in the New Testament.[459] It is also an important source for spiritual warfare issues.[460] The main purpose of this passage, as many scholars indicate, is to exhort the letter's readers to be strong in God as they are engaged in warfare with their spiritual enemies.[461]

Structurally speaking, a number of scholars consider Ephesians 6:10–20 as the conclusion to the parenetic section of the letter (chs. 4–6).[462] Others attest that Ephesians 6:10–20 is a summary of the entire epistle.[463] Most scholars agree that this passage contains subunits, but different proposals regarding the division of this passage have been suggested. For example, Brian Wintle and Ken Gnanakan attest that the passage is divided into three subunits. In verses 10–13, the first subunit, Paul encourages his readers to be strong in the Lord and to equip themselves for battle against the spiritual forces of evil. The second subunit is found in verses 14–17. In this subunit, Paul lists the pieces of armor that Christians must put on. Verses 18–20 constitute the third subunit, in which Paul exhorts his readers to pray and be watchful.[464] Harold W. Hoehner proposes a similar division of the passage, but he considers verses 17–20 as the third subunit, which focuses on receiving the final pieces of armor.[465] Charles H. Talbert, on the other hand, considers verse 10 as a general exhortation, followed by three subsections: verses 11–13, 14–16, and 17–20.[466]

---

458. Arthur E. Travis, "The Christian's Warfare: An Exegetical Study of Ephesians Six (Ephesians 6:10–18)," *SwJT* 6 (1963): 71–80 (71).

459. J. Ayodeji Adeweya, "The Spiritual Powers of Ephesians 6:10–18 in the Light of African Pentecostal Spirituality," *BBR* 22 (2012): 251–258 (251).

460. David H. Wenkel, "The 'Breastplate of Righteousness' in Ephesians 6:14, Imputation or Virtue?," *TynBul* 58 (2007): 275–287 (275).

461. Timothy G. Gombis, *The Drama of Ephesians: Participating in the Triumph of God* (Downers Grove, IL: IVP Academic, 2010), 156.

462. Robert A. Wild, "The Warrior and The Prisoner: Some Reflections on Ephesians 6:10–20," *CBQ* 46 (1984): 284–298 (284). See also Harold W. Hoehner, *Ephesians*, An Exegetical Commentary (Grand Rapids, MI: Baker Academic, 2002), 817.

463. Peter T. O'Brien, *The Letter to the Ephesians*, The Pillar New Testament Commentary (Grand Rapids, MI: Eerdmans, 1999), 81. See also Andrew Lincoln, *Ephesians*, Word Biblical Commentary (Dallas: Word, 1990), 433. Andrew Lincoln suggests that Ephesians 6:10–20 is a *peroration (epilogos)* for the whole letter.

464. Brian Wintle and Ken Gnanakan, *Ephesians*, Asia Bible Commentary (Bangalore: Asia Theological Association, 2004), 171–180. See also Lincoln, *Ephesians*, 430.

465. Hoehner, *Ephesians*, 819.

466. Charles H. Talbert, *Ephesians and Colossians* (Grand Rapids, MI: Baker Academic, 2007), 161.

Scholarly opinion is also divided regarding the rhetorical genre of Ephesians 6:10–20. Some believe that the passage is an adaptation of a type of ancient hortatory speech before battle. For instance, Andrew Lincoln believes that this passage contains elements in common with ancient military exhortation in ancient Greek.[467] It is considered as like ancient pre-battle speeches.[468] Frank Thielman, however, points out that the passage is too short to be considered as a typical pre-battle speech. He also indicates that, unlike ancient pre-battle speeches which emphasize the weakness of the enemies, 6:10–20 emphasizes the strength of the enemies.[469]

In terms of structural analysis, Robert A. Wild attests that Ephesians 6:12 functions as the center element in the passage[470] and particularly the idea of the evil powers takes center stage.[471] Obviously, the concept of power is an important theme of the entire letter of Ephesians.[472] However in verse 12, Paul further reminds his readers of the importance of recognizing the power of the hosts of the dark world. Christians must stand against the spiritual forces of evil.

The teaching of spiritual warfare in Ephesians 6:10–20 is vital for believers. Several salient points of this passage must be highlighted. First, it helps us to recognize the reality of the demonic realm and the leader of the demonic realm, which is Satan.[473] As Stott asserts, "A thorough knowledge of the enemy and a healthy respect for his prowess are a necessary preliminary to victory in war."[474] Second, Paul reminds us to be active participants in spiritual warfare. Ephesians 6 commands believers to take an active role in spiritual defence.[475] Third, Paul's message is to the whole church, not just to individual

---

467. Andrew Lincoln, "'Stand therefore . . .' Ephesians 6:10–20 as *Peraratio*," *BibInt* 3 (1995): 99–114 (110–111).

468. Talbert, *Ephesians and Colossians*, 158–159.

469. Frank Thielman, *Ephesians*, Baker Exegetical Commentary on the New Testament (Grand Rapids, MI: Baker Academic, 2010), 413–414.

470. Wild, "The Warrior and The Prisoner," 286.

471. Paul T. Eckel, "Ephesians 6:10–20," *Int* 45 (1991): 288–293 (289).

472. Arnold, *Ephesians: Power and Magic*, 41.

473. Wintle and Gnanakan, *Ephesians*, 180.

474. John R. W. Stott, *The Message of Ephesians: God's New Society*, The Bible Speaks Today (Leicester: Inter-Varsity Press, 1979), 263.

475. Neil T. Anderson, *The Bondage Breaker* (Eugene, OR: Harvest House, 1990), 77–78.

Christians.[476] Significantly, the Christian armor in Ephesians 6 is described in "corporate terms."[477] The whole church must put on the full armor of God.[478] As Kinnaman explains, "Spiritual warfare is an activity of the whole Body of Christ working together."[479] Every believer in the body of Christ is inevitably involved in spiritual warfare with evil spirits. Lastly, spiritual warfare in this passage is mainly connected with Christian conduct.[480]

7.3 Summary

This chapter includes two main sections. The first section underlines a brief survey on the cult of the dead in the ancient Near Eastern and ancient Greco-Roman worlds. This section also reviews the history of Christianity's encounter with Chinese ancestor worship. At the end of the first section, a theological reflection on the issue of the afterlife is presented. The second section in this chapter addresses the issues of the spiritual realm. This section demonstrates that the Bible acknowledges the existence of Satan and demons and highlights the differences between the concepts of ghosts and demons. This section also discusses various views of the biblical material on the origins of Satan and demons. Finally, it presents a biblical understanding of Christ's supremacy over evil powers and underlines the current discussion of spiritual warfare. Furthermore, it points to Ephesians 6 as a reflection on the issue of spiritual warfare.

---

476. Gombis, *Drama of Ephesians*, 156–157.

477. Clinton E. Arnold, *Power of Darkness: A Thoughtful, Biblical Look at an Urgent Challenge Facing the Church* (Leicester: Inter-Varsity Press, 1992), 159.

478. Arnold, *Power of Darkness*, 159.

479. Gary D. Kinnaman, *Overcoming the Dominion of Darkness* (Cambridge: Crossway, 1992), 69.

480. Clinton Arnold, "Giving the Devil His Due," *Christianity Today* 34 (1990): 17–19 (19).

CHAPTER 8

Principles for Formulating Contextualized Preaching to Chinese People

Key outcomes from the analysis of the field research observations and of the interviews with six Chinese preachers are reported in chapter 5 and chapter 6 respectively. Chapter 7 presents the theological reflections on the cult of the dead and the spiritual realm. Based on the findings and the theological reflections, the current chapter addresses six underlying principles involved in formulating contextualized preaching to the Chinese people during the Spring Festival, the Qing Ming Festival, and the Hungry Ghost Festival. The first two principles are related to contextualization in a broader sense. The first principle reemphasizes the importance of contextualization which has been stressed by many scholars, as we see in chapter 2.[1] The second principle, similarly to Paul Hiebert's approach of critical contextualization,[2] underlines the significance of constructive engagement with the recipients' culture. The other four principles specifically deal with contextualized preaching during the festivals.

---

1. See sections 2.7, pp. 77–80, and 2.8, pp. 81–86.
2. See section 2.4, pp. 64–65.

291

8.1 Principle 1:
Contextualization is important in preaching, even when the Chinese preacher shares the same cultural background with the audience.

Many agree that contextualization is crucial in communicating the gospel. As Charles R. Taber says, contextualization is important because Christians always have to deal with the various dimensions of the context in which they live – social, cultural, political, economic, and religious.[3] However, the discussion on contextualization usually focuses on missiology or cross-cultural ministry.[4] Kortright Davis, for instance, points out that the concept of contextualization has helped align Western missionaries with contemporary modes of understanding international relationships and with the inherent dignity and worth of each other's traditions and cultures.[5] Undeniably, as Craig Blomberg rightly attests, "Every successful cross-cultural communication of the gospel that has led to a truly indigenous church with significant social impact throughout church history has involved contextualization, whether implemented consciously or not."[6] In missiology, contextualization is noticeably a three-culture model: "the Bible's culture, the missionary's culture, and the respondent's culture."[7] Communicating the gospel involves a complex cultural matrix: the culture of the biblical world (the source), the culture of the messenger, and the culture of the receptor.[8]

The findings of this study highlight the importance that contextualization not be limited only to cross-cultural communication. In any preaching event, even when the speaker and the audience share the same culture, contextualization still plays a vital role. The contextual factor in preaching is

---

3. Charles R. Taber, "Contextualization," *RelSRev* 13 (1987): 33–36 (33).

4. Bardshaw, for example, insists that contextualization plays an important role in Christian missions. See Bruce Bradshaw, *Bridging the Gap: Evangelism, Development and Shalom* (Monrovia, CA: MARC, 1993), 52.

5. Kortright Davis, "Bilateral Dialogue and Contextualization," *JES* 23 (1986): 386–399, (387).

6. Craig Blomberg, "We Contextualize More Than We Realize," in *Local Theology for the Global Church: Principles for an Evangelical Approach to Contextualization*, ed. Matthew Cook, et al. (Pasadena, CA: William Carey Library, 2010), 37–55 (40).

7. Jonathan Lewis, *World Mission: An Analysis of the World Christian Movement – Cross-Cultural Considerations*, 2nd ed. (Pasadena, CA: William Carey Library, 1994), section 13 33.

8. R. Daniel Shaw, *Transculturation: The Cultural Factor in Translation and Other Communication Tasks* (Pasadena, CA: William Carey Library, 1988), 30–31.

always crucial.⁹ The findings show that all six Chinese preachers, who share essentially the same cultural background with their audience, agreed that contextualized preaching is also important in their own contexts. As Andrew Walls argues, no society in the East or the West, in ancient or modern times, has been able to absorb the biblical truth painlessly into its system.¹⁰ In his recent book *Evangelism in the Skeptical World*, Sam Chan reminds us that the gospel "is deeply enculturated."¹¹ Therefore, communication of the gospel within any culture in the world is, to some extent, "cross-cultural" communication because the gospel has to be extracted from the culture of the biblical world and embedded in the receptor's culture.¹²

John Stott employs the bridge-building metaphor to describe the ministry of preaching because preaching bridges the cultural chasm of the biblical world and the audience's world.¹³ As Matthew D. Kim observes, "By our very vocation, pastors and preachers are bridgers of cultures."¹⁴ An authentic preacher must be faithful to the Word of God and sensitive to the world of the audience.¹⁵ To become effective bridge-building preachers, therefore, requires preachers to take the main idea of the scriptural text into the deeper alcoves of the listeners' hearts and minds.¹⁶ Faithful communicators of the gospel not only must learn to listen to biblical texts but also must pay attention to the people around them.¹⁷ Paul, an example for all gospel communicators, always listened to his listeners. Paul preached to both Jews and Gentiles, including elites of the Greco-Roman world, uneducated people, and people from other cultures. Whenever Paul preached, he depended on the receptors

---

9. James F. Kay, *Preaching and Theology* (St. Louis, MS: Chalice, 2007), 132.

10. Andrew F. Walls, *The Missionary Movement in Christian History: Studies in the Transmission of Faith* (Edinburgh: T&T Clark, 1996), 8.

11. Sam Chan, *Evangelism in a Skeptical World: How to Make the Unbelievable News about Jesus More Believable* (Grand Rapids, MI: Zondervan, 2018), 132.

12. R. Daniel Shaw believes that the cultural difference between the biblical world and the receptor's world always exists. See Shaw, *Transculturation*, 30–31.

13. John R. W. Stott, *I Believe in Preaching* (London: Hodder & Stoughton, 1982), 137–139.

14. Matthew D. Kim, *Preaching with Cultural Intelligence: Understanding the People Who Hear Our Sermons* (Grand Rapids, MI: Baker Academic, 2017), 8.

15. John R. W. Stott, *The Contemporary Christian: Applying God's Word to Today's World* (Downers Grove, IL: InterVarsity Press, 1992), 213.

16. Kim, *Preaching with Cultural Intelligence*, 9.

17. R. Daniel Shaw and Charles E. Van Engen, *Communicating God's Word in a Complex World: God's Truth or Hocus Pocus* (Lanham, MD: Rowman & Littlefield, 2003), 213.

of his message.[18] He became all things to all people in order to save some (1 Cor 9:22).

One problem preachers face today is a lack of understanding the congregation. They fail to understand how worldview assumptions and culture influence their listeners.[19] Some preachers neglect the responsibility of exegeting their listeners.[20] As Keith Willhite attests, preachers have two essential tasks: "accurately explaining the biblical text and clearly demonstrating the relevance of the text to the audience."[21] Regarding relevance of the sermon, Sidney Greidanus reminds modern preachers to pay attention to the discontinuity between the biblical world (including the societies of both the Old Testament and the New Testament) and modern societies. Greidanus rightly states, "Cultural changes do not negate the original message but make transformation in the light of our present culture mandatory."[22] In other words, effective preaching involves a correct understanding of the biblical truth as well as the world of the audience. Thus, contextualization is vital to preaching. As Padilla affirms, "Without the contextualization of the gospel there can be no real communication of the Word of God."[23] Contextualization helps preachers listen carefully and respond properly to the world of the audience. Contextualized sermons, to some extent, directly address the issues that pertain to life in a particular social and cultural situation.[24]

Audience is an important context to consider when preaching. The more the preacher understands the audience, the more relevantly he or she will

---

18. Ecknard J. Schnabel, *Paul the Missionary: Realities, Strategies and Methods* (Downers Grove, IL: IVP Academic, 2008), 336–337.

19. Greg R. Scharf, *Let The Earth Hear His Voice: Strategies for Overcoming Bottlenecks in Preaching God's Word* (Phillipsburg, NJ: P&R, 2015), 128.

20. Scott M. Gibson, *Preaching with a Plan: Sermon Strategies for Growing Mature Believers* (Grand Rapids, MI: Baker, 2012), 58.

21. Keith Willhite, "Connecting with Your Congregation," in *Preaching to a Shifting Culture: 12 Perspectives on Communication that Connects* (Grand Rapids, MI: Baker, 2004), 95–111 (96).

22. Sidney Greidanus, *The Modern Preacher and the Ancient Text: Interpreting and Preaching Biblical Literature* (Grand Rapids, MI: Eerdmans, 1988), 169.

23. C. René Padilla, *Mission Between the Times*, rev. ed. (Carlisle: Langham Monographs, 2010), 114.

24. John S. McClure, *Preaching Words: 144 Key Terms in Homiletics* (Louisville, KY: Westminster John Knox, 2007), 17.

preach.²⁵ Timothy Keller is right when he insists that preachers need to be culturally resourceful. According to Keller, "Most people know what IQ is, and many speak of EQ, but ministry leaders should also be characterized by CQ (cultural quotient)."²⁶ Cultural quotient is also known as cultural intelligence. It is the capability to relate effectively across cultures.²⁷ David A. Livermore asserts that cultural intelligence "measures the ability to effectively reach across the chasm of cultural differences in ways that are loving and respectful."²⁸ As mentioned previously, biblical preaching within any culture, to some extent, is "cross-cultural" communication. Therefore, all preachers should be equipped to become culturally intelligent preachers.²⁹

8.2 Principle 2:
Contextualized preaching includes both affirmation and confrontation.

The results of this study show that all six experienced Chinese preachers in their practices of contextualized preaching engage constructively with their own culture. On one hand, they are well aware of the ideas and beliefs of the Chinese and affirm some aspects of Chinese culture. They affirm, for example, the virtue of filial piety in Chinese culture. They believe the virtue of filial piety is in harmony with biblical teaching. They also agree that the concept of reunion with family and renewal of life during the Chinese New Year is a cultural contact point for contextualized preaching.

On the other hand, these Chinese preachers confront incorrect worldviews and superstitious beliefs and practices within the Chinese culture. They criticize, for example, idol worship and the practice of fortune telling during the Spring Festival. Moreover, they insist that the Hungry Ghost Festival should be discarded due to its involvement with worship of demons. These Chinese

---

25. 梁家麟, 愛主優先 *(The Lord's Priority Over)* (香港 [Hong Kong]: 建道神學院, 2003), 167.

26. Timothy Keller, *Center Church: Doing Balanced, Gospel-Centered Ministry in Your City* (Grand Rapids, MI: Zondervan, 2012), 121.

27. Kim, *Preaching with Cultural Intelligence*, 5.

28. David A. Livermore, *Cultural Intelligence: Improving Your CQ to Engage Our Multicultural World* (Grand Rapids, MI: Baker Academic, 2009), 13.

29. Kim, *Preaching with Cultural Intelligence*, 9–10.

preachers also reject the idea that the souls of the dead can continue to communicate with the living.

The approach of these six Chinese preachers to contextualization seems compatible with the apostle Paul's approach. Paul's preaching to the Athenians (Acts 17:16–32), as we have seen, is a good biblical example of constructive engagement with the recipients' culture.[30] Overall, in his speech to the Athenians, Paul affirms beliefs that are in harmony with the biblical truth and also confronts incorrect worldviews. Paul applies "points of agreement" as well as "points of contradiction" to communicate the gospel message to the Athenians.[31] As Paul G. Hiebert argues, "Contextualization must mean the communication of the gospel in ways the people understand but that also challenge them individually and corporately to turn from their evil ways."[32] In reality, all cultures have practices that can be redeemed and also practices that must be discarded.[33] Some neutral cultural norms are biblically permissible, but some must be rejected if they "carry functions and meanings that are against the Bible."[34] Contextualization is a dynamic and comprehensive process. It seeks not only to express the gospel authentically in the local context but also to transform the context at the same time.[35]

8.3 Principle 3:
The theme of harmony is appropriate for contextualized preaching among the Chinese, particularly during the Spring Festival.

The theme of harmony involves the elements of reunion and renewal because the underlying goal of reunion and renewal is to restore harmony in life. This study demonstrates that concepts of both reunion and renewal are key

---

30. William J. Larkin, Jr., *Culture and Biblical Hermeneutics: Interpreting and Applying the Authoritative Word in a Relativistic Age* (Grand Rapids, MI: Baker, 1988), 319–320. See also section 2.6.2.

31. Schnabel, *Paul the Missionary*, 171–183.

32. Paul G. Hiebert, *Anthropological Insights for Missionaries* (Grand Rapids, MI: Baker, 2004), 185.

33. Bradshaw, *Bridging the Gap*, 52.

34. Teresa Chai, "A Look at Contextualization: Historical Background, Definition, Function, Scope and Models," *AJPS* 18 (2015): 3–19 (18).

35. Dean Flemming, *Contextualization in the New Testament: Patterns for Theology and Mission* (Nottingham: Apollos, 2005), 19.

elements in the Spring Festival. Therefore, the theme of harmony, which is closely related to the concepts of reunion and renewal, can help contextualize the preaching of the gospel effectively during the Spring Festival.

The concepts of renewal and reunion are important to the Chinese, particularly during the Spring Festival. Through emphasizing renewal and reunion each year, the Chinese seek harmony in all aspects of life. One example is sending the kitchen god to heaven during the Spring Festival. By sending the kitchen god to heaven with sticky candy and other foods, the Chinese hope to restore or maintain harmonious relationships with the deities in heaven. Another example is the New Year's Eve reunion dinner. This dinner symbolizes harmony in the family. The key Chinese character for harmony is he 和. Etymologically, he 和 is made up of two parts, "grain" (禾) and "mouth" (口). Ancient China was an agricultural society. Therefore, "grain" and "mouth" means eating together. The Chinese believe that whenever people share their food together around the table, they have he 和, peace or harmony.[36]

Living in harmony is vital to the Chinese.[37] Chenyang Li states, "If we were to choose one word to characterize the Chinese ideal way of life, the word would be 'harmony.'"[38] The concept of harmony always plays an important role in Chinese thinking. In Chinese cosmology, the basic principle for the smooth operation of the universe is harmony.[39] As stated in the teaching of *The Book of Changes* (*Yi Jing* 易經), "The superior leader (also translated as 'the great man') displays benevolence, harmony in all that is right, complete propriety, and perseverance in correct behaviour (夫大人者，與天地合其德)."[40] Thus harmony is considered the measure of all things.[41] According to *The Analects*, "When practicing the ritual, what matters most is harmony. This is what made the beauty of the way of the ancient kings; it inspired their every move, great

---

36. Ching-Fen Hsiao, "Harmony Is Good and Good Is Harmony," *The Living Pulpit* 15 (2006): 24–26 (24).

37. David J. Hesselgrave, *Communicating Christ Cross-Culturally* (Grand Rapids, MI: Zondervan, 1978), 226.

38. Chenyang Li, *The Confucian Philosophy of Harmony* (New York: Routledge, 2014), 1.

39. Yih-Yuan Li, "In Search of Harmony and Equilibrium," *Dialogue & Alliance* 4 (1990): 15–30 (15).

40. This statement is in the first hexagram of *The Book of Changes*. See R. G. H. Siu, *The Man of Many Qualities: The Legacy of the I Ching* (Cambridge, MA: MIT Press, 1968), 15.

41. Ralph R. Covell, *Confucius, the Buddha, and Christ: A History of the Gospel in Chinese* (New York: Orbis, 1986), 11.

or small (禮之用, 和為貴. 先王之道, 斯為美)."[42] Harmony is believed to be the foundation of all things in the universe.[43] In Confucianism, harmony is also the ultimate purpose of all virtues (*li* 禮).[44]

According to the ancient Chinese philosophers, human beings and the universe constitute "a system of comprehensive harmony."[45] As Xinzhong Yao attests, three principles compose the backbone of Confucianism: harmony and unity between humanity and heaven, harmony and unity between descendants and ancestors, and harmony and unity between the secular and the sacred.[46] Instructing people how to live in harmony with one another is essential in the teachings of Confucius.[47] Confucians believe that harmony is closely related to nature, politics, ethics, and daily life. Harmony is "central to all existence and all activities and is rooted in innate centrality and equilibrium."[48] Indeed, Confucianism was founded on the belief that heaven and earth coexist in harmony and balanced strength while maintaining a perpetual dynamic. People on earth are sustained by these conditions and must strive to emulate the cosmic model.[49] From Confucius onward, "Chinese philosophers have always aspired to the creation of harmonious societies and have attempted to bring them into being."[50] In traditional Chinese thinking, the major role of human beings is to pursue the ideal of a harmonious society.[51]

---

42. "Chapter 1," *The Analects of Confucius*, trans. and ed. Simon Leys (New York: W. W. Norton, 1997), 5.

43. 陳谷嘉, "中國傳統文化的基本精神" (The Basic Spirit of Traditional Chinese Culture), 於中國傳統文化導論 (*An Introduction to Chinese Traditional Culture*), 朱漢民編 (長沙 [Changsha]: 湖南大學出版社, 2016), 36.

44. 石衡潭, 49.

45. Thome H. Fang, *The Chinese View of Life: The Philosophy of Comprehensive Harmony* (Taipei: Linking, 1981), 82. According to Fang, six different types of theories about the harmonious relations between human beings and the universe are evident throughout the entire development of Chinese philosophy. For details, see 82–88.

46. Xinzhong Yao, *An Introduction to Confucianism* (Cambridge: Cambridge University Press, 2000), 45.

47. *The Sacred Books of Confucius and Other Confucian Classics*, trans. and ed. Ch"u Chai and Winberg Chai (New Hyde Park, NY: University Books, 1965), 39.

48. Yao, *Introduction to Confucianism*, 172.

49. Diane Collinson, Kathryn Plant, and Robert Wilkinson, *Fifty Eastern Thinkers* (London: Routledge, 2000), 218.

50. Yi-Jie Tang, *Confucianism, Buddhism, Daoism, Christianity and Chinese Culture* (Washington, DC: Council for Research in Values and Philosophy, 1991), 55.

51. Tang, 56

8.3.1 The Biblical Concept of *Shalom* and the Theme of Harmony

In his article "Shalom and Confucian Harmony," Richard J. Mouw links the biblical concept of *shalom* to the Confucian idea of social harmony.⁵² He argues that the two concepts are parallel to one another. Mouw says, "As Christians, we need to think of social harmony, of *shalom*, as agents of the kingdom of Jesus Christ."⁵³ Noticeably, the Chinese concept of harmony is similar to the Old Testament concept of *shalom*, as well as to the New Testament concept of *eirene*.⁵⁴

As Chenyang Li insightfully notes, "Confucian harmony is multilateral and multifaceted."⁵⁵ According to Confucianism, harmony can occur within the individual, between individuals at various levels (familial, communal, national, and global), and between individuals and the natural universe.⁵⁶ In this regard, the concept of harmony in Chinese culture is similar to the Hebrew concept of שָׁלוֹם (*shalom*) in the Old Testament.

The basic meaning of שָׁלוֹם, according to *The Hebrew and Aramaic Lexicon of the Old Testament*, is completeness and intactness.⁵⁷ Thus Al Tizon suggests defining the term *shalom* as "the fullness of life."⁵⁸ *Shalom* can also signify "peace, friendship, happiness, well-being, prosperity, health, luck, kindness," and "salvation."⁵⁹ It represents one of the more prominent theological concepts in the Old Testament. Perry B. Yoder highlights three realms of meaning for the term *shalom* in the Old Testament. The first major realm to which *shalom* is linked is the material and physical realm. As Yoder asserts, "*Shalom* is most used to talk about material, physical circumstances."⁶⁰ He notes that

---

52. Richard J. Mouw, "Shalom and Confucian Harmony," *SANACS Journal* (2012–2013): 57–63.
53. Mouw, 62.
54. Hsiao, "Harmony Is Good and Good Is Harmony," 24–26.
55. Chenyang Li, *Confucian Philosophy of Harmony*, 9.
56. Chenyang Li, "The Confucian Ideal of Harmony," *Philosophy East and West* 56 (2006): 583–603 (588).
57. שָׁלוֹם, *HALOT*, ed. Ludwig Köhler et al. (Leiden: Brill, 1999), 1507.
58. Al Tizon, "Preaching for Shalom: Life and Peace," *AJPS* 19 (2016): 17–29 (19).
59. Philip J. Nel, "שׁלמ," in *NIDOTTE*, vol. 4, ed. Willem A. VanGemeren (Carlisle: Paternoster, 1997), 130–135 (130).
60. Perry B. Yoder, *Shalom: The Bible's Word for Salvation, Justice and Peace* (Eugene, OR: Wipf & Stock, 1997), 10–11.

shalom refers to a state of well-being in the material, physical realm.[61] Yoder further explains, "*Shalom* is marked by the presence of physical well-being and by the absence of physical threats like war, disease, and famine."[62] The second major realm to which the word *shalom* is applied is the social realm. Yoder attests that in the realm of human relations, "*shalom* describes the way things ought to be, whether between individuals or states."[63] He stresses that the concept of *shalom* points to the presence of positive and good relations as marked by justice, not just the absence of conflict.[64] Yoder points out that the third major realm to which *shalom* is related is the moral or ethical realm. In this regard, he notes that *shalom* refers to the absence of fault, guilt, or blame. *Shalom*, according to Yoder, also refers to the presence of integrity and straightforwardness.[65] As a religious concept, *shalom* is an essential part of God's plan of salvation. As Philip J. Nel explains, "All peace comes from him and he is the foundation of peace."[66]

In the New Testament, the Greek word εἰρήνη (*eirene*) occurs approximately one hundred times[67] and appears in almost every book.[68] *Eirene* is the Greek word for "peace." As William Klassen indicates, the concept of *eirene* in the New Testament is deeply influenced by the Jewish concept of *shalom*.[69] Many commentators seem to hold a similar view. Ernest Best believes that the meaning of *eirene* in Ephesians 2:14 should be understood "in its wider Jewish sense where it refers to both physical and spiritual well-being, [it] comes close to meaning salvation and attains eschatological significance."[70] D. A. Carson attests that *eirene* in John 14:27 reflects Hebrew *shalom*. Carson also believes that *eirene* is associated with the messianic kingdom anticipated

---

61. Yoder, 12.
62. Yoder, 13.
63. Yoder, 15.
64. Yoder, 15.
65. Yoder, 15–16.
66. Nel, "שׁלמ‎," 132.
67. Willard M. Swartley, "The Relation of Justice/Righteousness to *Shalom/Eirene*," *ExAud* 22 (2006): 29–53 (29).
68. William Klassen, "Peace: New Testament," in *The Anchor Bible Dictionary: Volume 5*, ed. David Noel Freedman (New York: Doubleday, 1992), 207–212 (207).
69. Klassen, 208.
70. Ernest Best, *Ephesians*, International Critical Commentary (London: T&T Clark, 1998), 252.

in the Old Testament.⁷¹ Thus Yoder is correct to maintain that *eirene* in the New Testament is "used in much the same way as *shalom* – for material and physical well-being, good relationships, and moral character."⁷² In summary, *shalom* in the Old Testament and *eirene* in the New Testament have a wide range of meaning in addition to "peace." Therefore, it is reasonable to conclude that the biblical concept of *shalom* is certainly related to the Chinese idea of harmony.

8.3.2 The Doctrine of Reconciliation and the Theme of Harmony

Since harmony is highly prized in Chinese culture, some consider the Christian doctrine of reconciliation as a good launch pad for proclaiming the gospel to the Chinese.⁷³ Biblically speaking, reconciliation is "the restoration of the justified person to fellowship with God."⁷⁴ Although the term *reconciliation* (καταλλάσσω – verb; καταλλαγή – noun) in its various forms is relatively rare in the New Testament, the doctrine of reconciliation is one of the main Christian concepts that attests to the reality of salvation.⁷⁵ In his work *Church Dogmatics*, Karl Barth allocated the discussion of salvation under the heading of "Reconciliation."⁷⁶ More recently, Stanley E. Porter attests that the notion of reconciliation "provides the basic and the major essential component" of Paul's missiological theology.⁷⁷ For Paul, reconciliation is the basis of Christian proclamation to non-believers.⁷⁸

---

71. D. A. Carson, *The Gospel According to John*, The Pillar New Testament Commentary (Nottingham: Apollos, 1991), 505.
72. Yoder, *Shalom*, 19.
73. Covell, *Confucius, the Buddha, and Christ*, 19.
74. Ladd, *Theology of the New Testament*, 492.
75. Phillip Gordon Ziegler, "A Brief Theology of Reconciliation," *Touchstone* 34 (2016): 7–13 (7). The term "reconciliation" appears mainly in the collection of Pauline letters. However, as Gary Shultz. Jr. reminds us, this does not mean that Paul is the only one who talks about reconciliation in the New Testament. Sometimes different words are used for the same concept of reconciliation. See Gary L. Shultz Jr., "The Reconciliation of All Things in Christ," *BSac* 167 (2010): 442–459 (442).
76. See Karl Barth, *Church Dogmatics, IV: The Doctrine of Reconciliation*, eds. G. W. Bromiley and T. F. Torrance (Edinburgh: T&T Clark, 1956).
77. Stanley E. Porter, "Reconciliation as the Heart of Paul's Missionary Theology," in *Paul as Missionary: Identity, Activity, Theology, and Practice*, eds. Trevor J. Burke and Brian S. Rosner (London: T&T Clark International, 2011), 169–179 (179).
78. Porter, 176.

Compared to other concepts used to explain the effects of the cross, such as the concepts of justification or redemption, Marshall believes that the concept of reconciliation "is the one which belongs most clearly to the sphere of personal relationship."[79] Concerning the salvation of human beings, the doctrine of reconciliation refers to "God's work in which he acts out his love to bring about harmonious relations between himself and others."[80] The key issue of reconciliation is the restoration of a harmonious relationship between human beings and their Creator. God's *shalom* intention for people was established through the reconciling work of Jesus Christ.[81] As Enoch Wan attests, for many generations the Chinese always put emphasis on harmonious relationships. Therefore, the doctrine of reconciliation has particular appeal and relevance for the Chinese mentality.[82]

Biblical passages closely related to the doctrine of reconciliation include Romans 5:1–11; 2 Corinthians 5:17–21; Ephesians 1:10, 2:11–22; and Colossians 1:11–22. Second Corinthians 5:17–21, particularly, can help the Chinese understand the doctrine of reconciliation. Porter asserts that 2 Corinthians 5:17–21 is perhaps the most important of Paul's reconciliation passages.[83] In this passage, Paul connects the idea of "reconciliation" with the idea of the "new creation."[84] This connection indicates a significant relationship between the "new creation" and "reconciliation." Every genuine believer of Christ has become a new person. "In Christ" God gives new life.[85] The relationship between the new creation and reconciliation is relevant to the Chinese, especially since the concepts of "renewal of life" and "reunion

---

79. I. Howard Marshall, "The Meaning of Reconciliation," in *Unity and Diversity in New Testament Theology: Essays in Honor of George E. Ladd*, ed. Robert A. Guelich (Grand Rapids, MI: Eerdmans, 1978), 117–132 (117).

80. Shultz, "Reconciliation of All Things," 442.

81. John Driver, *Understanding the Atonement for the Mission of the Church* (Scottdale, PA: Herald, 1986), 186.

82. 溫以諾, "榮耀的基督與人類文化" (The Glory of Christ and Human Culture), 於榮耀的基督與當代信徒 (*The Glorious Christ and the Contemporary Christian*) (加州 [California]: 基督工人神學院, 2003), 268–284 (280–282).

83. Porter, "Reconciliation as the Heart," 172.

84. G. K. Beale, *A New Testament Biblical Theology: The Unfolding of the Old Testament in the New* (Grand Rapids, MI: Baker Academic, 2011), 529. Beale presents a helpful discussion about the link between "reconciliation" and "new creation." He also refers this connection to the idea of "restoration" in the Old Testament. See 528–538.

85. Wayne Grudem, *Bible Doctrine: Essential Teachings of the Christian Faith*, ed. Jeff Purswell (Grand Rapids, MI: Zondervan, 1999), 302.

with family" are emphasized every Spring Festival. Nonetheless, the biblical concept of the "new creation" never refers only to the regeneration of a few individuals but to the regeneration of a whole new world. N. T. Wright claims that the new creation is "a whole new world coming to birth with the arrival of renewed and transformed humans."[86] As he explains, "Each personal 'new creation,' through Messiah-faith and baptism, was another signpost to the larger 'new creation' of which the Psalms and the prophets had spoken."[87] Similarly, John Stott attests, "Our hope for the future, however, is also cosmic."[88] Stott explains that Jesus "will not only raise the dead but regenerate the universe; he will make all things new."[89] Derek Tidball indicates that the death of Christ "has made it possible for the universe to be restored to peace with God and to be brought once again to a state of order under his control."[90] At some future time, the whole of God's creation will be brought into submission to God's reign.[91] The summing up of the universe in Christ, according to Ephesians 1:10, is the final goal of God's plan.[92] This does not mean universal salvation. As Tidball reminds us, "We must disabuse ourselves of any thoughts of universalism."[93] He clearly points out that "it is very hard to find a doctrine of universalism in the New Testament."[94]

In 2 Corinthians 5:18–19, Paul reminds us that no human action initiates and conveys reconciliation. Reconciliation is the "solemn act of God in Christ."[95] Porter rightly indicates that "all elements of this reconciling work come from God, and it is God who reconciles us all to himself through Christ."[96] This is a major difference between Christianity and traditional

---

86. N. T. Wright, *Paul and the Faithfulness of God* (Minneapolis: Fortress, 2013), 1489.
87. Wright, 1489.
88. John R. W. Stott, *Authentic Christianity: From the Writings of John Stott*, ed. Timothy Dudley-Smith (Downers Grove, IL: InterVarsity Press, 1995), 402.
89. Stott, 402.
90. Derek Tidball, *The Message of the Cross* (Leicester: Inter-Varsity Press, 2001), 229.
91. Derek Tidball, "Can Evangelicals Be Universalists?," *EvQ* 84 (2012): 19–32 (29).
92. Peter T. O'Brien, *The Letter to the Ephesians*, The Pillar New Testament Commentary (Grand Rapids, MI: Eerdmans, 1999), 114.
93. Tidball, *Message of the Cross*, 229.
94. Tidball, "Can Evangelicals," (29).
95. Svetlana Khobnya, "Reconciliation Must Prevail: A Fresh Look at 2 Corinthians 5:14–6:2," *EJT* 25 (2016): 128–136 (129).
96. Porter, "Reconciliation as the Heart," 173.

Chinese religious belief. In Chinese culture, human beings must take the initiative to reconcile with the deities. This belief is similar to a belief in Greco-Roman religions and myths, in which deities were the objects of human beings' reconciliation efforts.[97] Moreover, as Wing-Tsit Chan points out, "Humanism is evident in all aspects of Chinese life."[98] According to Confucius, "It is man that can make the Way great, and not the Way that can make man great (人能弘道, 非道弘人)."[99] Thus, Confucian humanism teaches that human beings must always take initiative to solve their own problems and direct their own destinies.[100]

According to the Bible, on the other hand, the process of reconciliation originates with God. Out of his love, God inaugurates the process of reconciliation with human beings so that they can be brought into right relationship with him.[101] In reconciliation, God and human beings are never equal partners. Reconciliation is initiated from God's side.[102] As Khobnya attests, "God is not the object of reconciliation but the subject and the source, and Christ is the agent."[103] Indeed, "God is both the initiator of reconciliation and the one toward whom reconciliation is directed."[104] In this respect, the biblical view of reconciliation is a novelty for the Chinese.

Although reconciliation was wrought first by God, it does not become efficacious until one has accepted God's proffered reconciliation (2 Cor 5:20). The relationship is restored only when a person has embraced the offer of reconciliation.[105] As I. Howard Marshall explains, the process of reconciliation involves three stages. The first stage is the reconciling act of God through the death of Jesus Christ. The second stage is the proclamation of reconciliation

---

97. Khobnya, "Reconciliation Must Prevail," 129.

98. Wing-Tsit Chan, "Chinese Theory and Practice, with Special Reference to Humanism," in *The Chinese Mind: Essentials of Chinese Philosophy and Culture*, ed. Charles A. Moore (Honolulu: University of Hawaii Press, 1967), 11–30 (18). Chan believes the word "humanism" could characterize the whole history of Chinese philosophy. See *A Source Book in Chinese Philosophy*, ed. and compiled by Wing-Tsit Chan (Princeton, NJ: Princeton University, 1963), 3.

99. *The Analects* (lun y u 論語) 15:28. See *A Source Book in Chinese Philosophy*, 44.

100. Wing-Tsit Chan, "Chinese Theory and Practice," 19.

101. Leon Morris, *The Apostolic Preaching of the Cross* (Grand Rapids, MI: Eerdmans, 1955), 192.

102. Marshall, "Meaning of Reconciliation," 128.

103. Khobnya, "Reconciliation Must Prevail," 130.

104. Porter, "Reconciliation as the Heart," 174.

105. Ladd, *Theology of the New Testament*, 496.

by God's messengers. The last stage, then, is the acceptance of God's act of reconciliation by faith. The process of reconciliation is not complete until all three stages have taken place.[106]

8.4 Principle 4:
The theme of filial piety is appropriate for contextualized preaching among the Chinese, particularly during the Qing Ming Festival.

The practice of ancestral veneration during the Chinese festivals is rooted in the ethics of filial piety,[107] a prime virtue in Chinese culture.[108] Moreover, the celebration of the Qing Ming Festival reinforces the teaching of filial piety every year. In Chinese culture, filial piety underlines the affection and duty of the children in parent-child relationship.[109] The Chinese character for filial piety is *xiao* 孝. Etymologically, *xiao* 孝 symbolizes a hierarchical parent-child relationship in which the aged person (*lao* 老) is positioned above the child (*zi* 子).[110] In this regard, the Chinese understanding of filial piety is similar to that of the ancient Roman understanding.[111] The word *piety* originates from the Latin word *pietas*. As is true today in Chinese culture, a father in ancient Roman culture maintained paternal authority throughout his life.[112]

In Chinese culture, filial piety stresses the obligation of children to obey, support, and honor their parents.[113] Filial piety emphasizes gratitude toward the parents. According to a Chinese saying, everyone should be grateful to

---

106. Marshall, "Meaning of Reconciliation," 128.

107. Khiok-Khng Yeo, "Paul's Theological Ethic and the Chinese Morality of Ren Ren," in *Cross-Cultural Paul: Journeys to Others, Journeys to Ourselves*, ed. Charles H. Cosgrove, Herold Weiss, and Khiok-Khng Yeo (Grand Rapids, MI: Eerdmans, 2005), 138. The problem of ancestral worship in Chinese culture, as well as the cult of the dead, is discussed in chapter 7. The current section focuses on using the concept of filial piety as a cultural contact point in contextualized preaching.

108. See pages 20, 92, 93, and 116 in this book.

109. Daniel Qin, "Confucian Filial Piety and the Fifth Commandment: A Fulfillment Approach," *AJPS* 16 (2013): 139–164 (140).

110. Heng Sure, "Filial Respect and Buddhist Meditation," *Religion East & West* 1 (2001): 57–65 (58).

111. G. Wright Doyle, *Jesus: The Complete Man* (Bloomington, IN: Author House, 2008), 25–26.

112. Meyer Fortes, *Time and Social Structure and Other Essays* (London: University of London, Athlone, 1970), 181–183.

113. Qin, "Confucian Filial Piety," 140.

their parents and repay their parents for their care (孝親報恩).¹¹⁴ However, filial piety in Chinese culture involves more than just supporting the parents. Confucius also stressed the importance of paying respect to the parents. In *The Analects* he states, "Nowadays people think they are dutiful sons when they feed their parents. Yet they also feed their dogs and horses. Unless there is respect, where is the difference? (今之孝者, 是謂能養。至于犬馬, 皆能有養; 不敬, 何以別乎)." ¹¹⁵

Classical Chinese philosophers believed that filial piety is the foundation of virtue.¹¹⁶ According to *The Classic of Filial Piety (xiao jing)*, "Filiality is the foundation of virtue and the root of civilization (夫孝, 德之本也, 教之所由生也)."¹¹⁷ *The Classic of Filial Piety* also declares, "Man excels all the beings in heaven and on earth. Of all man's acts none is greater than filiality (天地之性人為貴。人之行莫大於孝)."¹¹⁸ In Confucianism, filial piety is also considered the root of benevolence (*ren* 仁), which is the supreme virtue (孝弟也者, 其為仁之本與).¹¹⁹ Today, filial piety is still regarded as the primary culture spirit for the Chinese.¹²⁰ Thus, Hinsch attests that filial piety is the most fundamental organizing principle of Chinese society.¹²¹

It is not surprising, therefore, that the six preachers interviewed for this study suggest implementing the concept of filial piety as a cultural contact point in contextualized preaching among the Chinese. Indeed, filial piety is also an important ethical teaching in the Bible. Although the term "filial piety" does not exist in the Bible, the teaching of filial piety is asserted in various

---

114. 黃孝光, 與全人相遇 *(The Holistic Encounter)* (新北市 [New Taipei]: 華宣出版, 2009) 39.

115. "Chapter 2," *The Analects of Confucius*, trans. and ed. Simon Leys (New York: W. W. Norton, 1997), 7.

116. Yu-Wei Hsieh, "Filial Piety and Chinese Society," in *The Chinese Mind*, 167–187 (172).

117. *The Hsiao Ching*, ed. Paul K. T. Sih and trans. Mary Lelia Makra (New York: St. John University Press, 1961), 2–3. According to another translation, "Filial piety is the basis of virtue and the source of culture." See *The Sacred Books of Confucius*, 326.

118. *The Hsiao Ching*, ed. Paul K. T. Sih and trans. Mary Lelia Makra, 18–19. The last two Chinese words *yan fu* 嚴父 imply giving the highest honor to the father. See 56.

119. 何世明, 從基督教看中國孝道 *(A Christian's Perspective towards Filial Piety)* (北京 [Beijing]: 宗教文化出版社, 1999), 3–4.

120. Qing Wang, "A Tentative Study on Differences and Integration of Sino-Western Filial Piety Culture," *Asian Social Science* 7 (2011): 97–106 (97).

121. Bret Hinsch, "Confucian Filial Piety and the Construction of the Ideal Chinese Buddhist Woman," *Journal of Chinese Religions* 30 (2002): 49–75 (49).

passages.¹²² The following sections will highlight some features of the biblical teaching of filial piety.

8.4.1 Emphasis on Filial Piety in Both the Old Testament and the New Testament

First, filial piety is one of the Ten Commandments in the Bible.¹²³ As Snyder and Ramirez attest, "Few biblical passages are as important in the everyday life of Judeo-Christian people than the Ten Commandments."¹²⁴ Indeed, the Ten Commandments are a vital part of the Christian faith. The commandments were given by God to his people face to face. They were written by the finger of God on two stone tablets. Moreover, the tablets of the Ten Commandments were later placed in the ark of the covenant.¹²⁵ The first four commandments focus on human beings' relationship with God. Commandments five to ten apply to human beings' relationship with one another.¹²⁶ Thus, the fifth commandment is the first of the commands directed to humanity as social beings.¹²⁷ This commandment "underscores the importance and maintenance of the most fundamental unit of society, the family."¹²⁸ Although sometimes the fifth commandment has been called "the children's commandment," Hayes rightly points out that the fifth commandment applies not only to young children but also to adults.¹²⁹

---

122. Qin, "Confucian Filial Piety," 148.

123. Peter T. Cha, "Constructing New Intergenerational Ties, Cultures, and Identities among Korean American Christians: A Congregational Case Study," in *This Side of Heaven: Race, Ethnicity, and Christian Faith*, eds. Robert J. Priest and Alvaro L. Nieves (Oxford: Oxford University Press, 2007), 259–274 (265).

124. Graydon F. Snyder and Frank Ramirez, "The Ten Commandments," *Brethren Life and Thought* 55 (2010): 99–105 (99).

125. Patrick D. Miller, *The Ten Commandments, Interpretation: Resources for the Use of Scripture in the Church* (Louisville, KY: Westminster John Knox, 2009), 3–4.

126. Miller, 168.

127. Gerald Blidstein, *Honor Thy Father and Mother: Filial Responsibility in Jewish Law and Ethics* (New York: KTAV, 1976), 1. Filial piety is the center of Jewish family ethics, and Blidstein's work is considered one of the key resources on Jewish tradition. Grant highlights the longevity of the Jewish tradition and commentary on the fifth commandment. See Brian W. Grant, *The Social Structure of Christian Families: A Historical Perspective* (St. Louis, MS: Chalice, 2000), 14.

128. Joseph Hester, *The Ten Commandments: A Handbook of Religious, Legal and Social Issues* (Jefferson, NC: McFarland, 2003), 21.

129. John Alexander Hayes, *The Ten Commandments: A Present-Day Interpretation* (New York: Fleming H. Revell, 1931), 84.

The fifth commandment states, "Honor your father and your mother, that your days may be prolonged in the land which the LORD your God gives you" (Exod 20:12).[130] The fifth commandment is the first commandment with a promise attached. God commands us to honor our parents and promises long life as a reward. The Hebrew term for "honor" in this verse is כָּבֵד (kabed). The Hebrew root comes from a verb that means "to give weight" or "to make heavy."[131] This term refers to the high regard or position of an individual. Thus in the fifth commandment, God exhorts us to regard our parents as persons of great weight and to treat them with high regard.[132] In this respect, the idea of treating parents with high regard is similar to the Chinese teaching of filial piety, which puts parents in a higher position than children. The punishment for dishonoring parents is serious. The negative counterpart of the fifth commandment is in Leviticus 20:9: "If there is anyone who curses his father or his mother, he shall surely be put to death." The word "curse" in Hebrew is קָלַל (qalal), which means "to be light" or "to dishonor."[133] Dishonoring parents led to the death penalty in the Mosaic Law.[134] Similarly, unfiliality was also a serious offence in ancient China. According to *The Classic of Filial Piety*, "There are five punishments for three thousand offences, and of these offences there is none greater than unfiliality (五刑之屬三千, 而罪莫大於不孝)."[135]

The usage of the verb "to honor" in the fifth commandment, however, means more than just showing respect. It also means highly prizing, caring, and showing affection for parents.[136] J. Douma has identified several practical aspects of honoring parents from a biblical perspective. First, to honor is to listen carefully to the instruction given by parents. Second, honoring involves

---

130. The Deuteronomy version of the fifth commandment has two differences compared to the Exodus version. First, Deuteronomy 5:16 includes the phrase "as the Lord your God has commanded you" after the word "mother." Second, the phrase "and that it may go well with you" was added after the phrase "that your days may be prolonged." See Victor Hamilton, *Exodus: An Exegetical Commentary* (Grand Rapids, MI: Baker Academic, 2011), 325. For citations of the fifth commandment in the New Testament see Matt 15:4; 19:19; Mark 7:10; 10:19; Luke 18:20; Eph 6:2–3.

131. R. Kent Hughes, *Disciplines of Grace* (Wheaton, IL: Crossway, 1993), 98–99.

132. Miller, *Ten Commandments*, 176.

133. Hamilton, *Exodus*, 340.

134. Hamilton, 340.

135. *The Hsiao Ching*, 24–25.

136. Walter C. Kaiser Jr., *Toward Old Testament Ethics* (Grand Rapids, MI: Zondervan, 1983), 156.

showing deference toward parents. Third, to honor is to love one's parents. Douma believes that the general rule of loving our neighbor as ourselves applies to loving parents as well. Fourth, honoring parents includes being faithful in taking care of one's parents.[137]

Joseph, the son of Jacob, is considered a good example of filial piety in the Old Testament. After Joseph reconciled with his brothers, he asked them to bring his father, Jacob, and his father's household to Egypt so that he could take care of them (Gen 45:1–28). When Joseph met Jacob in Goshen, Joseph "fell on Jacob's neck and wept on his neck for a long time" (Gen 45:29). Joseph was affectionate toward his father and took good care of him in his old age. As Heng Tan Shi asserts, Joseph was a son with great filial piety even according to the standard of Confucius.[138]

The book of Proverbs also contains important instructions about filial piety. In Proverbs 13:1, the son is encouraged to listen to parental instruction. The passage contrasts a wise son who listens to his father's chastening instruction with a mocker who does not listen to rebuke.[139] Proverbs 23:22–25 reminds children to be grateful to their parents and attentive to their teaching.[140] Proverbs 19:26 also expresses condemnation toward the wicked son who does not provide proper care and protection for his elderly parents.[141]

In the New Testament the Decalogue is restated,[142] including the fifth commandment concerning filial piety. In Mark 7:6–13, Jesus affirms the mandate of the fifth commandment and rebukes the Pharisees and the scribes for invalidating God's commandment.[143] In Ephesians 6:1–4, Paul quotes the fifth

---

137. J. Douma, *The Ten Commandments: Manual for the Christian Life*, trans. Nelson D. Kloosterman (Phillipburg, NJ: P&R, 1996), 172–173.

138. 石衡潭, 30–31.

139. Bruce K. Waltke, *The Book of Proverbs 1–15*, The New International Commentary on the Old Testament (Grand Rapids, MI: Eerdmans, 2004), 551.

140. Ernest C. Lucas, *Proverbs*, The Two Horizons Old Testament Commentary (Grand Rapids, MI: Eerdmans, 2015), 157.

141. Roland E. Murphy, *Proverbs*, Word Biblical Commentary (Nashville, TN: Thomas Nelson, 1998), 146.

142. Christopher R. Seitz, "The Ten Commandments: Positive and Natural Law and the Covenants Old and New – Christian Use of the Decalogue and Moral Law," in *I Am the Lord Your God: Christian Reflections on the Ten Commandments*, eds. Carl E. Braaten and Christopher R. Seitz (Grand Rapids, MI: Eerdmans, 2005), 20.

143. Anathea E. Portier-Young, "Response to Honoring Parents," in *The Ten Commandments for Jews, Christians, and Others*, ed. Roger E. Van Harn (Grand Rapids, MI: Eerdmans, 2007), 100–111 (105). See also Matt 15:1–9.

commandment and urges children to be obedient to their parents. Clinton E. Arnold points out that the apostle Paul employed the Greek word ὑπακούω ("obey") to convey the idea of "unquestioning compliance expected from children toward their parents."[144] Moreover, "obedience is further motivated by and based on the fact that it is 'right' (δίκαιον)," Arnold asserts.[145]

In Colossians 3:20, Paul again urges children to obey their parents because "it is well pleasing to the Lord." R. Kent Hughes indicates that the word "obey" can be read literally as "listen under your parents" or "really listen to your parents and do it!"[146] This command is a call for "a heart obedience to parents."[147] Therefore, we conclude that in both the Old and New Testaments, the importance of filial piety is consistently emphasized. In fact, while filial piety is a cultural norm for the Chinese, it is a divine order in the Bible.[148]

On the other hand, the Bible also emphasizes parents' responsibility to instruct and train their children.[149] Various passages in the book of Proverbs draw attention to the importance of parental discipline, nurture, and education.[150] For instance, Proverbs 13:24 encourages parents to correct the faults of their children.[151] Proverbs 23:13–14 reminds parents not to hold back discipline from the child: "You shall strike him with the rod and rescue his soul from Sheol" (Prov 23:14). Moreover, Proverbs 19:18 reminds parents that withholding discipline from children is regarded as killing them.[152] Similar teaching is also found in the New Testament. In Ephesians 6:4, Paul urges parents to raise their children with the discipline and instruction that comes

---

144. Clinton E. Arnold, *Ephesians*, Zondervan Exegetical Commentary on the New Testament (Grand Rapids, MI: Zondervan, 2010), 415.

145. Arnold, 416.

146. R. Kent Hughes, *Colossians and Philemon: The Supremacy of Christ*, Preaching the Word (Westchester, IL: Crossway, 1989), 124.

147. Hughes, 125.

148. Qin, "Confucian Filial Piety," 156.

149. John M. McBain, *The Ten Commandments in the New Testament* (Nashville, TN: Broadman, 1977), 50. See Deut 6:20–24.

150. Robert M. Hicks, *The Christian Family in Changing Times: The Myths, Models, and Mystery of Family Life* (Grand Rapids, MI: Baker, 2002), 92. See Prov 22:6; 29:17.

151. Waltke, *Book of Proverbs 1–15*, 574.

152. Tremper Longman III, *Proverbs*, Baker Commentary on the Old Testament Wisdom and Psalms (Grand Rapids, MI: Baker Academic, 2006), 370.

from the Lord.¹⁵³ In Colossians 3:21, Paul warns parents not to cause their children to become discouraged or "lose heart."

8.4.2 Jesus the Son of God as a Perfect Model of Filial Piety

A discussion of Jesus's filial piety as the Son of God requires a brief preliminary evaluation of the phrase "Son of God" in the Bible. This phrase refers not only to Jesus but also to a diverse range of beings, including human beings and angels.¹⁵⁴ In the book of Job, angels are called "sons of God" (Job 1:6; 2:1). Adam is called "son of God" (Luke 3:38). The nation of Israel is also called "son of God" (Exod 4:22).¹⁵⁵ However, when applied to Jesus, the phrase "Son of God" is used in a unique christological way.

"Son of God" is probably "the most significant christological title" in the New Testament.¹⁵⁶ As David R. Bauer explains, "The New Testament characteristically describes Jesus' relationship to God in terms of divine sonship."¹⁵⁷ The concept of Jesus's divine sonship indeed plays a significant role in the New Testament. For the authors of the four gospels, Jesus's sense of sonship is distinctive.¹⁵⁸ The christological title "Son of God" in the New Testament, as D. A. Carson reminds us, "is not a *terminus technicus*" – "a technical term that always carries the same associations."¹⁵⁹ Collin Hansen attests that "Son of God" is indeed "a rich, multilayered title whose meaning defies simple explanation."¹⁶⁰ In this respect, N. T. Wright's explanation is helpful. Wright indicates that the christological title "Son of God" has three levels of meaning. The first level of the title constitutes Jesus as Israel's Messiah. The second level

---

153. "Fathers, do not provoke your children to anger, but bring them up in the discipline and instruction of the Lord" (Eph 6:4).

154. D. A. Carson, *Jesus the Son of God: A Christological Title Often Overlooked, Sometimes Misunderstood, and Currently Disputed* (Wheaton, IL: Crossway, 2012), 24.

155. Ladd, *Theology of the New Testament*, 159.

156. David R. Bauer, "Son of God," in *Dictionary of Jesus and the Gospel* (Downers Grove: InterVarsity Press, 1992), 769.

157. Bauer, 770.

158. James D. G. Dunn, *Jesus and the Spirit: A Study of the Religious and Charismatic Experience of Jesus and the First Christians as Reflected in the New Testament* (London: SCM, 1975), 26–27.

159. Carson, *Jesus the Son of God*, 74. In the third chapter of his book, Carson also provides a helpful evaluation of the current debates over translating the phrase "the Son of God" for Muslims.

160. Collin Hansen, "The Son and the Crescent," *Christianity Today* 55 (2011): 18–23 (23).

refers to Jesus as the world's true sovereign. The third and final meaning of the title constitutes Jesus as the unique Son of God, the personal embodiment and revelation of the one true God.[161] Wright further emphasizes, "The third sense of 'Son of God', then, does not leave the first two behind, but integrates them within a larger picture of who the one true God, Israel's God, actually is."[162]

The Lukan account of the boy Jesus in the temple (Luke 2:41–51) shows that his sense of divine sonship was already deep-rooted and mature when he was still a young boy.[163] Matthew 11:25–27 clearly describes the unique relationship between God the Heavenly Father and Jesus, God's Son, who redeems his Father's people. The Son of God is the exclusive revelator of the Father.[164] Jesus regards his relationship with the Father as something unique. Jesus's sonship is different from his disciples' status as children of God.[165]

In the Gospel of Mark, "Son of God" appears within the general heading of the gospel (Mark 1:1).[166] Moreover, the specific meaning of Jesus's divine sonship was acclaimed by a heavenly voice (Mark 1:9–11).[167] Jesus's eternal sonship was confirmed during his baptism by the Heavenly Father[168] and in Luke 3:21–22 and Matthew 3:13–17.[169] The narratives of Jesus's experience at his baptism signify that Jesus knew himself to be the Son of God, and his sense of sonship was fundamental to his ministry.[170] Furthermore, Jesus's use of the word "Abba" in his prayer expresses his complete surrender to the Father's will (Mark 14:36).[171]

---

161. N. T. Wright, *The Resurrection of the Son of God* (London: SPCK, 2003), 724–733.

162. Wright, 735.

163. Dunn, *Jesus and the Spirit*, 27.

164. David L. Turner, *Matthew*, Baker Exegetical Commentary on the New Testament (Grand Rapids, MI: Baker Academic, 2008), 303.

165. Craig L. Blomberg, *Matthew*, The New American Commentary (Nashville, TN: Broadman, 1992), 193.

166. The phrase "Son of God" does not appear in some Greek manuscripts. See Mark L. Strauss, *Mark*, Exegetical Commentary on the New Testament, vol. 2 (Grand Rapids, MI: Zondervan, 2014), 60.

167. Bauer, "Son of God," 772–773.

168. Ladd, *Theology of the New Testament*, 163–164.

169. Compared with Luke and Mark, Matthew's account alone presents the dialogue between Jesus and John. Moreover, Matthew alone presents the Father's words in the third person instead of second person. See Turner, *Matthew*, 121.

170. Dunn, *Jesus and the Spirit*, 27.

171. Dunn, 39.

In the Gospel of John, the term "Son (of God)" appears twenty-nine times and "Father" (referring to God) appears more than one hundred times. According to John, the gospel was written in order to confirm for his readers that "Jesus is the Christ, the Son of God" (John 20:31).[172] In addition, John presents Jesus as the eternal Son.[173] Selvam Robertson argues that the divine sonship of Jesus is "the deepest theological teaching" in the Gospel of John. He further attests, "Sonship connotes the perfect unity of Christ with the Father which is established upon the basis of the perfect obedience of the Son, whose meat and drink is to do the Father's will (John 4:34; 8:29)."[174]

A close and intimate relationship exists between Jesus and God the Father.[175] As Brian Edgar emphasizes, "Love and obedience are at the heart of the inner relationships of the Trinity."[176] Regarding the roles and relationships within the Trinity, Bruce A. Ware highlights the fact that Jesus always obeys the Father and seeks to glorify him.[177] Similarly, Tidball asserts that Jesus "lived in complete dependence on and obedience to his Father."[178] Jesus's voluntary obedience became the "hallmark of his life and of his death."[179] Christ's filial obedience can be discussed both christologically and soteriologically. "From a christological perspective," Kevin Giles explains, "the incarnate Christ's will to do his Father's will is indicative of the perfect harmony of mind and will between the Father and the Son."[180] From a soteriological perspective, Giles indicates that Jesus is the second Adam "who perfectly does the will of God and thereby wins our salvation."[181] Jesus's complete obedience is imputed to

---

172. Bauer, "Son of God," 774.
173. Donald Macleod, *The Person of Christ* (Leicester: Inter-Varsity Press, 1998), 73.
174. S. Robertson, "Sonship in John's Gospel," *AJT* 25 (2011): 315–333 (323).
175. Allan Coppedge, *The God Who Is Triune: Revisioning the Christian Doctrine of God* (Downers Grove, IL: IVP Academic, 2007), 171.
176. Brian Edgar, *The Message of the Trinity: Life in God* (Leicester: Inter-Varsity Press, 2004), 176.
177. Bruce A. Ware, "The Father, the Son, and the Holy Spirit: The Trinity as Theological Foundation for Family Ministry," *JFM* 1 (2011): 6–13 (8).
178. Tidball, *Voices of the New Testament*, 91.
179. Tidball, 111.
180. Kevin Giles, *Jesus and the Father: Modern Evangelicals Reinvent the Doctrine of the Trinity* (Grand Rapids, MI: Zondervan, 2006), 203.
181. Giles, 203.

those who believe in him.[182] According to Tidball, "The whole life of Christ, including the manner of his death, exhibits an active obedience which resulted in our salvation."[183]

Jesus Christ, therefore, is viewed as a model of filial devotion and obedience toward God the Father.[184] Qin believes that Jesus reveals to us "the true meaning and practice of filial piety."[185] Regarding filial piety, Qin rightly attests that Jesus Christ sets "an ideal example for Confucians' cultural aspiration."[186] Moreover, Qin believes that the Chinese people will be more open to Christianity if they understand that the fulfillment of filial piety is found in the Christian faith.[187]

8.4.3 Honoring God Takes Precedence over Honoring Parents

In the biblical teaching of filial piety, several scholars suggest a close connection exists between respecting parents and respecting God. One's relationship with his or her parents is an extension of one's relationship with God.[188] In fact, the Hebrew word for honoring parents, כָּבֵד (kabed), also appears in several passages for honoring God.[189] However, the fifth commandment does not suggest that parental authority is equal to God's authority. Jan Milic Lochman cautions misunderstanding the fifth commandment by emphasizing, "We are not required to worship our parents."[190] As Blidstein has noted, loyalty to God always takes precedence over filial piety toward parents.[191] McBain rightly attests that the Ten Commandments are interrelated with one another. Moreover, he believes that the first four commandments, which apply to one's

---

182. Richard W. Daniels, "'To Fulfill All Righteousness': The Saving Merit of Christ's Obedience," *PRJ* 5 (2013)1 19–64 (51).

183. Tidball, *Voices of the New Testament*, 112.

184. Portier-Young, "Response to Honoring Parents," 109.

185. Qin, "Confucian Filial Piety," 159.

186. Qin, 160.

187. Qin, 160.

188. David Klinghoffer, *Shattered Tablets: Why We Ignore the Ten Commandments at Our Peril* (New York: Doubleday, 2007), 106.

189. Hamilton, *Exodus*, 341.

190. Jan Milic Lochman, *Signposts to Freedom: The Ten Commandments and Christian Ethics*, trans. David Lewis (Minneapolis: Augsburg, 1982), 79.

191. Blidstein, *Honor Thy Father and Mother*, 81.

relationship with God, are foundational for the rest of the commandments.[192] Therefore, the obligation to observe the commandments, such as keeping the Sabbath and not worshipping other gods, trumps the obligation to honor one's parents.[193]

One good example of honoring God over other things is the biblical record of Abraham. In Joshua 24, Joshua relayed God's message to the Israelites by reviewing the history of God's gracious provision for Abraham and his descendants, the Israelites.[194] In Joshua 24:2-3, God said that he took Abraham out from his family, who lived in a polytheistic culture, and gave him descendants.[195] Terah, and possibly his sons Abraham and Nahor as well, worshipped other gods in Mesopotamia.[196] The deities whom Terah and his sons worshipped may have included Aramean gods and goddess.[197] Abraham, however, abandoned the polytheistic worship of his family when he encountered Yahweh (Gen 11:31-12:3).[198] Although Terah also set out from Ur with Abraham and his family, there is no explanation given for his departure or his later residency in Haran.[199] Stephen's speech in Acts 7 regarding the call of Abraham helps us to focus on the main theological point in the narrative of Genesis 11:31-12:3. As David G. Peterson explains, "God was directing and using Abraham, whatever the role of Terah in the movement of the family

---

192. McBain, *Ten Commandments*, 50.

193. Bryon L. Sherwin, "The Fifth Word: Honouring Parents," in *Ten Commandments for Jews, Christians, and Others*, 87-99 (90).

194. Joshua began his address with the phrase "Thus says the LORD," which is a common formula in prophetic messages. See L. Daniel Hawk, *Joshua*, Berit Olam Studies in Hebrew Narrative and Poetry (Collegeville, MN: Liturgical Press, 2000), 267.

195. "Joshua said to all the people, 'Thus says the LORD, the God of Israel, "From ancient times your fathers lived beyond the River, *namely*, Terah, the father of Abraham and the father of Nahor, and they served other gods. Then I took your father Abraham from beyond the River, and led him through all the land of Canaan, and multiplied his descendants and gave him Isaac"'" (Josh 24:2-3).

196. Marten H. Woudstra, *The Book of Joshua*, The New International Commentary on the Old Testament (Grand Rapids, MI: Eerdmans, 1981), 344. See also David M. Howard Jr., *Joshua*, The New American Commentary (Nashville, TN: B&H, 1998), 430.

197. Joseph Blenkinsopp, "The First Family: Terah and Sons," *JSOT* 41 (2016): 3-13 (9).

198. J. Gordon McConville and Stephen N. Williams, *Joshua*, The Two Horizons Old Testament Commentary (Grand Rapids, MI: Eerdmans, 2010), 89.

199. Kenneth A. Mathews, *Genesis 11:27-50:26*, The New American Commentary (Nashville, TN: B&H, 2005), 102.

from Mesopotamia to Haran."[200] The divine calling of Abraham plays a central role in the patriarchal narratives,[201] and it shows that commitment to country and family must give way to allegiance to God.[202] After his encounter with God, Abraham worshipped only Yahweh and responded to Yahweh's call to leave his father's household and his country. Abraham lived for 175 years, and apparently God never regarded him as unfilial to his ancestors. Instead, Abraham was greatly blessed by God and became a father of many nations.

Other examples from the Old Testament include Ruth and Hezekiah. When Ruth followed Naomi back to Bethlehem, she left her country behind, including her parents and her parents' religion. She made a decision to worship Yahweh instead of Chemosh, the deity of the Moabites.[203] Ruth was blessed by God and eventually became the great-grandmother of David. A new trajectory of Israel's history began with Ruth's decisions.[204] Hezekiah was a highly praised Judean king (2 Kgs 18:5).[205] He refused to follow the religious path of his father, Ahaz, one of the worst kings in the history of Judah, who worshipped and promoted the worship of foreign gods.[206] Instead, Hezekiah demolished pagan places of worship and undertook cultic reforms.[207] Hezekiah also crushed the fertility symbol, the bronze serpent that Israel had traditionally worshipped since the time of Moses.[208] Hezekiah kept God's commandments, and the Lord was with him (2 Kgs 18:3–7).

As the incarnate obedient Son, Jesus did show filial piety toward his human parents. When Jesus was hanging on the cross, for example, he continued to

---

200. David G. Peterson, *The Acts of the Apostles*, The Pillar New Testament Commentary (Grand Rapids, MI: Eerdmans, 2009), 272.

201. Mathews, *Genesis 11:27–50:26*, 104.

202. Mathews, 109.

203. James McKeown, *Ruth*, The Two Horizons Old Testament Commentary (Grand Rapids, MI: Eerdmans, 2015), 25.

204. L. Daniel Hawk, *Ruth*, Apollos Old Testament Commentary (Nottingham: Apollos, 2015), 141.

205. Lissa M. Wray Beal, *1 and 2 Kings*, Apollos Old Testament Commentary (Nottingham: Apollos, 2014), 464.

206. Steven L. McKenzie, *1–2 Chronicles*, Abingdon Old Testament Commentaries (Nashville, TN: Abingdon, 2004), 334–335.

207. Roger L. Omanson and John E. Ellington, *A Handbook on 1–2 Chronicles*, vol. 2 (Miami: United Bible Societies, 2014), 1226.

208. Marvin A. Sweeney, *1 and 2 Kings*, The Old Testament Library (Louisville, KY: Westminster John Knox, 2007), 403.

demonstrate his love, concern, and provision for his mother (John 19:26–27).[209] However, in Jesus's teaching, allegiance to the kingdom of God unquestionably precedes allegiance to the biological family.[210] In the incident of Mark 3:31–35, Jesus clearly places the honor of God above his physical family, albeit not in any way dishonoring his family.[211] As Greg Jao asserts, "In his actions and statements, Jesus places the biological family in a position of secondary importance to the kingdom of God."[212]

In addition, Jesus proclaims a new concept of God's family which is defined by obedience to God's will.[213] Walking in obedience to God is considered an act of filial piety. Allen Mawhinney reminds us that Christians, as the children of God, have filial obligations toward our Heavenly Father.[214] In this regard, Paul Woods helpfully suggests "to refocus filial piety away from earthly superiors and elders and onto God himself, thus attributing to him all loyalty and obligation due a father from a son."[215]

8.4.4 Biblical Filial Piety Honors Both Father and Mother

Regarding the equality of fathers and mothers, the biblical teaching on filial piety differs from the Chinese teaching on filial piety.[216] Although respecting the mother is mentioned a few times in *The Classic of Filial Piety* (*xiao jing*),[217] the mother's status is never equal with the father's status in traditional Chinese culture. According to *The Classic of Filial Piety*, "In the practice of

---

209. T. B. Maston, *The Bible and Family Relations* (Nashville, TN: Broadman, 1983), 245.

210. Rodney Clapp, *Families at the Crossroads: Beyond Traditional and Modern Options* (Downers Grove, IL: InterVarsity Press, 1993), 77.

211. Ben Witherington III, *The Gospel of Mark: A Socio-Rhetorical Commentary* (Grand Rapids, MI: Eerdmans, 2001), 160.

212. Greg Jao, "Honor and Obey," in *Following Jesus without Dishonoring Your Parents: Asian American Discipleship*, eds. Jeanette Yep et al. (Downers Grove, IL: IVP, 1998) 43–56 (52).

213. Kim Huat Tan, *The Gospel According to Mark*, Asia Bible Commentary Series (Manila: Asia Theological Association, 2011), 91.

214. Allen Mawhinney, "God as Father: Two Popular Theories Reconsidered," *JETS* 31 (1988): 181–189 (189).

215. Paul R. Woods, "Towards a Contextualized Spirituality for Chinese Diaspora Christians" (unpublished master of theology dissertation, Spurgeon's College, 2006), 52.

216. Qin, "Confucian Filial Piety," 156–157.

217. *The Classic of Filial Piety* states, "Restricting one's personal desires and enjoyment in order to support one's parents ("one's father and mother," my translation) - this is the filiality of the common people (謹身節用, 以養父母, 此庶人之孝也)." See *The Hsiao Ching*, 12–13.

filiality, nothing is greater than to reverence one's father (孝莫大於嚴父)."[218] As Daniel Qin points out, the characteristic of the Confucian family is the extraordinary emphasis on the father-son relationship. Mothers, wives, and daughters are marginalized in the Confucian family.[219] Therefore, Qin concludes that Confucian filial piety is primarily based on a male-dominated mindset. On the other hand, he emphasizes that biblical filial piety has no gender prejudice.[220]

The fifth commandment calls for honoring both father and mother.[221] The teaching of the fifth commandment implies that the mother deserves to be treated with as much respect as the father.[222] This commandment attributes equal status to the mother.[223] In view of the inferior status of women in ancient cultures, it is worthy to note that the fifth commandment emphasizes the mother's position of equality with the father.[224] This emphasis on the equality of the parents is exceptional in the ancient Near East.[225] Some biblical passages, such as Leviticus 19:3,[226] give precedence to the respect owed to the mother.[227] As John E. Hartley points out, "The initial position of the mother in this command is striking. Clearly the mother is being honored."[228] Thus, Hayes calls the fifth commandment "the first step in the elevation of womanhood" in ancient customs.[229]

---

218. *The Hsiao Ching*, 18–19.
219. Qin, "Confucian Filial Piety," 156.
220. Qin, 157.
221. Douma, *Ten Commandments*, 161.
222. Douma, 161–162.
223. T. Desmond Alexander, *Exodus*, Apollos Old Testament Commentary (London: Apollos, 2017), 414.
224. Walther Eichrodt, "The Law and the Gospel," trans. Charles F. McRae, *Int* 11 (1957): 23–40 (31).
225. John I. Durham, *Exodus*, Word Biblical Commentary (Waco, TX: Word, 1987), 291.
226. "Every one of you shall reverence his mother and his father, and you shall keep my Sabbaths; I am the Lord your God" (Lev 19:3).
227. Blidstein, *Honor Thy Father and Mother*, 31. Blidstein believes that the father-mother equality teaching may have had significant influence on later Roman law, which "elevated the status of the mother and expected the son to give her much the same loyalty proffered his father." See also Blidstein, 32.
228. John E. Hartley, *Leviticus*, Word Biblical Commentary (Waco, TX: Word, 1992), 313.
229. Hayes, *Ten Commandments*, 87.

8.5 Principle 5:
Preaching about the spiritual realm is appropriate during the Hungry Ghost Festival.

Among the three festivals studied in this research, the Hungry Ghost Festival was considered the most controversial by the interviewees. This study discovered that the beliefs and practices associated with the Hungry Ghost Festival are contrary to Christian faith. Therefore, this study argues that Chinese Christians should not in any way participate in the Hungry Ghost Festival. On the other hand, this research highlights the importance of helping the Chinese understand the It suggests that preaching about issues such as ghosts, demons, or Satan is appropriate during the Hungry Ghost Festival. In fact, Charles H. Kraft in his recent book *Issues in Contextualization* also asserts that the discussion of spiritual powers is essential to contextualization.[230]

In chapter 7, the spiritual realm as well as the cult of the dead are discussed. The current section will not repeat the discussions. Regarding to preaching during the Hungry Ghost Festival, however, several main points are worth highlighting. First, preaching of the reality of the spiritual realm is considered as a good starting point of contextualized preaching during the Hungry Ghost Festival. As a matter of fact, the very concept of an invisible domain of spirits plays a central role during the Hungry Ghost Festival. For example, the first row of priority seats in the canopy of the Hungry Ghost Festival was reserved to entertain the invisible spirits, and foods are offered to them as well. Unlike the Western rational worldview which tends to exclude the unseen world, the traditional Chinese worldview generally accepts the reality of the spiritual realm. Thus in regards to the reality of the spiritual realm, the Chinese perspective, compared to the rationalist perspective, with only two tiers of reality, is closer to the biblical perspective. In the preceding chapter, this study argues that the biblical worldview affirms the reality of evil spirit powers, pointing out that the existence of the devil and demons is neither a myth nor merely structural societal evil. According to the biblical perspective, evil spiritual beings have their own independent existence. This acknowledgement of the reality of the spiritual realm is essential to preaching during the Hungry Ghost Festival.

---

230. Charles H. Kraft, *Issues in Contextualization* (Pasadena, CA: William Carey Library, 2016), 173

Second, the fundamental differences between Chinese and biblical perceptions on ghosts and demons must be clarified when preaching during the Hungry Ghost Festival. In the traditional Chinese worldview, a person becomes a ghost after dying and might haunt the living. However, there is little biblical warrant for believing spirits of the dead can influence the living. According to the Bible, ghosts or spirits of the dead are not the same as demons. Furthermore, the Chinese preachers interviewed in this study maintain that Satan and demons are all fallen angels behind the Chinese ghost culture. The Hungry Ghost Festival is considered as worship of demons. Consequently, preaching to the Chinese about satanic deception and fallen angels is also crucial. In 2 Corinthians 11:14, we are reminded that Satan disguises himself as an angel of light. Paul describes Satan as presenting the danger of deception in false appearance.[231] It is possible, therefore, for Satan and his demons to impersonate the dead. Chinese must understand the possibility of the manipulation of spiritual powers behind the Hungry Ghost Festival in order to be free from deception.

Third, Christ's supremacy over the spiritual realm must be emphasized within contextualized preaching during the Hungry Ghost Festival. Preaching about evil spiritual powers or satanic deception should never be an end in itself. Christ has defeated Satan and his demons. In the epistle to the Colossians, Paul exhorts his readers to fix their gaze on Jesus Christ, the head over all things, and to be sure that no one stands as Jesus's rival (Col 1:15–20; 2:9–15; 3:1–3).[232] Furthermore in 1 Peter 3:22, Peter also declares that Christ by his resurrection and ascension is victorious over all evil for all time.[233] By implication, believers of Jesus Christ will reign together with him.[234] As Paul says in Romans 8:37, "But in all these things we overwhelmingly conquer through Him who loved us." Literally, Paul is saying that believers are completely

---

231. Mark A. Seifrid, *The Second Letter to the Corinthians*, The Pillar New Testament Commentary (Grand Rapids, MI: Eerdmans, 2014), 419.

232. Stephen Seamands, *Give Them Christ: Preaching His Incarnation, Crucifixion, Resurrection, Ascension and Return* (Downers Grove, IL: IVP Books, 2012), 11–12. See also section 7.2.4.

233. Karen H. Jobes, *1 Peter*, Baker Exegetical Commentary on the New Testament (Grand Rapids, MI: Baker Academic, 2005), 258.

234. Thomas R. Schreiner, *1, 2 Peter, Jude*, The New American Commentary (Nashville, TN: B&H, 2003), 198.

victorious.²³⁵ Christ's followers must realise that Christ gives them power and authority to overcome evil spirits. As Kraft rightly states, "We can't be either biblical or relevant to most of the people of the world without a solid approach to spiritual power."²³⁶

8.6 Principle 6:
Choosing an appropriate metaphor for contextualized preaching in the Chinese culture is essential.

Several scholars have emphasized the importance of metaphor in preaching. David Buttrick advocates the use of metaphorical language in preaching because he believes that "metaphor making is native to human consciousness."²³⁷ He believes that metaphorical language makes preaching authentic. According to Buttrick, "What is artificial is attempting to preach without metaphorical language."²³⁸ In fact, Buttrick believes that "the language of preaching is essentially metaphorical."²³⁹ Eduard R. Riegert holds a similar position with Buttrick. Riegert believes metaphor redescribes reality and discloses a world of new possibilities for perception, understanding, and action.²⁴⁰ Thus he urges never to neglect the importance of metaphor in preaching.²⁴¹ Liske also highly values metaphor. He points out that metaphor has "great picture-evoking power."²⁴² In fact, some modern linguists and philosophers

---

235. Colin G. Kruse, *Paul's Letter to the Romans*, The Pillar New Testament Commentary (Grand Rapids, MI: Eerdmans, 2012), 364.

236. Kraft, *Issues in Contextualization*, 174.

237. David Buttrick, *Homiletic: Moves and Structures* (Philadelphia: Fortress, 1987), 192.

238. Buttrick, 192.

239. Buttrick, 125. Buttrick is surely right about the importance of metaphor in preaching. However, his symbolic orientation of the doctrine of salvation and other historical events in the Bible is questionable. Battrick says, "While the resurrection was surely an event, stories of the risen Christ speak of faith symbolically." See also 400.

240. Eduard R. Riegert, *Imaginative Shock: Preaching and Metaphor* (Burlington, ON: Trinity, 1990), 10–12.

241. Riegert, 14. Riegert views metaphor as not only a trope but also a process. He identifies three activities of metaphor: instructs, provides access to reality, and redescribes reality. See also 69–72.

242. Thomas V. Liske, *Effective Preaching* (New York: Macmillan, 1960), 193.

even suggest that metaphorical language is a basic part of all types of human communication.[243]

What is metaphor? Colin E. Gunton has warned that giving a satisfactory definition of metaphor is never an easy task. He argues, "Metaphor is such a pervasive feature of our language that any tight definition would very likely exclude many respectable instances."[244] The word *metaphor* originally comes from two Greek words *meta* ("across" or "over") and *pherein* ("carry" or "bring").[245] Aristotle's definition of metaphor is well-known: "Metaphor consists in giving the thing a name that belongs to something else; the transference being either from genus to species, or from species to genus, or from species to species, or on grounds of analogy."[246] Nevertheless in the modern study of metaphor, scholars with various perspectives and interests have diversely defined metaphor. These varying perspectives and interests include disciplines of linguistics, psychology, literary criticism, philosophy of science, and philosophy of religion.[247]

Some have defined metaphor simply. Robert Smith Jr. defines metaphor as "an extension of meaning through the comparison of one thing to another."[248] Other definitions of metaphor are more complicated. For Nisbet, metaphor is "a way of proceeding from the known to the unknown. It is a way of cognition in which the identifying qualities of one thing are transferred in an instantaneous, almost unconscious, flash of insight to some other thing that is, by remoteness of complexity, unknown to us."[249] In his explanation of metaphor, I. A. Richards claims, "When we use a metaphor we have two thoughts of different things active together and supported by a single word,

---

243. Marc Zvi Brettler, *God Is King: Understanding an Israelite Metaphor* (Sheffield: JSOT, 1989), 17.

244. Colin E. Gunton, *The Actuality of Atonement: A Study of Metaphor, Rationality and the Christian Tradition* (Grand Rapids, MI: Eerdmans, 1989), 27–28.

245. John R. Donahue, *The Gospel in Parable: Metaphor, Narrative, and Theology in the Synoptic Gospels* (Philadelphia, PA: Fortress, 1988), 6.

246. Quoted by Paul Ricoeur, *The Rule of Metaphor* (Toronto: University of Toronto Press, 1975), 13.

247. Peter W. Macky, *The Centrality of Metaphors to Biblical Thought: A Method for Interpreting the Bible* (Lewiston, NY: Edwin Mellen, 1990), 42.

248. Robert Smith, Jr., *Doctrine That Dances: Bringing Doctrinal Preaching and Teaching to Life* (Nashville, TN: B&H, 2008), 30.

249. Robert A. Nisbet, *Social Change and History: Aspects of the Western Theory of Development* (Oxford: Oxford University Press, 1969), 4.

or phrase, whose meaning is a resultant of their interaction."[250] On the other hand, Lakoff and Johnson explain metaphor in this way: "We have found that metaphors allow us to understand one domain of experience in terms of another. This suggests that understanding takes place in terms of entire domain of experience and not in terms of isolated concepts."[251]

For the purpose of this study, further discussion on the definitions of metaphor is unnecessary.[252] A simple yet useful working definition of metaphor is found in Janet Martin Soskice's work *Metaphor and Religious Language*. For Soskice, metaphor is "that figure of speech whereby we speak about one thing in terms which are seen to be suggestive of another."[253] Soskice emphasizes that metaphor is a mode of language use. She is against the claim that metaphor is a mental event. For Soskice, metaphor is mainly a linguistic phenomenon.[254] This understanding of metaphor will be applied in our current discussion.

In this study, the interviewees admitted that they incorporate metaphors in their sermons during the Chinese festivals. Preaching the "lost sheep" metaphor during the Chinese "Year of the Sheep" is one example. However, the wide variety of metaphors must be acknowledged. Generally speaking, metaphors "may be taken from all things in the world, whether substances or accidents, natural or artificial."[255] Even though many elements employed during the Chinese festivals are related to Chinese religions or myths, applying these elements metaphorically in contextualized preaching is still possible. When communicating the gospel, sometimes non-Christian elements can be helpful for an explanation or argument.

Discernment is needed when choosing or creating an appropriate metaphor for contextualized preaching in the Chinese culture, otherwise

---

250. Richards called these two thoughts the "tenor" (the underlying subject) and the "vehicle" (the symbols used to illuminate the subject) of the metaphor. See Ivor Armstrong Richards, *The Philosophy of Rhetoric* (Oxford: Oxford University Press, 1936), 93.

251. George Lakoff and Mark Johnson, *Metaphors We Live By* (Chicago: University of Chicago Press, 1980), 117.

252. For discussions on the modern study of metaphor regarding its definition, Macky provides a helpful overview in his book *The Centrality of Metaphors to Biblical Thought*. See 31–56.

253. Janet Martin Soskice, *Metaphor and Religious Language* (Oxford: Oxford University Press, 1985), 15.

254. Soskice, 16.

255. Benjamin Keach, *Preaching from the Types and Metaphors of the Bible* (Grand Rapids, MI: Kregel, 1972), 38.

metaphors may be misleading. Appropriateness and potential fruitfulness must be taken into account when expressing something metaphorically.[256] In this regard Buttrick's suggestion is helpful. He urges us to consider our usage of metaphor in two directions: toward social usage and toward theological intent. The direction of social usage applies to the social function of an image (or a symbol), basically its value, meaning, or emotional baggage. The direction of theological intent considers what theological understanding we are attempting to convey.[257]

In the context of Chinese culture, for instance, the "church as family" metaphor is considered very meaningful. Most mature readers of the Bible are familiar with the "church as family" metaphor.[258] Family and kinship groups always hold a prominent place in Chinese society.[259] As Scharfstein points out, the Chinese consider the family as the centre of human existence.[260] To some extent, the ancestral veneration, the reunion dinner on New Year's Eve, and the family gathering for tomb sweeping during the Qing Ming Festival are all family centred. Therefore, the "church as family" metaphor is more appropriate within contextualized preaching during the Spring Festival and the Qing Ming Festival, compared to other church metaphors such as the "church as Christ's body" metaphor.[261]

---

256. Victor Turner, *Dramas, Fields, and Metaphors: Symbolic Action in Human Society* (London: Cornell University Press, 1974), 25.

257. Buttrick, *Homiletic*, 119.

258. The "church as family" metaphor is viewed as one of the standard metaphors in the Bible. See 1 Peter 4:17 and Hebrews 3:6.

259. Martin J. Gannon, *Understanding Global Cultures: Metaphorical Journeys Through 28 Nations, Clusters of Nations, and Continents*, 3rd ed. (Thousand Oaks, CA: SAGE, 2004), 390.

260. Ben-Ami Scharfstein, *The Mind of China* (New York: Basic, 1974), 4.

261. A Catholic bishop in Vietnam, Simon Hoa Nguyen-Van Hien, argues that the "church as body of Christ" metaphor is too abstract and too organic for Vietnamese to come to terms with the nature of the church. He believes that the "church as family of God" metaphor is more meaningful to the Vietnamese people. Seemingly, the "church as family of God" metaphor also works well in African culture. See Francis Appiah-Kubi, "The Church, Family of God: Relevance and Pastoral Challenges of a Metaphor from an African Perspective," in *The Household of God and Local Households: Revisiting the Domestic Church*, eds. Thomas Knieps-Port Le Toi, Gerard Mannion, and Peter De Mey (Leuven: Peeters, 2013), 67–80 (67–68).

8.7 Summary

This chapter identifies five main principles involved in formulating contextualized preaching to the Chinese people. The first principle attests that contextualization is important in preaching, even when the Chinese preacher shares the same cultural background with the audience. The second principle maintains that the contextualized preaching should include both affirmation and confrontation while seeking to express the gospel authentically in the local context. The third principle brings out the theme of harmony which is appropriate for contextualized preaching among the Chinese, particularly during the Spring Festival. The fourth principle emphasizes that the theme of filial piety is appropriate for contextualized preaching among the Chinese, particularly during the Qing Ming Festival. The fifth principle suggests the preaching of the topic of the spiritual realm is appropriate during the Hungry Ghost Festival. The sixth principle advocates the importance of selecting appropriate metaphors for contextualized preaching in the Chinese culture.

CHAPTER 9

Summary, Conclusions, and Recommendations

The overall aim of this study was to investigate the principles involved in formulating contextualized preaching for the Chinese people during the Spring Festival, the Qing Ming Festival, and the Hungry Ghost Festival. To achieve the goal of this study, six research questions were developed. A qualitative field research and a qualitative interviewing method were both employed to gather the necessary information to answer these questions. In this final chapter, a summary of previous chapters is presented, conclusions derived from the findings are addressed, and recommendations for future research are identified.

9.1 Summary

Chapter 1 gave the background of this study by addressing the need of contextualization in the Chinese church. It highlighted the importance and urgency of making the gospel culturally relevant and understood by the Chinese people. Three objectives were identified in chapter 1. The first objective sought to identify biblical principles in response to religious beliefs and cultural values and practices associated with the three aforementioned major festivals. The second objective was to investigate the perception and practices of Chinese preachers with regard to contextualized preaching during these three major festivals. The third objective was to clarify the principles implicated in preparing contextualized preaching to the Chinese people in Malaysia. Furthermore, six research questions were identified. Chapter 1 also briefly introduces the research methodology, which is later discussed in detail in chapter 4. In addition, justification of the study and the definition of the key terms are outlined in chapter 1, which concludes with an overview of each following chapter.

The review of literature was undertaken in chapter 2 and chapter 3. Chapter 2 reviews major issues of contextualization and also addresses the necessity of contextualization. This chapter introduces a brief survey on the history of the ecumenical movement and the emergence of contextualization in the twentieth century. Moreover, chapter 2 also demonstrates the importance of contextualization, the approaches of contextualization, and the concern of syncretism. Examples of contextualization from the New Testament are reviewed as well, particularly the account of Paul's contextualized preaching in Lystra and Athens. Chapter 3 outlines the backgrounds and basic tenets of Confucianism, Taoism, Buddhism, and Chinese folk religion. The review of literature in both chapters substantiates the rationale and framework used in the study.

Chapter 4 gives a detailed explanation about the two research methods employed in this study. The first research method used was qualitative field research, conducted within Chinese communities in Malaysia. This chapter describes the field sites of the observations and the procedures utilized. The second research method employed was qualitative interviewing with six Chinese preachers. The selection of interviewees and procedures of the interviewing are also explained in chapter 4.

Data from field research observations is analysed and reported in three sections in chapter 5, covering findings regarding the Spring Festival, the Qing Ming Festival, and the Hungry Ghost Festival. The first section of chapter 5 reveals that influence from Chinese legends and the Chinese zodiac is present during the Spring Festival. Data also reveals that the Chinese people seek good fortune and ask for the blessing of deities during the festival. Remarks on the lion dance performed during the celebration concluded the analysis on the Spring Festival. The second section of chapter 5 covers the Qing Ming festival. Ancestral worship is the main theme of the festival, with varying methods of practices dependent upon specific circumstances and settings. The basis of ancestral worship is the belief that the dead have similar needs as the living. These needs even include divine protection, which is noted in the conclusion of this section. The third section of chapter 5 addresses the Hungry Ghost Festival, which reflects the belief that ghosts are the actual spirits of the deceased. In contrast to ancestral worship, however, the Chinese worship hungry ghosts out of fear. Fueled by this slightly twisted incentive, the Chinese people perform charitable acts for both the needy and the deceased during the period of the Hungry Ghost Festival. The parameters of this festival include a prominent utilitarian character, which becomes yet another focus of worship.

Chapter 6 records the analysis of interviews with Chinese preachers on contextualized preaching regarding the Spring Festival, Qing Ming Festival, and Hungry Ghost Festival. The interviews indicated that contextualized preaching in Chinese churches is necessary to help Chinese believers understand biblical teaching through the respect of their own culture. The analysis also highlights that some of the beliefs and practices associated with the Spring Festival, the Qing Ming Festival, and the Hungry Ghost Festival are contrary to the Christian faith. Among the three festivals, the Hungry Ghost Festival seems to be the most contrary to the Christian faith. For effective contextualized preaching during the three festivals, some cultural contact points, suitable preaching topics, and biblical passages are revealed in the findings.

Chapter 7 includes two main sections. The first section underlines a brief survey on the cult of the dead in the ancient Near Eastern and ancient Greco-Roman worlds. This section also reviews the history of Christianity's encounter with Chinese ancestral worship. Therefore, a theological reflection on the afterlife is presented. The second section of chapter 7 addresses the issues of the spiritual realm. This section demonstrates that the Bible acknowledges the existence of Satan and demons and highlights the differences between the concepts of ghosts and demons. Various views of the biblical material on the origins of Satan and demons are presented. Finally, a biblical understanding of Christ's supremacy over evil powers underlines the discussion of spiritual warfare, pointing to Colossians 1 and 2 and Ephesians 6 as germane to the discussion.

Based on previous findings and theological reflection, chapter 8 identifies six main principles involved in formulating contextualized preaching to the Chinese people. The first principle attests the importance of contextualization in preaching. Even though the Chinese preachers share the same cultural background with the audience, the preaching needs to be contextualized in order to be effective. The second principle maintains that contextualized preaching should include both affirmation and confrontation while seeking to express the gospel authentically in the local context.

Following these two underlying principles for contextualized preaching, the third to fifth principles identify a unique perspective for each of the three festivals discussed earlier. The third principle underscores the significance of the theme of harmony for contextualized preaching during the Spring Festival. Under this principle, the biblical concept of *shalom* and the doctrine of reconciliation is discussed. The fourth principle suggests utilizing the theme of filial piety, particularly during the Qing Ming Festival. The emphasis of filial piety in the Bible is highlighted, and Jesus is presented as the perfect model of filial piety. Biblical teaching of filial piety, in which honoring God takes precedence over honoring parents, is addressed, and the equality of fathers and mothers is also highlighted. The fifth principle demonstrates that the biblical view of the spiritual realm is appropriate for preaching during the Hungry Ghost Festival. The sixth principle is a general principle advocating the importance of appropriate metaphors from the perspective of the Chinese audience.

9.2 Conclusions

The main research question of this study is as follows: What are experienced Chinese preachers' perceptions and practices with regard to contextualized preaching during the Spring Festival, the Qing Ming Festival, and the Hungry Ghost Festival? As a result of the findings from the field research observations and the qualitative interviewing, alongside the theological reflections, the following conclusions are derived to answer the six sub-questions in this study.

Research Question 1: How do experienced Chinese preachers perceive contextualized preaching during the Spring Festival, the Qing Ming Festival, and the Hungry Ghost Festival?

Conclusion 1: Overall, the Chinese preachers agreed that contextualized preaching is important in their own contexts. They believe that there is a great need for contextualized preaching in Chinese churches. They agreed that contextualized preaching during the three festivals, the Spring Festival, the Qing Ming Festival, and the Hungry Ghost Festival, plays a vital role.

Research Question 2: What are experienced Chinese preachers' experiences of preaching during the Spring Festival, the Qing Ming Festival, and the Hungry Ghost Festival?

Conclusion 2: All six interviewees have experience preaching during the three festivals. Overall, their preaching experiences during these festivals were positive because they believe that their contextualized sermons were well-received by the congregation. Although they did not agree with the participation of Christians in the Hungry Ghost Festival, the preachers all think that the Hungry Ghost Festival is a good season for evangelistic preaching.

Research Question 3: According to experienced Chinese preachers, which aspects of the religious beliefs, cultural values, and practices associated with the Spring Festival, the Qing Ming Festival, and the Hungry Ghost Festival are in harmony with the Christian faith?

Conclusion 3: According to the interviewees, all three festivals contain elements in harmony with the Christian faith in varying degrees. Regarding the Spring Festival, the concepts of renewal and reunion, which have the underlying goal to restore harmony in life, are in consonance with the Christian faith. As for the Qing Ming Festival, the virtue of filial piety is in harmony with the Christian faith, since there is emphasis on filial piety in both the Old Testament and the New Testament. Concerning the Hungry Ghost Festival, the acknowledgement of the reality of the spiritual realm, although not identical to the Christian perspective, is considered similar to the Christian understanding.

Research Question 4: According to experienced Chinese preachers, which aspects of the religious beliefs, cultural values, and practices associated with the Spring Festival, the Qing Ming Festival, and the Hungry Ghost Festival are contrary to the Christian faith?

Conclusion 4: According to the interviewees, all three festivals contain elements contrary to the Christian faith in varying degrees. Regarding the Spring Festival, the worship of Chinese deities, belief in the Chinese zodiac, and participation in fortune telling are contrary to the Christian faith. The practice of tomb sweeping during the Qing Ming Festival is acceptable for Christians, but not the practice of ancestral worship. Ancestral worship and the worship of the hungry ghosts during the Hungry Ghost Festival are considered as a cult of the dead which is contrary to the Christian faith.

Research Question 5: According to experienced Chinese preachers, which elements of the religious beliefs, cultural values, and practices associated with the Spring Festival, the Qing Ming Festival, and the Hungry Ghost Festival, either contrary to or in harmony with the Christian faith, can be used to contextualize the preaching of the gospel effectively?

Conclusion 5: Some elements have been identified by the interviewees for effective contextualized preaching during all three festivals. The theme of harmony, which is closely related to the concepts of reunion and renewal, can help contextualize the preaching of the gospel effectively during the Spring Festival. As for the Qing Ming Festival, the concept of filial piety could be used as a cultural contact point in contextualized preaching among the Chinese. Among the three festivals studied in this research, the Hungry Ghost Festival is considered the most controversial. However, this study suggests that the preaching of the reality of spiritual realm is considered a good starting point of contextualized preaching during the Hungry Ghost Festival.

Research Question 6: According to experienced Chinese preachers, what theological resources can be used in contextualizing the preaching of the gospel during the Spring Festival, the Qing Ming Festival, and the Hungry Ghost Festival?

Conclusion 6: According to the interviewees, theological resources that can be used in contextualizing preaching during the three festivals are plentiful. For the Spring Festival, the Old Testament concept of *shalom* and the New Testament concept of *eirene* are considered useful in preaching the theme of harmony. Moreover, the doctrine of reconciliation is believed to be relevant to preaching about harmony during the Spring Festival. Bible passages suitable for contextualized preaching during the Spring Festival include the creation account in the book of Genesis (Gen 1:1–2:25) as well as passages about God's nature, promises, and love (Exod 34:6–8; Deut 8:1–20; 11:8–16). Other relevant Scripture during the Spring Festival include passages about family relationships (Exod 20:12; Josh 24:15) crossing the Jordan River (Josh 3:1–4:24), Psalm 1, the book of Ecclesiastes, the Beatitudes of Jesus (Matt 5:3–10), the parable of the prodigal son (Luke 15:11–32), John 3:1–16, and 2 Corinthians 5:17.

For the Qing Ming Festival, the fifth commandment (Lev 20:9) and related teachings about honoring one's mother and father are considered useful for preaching about filial piety at this festival (Gen 45:1–28; Prov 13:1; 19:26; 23:22–25; Mark 7:6–13; Eph 6:1–4; Col 3:20). Jesus's relationship to God (Matt 11:25–27; John 20:31) in terms of divine sonship is another important doctrine for filial piety that can be helpful for preaching to the Chinese.

Moreover, biblical teachings about honoring God taking precedence over honoring parents (Mark 3:31–35) and the belief that filial piety honors both father and mother (Lev 19:3) are important to the contextualized preaching of filial piety during the Qing Ming Festival. The death and resurrection of Christ is also a suitable topic for contextualized preaching during the Qing Ming Festival since this festival is usually close to the date of Easter. Biblical views of the afterlife and of evil spiritual powers are believed to be very crucial to both the Qing Ming Festival and the Hungry Ghost Festival. Colossians 1:15–20; 2:8–15 and Ephesians 6:10–20 are relevant for preaching during the Hungry Ghost Festival.

9.3 Recommendations

This research is significant in that it has demonstrated principles involved in formulating contextualized preaching among the Chinese people during the Spring Festival, the Qing Ming Festival, and the Hungry Ghost Festival. Key themes which can be used to contextualize the preaching of the gospel effectively have been identified in this study as well. Since this study maintains that authentic contextualization must be consistent with Scripture and the historic Christian faith, these key themes were discussed from the perspective of biblical teaching. However, the theological reflection on these issues is not exhaustive. The discussions in this study tend to be illustrative, laying a foundation. A considerable amount of research on contextualization and Chinese culture remains to be conducted. Understanding the biblical principles of harmony, *shalom*, reconciliation, filial piety, afterlife, demonology, and spiritual warfare is important for contextualized preaching among the Chinese.

These biblical principles, when applied, are useful but can be further augmented via cross-referential study with other traditional Chinese festivals. Much could be inferred through the study of other major Chinese festivals, such as the Dragon Boat Festival, the Mid-Autumn Festival, and the Winter Solstice Festival, as well as the study of minor Chinese festivals. A possible future project could involve conducting qualitative field research on Chinese marriage and funeral customs, as they are living expressions of popular values and beliefs in Chinese culture as well. Moreover, further studies on Chinese legends, folk literature, and poems could be helpful to understand the moral values of the Chinese.

Another area that needs further research is the investigation of existing strategies for seminary instruction to prepare Chinese preachers to be effective in contextualized preaching. What are the theological institutions' curricula and models for training preachers among the Chinese? Does the training of preachers cover the issue of contextualization adequately? Does the curriculum in theological institutions include a course on contextualization? Courses on the intersection of the biblical perspective and the traditional Chinese perspective are quite necessary. Do curriculum subjects deal with theological issues such as harmony, filial piety, afterlife, demonology, and spiritual warfare?

This study was of the ideas and experiences of pastors. A study on the Chinese congregation would also be essential. Are Chinese congregations receiving relevant teachings from their preachers? Without proper guidance, Christian converts will likely not know that some practices long held as traditional, such as ancestral worship, are not in accordance with their Christian faith. Do Chinese believers realise from what they need to turn away? Do they have to deal with accusations of dishonoring their family? Are Chinese Christians still struggling with these issues?

Another important topic is the Westernization and secularization of the young Chinese generation and how much this is changing the importance of traditional Chinese culture. How is postmodernism influencing the Chinese today, and how is it changing the Chinese worldview and perspective?

Lastly, this study focused on contextualized preaching in a Chinese context, yet its relevance extends well beyond Chinese communities. After all, many cultures share common features. Almost every culture, for example, celebrates the New Year, albeit each culture's customs may differ significantly. The cult of the dead is also prevalent in many cultures. Therefore, similar research needs to be conducted in other cultures to find better ways of contextualizing preaching in particular cultural settings.

9.4 Concluding Remarks

Enoch Wan once asserted, "Evangelizing Chinese is one of the most challenging but imperative tasks of modern missions."[1] As the largest ethnic group in

---

1. Enoch Wan, "Mission among the Chinese Diaspora: A Case of Migration and Mission," *Missiology* 31 (2003): 35–43 (36).

the world, most Chinese live within the 10/40 Window, which includes the People's Republic of China, the world's most populous country today. Even though Christianity has made rapid progress in China and in the Chinese diaspora,[2] the majority of the Chinese population across the globe is still non-Christian. Moreover among millions of Chinese worldwide, the traditional Chinese culture continues to wield tremendous influence in all spheres of life. Therefore, gaining knowledge of preaching the gospel in culturally relevant ways to the Chinese is urgent and crucial.

The aim of this study has been to contribute to the knowledge of effective contextualized preaching among the Chinese by analyzing empirical evidence from field research on three Chinese festivals and by interviewing six Chinese preachers. The apostle Paul says, "I have become all things to all men, so that I may by all means save some" (1 Cor 9:22). He was well aware of the necessity of adapting the presentation of the gospel according to the particular contexts of his hearers.[3] Thus to win more Chinese for Christ today, proper and thorough contextualized preaching is fundamental for the Chinese church.

---

2. Phillip Jenkins, *The Next Christendom: The Coming of Global Christianity* (Oxford: Oxford University Press, 2002), 70.

3. M. David Sills, "Paul and Contextualization," in *Paul's Missionary Methods: In His Time and Ours*, eds. Robert L. Plummer and John Mark Terry (Leicester: Inter-Varsity Press, 2012), 196–215 (201–202).

Appendix

The Gospel of Jesus Christ: An Evangelical Celebration[1]

For God so loved the world that he gave his one and only Son, that whoever believes in him shall not perish but have eternal life.
– John 3:16

Sing to the Lord, for he has done glorious things; let this be known to all the world. – Isaiah 12:5

Preamble

The Gospel of Jesus Christ is news, good news: the best and most important news that any human being ever hears.

This Gospel declares the only way to know God in peace, love, and joy is through the reconciling death of Jesus Christ the risen Lord.

This Gospel is the central message of the Holy Scriptures, and is the true key to understanding them.

---

[1]. "The Gospel of Jesus Christ: An Evangelical Celebration" is copyright 1999 by the Committee on Evangelical Unity in the Gospel, PO Box 5551, Glendale Heights, IL 60139-5551. The drafting committee included J. I. Packer, John N. Akers, Timothy George, John Ankerberg, R. C. Sproul, Harold Myra, David Neff, John Armstrong, Thomas C. Oden, D. A. Carson, Scott Hafemann, Keith Davey, Maxie Dunnam, Erwin Lutzer, and John Woodbridge.

This Gospel identifies Jesus Christ, the Messiah of Israel, as the Son of God and God the Son, the second Person of the Holy Trinity, whose incarnation, ministry, death, resurrection, and ascension fulfilled the Father's saving will. His death for sins and his resurrection from the dead were promised beforehand by the prophets and attested by eyewitnesses. In God's own time and in God's own way, Jesus Christ shall return as glorious Lord and Judge of all (1 Thess. 4:13–18; Matt. 25:31–32). He is now giving the Holy Spirit from the Father to all those who are truly his. The three Persons of the Trinity thus combine in the work of saving sinners.

This Gospel sets forth Jesus Christ as the living Savior, Master, Life, and Hope of all who put their trust in him. It tells us that the eternal destiny of all people depends on whether they are savingly related to Jesus Christ.

This Gospel is the only Gospel: there is no other; and to change its substance is to pervert and indeed destroy it. This Gospel is so simple that small children can understand it, and it is so profound that studies by the wisest theologians will never exhaust its riches.

All Christians are called to unity in love and unity in truth. As evangelicals who derive our very name from the Gospel, we celebrate this great good news of God's saving work in Jesus Christ as the true bond of Christian unity, whether among organized churches and denominations or in the many transdenominational co-operative enterprises of Christians together.

The Bible declares that all who truly trust in Christ and his Gospel are sons and daughters of God through grace, and hence are our brothers and sisters in Christ.

All who are justified experience reconciliation with the Father, full remission of sins, transition from the kingdom of darkness to the kingdom of light, the reality of being a new creature in Christ, and the fellowship of the Holy Spirit. They enjoy access to the Father with all the peace and joy that this brings.

The Gospel requires of all believers worship, which means constant praise and giving of thanks to God, submission to all that he has revealed in his written word, prayerful dependence on him, and vigilance lest his truth be even inadvertently compromised or obscured.

To share the joy and hope of this Gospel is a supreme privilege. It is also an abiding obligation, for the Great Commission of Jesus Christ still stands: proclaim the Gospel everywhere, he said, teaching, baptizing, and making disciples.

By embracing the following declaration we affirm our commitment to this task, and with it our allegiance to Christ himself, to the Gospel itself, and to each other as fellow evangelical believers.

The Gospel

This Gospel of Jesus Christ which God sets forth in the infallible Scriptures combines Jesus' own declaration of the present reality of the kingdom of God with the apostles' account of the person, place, and work of Christ, and how sinful humans benefit from it. The Patristic Rule of Faith, the historic creeds, the Reformation confessions, and the doctrinal bases of later evangelical bodies all witness to the substance of this biblical message.

The heart of the Gospel is that our holy, loving Creator, confronted with human hostility and rebellion, has chosen in his own freedom and faithfulness to become our holy, loving Redeemer and Restorer. The Father has sent the Son to be the Savior of the world (1 John 4:14): it is through his one and only Son that God's one and only plan of salvation is implemented. So Peter announced: "Salvation is found in no one else, for there is no other name under heaven given to men by which we must be saved" (Acts 4:12). And Christ himself taught: "I am the way, the truth and the life. No one comes to the Father except through me" (John 14:6).

Through the Gospel we learn that we human beings, who were made for fellowship with God, are by nature – that is, "in Adam" (1 Cor. 15:22) – dead in sin, unresponsive to and separated from our Maker. We are constantly twisting his truth, breaking his law, belittling his goals and standards, and offending his holiness by our unholiness, so that we truly are "without hope and without God in the world" (Rom. 1:18–32; 3:9–20; Eph. 2:1–3, 12). Yet God in grace took the initiative to reconcile us to himself through the sinless life and vicarious death of his beloved Son (Eph. 2:4–10; Rom. 3:21–24).

The Father sent the Son to free us from the dominion of sin and Satan, and to make us God's children and friends. Jesus paid our penalty in our place on his cross, satisfying the retributive demands of divine justice by shedding his blood in sacrifice and so making possible justification for all who trust in him (Rom. 3:25–26). The Bible describes this mighty substitutionary transaction as the achieving of ransom, reconciliation, redemption, propitiation, and conquest of evil powers (Matt. 20:28; 2 Cor. 5:18–21; Rom. 3:23–25;

John 12:31; Col. 2:15). It secures for us a restored relationship with God that brings pardon and peace, acceptance and access, and adoption into God's family (Col. 1:20; 2:13–14; Rom. 5:1–2; Gal. 4:4–7; 1 Pet. 3:18). The faith in God and in Christ to which the Gospel calls us is a trustful outgoing of our hearts to lay hold of these promised and proffered benefits.

This Gospel further proclaims the bodily resurrection, ascension, and enthronement of Jesus as evidence of the efficacy of his once-for-all sacrifice for us, of the reality of his present personal ministry to us, and of the certainty of his future return to glorify us (1 Cor. 15; Heb. 1:1–4; 2:1–18; 4:14–16; 7:1–10:25). In the life of faith as the Gospel presents it, believers are united with their risen Lord, communing with him, and looking to him in repentance and hope for empowering through the Holy Spirit, so that henceforth they may not sin but serve him truly.

God's justification of those who trust him, according to the Gospel, is a decisive transition, here and now, from a state of condemnation and wrath because of their sins to one of acceptance and favor by virtue of Jesus' flawless obedience culminating in his voluntary sin-bearing death. God "justifies the wicked" (ungodly: Rom. 4:5) by imputing (reckoning, crediting, counting, accounting) righteousness to them and ceasing to count their sins against them (Rom. 4:1–8). Sinners receive through faith in Christ alone "the gift of righteousness" (Rom. 1:17; 5:17; Phil. 3:9) and thus be come "the righteousness of God" in him who was "made sin" for them (2 Cor. 5:21).

As our sins were reckoned to Christ, so Christ's righteousness is reckoned to us. This is justification by the imputation of Christ's righteousness. All we bring to the transaction is our need of it. Our faith in the God who bestows it, the Father, the Son, and the Holy Spirit, is itself the fruit of God's grace. Faith links us savingly to Jesus, but inasmuch as it involves an acknowledgement that we have no merit of our own, it is confessedly not a meritorious work.

The Gospel assures us that all who have entrusted their lives to Jesus Christ are born-again children of God (John 1:12), indwelt, empowered, and assured of their status and hope by the Holy Spirit (Rom. 7:6; 8:9–17). The moment we truly believe in Christ, the Father declares us righteous in him and begins conforming us to his likeness. Genuine faith acknowledges and depends upon Jesus as Lord and shows itself in growing obedience to the divine commands, though this contributes nothing to the ground of our justification (James 2:14–26; Heb. 6:1–12).

By his sanctifying grace, Christ works within us through faith, renewing our fallen nature and leading us to real maturity, that measure of development which is meant by "the fullness of Christ" (Eph. 4:13). The Gospel calls us to live as obedient servants of Christ and as his emissaries in the world, doing justice, loving mercy, and helping all in need, thus seeking to bear witness to the kingdom of Christ. At death, Christ takes the believer to himself (Phil. 1:21) for unimaginable joy in the ceaseless worship of God (Rev. 22:1–5).

Salvation in its full sense is from the guilt of sin in the past, the power of sin in the present, and the presence of sin in the future. Thus, while in foretaste believers enjoy salvation now, they still await its fullness (Mark 14:61–62; Heb. 9:28). Salvation is a Trinitarian reality, initiated by the Father, implemented by the Son, and applied by the Holy Spirit. It has a global dimension, for God's plan is to save believers out of every tribe and tongue (Rev. 5:9) to be his church, a new humanity, the people of God, the body and bride of Christ, and the community of the Holy Spirit. All the heirs of final salvation are called here and now to serve their Lord and each other in love, to share in the fellowship of Jesus' sufferings, and to work together to make Christ known to the whole world.

We learn from the Gospel that, as all have sinned, so all who do not receive Christ will be judged according to their just deserts as measured by God's holy law, and face eternal retributive punishment.

Unity in the Gospel

Christians are commanded to love each other despite differences of race, gender, privilege, and social, political, and economic background (John 13:34–35; Gal. 3:28–29), and to be of one mind wherever possible (John 17:20–21; Phil. 2:2; Rom. 14:1–15:13). We know that divisions among Christians hinder our witness in the world, and we desire greater mutual understanding and truth-speaking in love. We know too that as trustees of God's revealed truth we cannot embrace any form of doctrinal indifferentism, or relativism, or pluralism by which God's truth is sacrificed for a false peace.

Doctrinal disagreements call for debate. Dialogue for mutual understanding and, if possible, narrowing of the differences is valuable, doubly so when the avowed goal is unity in primary things, with liberty in secondary things, and charity in all things.

In the foregoing paragraphs, an attempt has been made to state what is primary and essential in the Gospel as evangelicals understand it. Useful dialogue, however, requires not only charity in our attitudes, but also clarity in our utterances. Our extended analysis of justification by faith alone through Christ alone reflects our belief that Gospel truth is of crucial importance and is not always well understood and correctly affirmed. For added clarity, out of love for God's truth and Christ's church, we now cast the key points of what has been said into specific affirmations and denials regarding the Gospel and our unity in it and in Christ.

Affirmations and Denials

1. We affirm that the Gospel entrusted to the church is, in the first instance, God's Gospel (Mark 1:14; Rom. 1:1). God is its author, and he reveals it to us in and by his Word. Its authority and truth rest on him alone.

We deny that the truth or authority of the Gospel derives from any human insight or invention (Gal. 1:1–11). We also deny that the truth or authority of the Gospel rests on the authority of any particular church or human institution.

2. We affirm that the Gospel is the saving power of God in that the Gospel effects salvation to everyone who believes, without distinction (Rom. 1:16). This efficacy of the Gospel is by the power of God himself (1 Cor. 1:18).

We deny that the power of the Gospel rests in the eloquence of the preacher, the technique of the evangelist, or the persuasion of rational argument (1 Cor. 1:21; 2:1–5).

3. We affirm that the Gospel diagnoses the universal human condition as one of sinful rebellion against God, which, if unchanged, will lead each person to eternal loss under God's condemnation.

We deny any rejection of the fallenness of human nature or any assertion of the natural goodness, or divinity, of the human race.

4. We affirm that Jesus Christ is the only way of salvation, the only mediator between God and humanity (John 14:6; 1 Tim. 2:5).

We deny that anyone is saved in any other way than by Jesus Christ and his Gospel. The Bible offers no hope that sincere worshipers of other religions will be saved without personal faith in Jesus Christ.

5. We affirm that the church is commanded by God and is therefore under divine obligation to preach the Gospel to every living person (Luke 24:47; Matt. 28:18–19).

We deny that any particular class or group of persons, whatever their ethnic or cultural identity, may be ignored or passed over in the preaching of the Gospel (1 Cor. 9:19–22). God purposes a global church made up from people of every tribe, language, and nation (Rev. 7:9).

6. We affirm that faith in Jesus Christ as the divine Word (or Logos, John 1:1), the second Person of the Trinity, co-eternal and co-essential with the Father and the Holy Spirit (Heb. 1:3), is foundational to faith in the Gospel.

We deny that any view of Jesus Christ which reduces or rejects his full deity is Gospel faith or will avail to salvation.

7. We affirm that Jesus Christ is God incarnate (John 1:14). The virgin-born descendant of David (Rom. 1:3), he had a true human nature, was subject to the Law of God (Gal. 4:5), and was like us at all points, except without sin (Heb. 2:17, 7:26–28). We affirm that faith in the true humanity of Christ is essential to faith in the Gospel.

We deny that anyone who rejects the humanity of Christ, his incarnation, or his sinlessness, or who maintains that these truths are not essential to the Gospel, will be saved (1 John 4:2–3).

8. We affirm that the atonement of Christ by which, in his obedience, he offered a perfect sacrifice, propitiating the Father by paying for our sins and satisfying divine justice on our behalf according to God's eternal plan, is an essential element of the Gospel.

We deny that any view of the Atonement that rejects the substitutionary satisfaction of divine justice, accomplished vicariously for believers, is compatible with the teaching of the Gospel.

9. We affirm that Christ's saving work included both his life and his death on our behalf (Gal. 3:13). We declare that faith in the perfect obedience of Christ by which he fulfilled all the demands of the Law of God in our behalf is essential to the Gospel.

We deny that our salvation was achieved merely or exclusively by the death of Christ without reference to his life of perfect righteousness.

10. We affirm that the bodily resurrection of Christ from the dead is essential to the biblical Gospel (1 Cor. 15:14).

We deny the validity of any so-called gospel that denies the historical reality of the bodily resurrection of Christ.

11. We affirm that the biblical doctrine of justification by faith alone in Christ alone is essential to the Gospel (Rom. 3:28; 4:5; Gal. 2:16).

We deny that any person can believe the biblical Gospel and at the same time reject the apostolic teaching of justification by faith alone in Christ alone. We also deny that there is more than one true Gospel (Gal. 1:6–9).

12. We affirm that the doctrine of the imputation (reckoning or counting) both of our sins to Christ and of his righteousness to us, whereby our sins are fully forgiven and we are fully accepted, is essential to the biblical Gospel (2 Cor. 5:19–21).

We deny that we are justified by the righteousness of Christ infused into us or by any righteousness that is thought to inhere within us.

13. We affirm that the righteousness of Christ by which we are justified is properly his own, which he achieved apart from us, in and by his perfect obedience. This righteousness is counted, reckoned, or imputed to us by the forensic (that is, legal) declaration of God, as the sole ground of our justification.

We deny that any works we perform at any stage of our existence add to the merit of Christ or earn for us any merit that contributes in any way to the ground of our justification (Gal. 2:16; Eph. 2:8–9; Titus 3:5).

14. We affirm that, while all believers are indwelt by the Holy Spirit and are in the process of being made holy and conformed to the image of Christ, those consequences of justification are not its ground. God declares us just, remits our sins, and adopts us as his children, by his grace alone, and through faith alone, because of Christ alone, while we are still sinners (Rom. 4:5).

We deny that believers must be inherently righteous by virtue of their cooperation with God's life-transforming grace before God will declare them justified in Christ. We are justified while we are still sinners.

15. We affirm that saving faith results in sanctification, the transformation of life in growing conformity to Christ through the power of the Holy Spirit. Sanctification means ongoing repentance, a life of turning from sin to serve Jesus Christ in grateful reliance on him as one's Lord and Master (Gal. 5:22–25; Rom. 8:4, 13–14).

We reject any view of justification which divorces it from our sanctifying union with Christ and our increasing conformity to his image through prayer, repentance, cross-bearing, and life in the Spirit.

16. We affirm that saving faith includes mental assent to the content of the Gospel, acknowledgement of our own sin and need, and personal trust and reliance upon Christ and his work.

We deny that saving faith includes only mental acceptance of the Gospel, and that justification is secured by a mere outward profession of faith. We further deny that any element of saving faith is a meritorious work or earns salvation for us.

17. We affirm that, although true doctrine is vital for spiritual health and well-being, we are not saved by doctrine. Doctrine is necessary to inform us how we may be saved by Christ, but it is Christ who saves.

We deny that the doctrines of the Gospel can be rejected without harm. Denial of the Gospel brings spiritual ruin and exposes us to God's judgment.

18. We affirm that Jesus Christ commands his followers to proclaim the Gospel to all living persons, evangelizing everyone everywhere, and discipling believers within the fellowship of the church. A full and faithful witness to Christ includes the witness of personal testimony, godly living, and acts of mercy and charity to our neighbor, without which the preaching of the Gospel appears barren.

We deny that the witness of personal testimony, godly living, and acts of mercy and charity to our neighbors constitutes evangelism apart from the proclamation of the Gospel.

Our Commitment

As evangelicals united in the Gospel, we promise to watch over and care for one another, to pray for and forgive one another, and to reach out in love and truth to God's people everywhere, for we are one family, one in the Holy Spirit, and one in Christ.

Centuries ago it was truly said that in things necessary there must be unity, in things less than necessary there must be liberty, and in all things there must be charity. We see all these Gospel truths as necessary.

Now to God, the Author of the truth and grace of this Gospel, through Jesus Christ, its subject and our Lord, be praise and glory forever and ever. Amen.

Bibliography

Bibles

King James Version (1611), BibleWorks 9.
Leningrad Hebrew Old Testament, BibleWorks 9.
New American Standard Bible (1995), BibleWorks 9.
New English Translation, BibleWorks 9.
New International Version (2011), BibleWorks 9.
New King James Version (1982), BibleWorks 9.
New Living Translation, BibleWorks 9.
Novum Testamentum Graece, Nestle-Aland 27, BibleWorks 9

English Works Cited

Adeweya, J. Ayodeji. "The Spiritual Powers of Ephesians 6:10–18 in the Light of African Pentecostal Spirituality." *BBR* 22 (2012): 251–258.

Adler, Joseph A. *Chinese Religious Traditions*. Upper Saddle River, NJ: Prentice Hall, 2002.

Aiken, Peter, "Should Reformed Believers Engage in Spiritual Warfare?" *PRJ* 7 (2015): 245–255.

Ajibade, Ezekiel A. "The Kingdom of God and Spiritual Warfare." *Ogbomoso Journal of Theology* 12 (2007): 107–116.

Akers, John N., John H. Armstrong, and John D. Woodbridge, eds. *This We Believe: The Good News of Jesus Christ for the World*. Grand Rapids: Zondervan, 2000.

Alden, Robert L., "Lucifer, Who or What?" *BETS* 11 (1968): 35–39.

Alexander, T. Desmond. *Exodus*. Apollos Old Testament Commentary. London: Apollos, 2017.

Alexander, T. Desmond et al., eds. *NDBT*. Leicester: Inter-Varsity Press, 2000.

Allan, Sarah. "Shang Foundations of Modern Chinese Folk Religion." In *Legend, Lore, and Religion in China: Essays in Honor of Wolfram Eberhard on His Seventieth Birthday*, edited by Sarah Allen and Alvin P. Cohen, 1–21. San Francisco: Chinese Materials Center, 1979.

———. *The Shape of the Turtle: Myth, Art, and Cosmos in Early China*. Albany: State University of New York Press, 1991.

Allan, Sarah, and Alvin P. Cohen, eds. *Legend, Lore, and Religion in China: Essays in Honor of Wolfram Eberhard on His Seventieth Birthday*. San Francisco: Chinese Materials Center, 1979.

Allen, Leslie C., *Ezekiel 20–48*. Word Biblical Commentary. Dallas: Word, 1990.

Allmen, Jean-Jacques von. *Preaching and Congregation*. London: Lutterworth, 1963.

Almond, Philip C. *The Devil: A New Biography*. Ithaca, NY: Cornell University Press, 2014.

Anderson, J. N. D. *Christianity and Comparative Religion*. London: Tyndale, 1970.

Anderson, Gary A. "The Exaltation of Adam and the Fall of Satan." *Journal of Jewish Thought and Philosophy* 6 (1997): 105–134.

Anderson, Neil T. *The Bondage Breaker*. Eugene, OR: Harvest House, 1990.

Arbel, Daphna, "Questions about Eve's Iniquity, Beauty, and Fall: The 'Primal Figure' in Ezekiel 28:11–19 and Genesis Rabbah traditions of Eve." *JBL* 124 (2005): 641–655.

Arbuckle, Gerald A. *Culture, Inculturation, and Theologians: A Postmodern Critique*. Collegeville, MN: Liturgical, 2010.

Archer, Gleason L. *Encyclopedia of Bible Difficulties*. Grand Rapids, MI: Regency Reference Library, 1992.

Ariarajah, S. Wesley. "Towards a Theology of Dialogue." *ER* 29 (1977): 3–11.

Arnold, Clinton E. *The Colossian Syncretism: The Interface Between Christianity and Folk Belief at Colossae*. Tubingen: J. C. B. Mohr, 1995.

———. *Ephesians*. Zondervan Exegetical Commentary on the New Testament. Grand Rapids, MI: Zondervan, 2010.

———. *Ephesians: Power and Magic – The Concept of Power in Ephesians in Light of Its Historical Setting*. Cambridge: Cambridge University Press, 1989.

———. "Giving the Devil His Due." *Christianity Today* 34 (1990): 17–19.

———. *Power of Darkness: A Thoughtful, Biblical Look at an Urgent Challenge Facing the Church*. Leicester: Inter-Varsity Press, 1992.

———. *Three Crucial Questions about Spiritual Warfare*. Grand Rapids, MI: Baker, 2001.

Atkins, Martyn D. *Preaching in a Cultural Context*. Peterborough: Foundry, 2001.

Babbie, Earl. *The Practice of Social Research*, 10th edition. Belmont, CA: Wadsworth/Thomson Learning, 2004.

Badham, Paul. "The Christian Hope Today." In *Death and Immortality in the Religions of the World*, edited by Paul Badham and Linda Badham, 37–50. New York: Paragon House, 1987.

Bailyes, Alan J. "Evangelical and Ecumenical Understandings of Mission." *IRM* 85 (1996): 485–503.

Baity, Philip C. "The Ranking of Gods in Chinese Folk Religion." *AFS* 36 (1977): 75–84.

Baldwin, Joyce G. *1 and 2 Samuel: An Introduction and Commentary*. Tyndale Old Testament Commentaries. Leicester: Inter-Varsity Press, 1988.

Barbour, Rosaline S. *Introducing Qualitative Research: A Student's Guide*, 2nd edition. London: Sage, 2014.

Barth, Karl. *Church Dogmatics, IV: The Doctrine of Reconciliation*. Edited by G. W. Bromiley and T. F. Torrance. Edinburgh: T&T Clark, 1956.

Bauer, David R. "Son of God." In *Dictionary of Jesus and the Gospel*, edited by Joel Green, 769–775. Downers Grove: InterVarsity Press, 1992.

Bautch, Kelley Coblentz. "The Fall and Fate of Renegade Angels: The Intersection of Watchers Traditions and the Book of Revelation." In *The Fallen Angels Traditions: Second Temple Developments and Reception History*, edited by Angela Kim Harkins, Kelley Coblentz Bautch, and John C. Endres, S.J., 69–93. Washington, DC: Catholic Biblical Association of America, 2014.

Bays, Daniel H. *A New History of Christianity in China*. West Sussex: Wiley-Blackwell, 2012.

Beal, Lissa M. Wray. *1 and 2 Kings*. Apollos Old Testament Commentary. Nottingham: Apollos, 2014.

Beale, G. K. *A New Testament Biblical Theology: The Unfolding of the Old Testament in the New*. Grand Rapids, MI: Baker Academic, 2011.

Bebbington, David W. *Evangelicalism in Modern Britain: A History form the 1730s to the 1980s*. London: Unwin Hyman, 1989.

Bell, Judith, and Stephen Waters. *Doing Your Research Project: A Guide for First-Time Researchers*, 6th edition. Maidenhead: McGraw-Hill, 2014.

Bell, Richard H. *Deliver Us from Evil: Interpreting the Redemption from the Power of Satan in New Testament Theology*. Tübingen: Mohr Siebeck, 2007.

Bergquist, James A. "TEF and the Uncertain Future of Third World Theological Education." *Theological Education* 9 (1973): 244–253.

Berkwitz, Stephen C. 'The History of Buddhism in Retrospect." In *Buddhism in World Cultures: Comparative Perspectives*, edited by Stephen C. Berkwitzm, 1–44. Santa Barbara, CA: ABC-CLIO.

Berling, Judith A. *A Pilgrim in Chinese Culture: Negotiating Religious Diversity*. Maryknoll, NY: Orbis, 1997.

Best, Ernest. *Ephesians*. International Critical Commentary. London: T&T Clark, 1998.

Beyer, Bryan E. *Encountering the Book of Isaiah: A Historical and Theological Survey*. Grand Rapids, MI: Baker Academic, 2007.

Beyer, Peter, "Social Forms of Religion and Religions in Contemporary Global Society." In *Handbook of the Sociology of Religion*, edited by Michele Dillon, 45–60. Cambridge: Cambridge University Press, 2003.

Bird, Michael F. *Evangelical Theology: A Biblical and Systematic Introduction*. Grand Rapids, MI: Zondervan, 2013.

———. "Mission as an Apocalyptic Event: Reflections on Luke 10:18 and Mark 13:10." *EvQ* 76 (2004): 117–134.

Blenkinsopp, Joseph. "The First Family: Terah and Sons." *JSOT* 41 (2016): 3–13.

Blidstein, Gerald. *Honor Thy Father and Mother: Filial Responsibility in Jewish Law and Ethics*. New York: KTAV, 1976.

Block, Daniel I. *The Book of Ezekiel: Chapters 25–48*. The New International Commentary on the Old Testament. Grand Rapids, MI: Eerdmans, 1998.

Bloch-Smith, Elizabeth. *Judahite Burial Practices and Beliefs about the Dead*. Sheffield: JSOT, 1992.

Blofeld, John. *Taoism: The Road to Immortality*. Boulder, CO: Shambhala, 1978.

Blomberg, Craig L. *Matthew*. The New American Commentary. Nashville, TN: Broadman, 1992.

Bloomfield, Freņa. *The Book of Chinese Beliefs: A Journey into the Chinese Inner World*. London: Arrow, 1986.

Blumenthal, Fred. "The Ghost of Samuel: Real or Imaginary?" *JBQ* 41 (2013): 104–106.

Bock, Darrell L. *Acts, Baker Exegetical Commentary on the New Testament*. Grand Rapids, MI: Baker Academic, 2007.

———. *Luke*. Vol. II: 9:51–24:53. Baker Exegetical Commentary on the New Testament. Grand Rapids, MI: Baker, 1996.

Bodde, Derk. *Festivals in Classical China: New Year and Other Annual Observances during the Han Dynasty 206 B.C. – A.D. 220*. Princeton, NJ: Princeton University Press, 1975.

Boice, James Montgomery. *Foundations of the Christian Faith*. Leicester: Inter-Varsity Press, 1986.

Bolt, Peter G. "Jesus, the Daimons and the Dead." In *The Unseen World: Christian Reflections on Angels, Demons and the Heavenly Realm*, edited by Anthony N. S. Lane, 75–102. Grand Rapids, MI: Baker, 1996.

———. "Towards a Biblical Theology of the Defeat of the Evil Powers." In *Christ's Victory Over Evil: Biblical Theology and Pastoral Ministry*, edited by Peter G. Bolt, 35–81. Nottingham: Apollos, 2009.

Bompiani, Brian Anthony. "The Development of the Concept of Satan." Unpublished MA thesis, Trinity Evangelical Divinity School, 2004.

Borg, Marcus. "Is Christianity about Heaven?" *WW* 31 (2011): 5–12.

Bosch, David J. "Ecumenicals and Evangelicals: A Growing Relationship?" *ER* 40 (1988): 458–72.

———. *Transforming Mission: Paradigm Shifts in Theology of Mission*. Maryknoll, NY: Orbis, 1991.

Bose, Bobby. *Reincarnation, Oblivion, or Heaven: A Christian Exploration*. Carlisle: Langham Global Library, 2016.

Bovon, François. *A Commentary on the Gospel of Luke 9:51–19:27*, translated by Donald S. Deer. Minneapolis: Fortress, 2013.

Boyd, Gregory A. *God at War: The Bible and Spiritual Conflict*. Downers Grove, IL: InterVarsity Press, 1997.

Boyd, James W. *Satan and Mara: Christian and Buddhist Symbols of Evil*. Leiden: E. J. Brill, 1975.

Bradshaw, Bruce. *Bridging the Gap: Evangelism, Development and Shalom*. Monrovia, CA: MARC, 1993.

Braswell, George W., Jr. *Understanding World Religions: Hinduism, Buddhism, Taoism, Confucianism, Judaism, Islam*, revised edition. Nashville: B&H, 1994.

Brettler, Marc Zvi. *God Is King: Understanding an Israelite Metaphor*. Sheffield: JSOT, 1989.

Briggs, John. "The First Industrial Nation." In *Introduction to the History of Christianity*, edited by Tim Dowley, 518–537. Minneapolis: Fortress, 1995.

Brinkmann, Svend, and Steinar Kvale. *InterViews: Learning the Craft of Qualitative Research Interviewing*. 3rd edition. Thousand Oaks, CA: SAGE, 2014.

Bryman, Alan. *Social Research Methods*. 5th edition. Oxford: Oxford University Press, 2016.

Bultmann, Rudolf et al. *Kerygma and Myth: A Theological Debate*. Edited by Hans Werner Bartsch. Revised edition. New York: Harper & Row, 1961.

Bunson, Margaret. *A Dictionary of Ancient Egypt*. Oxford: Oxford University Press, 1991.

Burckhardt, Valentine Rodolphe. *Chinese Creeds and Customs*. London: Kegan Paul, 2006.

Burke, T. Patrick. *The Major Religions: An Introduction with Texts*. Cambridge, MA: Blackwell, 1996.

Butler, Trent C. *Luke*. Holman New Testament Commentary. Edited by Max Anders. Nashville, TN: Holman Reference, 2000.

Buttrick, David. *Homiletic: Moves and Structures*. Philadelphia: Fortress, 1987.

Calvin, John. *Commentary on the Book of the Prophet Isaiah, vol. 1*. Translated by William Pringle. Grand Rapids, MI: Baker, 1999.

Cameron, Helen, and Catherine Duce. *Researching Practice in Ministry and Mission: A Companion*. London: SCM, 2013.

Candlish, Robert S. *Studies in First Corinthians 15: Life in a Risen Savior*. Grand Rapids, MI: Kregel, 1989.

Carman, John B. "Syncretism: Historical Phenomenon and Theological Judgement." *ANQ* 4 (1964): 30–43.

Carmody, Denise Lardner, and John Tully Carmody. *Ways to the Center: An Introduction to World Religions*. 2nd edition. Belmont, CA: Wadsworth, 1984.

Carroll, John T. *Luke: A Commentary*. The New Testament Library. Louisville, KY: Westminster John Knox, 2012.

Carson, D. A. *The Gospel According to John*. The Pillar New Testament Commentary. Nottingham: Apollos, 1991.

———. "The Gospel of Jesus Christ: 1 Corinthians 15:1–19." *TSFJ* (Spring 2008): 1–11.

———. *Jesus the Son of God: A Christological Title Often Overlooked, Sometimes Misunderstood, and Currently Disputed*. Wheaton, IL: Crossway, 2012.

———. "Preface." In *Coming Home: Essays on the New Heaven and New Earth*, edited by D. A. Carson and Jeff Robinson Sr., 9–11. Wheaton, IL: Crossway, 2017.

———. *Worship by the Book*. Grand Rapids: Zondervan, 2002.

Cathcart, Rochelle L. "Culture Matters: How Three Effective Preachers – Tim Keller, Rob Bell, Father Pfleger – Engage Culture in the Preaching Event." *TRINJ* 33 (2012): 209–222.

Cenkner, William. "Religions." In *The New Dictionary of Theology*, edited by Joseph A. Komonchak, Mary Collins, and Dermot A. Lane, 862–868. Dublin: Gill & Macmillan, 1987.

Cha, Peter T. "Constructing New Intergenerational Ties, Cultures, and Identities among Korean American Christians: A Congregational Case Study." In *This Side of Heaven: Race, Ethnicity, and Christian Faith*, edited by Robert J. Priest and Alvaro L. Nieves, 259–274. Oxford: Oxford University Press, 2007.

Chafer, Lewis Sperry. *Chafer Systematic Theology*. Vol. 2. Dallas: Dallas Seminary Press, 1980.

———. *Satan: His Motives and Methods*. Grand Rapids, MI: Kregel, 1990.

Chafin, Kenneth L. *1, 2 Corinthians*. The Communicator's Commentary. Waco, TX: Word, 1985.

Chai, Ch'u, and Winberg Chai, eds. *The Sacred Books of Confucius and Other Confucian Classics*. Translated by Ch'u Chai and Winberg Chai. New Hyde Park, NY: University Books, 1965.

Chai, Teresa. "A Look at Contextualization: Historical Background, Definition, Function, Scope and Models." *AJPS* 18 (2015): 3–19.

Chamberlain, Jonathan. *Chinese Gods*. Petaling Jaya: Pelanduk, 1987.

Chan, Sam. *Evangelism in a Skeptical World: How to Make the Unbelievable News about Jesus More Believable*. Grand Rapids, MI: Zondervan, 2018.

Chan, Shelly. *Diaspora's Homeland: Modern China in the Age of Global Migration*. Durham: Duke University Press, 2018.

Chan, Wing-Tsit. *A Source Book in Chinese Philosophy*. Princeton, NJ: Princeton University Press, 1963.
Chang, Eunhye et al. "Paul G. Hiebert and Critical Contextualization." *TRINJ* 30 (2009): 199–207.
Chang, Samuel Y. "A Comparison of the Diabologies of Tertullian and Origen." Unpublished masters thesis, Wheaton College, 1996.
Chao, Jonathan. "Christianization of Chinese Culture." 於基督教與中國文化更新: 研討會匯報, 55–81. Argyle, TX: 大使命中心, 2000.
Chao, Jonathan Tien-En. "The Chinese Indigenous Church Movement, 1917–1927: A Protestant Response to the Anti-Christian Movements in Modern China." Unpublished doctoral dissertation, University of Pennsylvania, 1986.
Chao, Samuel H. "Confucian Chinese and the Gospel: Methodological Considerations." *AJT* 1 (1987): 17–36.
Chapman, Stephen B. *1 Samuel as Christian Scripture: A Theological Commentary*. Grand Rapids, MI: Eerdmans, 2016.
Chard, Robert L. "Rituals and Scriptures of the Stove Cult." In *Ritual and Scripture in Chinese Popular Religion: Five Studies*, edited by David Johnson, 3–54. Berkeley, CA: IEAS, 1995.
Charles, J. Daryl. "Engaging the (Neo) Pagan Mind: Paul's Encounter with Athenian Culture as a Model for Cultural Apologetics (Acts 17:16–34)." *TRINJ* 16 (1995): 47–62.
Chen, Ellen M. *The Tao Te Ching: A New Translation with Commentary*. New York, NY: Paragon House, 1989.
Cheng, Manchao. *The Origin of Chinese Deities*. Beijing: Foreign Languages Press, 1995.
Chilcote, Paul W., and Laceye C. Warner, eds. *The Study of Evangelism: Exploring a Missional Practice of the Church*. Grand Rapids, MI: Eerdmans, 2008.
Childs, Brevard S. *Isaiah: A Commentary*. Louisville, KY: Westminster John Knox, 2001.
Ching, Julia. *Chinese Religions*. Maryknoll, NY: Orbis, 1993.
Chisholm, Robert B., Jr. *1 & 2 Samuel*. Teach the Text Commentary Series. Grand Rapids, MI: Baker, 2013.
Chou, Hsiang-Kuang. *A History of Chinese Buddhism*. Allahabad: Indo-Chinese Literature Publications, 1955.
Chu, Theresa. "Catholicism, Chinese Traditional Values and Marxist Thought: Searching for a Common Ground." *Missiology* 8 (1985): 337–346.
Chua, Wee Hian. "The Worship of Ancestors." In *Eerdmans' Handbook to the World's Religions*, revised edition. Grand Rapids, MI: Eerdmans, 1994.
Chuang, Tsu-Kung. *Ripening Harvest: Mission Strategy for Mainland Chinese Intellectuals in North America*. Paradise, PA: Ambassadors for Christ, 1995.

Clack, Beverley, and Brian R. Clack. *The Philosophy of Religion: A Critical Introduction.* Cambridge: Polity, 1998.

Clapp, Rodney. *Families at the Crossroads: Beyond Traditional and Modern Options.* Downers Grove, IL: InterVarsity Press, 1993.

Clark-Soles, Jaime. "The Afterlife: Considering Heaven and Hell." *Word & World* 31 (2011): 65–74.

Cline, Eric H. "Mycenae." In *The Oxford Encyclopedia of Ancient Greece and Rome* V, edited by Michael Gagarin, 22–23. Oxford: Oxford University Press, 2010.

Coe, Shoki. "Contextualizing Theology." In *Mission Trends No.3*, edited by Gerald H. Anderson and Thomas F. Stransky, 19–24. Grand Rapids, MI: Eerdmans 1976.

———. "In Search of Renewal in Theological Education." *Theological Education* 9 (1973): 233–243.

———. "Theological Education: A Worldwide Perspective." *Theological Education* 11 (1974): 5–12.

Cohen, Mark E. *The Cultic Calendars of the Ancient Near East.* Bethesda, MD: CDL, 1993.

Cole, Spencer. *Cicero and The Rise of Deification at Rome.* Cambridge: Cambridge University Press, 2013.

Collinson, Diane, Kathryn Plant, and Robert Wilkinson. *Fifty Eastern Thinkers.* London: Routledge, 2000.

Comber, Leon. *Chinese Ancestor Worship in Malaysia.* Singapore: Donald Moore, 1956.

Combs, Jason Robert. "Ghost on the Water?: Understanding an Absurdity in Mark 6:49–50." *JBL* 127 (2008): 345–358.

Congdon, David W. *Rudolf Bultmann: A Companion to His Theology.* Eugene, OR: Cascade, 2015.

Conn, Harvie M. "Contextual Theologies: The Problem of Agendas." *WTJ* 52 (1990): 51–63.

———. *Eternal Word and Changing Worlds: Theology, Anthropology, and Mission in Trialogue.* Phillipsburg, NJ: P&R, 1984.

Conybeare, Frederick Cornwallis. "The Demonology of the New Testament." *JQR* 8 (1896): 576–608.

Cook, Constance A. "Ancestor Worship during the Eastern Zhou." In *Early Chinese Religion, Part One: Shang through Han* (1250 BC–220 AD), edited by John Lagerwey and Marc Kalinowski, 237–279. Leiden: Brill, 2009.

———. *Death in Ancient China: The Tale of One Man's Journey.* Leiden: Brill, 2006.

Cook, Matthew et al., eds. *Local Theology for the Global Church: Principles for an Evangelical Approach to Contextualization.* Pasadena, CA: William Carey Library, 2010.

Cooper, Derek, and Martin Lohrmann, eds. *1–2 Samuel, 1–2 Kings, 1–2 Chronicles: Old Testament V, Reformation Commentary on Scripture*. Downers Grove: IVP Academic, 2016.

Cooper, Lamar Eugene, Sr. *Ezekiel*. The New American Commentary. Nashville, TN: B&H, 1994.

Coote, Robert T., and John Stott, eds. *Down to Earth: Studies in Christianity and Culture*. Grand Rapids, MI: Eerdmans, 1980.

Coppedge, Allan. *The God Who Is Triune: Revisioning the Christian Doctrine of God*. Downers Grove, IL: IVP Academic, 2007.

Corbin, Juliet, and Anselm Strauss. *Basics of Qualitative Research: Techniques and Procedures for Developing Grounded Theory*. 4th edition. Thousand Oaks, CA: SAGE, 2015.

Cortez, Marc. "Context and Concept: Contextual Theology and the Nature of Theological Discourse." *WTJ* 67 (2005): 85–102.

Cosgrove, Charles H., Herold Weiss, and Khiok-Khng Yeo, eds. *Cross-Cultural Paul: Journeys to Others, Journeys to Ourselves*. Grand Rapids, MI: Eerdmans, 2005.

Covell, Ralph. R. *Confucius, the Buddha, and Christ: A History of the Gospel in Chinese*. New York: Orbis, 1986.

Cox, James W. *Learning to Speak Effectively*. London: Hodder & Stoughton, 1966.

———. *Preaching*. San Francisco, CA: Harper & Row, 1985.

Craddock, Fred B. *Preaching*. Nashville, TN: Abingdon, 1985.

Craigie, Peter C., "Ugarit, Canaan, and Israel." *TynBul* 34 (1983): 145–167.

Creager, Harold L. "The Biblical View of Life after Death." *LQ* 17 (1965): 111–121.

Csikszentmihalyi, Mark, and Philip J. Ivanhoe, eds. *Philosophical Aspects of the Laozi*. Albany: State University of New York, 1999.

Da, Liu. *The Tao and Chinese Culture*. New York, NY: Schocken, 1979.

Daniel, Orville E. *A Harmony of the Four Gospels: The New International Version*, 2nd edition. Grand Rapids, MI: Baker, 1996.

Daniel Qin. "Confucian Filial Piety and the Fifth Commandment: A Fulfillment Approach." *AJPS* 16 (2013): 139–64.

Daniels, Richard W. "'To Fulfill All Righteousness': The Saving Merit of Christ's Obedience." *PRJ* 5 (2013): 49–64.

Daube, David. "On Acts 23: Sadducees and Angels." *JBL* 109 (1990): 493–497.

Davis, Kortright. "Bilateral Dialogue and Contextualization." *JES* 23 (1986): 386–399.

Davison, Gary Marvin, and Barbara E Reed. *Culture and Customs of Taiwan*. West Port, CT: Greenwood, 1998.

Dayton, Edward R., and David A. Fraser. *Planning Strategies for World Evangelization*. Grand Rapids, MI: Eerdmans, 1980.

DeBernardi, Jean. *The Way That Lives in the Heart: Chinese Popular Religion and Spirit Mediums in Penang, Malaysia*. Stanford, CA: Stanford University Press, 2006.

De Waal, Victor. "Death's Rituals." In *Beyond Death: Theological and Philosophical Reflections on Life After Death*, edited by Dan Cohn-Sherbok and Christopher Lewis, 95–103. New York: St. Martin's, 1995.

Donahue, John R. *The Gospel in Parable: Metaphor, Narrative, and Theology in the Synoptic Gospels*. Philadelphia: Fortress, 1988.

Dooley, David. *Social Research Methods*. 2nd edition. Englewood Cliffs, NJ: Prentice Hall, 1990.

Douglas, J. D., ed. *Let the Earth Hear His Voice*. Minneapolis: World Wide, 1975.

Douma, J. *The Ten Commandments: Manual for the Christian Life*. Translated by Nelson D. Kloosterman. Phillipburg, NJ: P&R, 1996.

Doyle, G. Wright. *Jesus: The Complete Man*. Bloomington, IN: AuthorHouse, 2008.

Driver, John. *Understanding the Atonement for the Mission of the Church*. Scottdale, PA: Herald, 1986.

Droogers, Andre. "Syncretism: The Problem of Definition, the Definition of the Problem." In *Dialogue and Syncretism: An Interdisciplinary Approach*, edited by J. D. Gort et al., 7–25. Grand Rapids, MI: Eerdmans, 1989.

Dunch, Ryan. "Christianity" and "Adaptation to Socialism." In *Chinese Religiosities: Afflictions of Modernity and State Formation*, edited by Mayfair Mei-hui Yang, 155–178. Berkeley: University of California Press, 2008.

Dunn, James D. G. *Jesus and the Spirit: A Study of the Religious and Charismatic Experience of Jesus and the First Christians as Reflected in the New Testament*. London: SCM, 1975.

Durham, John I. *Exodus*. Word Biblical Commentary. Waco, TX: Word, 1987.

Durkheim, Emile. *The Elementary Forms of Religious Life*. Translated by Karen E. Fields. New York: Free Press, 1995.

Dyrness, William A. *Learning about Theology from the Third World*. Grand Rapids, MI: Zondervan, 1990.

Eagleton, Terry. *The Idea of Culture*. Malden, MA: Blackwell, 2000.

Eberhard, Wolfram. *Chinese Festivals*. New York: Henry Schuman, 1952.

Ebrey, Patricia Buckley. *The Cambridge Illustrated History of China*. Cambridge: Cambridge University Press, 1996.

Eckel, Paul T. "Ephesians 6:10–20." *Int* 45 (1991): 288–93.

Edersheim, Alfred. *The Life and Times of Jesus The Messiah*. Vol. 2, New American edition. Grand Rapids, MI: Eerdmans, 1962.

Edgar, Brian. *The Message of the Trinity: Life in God*. Leicester: Inter-Varsity Press, 2004.

Edwards, James R. *The Gospel According to Luke*. The Pillar New Testament Commentary. Nottingham: Apollos, 2015.

———. *The Gospel According to Mark*. The Pillar New Testament Commentary. Grand Rapids, MI: Eerdmans, 2002.

Eichrodt, Walther. "The Law and the Gospel." Translated by Charles F. McRae. *Int* 11 (1957): 23–40.

Ellingsen, Mark. *The Evangelical Movement: Growth, Impact, Controversy, Dialog*. Minneapolis: Augsburg, 1988.

Elliston, Edgar J. *Introduction to Missiological Research Design*. Pasadena, CA: William Carey Library, 2011.

Elwell, Walter A., ed. *Baker Theological Dictionary of the Bible*. Grand Rapids, MI: Baker, 1996.

Erickson, Millard J. *Christian Theology*. 2nd edition. Grand Rapids, MI: Baker, 2001.

Erlandsson, Seth. "The Burden of Babylon: A Study of Isaiah 13:2–14:23." *Springfielder* 38 (1974): 1–12.

Evans, Christopher Francis. *Resurrection and the New Testament*. London: SCM, 1970.

Evans, Mary J. *The Message of Samuel*. The Bible Speaks Today. Leicester: Inter-Varsity Press, 2004.

Fang, Thome H. *The Chinese View of Life: The Philosophy of Comprehensive Harmony*. Taipei: Linking, 1981.

Fant, Clyde E. *Preaching for Today*. San Francisco: Harper & Row, 1987.

Farrar, Thomas J., and Guy J. Williams. "Diabolical Data: A Critical Inventory of New Testament Satanology." *JSNT* 39 (2016): 40–71.

———. "Talk of the Devil: Unpacking the Language of New Testament Satanology." *JSNT* 39 (2016): 72–96.

Ferdinando, Keith. *The Triumph of Christ in African Perspective: A Study of Demonology and Redemption in the African Context*. Carlisle: Paternoster, 1999.

Ferguson, Everett. *Demonology of the Early Christian World*. New York: E. Mellen, 1984.

Finlay, Anthony. *Demons: The Devil, Possession and Exorcism*. London: Blandford, 1999.

Firth, David G. *1 & 2 Samuel*. Apollos Old Testament Commentary. Leicester: Inter-Varsity Press, 2009.

Fleming, Bruce C. E. *Contextualization of Theology*. Pasadena, CA: William Carey Library, 1980.

Flemming, Dean. "Contextualizing the Gospel in Athens: Paul's Areopagus Address as a Paradigm for Missionary Communication." *Missiology* 30 (2002): 199–214.

———. *Contextualization in the New Testament: Patterns for Theology and Mission*. Nottingham: Apollos, 2005.

———. "The Third Horizon: A Wesleyan Contribution to the Contextualization Debate." *WesTJ* 30 (1995): 139–163.

Fortes, Meyer. *Time and Social Structure and Other Essays*. London: University of London, Athlone Press, 1970.

Fowler, Jeaneane, and Merv Fowler. *Chinese Religions: Beliefs and Practices*. Portland, OR: Sussex Academic, 2008.

France, R. T. *The Gospel of Mark: A Commentary on the Greek Text*. The New International Greek Testament Commentary. Grand Rapids, MI: Eerdmans, 2002.

Francis Appiah-Kubi. "The Church, Family of God: Relevance and Pastoral Challenges of a Metaphor from an African Perspective." In *The Household of God and Local Households: Revisiting the Domestic Church*, edited by Thomas Knieps-Port Le Toi, Gerard Mannion, and Peter De Mey, 67–80. Leuven: Peeters, 2013.

Frankfort, Henri. *Ancient Egyptian Religion: An Interpretation*. New York: Harper Torchbooks, 1961.

Fung, Yu Lan. *A History of Chinese Philosophy, Volume 1: The Period of the Philosophers* Translated by Derk Bodde. Princeton, NJ: Princeton University Press, 1952.

Gallou, Chrysanthi. *The Mycenaean Cult of the Dead*. Oxford: Archaeopress, 2005.

Gangel, Kenneth O. "Paul's Areopagus Speech." *BSac* 127 (1970): 308–312.

Gannon, Martin J. *Understanding Global Cultures: Metaphorical Journeys Through 28 Nations, Clusters of Nations, and Continents*. 3rd edition. Thousand Oaks, CA: SAGE, 2004.

Garcon, Maurice, and Jean Vinchon. *The Devil: An Historical Critical and Medical Study* Translated by Stephen Haden Guest. London: Victor Gollancz, 1929.

Garland, David E. *1 Corinthians*. Baker Exegetical Commentary on the New Testament. Grand Rapids, MI: Baker Academic, 2003.

Garland, Robert. *The Greek Way of Death*. Ithaca, NY: Cornell University Press, 1985.

Garrett, Duana A. *Angels and the New Spirituality*. Nashville, TN: B&H, 1995.

Garrett, Susan R. *The Demise of the Devil: Magic and the Demonic in Luke's Writings*. Minneapolis: Fortress, 1989.

Gates, Alan Frederick. *Christianity and Animism in Taiwan*. San Francisco: Chinese Materials Center, 1979.

Gathercole, Simon. "Jesus' Eschatological Vision of the Fall of Satan: Luke 10,18 Reconsidered." *ZNW* 94 (2003): 143–163.

Gehman, Richard J. *Who Are the Living-Dead?* Nairobi: Evangel, 1999.

Geisler, Norman L., and Thomas Howe. *The Big Book of Bible Difficulties: Clear and Concise Answers from Genesis to Revelation*. Grand Rapids, MI: Baker, 1992.

General Conference of the Protestant Missionaries of China. *Records of the General Conference of the Protestant Missionaries of China Held at Shanghai, May 7–20, 1890*. Shanghai: American Presbyterian Mission Press, 1890.

Germiquet, Edouard Ariste. "Paul and Barnabas in Lystra (Acts 14:8–20): The Contextualization of the Gospel in a Graeco-Roman City." Unpublished master's thesis, Rhodes University, 1992.

Gernet, Jacques. *A History of Chinese Civilization*. Translated by J. R. Foster and Charles Hartman. 2nd edition. Cambridge: Cambridge University Press, 1996.

Gibson, Scott M. *Preaching with a Plan: Sermon Strategies for Growing Mature Believers*. Grand Rapids, MI: Baker, 2012.

Gilbert, Greg. *What Is the Gospel?* Wheaton, IL: Crossway, 2010.

Giles, Kevin. *Jesus and the Father: Modern Evangelicals Reinvent the Doctrine of the Trinity*. Grand Rapids, MI: Zondervan, 2006.

Gillham, Bill. *Research Interviewing: The Range of Techniques*. Maidenhead: Open University Press, 2005.

Gilliland, Dean S., "The Incarnation as Matrix for Appropriate Theologies." In *Appropriate Christianity*, edited by Charles Kraft, 493–519. Pasadena, CA: William Carey Library, 2005.

———, ed. *The Word Among Us: Contextualizing Theology for Mission Today*. Dallas: Word, 1989.

Gnanakan, Ken. "Christ, Culture and Christianity in India." In *Doing Theology in Context: Festschrift in Honour of Dr. Bruce J. Nicholls*, edited by Sunand Sumithra, 67–78. Bangalore: Theological Book Trust, 1992.

Goering, Greg Schmidt. "Proleptic Fulfillment of the Prophetic Word: Ezekiel's Dirges over Tyre and Its Ruler." *JSOT* 36 (2012): 483–505.

Gokey, Francis X. *The Terminology for the Devil and Evil Spirits in the Apostolic Fathers*. Washington, DC: Catholic University of America Press, 1961.

Goldsworthy, Graeme. *Gospel-Centered Hermeneutics*. Nottingham: Apollos, 2006.

Gombis, Timothy G. *The Drama of Ephesians: Participating in the Triumph of God*. Downers Grove, IL: IVP Academic, 2010.

Goodall, Norman. "Evangelicalism and the Ecumenical Movement." *ER* 15 (1963): 399–409.

Gooding, David. *According to Luke: A New Exposition of the Third Gospel*. Leicester: Inter-Varsity Press, 1987.

Goodrich, Anne Swann. *Chinese Hell: The Peking Temple of Eighteen Hells and Chinese Conceptions of Hell*. St. Augustin: Monumenta Serica, 1981.

Gort, Gerald D. "Syncretism and Dialogue: Christian Historical and Earlier Ecumenical Perception." *Mission Studies* 6 (1989): 9–22.

Gould, Ezra P. *Gospel According to St. Mark*. Critical and Exegetical Commentary. Edinburgh: T&T Clark, 1982.

Graham, Billy. "Why Lausanne?" In *Let the Earth Hear His Voice*, edited by J. D. Douglas, 22–36. Minneapolis: World Wide, 1975.

Grant, Brian W. *The Social Structure of Christian Families: A Historical Perspective*. St. Louis: Chalice, 2000.

Gration, John. "Willowbank to Zaire: The Doing of Theology." *Missiology* 12 (1984): 297–309.

Gray, Patrick. "Implied Audiences in the Areopagus Narrative." *TynBul* 55 (2004): 205–218.

Green, Joel B., Scot McKnight, and I. Howard Marshall, eds. *DJG*. Downers Grove, IL: InterVarsity Press, 1992.

Green, Laurie. *Let's Do Theology: Resources for Contextual Theology*. London: Mowbray, 2009.

Green, Michael. *Exposing the Prince of Darkness*. Ann Arbor, MI: Servant, 1991.

———. *I Believe in Satan's Downfall*. London: Hodder & Stoughton, 1981.

Greidanus, Sidney. *The Modern Preacher and the Ancient Text: Interpreting and Preaching Biblical Literature*. Grand Rapids, MI: Eerdmans, 1988.

Grenz, Stanley J. *Revisioning Evangelical Theology: A Fresh Agenda for the 21st Century*. Downers Grove, IL: InterVarsity Press, 1993.

Grimes, Ronald L. *The Craft of Ritual Studies*. Oxford: Oxford University Press, 2014.

Grogan, Geoffrey W. "Isaiah." In *The Expositor's Bible Commentary: Proverbs-Isaiah, Vol.6*, revised edition, edited by Tremper Longman III and David E. Garland, 433–863. Grand Rapids, MI: Zondervan, 2008.

Grudem, Wayne. *Bible Doctrine: Essential Teachings of the Christian Faith*. Edited by Jeff Purswell. Grand Rapids, MI: Zondervan, 1999.

———. *Systematic Theology: An Introduction to Biblical Doctrine*. Leicester: InterVarsity Press, 1994.

Gruenthaner, Michael J. "The Demonology of the Old Testament." *CBQ* 6 (1944): 6–27.

Guanghu, He. "Thirty Years of Religious Studies in China." In *Social Scientific Studies of Religion in China : Methodology, Theories, and Findings*, edited by Fenggang Yang and Graeme Lang, 23–46. Leiden: Brill, 2011.

Gueli, John George, "Increasing Perceived Sermon Relevance through the Identification of Congregational Felt Needs." Unpublished doctoral thesis, Denver Conservative Baptist Seminary, 1993.

Gunde, Richard. *Culture and Customs of China*. Westport, CT: Greenwood, 2002.

Gunton, Colin E. *The Actuality of Atonement: A Study of Metaphor, Rationality and the Christian Tradition*. Grand Rapids, MI: Eerdmans, 1989.

Guo, Jue. "Concepts of Death and the Afterlife Reflected in Newly Discovered Tomb Objects and Texts from Han China." In *Mortality in Traditional Chinese*

Thought, edited by Amy Olberding and Philip J. Ivanhoe, 85–116. Albany, NY: SUNY, 2011.

Guthrie, Stewart Elliott. "Opportunity, Challenge and a Definition of Religion." *JSRNC* 1 (2007): 58–67.

Habel, Norman C. "Ezekiel 28 and the Fall of the First Man." *CTM* 38 (1967): 516–524.

Haleblian, Krikor. "The Problem of Contextualization." *Missiology* 11 (1983): 95–111.

Hallote, Rachel S. *Death, Burial, and Afterlife in the Biblical World: How the Israelites and Their Neighbors Treated the Dead*. Chicago: Ivan R. Dee, 2001.

Halverson, Dean C. "Buddhism." In *The Compact Guide to World Religions*, edited by Dean C. Halverson, 58. Minneapolis, MN: Bethany House, 1996.

Hamilton, Victor P. *Exodus: An Exegetical Commentary*. Grand Rapids, MI: Baker Academic, 2011.

Hamori, Esther J. "The Prophet and the Necromancer: Women's Divination for Kings." *JBL* 132 (2013): 827–843.

Han, Christina. "Cremation and Body Burning in Five Dynasties China." *Journal of Chinese Studies* 55 (2012): 1–22.

Hansen, Collin. "The Son and the Crescent." *Christianity Today* 55 (2011): 18–23.

Harris, Murray J. *Raised Immortal: Resurrection and Immortality in the New Testament*. Grand Rapids, MI: Eerdmans, 1985.

Harrison, Everett F. "Worship." In *Evangelical Dictionary of Theology*, edited by Walter A. Elwell, 1192–1193. Grand Rapids, MI: Baker, 1984.

Harrison, R. K. "Demon." In *The Zondervan Encyclopedia of the Bible*, vol. 2, edited by Merrill C. Tenney, 95–105. Grand Rapids, MI: Zondervan, 2009.

Hartley, John E. *Leviticus*. Word Biblical Commentary. Waco, TX: Word, 1992.

Harvey, Peter. *An Introduction to Buddhism: Teachings, History and Practices*. Cambridge: Cambridge University Press, 1990.

Hattaway, Paul. *Operation China: Introducing all the Peoples of China*. Pasadena, CA: William Carey Library, 2000.

Hawk, L. Daniel. *Joshua*. Berit Olam Studies in Hebrew Narrative and Poetry. Collegeville, MN: Liturgical Press, 2000.

———. *Ruth*. Apollos Old Testament Commentary. Nottingham: Apollos, 2015.

Hayes, John Alexander. *The Ten Commandments: A Present-Day Interpretation*. New York: Fleming H. Revell, 1931.

Hayes, John H., and Stuart A. Irvine. *Isaiah the Eighth-century Prophet: His Times and His Preaching*. Nashville, TN: Abingdon, 1987.

Haykin, Michael A. G., and Kenneth J. Stewart, eds. *The Emergence of Evangelicalism: Exploring Historical Continuities*. Nashville, TN: B&H Academic, 2008.

Heideman, Eugene S. "Syncretism, Contextualization, Orthodoxy, and Heresy." *Missiology* 25 (1997): 37–49.

Hemer, Colin J. "The Speeches of Acts II: The Areopagus Address." *TynBul* 40 (1989): 239–259.

Henry Newton Smith. "Chinese Ancestor Practice and Christianity: Toward a Viable Contextualization of Christian Ethics in a Hong Kong Setting." Unpublished doctoral dissertation, Southwestern Baptist Theological Seminary, 1987.

Herzog, Thomas. *Research Methods in the Social Sciences*. New York: HarperCollins, 1996.

Hess, Richard S. *Israelite Religions: An Archaeological and Biblical Survey*. Grand Rapids, MI: Baker Academic, 2007.

Hesse-Biber, Sharlene Nagy, and Patricia Leavy. *The Practice of Qualitative Research*. 2nd edition. Thousand Oaks, CA: SAGE, 2011.

Hesselgrave, David J. "Christian Communication and Religious Pluralism: Capitalizing on Differences." *Missiology* 18 (1990): 131–138.

———. *Communicating Christ Cross-Culturally*. Grand Rapids, MI: Zondervan, 1978.

———, ed. *Theology and Mission: Paper Given at Trinity Consultation No. 1*. Grand Rapids, MI: Baker, 1978.

Hesselgrave, David J., and Edward Rommen. *Contextualization: Meanings, Methods, and Models*. Nottingham: Apollos, 1989.

Hester, Joseph P. *The Ten Commandments: A Handbook of Religious, Legal and Social Issues*. Jefferson, NC: McFarland, 2003.

Hicks, Robert M. *The Christian Family in Changing Times: The Myths, Models, and Mystery of Family Life*. Grand Rapids, MI: Baker, 2002.

Hiebert, Paul G. *Anthropological Insights for Missionaries*. Grand Rapids, MI: Baker, 2004.

———. "Critical Contextualization." *IBMR* 11 (1987): 104–112.

———. *Cultural Anthropology*. Grand Rapids, MI: Baker, 1983.

———. "The Flaw of the Excluded Middle." *Missiology* 10 (1982): 35–47.

———. *Transforming Worldviews: An Anthropological Understanding of How People Change*. Grand Rapids, MI: Baker, 2008.

Hiebert, Paul G., R. Daniel Shaw, and Tite Tienou. *Understanding Folk Religion*. Grand Rapids, MI: Baker, 1999.

Hill, Charles. "The Ecumenical Movement." In *Zondervan Handbook to the History of Christianity*, edited by Jonathan Hill, 435. Grand Rapids, MI: Zondervan, 2006.

Hill, Jonathan. *History of Christianity*. Grand Rapids, MI: Zondervan, 2006.

Hinsch, Bret. "Confucian Filial Piety and the Construction of the Ideal Chinese Buddhist Woman." *Journal of Chinese Religions* 30 (2002): 49–75.

Hoad, T. F., ed. "Ghost." In *The Concise Oxford Dictionary of English Etymology*. Oxford: Oxford University Press, 2003. Oxford Reference. http://www.oxfordreference.com/view/10.1093/acref/9780192830982.001.0001/acref-9780192830982-e-6428?rskey=dtgrv5&result=6429.

Hoebel, E. Adamson, and Thomas Weaver. *Anthropology and the Human Experience*. New York: McGraw-Hill, 1979.

Hoehner, Harold W. *Ephesians: An Exegetical Commentary*. Grand Rapids, MI: Baker Academic, 2002.

Hofstede, Geert, and Gert Jan Hofstede. *Cultures and Organizations: Software of the Mind*. New York: McGraw-Hill, 2005.

Honeycutt, Dwight. "Contextualization: A Valuable Missiological Concept." *TTE* 36 (1987): 9–15.

Howard, David M., Jr. *Joshua*. The New American Commentary. Nashville, TN: B&H, 1998.

Howell, Brian M. "Multiculturalism, Immigration and the North American Church." *Missiology* 39 (2011): 79–85.

Howell, Brain M., and Jenell Williams Paris. *Introducing Cultural Anthropology: A Christian Perspective*. Grand Rapids, MI: Baker Academic, 2011.

Hsiao, Ching-Fen. "Harmony Is Good and Good Is Harmony." *The Living Pulpit* 15 (2006): 24–26.

Hsieh, Jiann, and Ying-Hsiung Chou. "Public Aspirations in the New Year Couplets: A Comparative Study Between the People's Republic and Taiwan." *AFS* 40 (1981): 125–149.

Hsu, Chiung-Yin, Margaret O'Connor, and Susan Lee. "Understandings of Death and Dying for People of Chinese Origin." *Death Studies* 33 (2009): 153–174.

Hughes, R. Kent. *Colossians and Philemon: The Supremacy of Christ*. Preaching the Word. Westchester, IL: Crossway, 1989.

———. *Disciplines of Grace*. Wheaton, IL: Crossway, 1993.

Hutchinson, Mark, and John Wolffe. *A Short History of Global Evangelicalism*. New York: Cambridge University Press, 2012.

Hwa, Yung. "Strategic Issues in Missions – An Asian Perspective." In *The Study of Evangelism: Exploring a Missional Practice of the Church*, edited by Paul W. Chilcote and Laceye C. Warner, 374–383. Grand Rapids, MI: Eerdmans, 2008.

Ikeda, Daisaku. *The Flower of Chinese Buddhism*. New York: Weatherhill, 1986.

Innes, D. K. "Sheol." In *The Illustrated Bible Dictionary*, 1435–1436. Leicester: Inter-Varsity Press, 1980.

Jackson, James. "Ancestral Worship." In China Centenary Missionary Conference, Held at Shanghai, April 25 to May 8, 1907, 215–246. Shanghai: Centenary Conference Committee, 1907.

James, E. O. *Seasonal Feasts and Festivals*. London: Thames & Hudson, 1961.

Jao, Greg. "Honor and Obey." In *Following Jesus without Dishonoring Your Parents: Asian American Discipleship*, edited by Jeanette Yep et al., 43–56. Downers Grove, IL: InterVarsity Press, 1998.

Jeffrey, David Lyle. *Luke*. Brazos Theological Commentary on the Bible. Grand Rapids, MI: Brazos, 2012.

Jenkins, Phillip. *The Next Christendom: The Coming of Global Christianity*. Oxford: Oxford University Press, 2002.

Jerome. "Ezekiel 28:11–19: The Fall of Satan." In *Ezekiel, Daniel*. Ancient Christian Commentary on Scripture, Old Testament 13, edited by Kenneth Stevenson and Michael Glerup, 93–97. Downers Grove, IL: InterVarsity Press, 2008.

Jin, Nailu, ed. *A Hundred Questions on the Chinese Culture*. Beijing: Beijing Language and Culture University Press, 2005.

Jipp, Joshua W. "Paul's Areopagus Speech of Acts 17:16–34 as Both Critique and Propaganda." *JBL* 131 (2012): 567–588.

Jobes, Karen H. *1 Peter*. Baker Exegetical Commentary on the New Testament. Grand Rapids, MI: Baker Academic, 2005.

Johnson, David, ed. *Ritual and Scripture in Chinese Popular Religion: Five Studies*. Berkeley, CA: IEAS, 1995.

Johnston, Philip S. "Afterlife." In *Dictionary of the Old Testament: Prophets*, edited by J. Gordon, 1–5. Downers Grove, IL: InterVarsity Press, 2012.

———. *Shades of Sheol: Death and Afterlife in the Old Testament*. Downers Grove, IL: InterVarsity Press, 2002.

———. "The Underworld and the Dead in the Old Testament." *TynBul* 45 (1994): 415–419.

Jordan, David K. *Gods, Ghosts, and Ancestors: Folk Religion in a Taiwanese Village*. Berkeley, CA: University of California Press, 1972.

Just, Arthur A., Jr. *Luke 9:51–24:53*. Concordia Commentary: A Theological Exposition of Sacred Scripture. St. Louis: Concordia, 1997.

Kaiser, Walter C., Jr. *More Hard Sayings of the Old Testament*. Downers Grove, IL: InterVarsity Press, 1992.

———. *Toward Old Testament Ethics*. Grand Rapids, MI: Zondervan, 1983.

Kaltenmark, Max. *Lao Tzu and Taoism*. Translated by Roger Greaves. Stanford, CA: Stanford University Press, 1969.

Kan, Baoping. "Theology in the Contemporary Chinese Context." *WW* 17 (1997): 161–167.

Kanyakumari, D. "Malaysia's Population to Number 30 Million on Thursday." *The Star*, 26 February 2014. http://www.thestar.com.my/News/Nation/2014/02/26/Malaysia-30-mil-population/.

Kay, James F. *Preaching and Theology*. St. Louis: Chalice, 2007.

Keach, Benjamin. *Preaching from the Types and Metaphors of the Bible*. Grand Rapids, MI: Kregel, 1972.

Keats, Daphne M. *Interviewing: A Practical Guide for Students and Professionals.* Buckingham: Open University Press, 2010.
Keesing, Roger M., and Felix M. Keesing. *New Perspectives in Cultural Anthropology.* New York: Holt, Rinehart, & Winston, 1971.
Kelleher, Margaret Mary. "Worship." In *The New Dictionary of Theology*, edited by Joseph A. Komonchak, Mary Collins, and Dermot A. Lane, 1105–1106. Dublin: Gill & Macmillan, 1987.
Keller, Timothy. *Center Church: Doing Balanced, Gospel-Centered Ministry in Your City.* Grand Rapids, MI: Zondervan, 2012.
Kelly, Henry Ansgar. *Satan: A Biography.* Cambridge: Cambridge University Press, 2006.
Kent, Greenvillen J. R. "'Call Up Samuel': Who Appeared to the Witch at En-Dor (1 Samuel 28:3–25)." *Andrews University Seminary Studies* 52 (2014): 141–160.
Keown, Damien. *Buddhism: A Brief Insight.* New York: Sterling, 1996.
Khatry, Ramesh. "Witchcraft and Demons." In *South Asia Bible Commentary: A One-Volume Commentary on the Whole Bible*, edited by Brian Wintle. Rajasthan: Open Door, 2015.
Khobnya, Svetlana. "Reconciliation Must Prevail: A Fresh Look at 2 Corinthians 5:14–6:2." *EJT* 25 (2016): 128–136.
Khoo, Kay Keng. "The Tao and the Logos: Lao Tzu and the Gospel of John." *IRM* 87 (1998): 77–84.
Khoo, Kay Kim. "The Emergence of Plural Communities in the Malay Peninsula before 1874." In *Multiethnic Malaysia: Past, Present and Future*, edited by Teck Ghee Lim, Alberto Gomes, and Azly Rahman, 11–31. Petaling Jaya: SIRD, 2009.
Kieschnick, John. "Buddhist Monasticism." In *Early Chinese Religion, Part Two: The Period of Division (220–589 AD)*, edited by John Lagerwey and Marc Kalinowski, 545–574. Leiden: Brill, 2009.
Kim, Matthew D. *Preaching with Cultural Intelligence: Understanding the People Who Hear Our Sermons.* Grand Rapids, MI: Baker Academic, 2017.
Kim, Young Oon. *World Religions Volume 3: Faiths of the Far East.* New York: Golden Gate, 1976.
Kinnaman, Gary D. *Overcoming the Dominion of Darkness.* Cambridge: Crossway, 1992.
Kinnamon, Michael. *Truth and Community: Diversity and Its Limits in the Ecumenical Movement.* Grand Rapids, MI: Eerdmans, 1988.
Kinnamon, Michael, and Brian E. Cope. "General Introduction." In *The Ecumenical Movement: An Anthology of Key Texts and Voices*, edited by Michael Kinnamon and Brian E. Cope, 1–8. Geneva: WCC, 1997.
Klassen, William. "Peace: New Testament." In *The Anchor Bible Dictionary: Volume 5*, edited by David Noel Freedman, 207–212. New York: Doubleday, 1992.

Klauck, Hans-Josef. *The Religious Context of Early Christianity: A Guide to Graeco-Roman Religions*. Translated by Brian McNeil. Edinburgh: T&T Clark, 2000.

Klein, Ralph W. *Ezekiel: The Prophet and His Message*. Columbia: University of South Carolina, 1988.

———. *1 Samuel*. Word Biblical Commentary. Waco, TX: Word, 1983.

Klinghoffer, David. *Shattered Tablets: Why We Ignore the Ten Commandments at Our Peril*. New York: Doubleday, 2007.

Köhler, Ludwig et al., eds. *HALOT*. Leiden: Brill, 1999.

Kohn, Livia. *Early Chinese Mysticism: Philosophy and Soteriology in the Taoist Tradition*. Princeton, NJ: Princeton University Press, 1992.

———. "Laozi: Ancient Philosopher, Master of Immortality, and God." In *Religions of China in Practice*, edited by Donald S. Lopez Jr., 52–63. Princeton, NJ: Princeton University Press, 1996.

———. *Taoist Mystical Philosophy: The Scripture of Western Ascension*. New York: State University of New York Press, 1991.

Kong, Stephen Wai. "Evaluating the Effect of Inductive Narrative Sermons Compared to Deductive Didactic Sermons to Increase Memory Retention of Chinese Church Members." Unpublished doctoral thesis, Denver Seminary, 2005.

Kraemer, H. *The Christian Message in a Non-Christian World*. Grand Rapids, MI: Kregel, 1969.

———. *Religion and the Christian Faith*. Cambridge: James Clarke, 1956.

Kraft, Charles H. *Christianity in Culture: A Study in Dynamic Biblical Theologizing in Cross-Cultural Perspective*. Maryknoll, NY: Orbis, 1981.

———. *Issues in Contextualization*. Pasadena, CA: William Carey Library, 2016.

———. *Worldview for Christian Witness*. Pasadena, CA: William Carey Library, 2008.

Kramer, Kenneth. *The Sacred Art of Dying: How World Religions Understand Death*. New York: Paulist, 1988.

Kreitzer, Beth, ed. *Luke*. Reformation Commentary on Scripture. Downers Grove, IL: IVP Academic, 2015.

Kruse, Colin G. *Paul's Letter to the Romans*. The Pillar New Testament Commentary. Grand Rapids, MI: Eerdmans, 2012.

Kuper, Adam. *Culture: The Anthropologists' Account*. Cambridge, MA: Harvard University Press, 1999.

Kvale, Steinar, and Svend Brinkmann. *InterViews: Learning the Craft of Qualitative Research Interviewing*. 2nd edition. Thousand Oaks, CA: SAGE, 2009.

Kwan, Simon S. M. "From Indigenization to Contextualization: A Change in Discursive Practice Rather than a Shift in Paradigm." *StudWorldChr* 11 (2005): 236–250.

Ladd, George Eldon. *I Believe in the Resurrection of Jesus*. London: Hodder & Stoughton, 1975.

———. *A Theology of the New Testament*. Revised edition. Edited by Donald A. Hagner. Grand Rapids, MI: Eerdmans, 1993.

Lagerwey, John. *Taoist Ritual in Chinese Society and History*. New York: Macmillan, 1987.

Lai, Chi-Tim. "Daoism in China Today, 1980–2002." In *Religion in China Today: The China Quarterly Special Issues No. 3*, edited by Daniel L. Overmyer, 107. Cambridge: Cambridge University Press, 2003.

Lai, Pan-Chiu. "Chinese Culture and the Development of Chinese Christian Theology." *StudWorldChr* 7 (2001): 219–240.

Lai, Pan-chui. "Theological Translation and Transmission between China and the West." In *Sino-Christian Theology: A Theological Qua Cultural Movement in Contemporary China*, edited by Pan-chui Lai and Jason Lam, 83–100. Frankfurt: Peter Lang, 2010.

Lakoff, George, and Mark Johnson. *Metaphors We Live By*. Chicago: University of Chicago Press, 1980.

Lakos, William. *Chinese Ancestor Worship: A Practice and Ritual Oriented Approach to Understanding Chinese Culture*. Newcastle upon Tyne: Cambridge Scholars, 2010.

Lam, Wing-hung. "Patterns of Chinese Theology." *OBMR* 4 (1980): 20–24.

Lane, Anthony N. S., ed. *The Unseen World: Christian Reflections on Angels, Demons and the Heavenly Realm*. Grand Rapids, MI: Baker, 1996.

Larkin, William J., Jr. *Culture and Biblical Hermeneutics: Interpreting and Applying the Authoritative Word in a Relativistic Age*. Grand Rapids, MI: Baker, 1988.

Larsen, David L. *The Anatomy of Preaching*. Grand Rapids, MI: Baker, 1989.

———. "Heaven and Hell in the Preaching of the Gospel." *TRINJ* 22 (2001): 237–258.

Larsen, Timothy. "Defining and Locating Evangelism." In *The Cambridge Company to Evangelical Theology*, edited by Timothy Larsen and Daniel J. Treier, 1–14. New York: Cambridge University Press, 2007.

Larson, Bruce. *Luke*. The Communicator's Commentary. Waco, TX: Word, 1983.

Latourette, Kenneth Scott. *A History of Christian Missions in China*. Taipei: Cheng-Wen, 1975.

Lausanne Committee for World Evangelization. "Willowbank Report: Report of a Consultation on Gospel and Culture." *IRM* 67 (1978): 211–221.

Law, Gail. *Chinese Churches Handbook*. Hong Kong: CCCOWE, 1981.

Lee, Kam Hing. "The Christian Brethren." In *Christianity in Malaysia: A Denominational History*, edited by Robert Hunt, Lee Kam Hing, and John Roxborogh, 34–74. Petaling Jaya: Pelanduk, 1992.

Lehtipuu, Outi. *The Afterlife Imagery in Luke's Story of the Rich Man and Lazarus.* Leiden: Brill, 2007.

Lenski, R. C. H. *The Interpretation of St. Luke's Gospel.* Commentary on the New Testament. Peabody, MA: Hendrickson, 1961.

Leon-Dufour, Xavier. *Life and Death in The New Testament: The Teachings of Jesus and Paul.* Translated by Terrence Prendergast. San Francisco: Harper & Row, 1986.

Lete, G. del Olmo. *Canaanite Religion: According to the Liturgical Texts of Ugarit.* Winona Lake, IN: Eisenbrauns, 2004.

Leung, Man Kam. "The Study of Religious Taoism in the People's Republic of China (1949–1990): A Bibliographical Survey." *JCR* 19 (1991): 113–126.

Levinskaya, Irina A. "Syncretism – The Term and Phenomenon." *TynBul* 44 (1993): 117–128.

Lewis, Jonathan. *World Mission: An Analysis of the World Christian Movement – Cross-Cultural Considerations.* 2nd edition. Pasadena, CA: William Carey Library, 1994.

Lewis, Theodore J. *Cults of the Dead in Ancient Israel and Ugarit.* Atlanta: Scholars, 1989.

Lewis, Todd T. "Karma." In *Buddhism: The Illustrated Guide,* edited by Kevin Trainor, 60–61. London: Duncan Braid, 2001.

Leys, Simon, ed. *The Analects of Confucius.* Edited and translated by Simon Leys. New York: W. W. Norton, 1997.

Li, Chenyang. "The Confucian Ideal of Harmony." *Philosophy East and West* 56 (2006): 583–603.

———. *The Confucian Philosophy of Harmony.* New York: Routledge, 2014.

Li, Yih-Yuan. "In Search of Harmony and Equilibrium." *Dialogue & Alliance* 4 (1990): 15–30.

Liaw, Stephen. "Ancestor Worship in Taiwan and Evangelism of the Chinese." In *Christian Alternatives to Ancestor Practices,* edited by Bong Rin Ro, 181–193. Taichung: Asia Theological Association, 1985.

Liddell, H. G., R. Scott, and H. S. Jones. *LSJ,* 9th edition with revised supplement. Oxford: Clarendon, 1996.

Lim, Mooyoung. "Preaching and Culture: A Phenomenological Study to Korean American Immigrant Church Pastors' Communication Skills in a Changing Culture." *TRINJ* 33 (2012): 259–271.

Lincoln, Andrew. *Ephesians.* Word Biblical Commentary. Dallas: Word, 1990.

———. "'Stand therefore . . .' Ephesians 6:10–20 as *Peraratio.*" *BibInt* 3 (1995): 99–114.

Ling, Trevor. *The Significance of Satan: New Testament Demonology and Its Contemporary Relevance.* London: SPCK, 1961.

Liske, Thomas V. *Effective Preaching.* New York: Macmillan, 1960.

Liu, Tik-sang. "A Nameless but Active Religion: An Anthropologist's View of Local Religion in Hong Kong and Macau." In *Religion in China Today: The China Quarterly Special Issues No. 3*, edited by Daniel L. Overmyer, 67–88. Cambridge: Cambridge University Press, 2003.

Livermore, David A. *Cultural Intelligence: Improving Your CQ to Engage Our Multicultural World*. Grand Rapids, MI: Baker Academic, 2009.

Livingston, James C. "Study of Religion." In *The Dictionary of Bible and Religion*, edited by William H. Gentz, 880–881. Nashville: Abingdon, 1986.

Lo, Lung-Kwong. "The Nature of the Issue of Ancestral Worship among Chinese Christians." *StudWorldChr* 9 (2003): 30–42.

Lo, Yuet-Keung. "Destiny and Retribution in Early Medieval China." In *Philosophy and Religion in Early Medieval China*, edited by Alan K. L. Chan and Yuet-Keung Lo, 319–356. Albany: State University of New York Press, 2010.

Lochman, Jan Milic. *Signposts to Freedom: The Ten Commandments and Christian Ethics* Translated by David Lewis. Minneapolis: Augsburg, 1982.

Löfstedt, Torsten. "Satan's Fall and the Mission of the Seventy-Two." *SEÅ* 76 (2011): 95–114.

Long, Thomas G. *The Witness of Preaching*. 2nd edition. Louisville, KY: Westminster John Knox, 2005.

Longenecker, Richard N., ed. *Life in the Face of Death: The Resurrection Message of the New Testament*. Grand Rapids, MI: Eerdmans, 1998.

Longman, Tremper, III. *Proverbs*. Baker Commentary on the Old Testament Wisdom and Psalms. Grand Rapids, MI: Baker Academic, 2006.

Lopez, Donald S., Jr. *Buddhism*. London: Penguin, 2001.

———. "Introduction." In *Buddhism in Practice*, edited by Donald S. Lopez Jr., 3–36. Princeton, NJ: Princeton University Press, 1995.

Louie, Kam. "Defining Modern Chinese Culture." In *The Cambridge Companion to Modern Chinese Culture*, edited by Kam Louie, 1–19. Cambridge: Cambridge University Press, 2008.

———. "Introduction – Hong Kong on the Move: Creating Global Cultures." In *Hong Kong Culture: Word and Image*, edited by Kam Louie, 1–7. Hong Kong: Hong Kong University Press, 2010.

Lowe, Chuck. *Honouring God and Family: A Christian Response to Idol Food in Chinese Popular Religion*. Bangalore: Theological Book Trust, 2001.

Lucas, Ernest C. *Proverbs*. The Two Horizons Old Testament Commentary. Grand Rapids, MI: Eerdmans, 2015.

Luzbetak, L. J. "Unity in Diversity: Ethnotheological Sensitivity in Cross-Cultural Evangelism." *Missiology* 4 (1976): 207–216.

Macky, Peter W. *The Centrality of Metaphors to Biblical Thought: A Method for Interpreting the Bible*. Lewiston, NY: Edwin Mellen, 1990.

Macleod, Donald. *The Person of Christ*. Leicester: Inter-Varsity Press, 1998.

Mah, Yeow Beng. "Critical Contextualization of Chinese Folk Beliefs and Practices: Feng Shui as a Case Study." Unpublished doctoral dissertation, Asbury Theological Seminary, 2004.

Malefijt, Annemarie De Waal. *Religion and Culture: An Introduction to Anthropology of Religion*. London: Collier-Macmillan, 1968.

Malaysia, Department of Statistics. *Population and Housing Census of Malaysia 2010: Population Distribution and Basic Demographic Characteristics*. Putrajaya: DSM, 2010.

Mandryk, Jason. *Operation World: The Definitive Prayer Guide to Every Nation*. 7th edition. Downers Grove, IL: InterVarsity Press, 2010.

Maroney, Eric. *Religious Syncretism*. London: SCM, 2006.

Marshall, I. Howard. *The Gospel of Luke: A Commentary on the Greek Text*. The New International Greek Testament Commentary. Exeter: Paternoster, 1978.

———. "The Meaning of Reconciliation." In *Unity and Diversity in New Testament Theology: Essays in Honor of George E. Ladd*, edited by Robert A. Guelich, 117–132. Grand Rapids, MI: Eerdmans, 1978.

Martens, John W. "Holy Ghost Story." *America* 211 (2014): 37.

Martyn Denscombe. *The Good Research Guide for Small-Scale Social Research Projects*. 3rd edition. Maidenhead: Open University Press, 2007.

Mason, Jennifer. *Qualitative Researching*. 2nd edition. London: SAGE, 2002.

Maston, T. B. *The Bible and Family Relations*. Nashville, TN: Broadman, 1983.

Mathews, Kenneth A. *Genesis 11:27–50:26*. The New American Commentary. Nashville, TN: B&H, 2005.

Mawhinney, Allen. "God as Father: Two Popular Theories Reconsidered." *JETS* 31 (1988): 181–189.

McBain, John M. *The Ten Commandments in the New Testament*. Nashville, TN: Broadman, 1977.

McClure, John S. *Preaching Words: 144 Key Terms in Homiletics*. Louisville, KY: Westminster John Knox, 2007.

McConville, J. Gordon, and Stephen N. Williams. *Joshua*. The Two Horizons Old Testament Commentary. Grand Rapids, MI: Eerdmans, 2010.

McCutcheon, Russell T. *Studying Religion: An Introduction*. Abingdon: Routledge, 2014.

McDermott, Gerald R., ed. *The Oxford Handbook of Evangelical Theology*. Oxford: Oxford University Press, 2010.

McKenna, David L. *Isaiah 1–39*. The Communicator's Commentary. Dallas: Word, 1993.

McKenzie, Steven L. *1–2 Chronicles*. Abingdon Old Testament Commentaries. Nashville, TN: Abingdon, 2004.

McKeown, James. *Ruth*. The Two Horizons Old Testament Commentary. Grand Rapids, MI: Eerdmans, 2015.

McKnight, Scot. *The King Jesus Gospel: The Original Good News Revisited.* Grand Rapids, MI: Zondervan, 2011.

———. *The Letter to the Colossians.* New International Commentary on the New Testament. Grand Rapids, MI: Eerdmans, 2018.

McNeill, Patrick, and Steve Chapman. *Research Methods* 3rd edition. London: Routledge, 2006.

McRay, John R. "Worship." In *The Dictionary of Bible and Religion*, edited by William H. Gentz, 1122–1124. Nashville, TN: Abingdon, 1986.

M'Donald, W. *Spiritualism: Identical with Ancient Sorcery, New Testament Demonology, and Modern Witchcraft: With the Testimony of God against It.* New York: Carlton & Porter, 1866.

Melick, Richard R., Jr. *Philippians, Colossians, Philemon.* The New American Commentary. Nashville, TN: Broadman, 1991.

Mettinger, Tryggve N. D. *The Riddle of Resurrection: Dying and Rising Gods in the Ancient Near East.* Stockholm: Almqvist & Wiksell International, 2001.

Middleton, J. Richard. *A New Heaven and a New Earth: Reclaiming Biblical Eschatology.* Grand Rapids, MI: Baker Academic, 2014.

Miller, Patrick D. *The Ten Commandments, Interpretation: Resources for the Use of Scripture in the Church.* Louisville, KY: Westminster John Knox, 2009.

Milne, Bruce. *The Message of Heaven and Hell: Grace and Destiny.* Leicester: InterVarsity Press, 2002.

Minamiki, George. *The Chinese Rites Controversy from Its Beginning to Modern Times.* Chicago: Loyola University Press, 1985.

Mizrahi, Noam. "The Textual History and Literary Background of Isa 14, 4." *ZAW* 125 (2013): 433–447.

Mohler, R. Albert, Jr. "Modern Theology: The Disappearance of Hell." In *Hell under Fire: Modern Scholarship Reinvents Eternal Punishment*, edited by Christopher W. Morgan and Robert A. Peterson, 15–41. Grand Rapids, MI: Zondervan, 2004.

Mong, Ambrose Ih-Ren. "The Legacy of Matteo Ricci and His Companions." *Missiology* 43 (2015): 385–397.

Montanari, Franco, ed. *The Brill Dictionary of Ancient Greek.* Leiden: Brill, 2015.

Moo, Douglas J. *The Letters to the Colossians and to Philemon.* The Pillar New Testament Commentary. Nottingham: Apollos, 2008.

Moore, Aubrey. "Note on the Philosophy of Chaps. I–VII," In *Chuang Tzu.* 2nd edition. Translated by Herbert A. Giles. London: Bernard Quaritch, 1926.

Moore, Charles A., ed. *The Chinese Mind: Essentials of Chinese Philosophy and Culture.* Honolulu: University of Hawaii Press, 1967.

Moreau, A. Scott. *Contextualization in World Missions: Mapping and Assessing Evangelical Models.* Grand Rapids, MI: Kregel, 2012.

———, ed. *Evangelical Dictionary of World Missions*. Grand Rapids, MI: Baker, 2000.

———. *The World of the Spirits: A Biblical Study in the African Context*. Nairobi: Evangel, 1990.

Moreau, Jules Laurence. *Language and Religious Language: A Study in the Dynamics of Translation*. Philadelphia: Westminster, 1961.

Moreman, Christopher M. *Beyond the Threshold: Afterlife Beliefs and Experiences in World Religions*. Lanham, MD: Rowman & Littlefield, 2008.

Morey, Robert A. *Death and the Afterlife*. Minneapolis: Bethany, 1984.

Morris, Leon. *The Apostolic Preaching of the Cross*. Grand Rapids, MI: Eerdmans, 1955.

Mounce, William D., ed. *Mounce's Complete Expository Dictionary of Old and New Testament Words*. Grand Rapids, MI: Zondervan, 2006.

Mouw, Richard J. "Shalom and Confucian Harmony." *SANACS Journal* (2012–2013): 57–63.

Murphy, Ed. *The Handbook for Spiritual Warfare*. Revised and updated edition. Nashville, TN: Thomas Nelson, 2003.

Murphy, Francesca Aran. *1 Samuel*. Brazos Theological Commentary on the Bible. Grand Rapids, MI: Brazos, 2010.

Murphy, Roland E. *Proverbs*. Word Biblical Commentary. Nashville, TN: Thomas Nelson, 1998.

Nadeau, Randall L. *Confucianism and Taoism: Introduction to the World's Major Religions*, vol. 2. Westport, CT: Greenwood, 2006.

Nakhai, Beth Alpert. "Canaanite Religion." In *Near Eastern Archaeology: A Reader*, edited by Suzanne Richard, 343–348. Winona Lake, IN: Eisenbrauns, 2003.

Naugle, David K. *Worldview: The History of a Concept*. Grand Rapids, MI: Eerdmans, 2002.

Neff, David. "A Call to Evangelical Unity." *Christianity Today* 14 (June 1999): 49–50.

Nelson, William B., Jr. "Sheol: Old Testament." In *Baker Theological Dictionary of the Bible*, edited by Walter A. Elwell, 735. Grand Rapids, MI: Baker, 2000.

Nemet-Nejat, Karen Rhea. *Daily Life in Ancient Mesopotamia*. Peabody, MA: Hendrickson, 1998.

Ng, Peter Tze. *Ming, Chinese Christianity: An Interplay between Global and Local Perspectives*. Leiden: Brill, 2012.

Ng, Zhiru. *The Making of Savior Bodhisattva: Dizang in Medieval China*. Honolulu: University of Hawaii Press, 2007.

Nicholls, Bruce J. *Contextualization: A Theology of Gospel and Culture*. Downers Grove, IL: InterVarsity Press, 1979.

Nichols, Terence. *Death and Afterlife: A Theological Introduction*. Grand Rapids, MI: Brazos, 2010.

Nida, Eugene A. *Customs, Culture and Christianity*. London: Tyndale, 1954.

———. *Message and Mission: The Communication of the Christian Faith*. Revised edition. Pasadena, CA: William Carey Library, 1990.

Niebuhr, H. Richard. *Christ and Culture*. New York: Harper & Row, 1975.

Nielsen, Kirsten. *Satan – The Prodigal Son?: A Family Problem in the Bible*. Sheffield: Sheffield Academic Press, 1998.

Nilsson, Martin P. *A History of Greek Religion* Translated by F. J. Fielden. Oxford: Clarendon, 1949.

Nisbet, Robert A. *Social Change and History: Aspects of the Western Theory of Development*. Oxford: Oxford University Press, 1969.

Noll, Mark A. *The Rise of Evangelicalism: The Age of Edwards, Whitefield and the Wesleys*. Downers Grove, IL: IVP Academic, 2003.

Noll, Stephen F. *Angels of Light, Powers of Darkness: Thinking Biblically about Angels, Satan and Principalities*. Downers Grove, IL: InterVarsity Press, 1998.

O'Brien, Peter T. *Colossians, Philemon*. Word Biblical Commentary. Dallas: Word, 1982.

———. *The Letter to the Ephesians*. The Pillar New Testament Commentary. Grand Rapids, MI: Eerdmans, 1999.

O'Connell, Robert H. "Isaiah XIV 4B–23: Ironic Reversal Through Concentric Structure and Mythic Allusion." *VT* 38 (1988): 406–418.

O'Grady, Joan. *The Prince of Darkness: The Devil in History, Religion and the Human Psyche*. Shaftesbury: Element, 1989.

Oh, Hyunchul Henry. "Preaching as Interaction between Church and Culture: With Specific Reference to the Korean Church." *AJT* 19 (2005): 92–105.

Olagunju, O.S. "An Evaluation of Bevans' Models of Contextual Theology and Its Contributions to Doing Theology in the 21st Century Church." *Ogbomoso Journal of Theology* 17 (2012): 37–57.

Oldridge, Darren. *The Devil: A Very Short Introduction*. Oxford: Oxford University Press, 2012.

Olsen, Rolv. "The Wind Blows Wherever It Pleases: A Study of Contextualisation of Christian Worship Services at Tao Fong Shan Christian Center, Hong Kong." *Swedish Missiological Themes* 87 (1999): 555–632.

Omanson, Roger L., and John E. Ellington. *A Handbook on 1-2 Chronicles*. Vol. 2. Miami, FL: United Bible Societies, 2014.

Oppenheim, A. N. *Questionnaire Design, Interviewing and Attitude Measurement*. New edition. London: Continuum, 1992.

Osborne, Grant R. *The Hermeneutical Spiral: A Comprehensive Introduction to Biblical Interpretation*. Downers Grove, IL: InterVarsity Press, 1991.

Oswalt, John N. *The Book of Isaiah: Chapters 1–39*. Grand Rapids, MI: Eerdmans, 1986.

Overmyer, Daniel L. *Religions of China: The World as a Living System.* San Francisco: Harper & Row, 1986.
Packer, James I. "The Gospel: Its Content and Communication – A Theological Perspective." In *Down to Earth: Studies in Christianity and Culture,* edited by Robert T. Coote and John Stott, 97–114. Grand Rapids, MI: Eerdmans, 1980.
Padilla, C. René. "The Contextualization of the Gospel." *JTSA* 24 (1978): 12–30.
———. *Mission Between the Times.* Revised and updated edition. Carlisle: Langham Monographs, 2010.
Page, Sydney H. T. *Powers of Evil: A Biblical Study of Satan and Demons.* Grand Rapids, MI: Baker, 1995.
Palmer, David A., Glenn Shive, and Philip L. Wickeri, eds. *Chinese Religious Life.* New York: Oxford University Press, 2011.
Pang, Alan W. H. "A Biblically Foundational, Culturally Appealing, and Contextually Appropriate Discipleship Course for Mainland Chinese People." Unpublished doctoral thesis, Denver Conservative Baptist Seminary, 1995.
Pao, David W. *Colossians & Philemon.* Zondervan Exegetical Commentary on the New Testament. Grand Rapids, MI: Zondervan, 2012.
Park, Nam Shin. "Hermeneutic and Spiritual Warfare." *Did* 22 (2011): 85–103.
Parshall, Phil. *New Paths in Muslim Evangelism.* Grand Rapids, MI: Baker, 1980.
Patmore, Hector M. *Adam, Satan, and the King of Tyre: The Interpretation of Ezekiel 28:11–19 in Late Antiquity.* Leiden: Brill, 2012.
Payne, David F. *I & II Samuel.* The Daily Study Bible Series. Louisville, KY: Westminster John Knox, 1982.
Pelto, Pertti J. *Applied Ethnography: Guidelines for Field Research.* Walnut Creek, CA: Left Coast Press, 2013.
Pember, G. H. *Earth's Earliest Ages.* Grand Rapids, MI: Kregel, 1975.
Penelhum, Terence. "Christianity." In *Life after Death in World Religions,* edited by Harold Coward, 31–47. Maryknoll, NY: Orbis, 1997.
Peng, Mu. "The Invisible and the Visible: Communicating with the Yin World." *Asian Ethnology* 74 (2015): 335–362.
Peters, Ted. "What Is the Gospel?" *PRSt* 13 (1986): 21–43.
Peterson, David G. *The Acts of the Apostles.* The Pillar New Testament Commentary. Grand Rapids, MI: Eerdmans, 2009.
———. "Worship." In *New Dictionary of Biblical Theology,* edited by T. Desmond Alexander and Brian S. Rosner, 855–863. Leicester: Inter-Varsity Press, 2000.
Philip J. Nel. "שלמ." In *NIDOTTE,* vol. 4, edited by Willem A. VanGemeren, 130–135. Carlisle: Paternoster, 1997.
Phillipsen, Gerry. *Speaking Culturally: Exploration in Social Communication.* Albany, NY: State University of New York, 1992.
Philpott, Kent. *A Manual of Demonology and the Occult.* Grand Rapids, MI: Zondervan, 1973.

Pike, Kenneth L. "Language and Life: A Stereoscopic Window on the World." *BSac* 114 (1957): 141–156.

———. "My Pilgrimage in Mission." *IBMR* 21 (1997): 159–161.

Piper, John. *God Is the Gospel: Meditations on God's Love as the Gift of Himself.* Leicester: Inter-Varsity Press, 2005.

Poceski, Mario. *Introducing Chinese Religions.* London: Routledge, 2009.

Pocock, M., G. Van Rheenen, and D. McConnell. *The Changing Face of World Mission.* Grand Rapids, MI: Baker, 2005.

Pope, Marvin H. "The Cult of the Dead at Ugarit." In *Ugarit in Retrospect*, edited by Gordon Douglas Young, 159–179. Winona Lake, IN: Eisenbrauns, 1981.

Porter, Stanley E. "Reconciliation as the Heart of Paul's Missionary Theology." In *Paul as Missionary: Identity, Activity, Theology, and Practice*, edited by Trevor J. Burke and Brian S. Rosner, 169–179. London: T&T Clark, 2011.

Poston, Dudley L., Jr., and Juyin Helen Wong. "The Chinese Diaspora: The Current Distribution of the Overseas Chinese Population." *Chinese Journal of Sociology* 2 (2016): 348–373.

Powlison, David *Power Encounters: Reclaiming Spiritual Warfare.* Grand Rapids, MI: Baker, 1995.

Powys, David. *"Hell': A Hard Look at a Hard Question: The Fate of the Unrighteous in New Testament Thought.* Carlisle: Paternoster, 1997.

Puett, Michael J. *To Become a God: Cosmology, Sacrifice, and Self-Divinization in Early China.* Cambridge: Harvard University Asia Center, 2002.

Quicke, Michael J. *360 Degree Preaching: Hearing, Speaking, and Living the Word.* Grand Rapids, MI: Baker Academic, 2003.

———. *Preaching as Worship: An Integrative Approach to Formation in Your Church.* Grand Rapids, MI: Baker, 2011.

Rahula, Walpola Sri. *What the Buddha Taught.* Revised edition. Bedford: Gordon Fraser, 1967.

Raphals, Lisa. "Fate, Fortune, Change, and Luck in Chinese and Greek: A Comparative Semantic History." *Philosophy East and West* 53 (2003): 537–574.

Ray, Reginald A. *Indestructible Truth: The Living Spirituality of Tibetan Buddhism.* Boston: Shambhala, 2000.

Ren, Qiliang, et. al., eds. *Common Knowledge about Chinese Culture.* Revised edition. Xi'an: Shaanxi Normal University General Publishing, 2015.

Renn, Stephen D., ed. *Expository Dictionary of Bible Words: Word Studies for Key English Bible Words.* Peabody, MA: Hendrickson, 2005.

Richards, Ivor Armstrong. *The Philosophy of Rhetoric.* Oxford: Oxford University Press, 1936.

Richards, Larry. *Every Good and Evil Angel in the Bible.* Nashville, TN: Thomas Nelson, 1998.

Ricoeur, Paul. *The Rule of Metaphor.* Toronto: University of Toronto Press, 1975.

Riegert, Eduard R. *Imaginative Shock: Preaching and Metaphor*. Burlington, ON: Trinity, 1990.

Riley, G. J. "Demon." In *DDD*, 2nd revised and expanded edition, edited by Karel van der Toorn, Bob Becking, and Pieter W. van der Horst, 235–240. Leiden: Brill, 1999.

Robertson, S. "Sonship in John's Gospel." *AJT* 25 (2011): 315–333.

Robinson, Haddon W. *Biblical Preaching: The Development and Delivery of Expository Messages*. 3rd edition. Grand Rapids, MI: Baker Academic, 2014.

Roetz, Heiner. *Confucian Ethics of the Axial Age: A Reconstruction under the Aspect of the Breakthrough toward Postconventional Thinking*. Albany: State University of New York, 1993.

Roland, Barnabas. "Communicating the Gospel with Power among China's Animistic Peoples." *ChinaSource Quarterly* 20 (2018): 7–9.

Root, Michael, and James J. Buckley, eds. *Life amid the Principalities: Identifying, Understanding, and Engaging Created, Fallen, and Disarmed Powers Today*. Eugene, OR: Cascade, 2016.

Routledge, Robin L. "Death and Afterlife in the Old Testament." *Journal of European Baptist Studies* 9 (2008): 22–39.

Rule, Andrew Kerr. "Religion, Religious." In *Evangelical Dictionary of Theology*, edited by Walter A Elwell, 930–931. Grand Rapids, MI: Baker, 1984.

Ruokanen, Miikka, and Paulos Huang. "Preface." In *Christianity and Chinese Culture*, edited by Miikka Ruokanen and Paulos Huang, ix–xvii. Grand Rapids, MI: Eerdmans, 2010.

Russell, Jeffrey Burton. *The Devil: Perceptions of Evil from Antiquity to Primitive Christianity*. London: Cornell University Press, 1977.

———. *The Prince of Darkness: Radical Evil and the Power of Good in History*. London: Thames & Hudson, 1989.

Ryan, N. J. *The Cultural Heritage of Malaya*. 2nd edition. Kuala Lumpur: Longman Malaysia, 1971.

Ryken, Philip Graham. *Luke*. Vol. 1, Reformed Expository Commentary. Phillipsburg, NJ: P&R, 2009.

Sasson, Jack M., ed. *Civilizations of the Ancient Near East*. 4 vols. New York: Charles Scribner's Sons, 1995.

Saville, Andy. "Reconciliationism: A Forgotten Evangelical Doctrine of Hell." *EvQ* 79 (2007): 35–51.

Scharf, Greg R. *Let the Earth Hear His Voice: Strategies for Overcoming Bottlenecks in Preaching God's Word*. Phillipsburg, NJ: P&R, 2015.

Scharfstein, Ben-Ami. *The Mind of China*. New York: Basic, 1974.

Schatzman, Leonard, and Anselm L. Strauss. *Field Research: Strategies for a Natural Sociology*. Englewood Cliffs, NJ: Prentice Hall, 1973.

Schineller, Peter. "Inculturation and Syncretism: What Is the Real Issue?" *IBMR* 16 (1992): 50–53.
Schirokauer, Conrad. *A Brief History of Chinese Civilization*. Orlando, FL: Harcourt Brace, 1991.
Schlaffer, David J. *What Makes This Day Different: Preaching Grace on Special Occasions*. Cambridge: Cowley, 1998.
Schmidt, Brain B. *Israel's Beneficent Dead: Ancestor Cult and Necromancy in Ancient Israelite Religion and Tradition*. Tübingen: J. C. B. Mohr, 1994.
Schnabel, Eckhard J. *Acts*. Zondervan Exegetical Commentary on the New Testament. Grand Rapids, MI: Zondervan, 2012.
———. *Early Christian Mission*, II. Downers Grove, IL: InterVarsity Press, 2004.
———. *Mark: An Introduction and Commentary*. Tyndale New Testament Commentary. Downers Grove, IL: IVP Academic, 2017.
———. *Paul the Missionary: Realities, Strategies and Methods*. Downers Grove, IL: IVP Academic, 2008.
Schreiner, Thomas R. *1, 2 Peter, Jude*. The New American Commentary. Nashville, TN: B&H, 2003.
Schreiter, Robert J. *Constructing Local Theologies*. Maryknoll, NY: Orbis, 1986.
Scott, Janet Lee. *For Gods, Ghosts, and Ancestors: The Chinese Tradition of Paper Offerings*. Hong Kong: Hong Kong University Press, 2007.
Seamands, Stephen. *Give Them Christ: Preaching His Incarnation, Crucifixion, Resurrection, Ascension and Return*. Downers Grove, IL: InterVarsity Press, 2012.
Segal, Alan F. *Life after Death: A History of the Afterlife in the Religions of the West*. New York: Doubleday, 2004.
Seidel, Anna. "Chinese Concepts of the Soul and the Afterlife." In *Death, Afterlife, and the Soul*, edited by Lawrence E. Sullivan, 183–188. New York: Macmillan, 1989.
Seifrid, Mark A. *The Second Letter to the Corinthians*. The Pillar New Testament Commentary. Grand Rapids, MI: Eerdmans, 2014.
Seitz, Christopher R. "The Ten Commandments: Positive and Natural Law and the Covenants Old and New – Christian Use of the Decalogue and Moral Law." In *I Am the Lord Your God: Christian Reflections on the Ten Commandments*, edited by Carl E. Braaten and Christopher R. Seitz, 18–38. Grand Rapids, MI: Eerdmans, 2005.
Sharma, Arvind. "A Note on the Use of the Word Hinayana in the Teaching of Buddhism." *Eastern Buddhist* 9 (1976): 129–133.
Shaughnessy, Edward L. "The Religion of Ancient China." In *The Handbook of Ancient Religions*, edited by John R. Hinnells, 490–536. Cambridge: Cambridge University Press, 2007.

Shaw, Ian, and Paul Nicholson. *British Museum Dictionary of Ancient Egypt*. London: British Museum Press, 1995.

Shaw, R. Daniel. *Transculturation: The Cultural Factor in Translation and Other Communication Tasks*. Pasadena, CA: William Carey Library, 1988.

Shaw, R. Daniel, and Charles E. Van Engen. *Communicating God's Word in a Complex World: God's Truth or Hocus Pocus*. Lanham, MD: Rowman & Littlefield, 2003.

Shaw, Rosalind, and Charles Stewart, "Introduction: Problematizing Syncretism." In *Syncretism/Anti-Syncretism: The Politics of Religious Synthesis*, edited by Charles Stewart and Rosalind Shaw, 1–24. London: Routledge, 1994.

Sherman, Dean. *Spiritual Warfare for Every Christian*. Seattle, WA: Frontline Communications, 1990.

Shultz, Gary L. Jr. "The Reconciliation of All Things in Christ." *BSac* 167 (2010): 442–459.

Sih, Paul K. T., ed. *The Hsiao Ching*. Translated by Mary Lelia Makra. New York: St. John University Press, 1961.

Sills, M. David. "Paul and Contextualization." In *Paul's Missionary Methods: In His Time and Ours*, edited by Robert L. Plummer and John Mark Terry, 196–215. Leicester: Inter-Varsity Press, 2012.

Silverman, David. *Doing Qualitative Research*. 4th edition. London: SAGE, 2013.

Sing, Poh Boon. *The Christian in the Chinese Culture*. Serdang: Good News Enterprise, 1986.

Sire, James W. *Naming the Elephant: Worldview as a Concept*. Downers Grove, IL: InterVarsity Press, 2004.

———. *The Universe Next Door*. 5th edition. Downers Grove, IL: InterVarsity Press, 2009.

Siu, R. G. H. *The Man of Many Qualities: The Legacy of the I Ching*. Cambridge, MA: MIT Press, 1968.

Smelik, K. A. D. "The Witch of Endor: 1 Samuel 28 in Rabbinic and Christian Exegesis till 800 A.D." *VC* 33 (1979): 160–179.

Smith, Alex. "Counting the Buddhist World Fairly." In *Sharing Jesus Holistically with the Buddhist World*, edited by David Lim and Steve Spaulding, 1–10. Pasadena, CA: William Carey Library, 2005.

Smith, D. Howard. *Chinese Religions*. New York: Holt, Rinehart & Winston, 1968.

———. "Confucianism." In *The Encyclopedia of Word Faiths: An Illustrated Survey of the World's Living Religions*, edited by Peter Bishop and Michael Darton, 273–278. London: Macdonald, 1987.

Smith, Daniel A. "Seeing a Pneuma (tic Body): The Apologetic Interests of Luke 24:36–43." *CBQ* 72 (2010): 752–772.

Smith, David Raymond. *Hand This Man over to Satan: Curse, Exclusion and Salvation in 1 Corinthians 5*. London: T&T Clark, 2008.

Smith, Gary V. *Isaiah 1–39*. The New American Commentary. Nashville, TN: B&H, 2007.
Smith, Graham Russell. "The Church Militant: A Study of 'Spiritual Warfare' in the Anglican Charismatic Renewal." Unpublished doctoral dissertation, University of Birmingham, 2011.
Smith, Henry N. "Ancestor Practices in Contemporary Hong Kong: Religious Ritual or Social Custom?" *AJT* 3 (1989): 31–45.
Smith, Huston. "Chinese Religion in World Perspective." *Dialogue & Alliance* 4 (1990): 4–14.
Smith, Mark S. "Recent Study of Israelite Religion in Light of the Ugaritic Texts." In *Ugarit at Seventy-Five*, edited by K. Lawson Younger Jr., 1–25. Winona Lake, IN: Eisenbrauns, 2007.
Smith, Ralph L. "Hell." In *HolBD*, edited by Trent C. Butler, 631–632. Nashville, TN: Holman Bible, 1991.
———. *Old Testament Theology: Its History, Method, and Message*. Nashville, TN: B&H, 1993.
Smith, Robert Jerome. "Festivals and Celebrations." In *Folklore and Folklife: An Introduction*, edited by Richard M. Dorson, 159–172. Chicago: University of Chicago Press, 1972.
Smith, Robert, Jr. *Doctrine that Dances: Bringing Doctrinal Preaching and Teaching to Life*. Nashville, TN: B&H, 2008.
Smith, Timothy L. "An Historical Perspective on Evangelicalism and Ecumenism." *Mid-Stream* 22 (1983): 308–325.
Snelling, John. *The Buddhist Handbook: A Complete Guide to Buddhist Schools, Teaching, Practice, and History*. Rochester, VT: Inner Traditions, 1991.
Snodgrass, Klyne R. *Stories with Intent: A Comprehensive Guide to the Parables of Jesus*. Grand Rapids, MI: Eerdmans, 2008.
Snyder, Graydon F., and Frank Ramirez. "The Ten Commandments." *Brethren Life and Thought* 55 (2010): 99–105.
Sommer, Deborah. "The Book of Rites." In *Chinese Religion: An Anthology of Sources*, edited by Deborah Sommer, 31. New York: Oxford University Press, 1995.
Sommer, Robert, and Barbara Sommer. *A Practical Guide to Behavioral Research: Tools and Techniques*. 5th edition. Oxford: Oxford University Press, 2002.
Soothill, W. E. *The Three Religions of China: Lectures Delivered at Oxford*. London: Oxford University Press, 1930.
Sorensen, Eric. *Possession and Exorcism in the New Testament and Early Christianity*. Tübingen: Mohr Siebeck, 2002.
Soskice, Janet Martin. *Metaphor and Religious Language*. Oxford: Oxford University Press, 1985.

Spradley, James P., and David W. McCurdy. *The Cultural Experience: Ethnography in Complex Society*. Prospect Heights, IL: Waveland, 1988.

Sproul, R. C. *Getting the Gospel Right: The Tie That Binds Evangelicals Together*. Grand Rapids, MI: Baker, 1999.

Stanley, Brian. "The World Missionary Conference, Edinburgh 1910: Sifting History from Myth." *Touchstone* 28 (2010): 7–18.

Stein, Robert H. *Luke*. The New American Commentary. Nashville, TN: Broadman, 1992.

———. *Mark*. Baker Exegetical Commentary on the New Testament. Grand Rapids, MI: Baker Academic, 2008.

Stepanchuk, Carol, and Charles Wong. *Mooncakes and Hungry Ghosts: Festivals of China*. San Francisco: China Books & Periodicals, 1991.

Stephen B. Bevans. *Models of Contextual Theology*. Revised edition. Maryknoll, NY: Orbis, 2010.

Sterckx, Roel. *Food, Sacrifice, and Sagehood in Early China*. Cambridge: Cambridge University Press, 2011.

Stott, John R. W. *Authentic Christianity: From the Writings of John Stott*. Edited by Timothy Dudley-Smith. Downers Grove, IL: InterVarsity Press, 1995.

———. *The Contemporary Christian: Applying God's Word to Today's World*. Downers Grove, IL: InterVarsity Press, 1992.

———. *Evangelical Truth: A Personal Plea for Unity, Integrity and Faithfulness*. Revised edition. Downers Grove, IL: InterVarsity Press, 2003.

———. *I Believe in Preaching*. London: Hodder & Stoughton, 1982.

———. *Lausanne Occasional Paper No. 3: The Lausanne Covenant, An Exposition and Commentary*. Minneapolis: World Wide, 1975.

———. *The Message of Ephesians: God's New Society*. The Bible Speaks Today. Leicester: Inter-Varsity Press, 1979.

Stransky, Tom. "Criticism of the Ecumenical Movement and of the WCC." In *Dictionary of the Ecumenical Movement*, edited by Nicholas Lossky et al., 252–256. Grand Rapids, MI: Eerdmans, 1991.

Stuart, Douglas. *Ezekiel*. The Communicator's Commentary. Dallas: Word, 1989.

Sumiko, Yamamato. *History of Protestantism in China*. Tokyo: The Institute of Eastern Culture, 2000.

Sumithra, Sunand, ed. *Doing Theology in Context: Festschrift in Honour of Dr. Bruce J. Nicholls*. Bangalore: Theological Book Trust, 1992.

Sun, Anna. *Confucianism as a World Religion: Contested Histories and Contemporary Realities*. Princeton, NJ: Princeton University Press, 2013.

Sundberg, Walter. "Satan the Enemy." *WW* 28 (2008): 29–37.

Sung, Vivien. *Five-Fold Happiness: Chinese Concepts of Luck, Prosperity, Longevity, Happiness, and Wealth*. San Francisco: Chronicle, 2002.

Sure, Heng. "Filial Respect and Buddhist Meditation." *Religion East & West* 1 (2001): 57–65.
Swartley, Willard M. "The Relation of Justice/Righteousness to *Shalom/Eirene*." *ExAud* 22 (2006): 29–53.
Sweeney, Marvin A. *1 & 2 Kings*. The Old Testament Library. Louisville, KY: Westminster John Knox, 2007.
Taber, Charles R. "Contextualization." *RelSRev* 13 (1987): 33–36.
Talbert, Charles H. *Ephesians and Colossians*. Grand Rapids, MI: Baker Academic, 2007.
Tan, Betty O. S. "The Contextualization of the Chinese New Year Festival." *AJT* 15 (2001): 115–132.
Tan, Chee-Beng. "Chinese Religion in Malaysia: A General View." *AFS* 42 (1983): 217–252.
———. "Migration, Localization, and Cultural Exchange: Global Perspectives of Chinese Overseas." In *Migration, Indigenization, and Interaction: Chinese Overseas and Globalization*, edited by Leo Suryadinata, 15–38. Singapore: World Scientific Publishing, 2011.
———. "People of Chinese Descent: Language, Nationality and Identity." In *The Chinese Diaspora: Select Essays*, vol. 1, edited by Ling Chi Wang and Gung Wu Wang, 29–48. Singapore: Times Academic, 1998.
Tan, Kang San. "Evangelical Missiology from an East Asian Perspective: A Study on Christian Encounter with People of Other Faiths." In *Global Missiology for the 21st Century: The Iguassu Dialogue*, edited by William D. Taylor, 295–306. Grand Rapids, MI: Baker Academic, 2000.
Tan, Kim Hong. *The Chinese in Penang: A Pictorial History*. Penang: Areca, 2007.
Tan, Kim Huat. *The Gospel According to Mark*. Asia Bible Commentary Series. Manila: Asia Theological Association, 2011.
Tang, Yi-Jie. *Confucianism, Buddhism, Daoism, Christianity and Chinese Culture*. Washington, DC: The Council for Research in Values and Philosophy, 1991.
Tate, Marvin E. "Satan in the Old Testament." *RevExp* 89 (1992): 461–474.
Taylor, Richard P. *Death and the Afterlife: A Cultural Encyclopedia*. Santa Barbara, CA: ABC-CLIO, 2000.
Taylor, Rodney L. *The Religious Dimensions of Confucianism*. Albany: State University of New York, 1990.
Teiser, Stephen F. *The Ghost Festival in Medieval China*. Princeton, NJ: Princeton University Press, 1988.
Tenney, Merrill C., ed. *The Zondervan Encyclopedia of the Bible*. 5 vols. Grand Rapids, MI: Zondervan, 2009.
Tey, David Hock. *Chinese Culture and the Bible*. Singapore: Here's Life Books, 1988.
Tey, Nai Peng. "Demographic Trends and Human Capital: The Case of Malaysian Chinese." In *Malaysian Chinese and Nation-Building: Before Merdeka and

Fifty Years After, vol. 1, edited by Phin Keong Voon, 307–338. Kuala Lumpur: Centre for Malaysian Chinese Studies, 2007.

Theodore De Bary, William, Wing-Tsit Chan, and Burton Watson. *Sources of Chinese Tradition*. New York: Columbia University Press, 1960.

Thielman, Frank. *Ephesians*. Baker Exegetical Commentary on the New Testament. Grand Rapids, MI: Baker Academic, 2010.

Thiselton, Anthony C. *A Concise Encyclopedia of the Philosophy of Religion*. Grand Rapids, MI: Baker Academic, 2002.

Thomas, Derek W. H. *Acts*. Reformed Expository Commentary. Philipsburg, NJ: P&R, 2011.

Thomas, M. M. "The Absoluteness of Jesus Christ and Christ-Centred Syncretism." *ER* 37 (1985): 387–397.

Thomas, Norman E., ed. *Classic Texts in Mission and World Christianity*. Maryknoll, NY: Orbis, 1995.

Thompson, Laurence G. *Chinese Religion: An Introduction*. 4th edition. Belmont, CA: Wadsworth, 1989.

———. "The Festival Year." In *The Chinese Way in Religion*, 2nd edition, edited by Jordan Paper and Lawrence G. Thompson. Belmont, CA: Wadsworth Publishing, 1998.

Thompson, Marianne Meye. *Colossians and Philemon*. The Two Horizons New Testament Commentary. Grand Rapids, MI: Eerdmans, 2005.

Thompson, Stuart E. "Death, Food, and Fertility." In *Death Ritual in Late Imperial and Modern China*, edited by James L. Watson and Evelyn S. Rawski, 71–108. Berkeley: University of California Press, 1988.

Thondup, Tulku. *Joyful Rebirth: A Tibetan Buddhist Guidebook*. Edited by Harold Talbott. Boston: Shambhala, 2005.

Tidball, Derek. "Can Evangelicals Be Universalists?" *EvQ* 84 (2012): 19–32.

———. *The Message of the Cross*. Leicester: Inter-Varsity Press, 2001.

———. *The Voices of the New Testament: A Conversational Approach to the Message of Good News*. Leicester: Inter-Varsity Press, 2016.

———. *Who Are the Evangelicals?: Tracing the Roots of Today's Movements*. London: Marshall Pickering, 1994.

Tienou, Tite. "Contextualization of Theology for Theological Education." In *Evangelical Theological Education Today: Agenda for Renewal*, edited by Paul Bowers, 42–52. Nairobi: Evangel, 1982.

Till, Barry. *The Churches Search for Unity*. Harmondsworth: Penguin, 1972.

Tillich, Paul. *Systematic Theology: Three Volumes in One*. New York: Harper & Row, 1967.

Ting, Rachel Sing-Kiat, and Alvin Lai Oon Ng. "Use of Religious Resources in Psychotherapy from a Tradition-Sensitive Approach: Cases from Chinese in Malaysia." *Pastoral Psychology* 61 (2012): 941–957.

Tisdale, Leonora Tubbs. *Preaching as Local Theology and Folk Art*. Minneapolis: Fortress, 1997.

Tizon, Al. "Preaching for Shalom: Life and Peace." *AJPS* 19 (2016): 17–29.

Tjandra, Lukas. "Folk Religion among the Chinese in Singapore and Malaysia." Unpublished doctoral dissertation, Fuller Theological Seminary, 1988.

Tomlin, Eric Walter Frederick. *Great Philosophers of the East*. London: Arrow, 1959.

Tong, Daniel. *A Biblical Approach to Chinese Traditions and Beliefs*. New edition. Singapore: Genesis, 2012.

Toon, Peter. *Heaven and Hell: A Biblical and Theological Overview*. Nashville, TN: Thomas Nelson, 1986.

Toorn, Karel van der. *Family Religion in Babylonia, Syria and Israel: Continuity and Change in the Forms of Religious Life*. Leiden: Brill, 1996.

Torre, Miguel A. De La, and Albert Hernandez. *The Quest for the Historical Satan*. Minneapolis: Fortress, 2011.

Toru, Funayama. "The Work of *Paramārtha*: An Example of Sino-Indian Cross-Cultural Exchange." *JIABS* 31 (2010): 141–183.

Trainor, Kevin, ed. *Buddhism: The Illustrated Guide*. London: Duncan Braid, 2001.

Travis, Arthur E. "The Christian's Warfare: An Exegetical Study of Ephesians Six (Ephesians 6:10–18)." *SwJT* 6 (1963): 71–80.

Trites, Allison A. *The Gospel of Luke*. Cornerstone Biblical Commentary. Carol Stream, IL: Tyndale, 2006.

Turner, Bryan S., and Oscar Salemink. "Introduction: Constructing Religion and Religions in Asia." In *Routledge Handbook of Religions in Asia*, edited by Bryan S. Turner and Oscar Salemink, 1–14. Abingdon: Routledge, 2015.

Turner, David L. *Matthew*. Baker Exegetical Commentary on the New Testament. Grand Rapids, MI: Baker Academic, 2008.

Turner, Victor. *Dramas, Fields, and Metaphors: Symbolic Action in Human Society*. London: Cornell University Press, 1974.

Twelftree, G. H. "Spiritual Powers." In *NDBT*, edited by T. Desmond Alexander, Brian S. Rosner, D. A. Carson, and Graeme Goldsworthy, 796–802. Leicester: Inter-Varsity Press, 2000.

Tylor, Edward B. *Primitive Culture: Researches into the Development of Mythology, Philosophy, Religion, Language, Art, and Custom*. London: John Murray, 1871.

Ukpong, Justin S. "Contextualisation: A Historical Survey." *AFER* 29 (1987): 278–286.

Unger, Merrill F. *Biblical Demonology: A Study of Spiritual Forces at Work Today*. Grand Rapids, MI: Kregel, 1994.

———. *Demons in the World Today: A Study of Occultism in the Light of God's Word*. Wheaton, IL: Tyndale, 1971.

Van Harn, Roger E., ed. *The Ten Commandments for Jews, Christians, and Others*. Grand Rapids, MI: Eerdmans, 2007.

Vanhoozer, Kevin J. "One Rule to Rule Them All?" In *Globalizing Theology: Belief and Practice in an Era of World Christianity*, edited by Craig Ott and Harold A. Netland, 85–126. Grand Rapids, MI: Baker Academic, 2006.

Vannoy, J. Robert. *1–2 Samuel*. Cornerstone Biblical Commentary. Carol Stream, IL: Tyndale, 2009.

Veeravanitkul, Salinthip. "Burning Money: Exploring the Annual Qing Ming Celebration among the Thai-Chinese and Their Consumption Meanings." Unpublished master of arts dissertation, University of Nottingham, 2006.

Voon, Phin Keong. "Pioneers, Entrepreneurs, and Labourers: Building the Social and Economic Foundations of Statehood." In *Malaysian Chinese and Nation-Building: Before Merdeka and Fifty Years After*, vol. 1, edited by Phin Keong Voon, 43–94. Kuala Lumpur: Centre for Malaysian Chinese Studies, 2007.

Vroon-van Vugt, Miranda. *Dead Man Walking in Endor: Narrative Mental Spaces and Conceptual Blending in 1 Samuel 28*. Ridderkerk: Ridderprint BV, 2013.

Vyhmeister, Nancy Jean, and Terry Dwain Robertson. *Your Guide to Writing Quality Research Papers: For Students of Religion and Theology*. 3rd edition. Grand Rapids, MI: Zondervan, 2014.

Wagner, C. Peter. *Warfare Prayer: Strategies for Combating the Rulers of Darkness*. Tunbridge Wells: Monarch, 1992.

Wall, Robert W. *Colossians & Philemon*. The IVP New Testament Commentary Series. Downers Grove, IL: InterVarsity Press, 1993.

Walls, Andrew F. *The Missionary Movement in Christian History: Studies in the Transmission of Faith*. Edinburgh: T&T Clark, 1996.

Waltke, Bruce K. *The Book of Proverbs 1–15*. The New International Commentary on the Old Testament. Grand Rapids, MI: Eerdmans, 2004.

Wan, Enoch. "Mission among the Chinese Diaspora: A Case of Migration and Mission." *Missiology* 31 (2003): 35–43.

Wang, Qing. "A Tentative Study on Differences and Integration of Sino-Western Filial Piety Culture." *Asian Social Science* 7 (2011): 97–106.

Wang, Thomas, and Sharon Chan. "Christian Witness to the Chinese People." In *Perspectives on the World Christian Movement*, edited by Ralph D. Winter and Steven C. Hawthorne, 639–645. 3rd edition. Pasadena, CA: William Carey Library, 1999.

Wang, Xuefu. "On Becoming a Religious Therapist in Chinese Culture." *Pastoral Psychology* 61 (2012): 1007–1024.

Ward, Pete. *Introducing Practical Theology: Mission, Ministry, and the Life of the Church*. Grand Rapids, MI: Baker Academic, 2017.

Ware, Bruce A. "The Father, the Son, and the Holy Spirit: The Trinity as Theological Foundation for Family Ministry." *JFM* 1 (2011): 6–13.

Watts, Alan. *Taoism: Way Beyond Seeking*. Boston: Charles E. Tuttle, 1997.
Weber, Max. *The Sociology of Religion*. Translated by Ephraim Fischoff. Boston: Beacon, 1993.
Wehmeier, Sally, ed. *Oxford Advanced Learner's Dictionary of Current English*. 6th edition. Oxford: Oxford University Press, 2000.
Wei, Liming. *Chinese Festivals*. Cambridge: Cambridge University Press, 2011.
Wei, Xiang. *Chinese Customs*. New York: Better Link, 2008.
Welch, Holmes. *The Practice of Chinese Buddhism: 1900–1950*. Cambridge: Harvard University Press, 1967.
———. *Taoism: The Parting of the Way*. Boston: Beacon, 1965.
Wenig, Scott A. "Biblical Preaching that Adapts and Contextualizes." In *The Big Idea of Biblical Preaching: Connecting the Bible to People*, edited by Keith Willhite and Scott M. Gibson, 25–38. Grand Rapids, MI: Baker, 1998.
Wenkel, David H. "The 'Breastplate of Righteousness' in Ephesians 6:14, Imputation or Virtue?" *TynBul* 58 (2007): 275–287.
Wheeler-Barclay, Marjorie. *The Science of Religion in Britain, 1860–1915*. Charlottesville: University of Virginia Press, 2010.
Wheeler, Ray. "The Legacy of Shoki Coe." *IBMR* 26 (2002): 77–80.
Whiteman, Darrell L. "Contextualization: The Theory, the Gap, the Challenge." *IBMR* 21 (1997): 2–7.
Wiersbe, Warren. *Real Worship: Playground, Battle Ground, or Holy Ground?* 2nd edition. Grand Rapids, MI: Baker, 2000.
Wild, Robert A. "The Warrior and The Prisoner: Some Reflections on Ephesians 6:10–20." *CBQ* 46 (1984): 284–298.
Wilken, Robert Louis, Angela Russell Christman, and Michael J. Hollerich, eds. *Isaiah: Interpreted by Early Christian and Medieval Commentators*. Grand Rapids, MI: Eerdmans, 2007.
Wilkinson, Richard H. *The Complete Temples of Ancient Egypt*. London: Thames & Hudson, 2000.
Willhite, Keith. "Connecting with Your Congregation." In *Preaching to a Shifting Culture: 12 Perspectives on Communication that Connects*, edited by Scott M. Gibson, 95–111. Grand Rapids, MI: Baker, 2004.
Williams, Charles Alfred Speed. *Chinese Symbolism and Art Motifs: A Comprehensive Handbook on Symbolism in Chinese Art through the Ages*. 4th revised edition. Rutland, VT: Tuttle, 2012.
Williams, Raymond. *Keywords: A Vocabulary of Culture and Society*. London: Fontana, 1983.
Wilson, Paul Scott. *Setting Words on Fire: Putting God at the Center of the Sermon*. Nashville, TN: Abingdon, 2008.

Wind, A. "The Protestant Missionary Movement from 1789 to 1963." In *Missiology: An Ecumenical Introduction: Texts and Contexts of Global Christianity*, edited by A. Camps et al., 237–252. Grand Rapids, MI: Eerdmans, 1995.

Wink, Walter. "Demons and DMins: The Church's Response to the Demonic." *RevExp* 89 (1992): 503–513.

———. *Naming the Powers: The Language of Power in the New Testament*. Philadelphia: Fortress, 1984.

———. *Unmasking the Powers: The Invisible Forces that Determine Human Existence*. Philadelphia: Fortress, 1986.

Winter, Bruce W. "On Introducing Gods to Athens: An Alternative Reading of Acts 17:28–20." *TynBul* 47 (1996): 71–90.

Wintle, Brian, and Ken Gnanakan. *Ephesians*. Asia Bible Commentary. Bangalore: Asia Theological Association, 2004.

Winzeler, Robert L. *Anthropology and Religion: What We Know, Think, and Question*. 2nd edition. Plymouth: AltaMira Press, 2012.

Witherington, Ben, III. *The Acts of the Apostles: A Socio-Rhetorical Commentary*. Grand Rapids, MI: Eerdmans, 1998.

———. *The Gospel of Mark: A Socio-Rhetorical Commentary*. Grand Rapids, MI: Eerdmans, 2001.

Wolf, Arthur P. "Gods, Ghosts, and Ancestors." In *Religion and Ritual in Chinese Society*, edited by Arthur P. Wolf, 131–182. Stanford, CA: Stanford University Press, 1974.

Wong, Choon San. *A Cycle of Chinese Festivities*. Singapore: Malaysia Publishing, 1967.

Woo, Taek Joo. "The *Marzeah* Institution and Rites for the Dead: A Comparative and Systemic Study with Special Attention to the Eight-Century Prophets' Setting." Unpublished doctoral dissertation, University of California, 1998.

Woods, Paul R. "Towards a Contextualized Spirituality for Chinese Diaspora Christians." Unpublished master of theology dissertation, Spurgeon's College, 2006.

World Conference on Salvation Today, Bangkok. "Culture and Identity: Report of Section I of the Bangkok Conference." *IRM* 62 (1973): 185–197.

Woudstra, Marten H. *The Book of Joshua*. The New International Commentary on the Old Testament. Grand Rapids, MI: Eerdmans, 1981.

Wray, T. J., and Gregory Mobley. *The Birth of Satan: Tracing the Devil's Biblical Roots*. New York: Palgrave Macmillan, 2005.

Wright, Christopher J. H. "According to the Scriptures: The Whole Gospel in Biblical Revelation." *ERT* 33 (2009): 4–18.

———. *The Message of Ezekiel: A New Heart and a New Spirit*. The Bible Speaks Today. Leicester: Inter-Varsity Press, 2001.

Wright, N. T. *The Day the Revolution Began*. London: SPCK, 2016.

———. "Heaven Is Not Our Home: The Bodily Resurrection Is the Good News of the Gospel – and Thus Our Social and Political Mandate." *Christianity Today* 52 (2008): 36–39.

———. *Jesus and the Victory of God: Christian Origins and the Question of God.* Minneapolis: Fortress, 1996.

———. *Luke for Everyone.* London: SPCK, 2001.

———. *Paul and the Faithfulness of God.* Minneapolis: Fortress, 2013.

———. *The Resurrection of the Son of God.* London: SPCK, 2003.

———. *Surprised by Hope: Rethinking Heaven, the Resurrection, and the Mission of the Church.* New York: HarperCollins, 2008.

———. *What Saint Paul Really Said: Was Paul of Tarsus the Real Founder of Christianity?* Grand Rapids, MI: Eerdmans, 1997.

Wright, Nigel Goring. *The Theology of the Dark Side: Putting the Power of Evil in Its Place.* Carlisle: Paternoster, 2003.

Wright, Stephen I. *Alive to the Word: A Practical Theology of Preaching for the Whole Church.* London: SCM, 2010.

———. "Parables on Poverty and Riches (Luke 1:13–21; 16:1–13; 16:19–31)." In *The Challenge of Jesus' Parables*, edited by Richard N. Longenecker, 217–239. Grand Rapids, MI: Eerdmans, 2000.

Wu, Jackson. *One Gospel for All Nations: A Practical Approach to Biblical Contextualization.* Pasadena, CA: William Carey Library, 2015.

Yandell, Keith E. *Philosophy of Religion: A Contemporary Introduction.* London: Routledge, 1999.

Yang, Mayfair Mei-hui. "Introduction." In *Chinese Religiosities: Afflictions of Modernity and State Formation*, edited by Mayfair Mei-hui Yang, 1–40. Berkeley: University of California Press, 2008.

Yang, Zeng. "A Biographical Study on Bukong 不空 (aka. Amoghavajra, 705–774): Networks, Institutions, and Identities." Unpublished doctoral thesis, The University of British Columbia, 2018.

Yao, Xinzhong. *An Introduction to Confucianism.* Cambridge: Cambridge University Press, 2000.

Yao, Xinzhong, and Yanxia Zhao. *Chinese Religion: A Contextual Approach.* London: Continuum, 2010.

Yates, Matthew. "Ancestral Worship." In *Records of the General Conference of the Protestant Missionaries of China Held at Shanghai, May 10–24, 1877*, 367–387. Taipei: Cheng-Wen, 1973.

Yeo, Khiok-Khng. "Christian Chinese Theology: Theological Ethics of Becoming Human and Holy." In *Global Theology in Evangelical Perspective: Exploring the Contextual Nature of Theology and Mission*, edited by Jeffrey P. Greenman and Gene L. Green, 102–115. Downers Grove, IL: IVP Academic, 2012.

———. "Li and Law in the Analects and Galatians: A Chinese Christian Understanding of Ritual and Propriety." *AJT* 19 (2005): 309–332.

Yoder, Perry B. *Shalom: The Bible's Word for Salvation, Justice and Peace*. Eugene, OR: Wipf & Stock, 1997.

Young, Edward J. *The Book of Isaiah, Volume I: Chapters I–XVIII*. The New International Commentary on the Old Testament. Grand Rapids, MI: Eerdmans, 1965.

Young, John D. *East-West Synthesis: Matteo Ricci and Confucianism*. Hong Kong: University of Hong Kong, 1980.

Yow, Yit Seng. *Chinese Dimensions: Their Roots, Mindset and Psyche*. Subang Jaya, Malaysia: Pelanduk, 2006.

Zahniser, A. H. Mathias. *Symbol and Ceremony: Making Disciples across Cultures*. Monrovia, CA: MARC, 1997.

Ziegler, Phillip Gordon. "A Brief Theology of Reconciliation." *Touchstone* 34 (2016): 7–13.

Zurcher, Erik. "Buddhist Influence on Early Taoism: A Survey of Scriptural Evidence." In *Buddhism: Critical Concepts in Religious Studies, Volume VIII: Buddhism in China, East Asia, and Japan*, edited by Paul Williams, 367–419. London: Routledge, 2005.

Chinese Works Cited

Sorted ascending by stroke

王世禎, 迷信在中國 *(Superstition in China)*. 臺北 (Taipei): 星光出版社, 1981.

王治心, "中國本色教會的討論" ("The Discussion on the Indigenous Chinese Church"), 於本色之探: 20 世紀中國基督教文化學術論集 *(Indigenization: Essays on the Chinese Christianity in 20th Century)*, 張西平與卓新平編. 北京 (Beijing): 中國廣播電視出版社, 1999, 236–244.

———. "本色教會應創何種節期適合中國固有的風俗" ("Festivals for Indigenous Chinese Church"), 於本色之探: 20 世紀中國基督教文化學術論集 *(Indigenization: Essays on the Chinese Christianity in 20th Century)*, 張西平與卓新平編. 北京 (Beijing): 中國廣播電視出版社, 1999, 485–495.

王琛發, 馬來西亞華人民間節日研究 *(A Study of Festivals among Malaysian Chinese)*. 士拉央 (Selayang): 藝品多媒體傳播中心, 2001.

王錦發, "大馬華人與中華文化" ("Chinese Malaysian and Chinese Culture"), 於中華文化之路: 中華文化邁向二十一世紀國際學術研討會論文集 *(The Direction of Chinese Culture: Essays on Chinese Culture toward the 21st Century)*, 林水檺與何國忠編. 吉隆坡 (Kuala Lumpur): 馬來西亞中華大會堂聯合會, 1995, 263–273.

Bibliography

丘恩處, 新時代華人神學 (The New Age Chinese Theology). New York: 紐約神學教育中心, 1996.

史孝進和劉仲宇, 道教風俗談 (Taoist Customs). 上海 (Shanghai): 上海辭書出版社, 2003.

史慧玲, 傳統習俗事典 (The Tradition Handbook). 香港 (Hong Kong): 文化會社有限公司, 2014.

石衡潭, 東風破:《論語》之另類解讀 (An Alternative Interpretation of The Analects). 濟南 (Jinan): 山東畫報出版社, 2009.

何世明, 從基督教看中國孝道 (A Christian's Perspective towards Filial Piety). 北京 (Beijing): 宗教文化出版社, 1999.

吳宗文, "祭祖儀節及用品之處置等問題" ("Issues of Ancestral Rituals and Ceremonial Products"), 基督教週報 (Christian Weekly), 2230 (2007).

———. 傳統與信仰續編 (Traditions and Faith). 香港 (Hong Kong): 基督教卓越使團, 2004.

吳國安, 中國基督徒對時代的回應 (1919-1926): 以《生命月刊》和《真理周刊》為中心的探討 (The Contextual Responses of Chinese Christians as Revealed in Life Journal and Truth Weekly 1919-1926). 香港 (Hong Kong): 建道神學院, 2000.

呂一中, 江湖一點訣: 法術、預言、算命之研究 (A Study of Spells, Prophecies and Fortune-Telling). 臺北 (Taipei): 校園書房, 2007.

呂理政, 傳統信仰與現代社會 (Traditional Beliefs and Modern Society). 臺北 (Taipei): 稻香出版社, 1992.

巫美梅和劉銳宏, 拜祀衣紙扎作與香港民間風俗 (Paper Effigies and Customs in Hong Kong). 香港 (Hong Kong): 中華文教交流服務中心, 2011.

李亦園, 信仰與文化 (Belief and Culture). 臺北 (Taipei): 巨流圖書公司, 1983.

李志剛, 基督教與近代中國文化論文集 (Essays on Christianity and Modern China). 臺北 (Taipei): 宇宙光, 1994.

李秀娥, 臺灣民俗節慶:歲時節俗的民俗意涵與祭祀文化 (Festivals and Customs of Taiwan: Connotations of Customs During Seasonal Festivals and Sacrificial Culture). 臺中 (Taichung): 晨星出版有限公司, 2004.

汪桂平與郭清執, "道教信仰與傳統文化" ("Taoist Belief and Traditional Culture"), 於中國道教基礎知識 (Basic Knowledge about Taoism in China), 王卡編. 北京 (Beijing): 宗教文化出版社, 2006.

邢福增與梁家麟, 中國祭祖問題 (Chinese Ancestor Worship). 香港 (Hong Kong): 建道神學院, 1997.

易夫, 冥界諸神 (Deities of The Underworld). 北京 (Beijing): 大眾文藝出版社, 1999.

林金一, "土地公在臺灣" ("Earth God in Taiwan"), 於臺灣民間宗教信仰 (Folk Religion in Taiwan), 董芳苑編. 臺北 (Taipei): 長青文化事業股份有限公司, 1981.

林國興, "新馬華人民間宗教習俗的認識: 回應" ("A Response: Understanding of Religious Practices among the Singaporeans and Malaysians"), 於福音與新馬華人文化:研討會報告書 (A Seminar Report on Gospel and Singapore-Malaysian Chinese Culture), 週賢正編. 新加坡 (Singapore): 三一神學院, 1989, 158–160.

林富士, 孤魂與鬼雄的世界: 北臺灣的厲鬼信仰 (Lonely Souls and the Ghostly World: The Malicious Ghost Belief of Northern Taiwan). 臺北 (Taipei): 臺北縣立文化中心, 1995.

林雲和聶達, 祭拜趣談 (Discussions about Venerations of Deities). 上海 (Shanghai): 上海古籍出版社, 2005.

林嘉瓊等編, 馬來西亞華人農曆新年 (Lunar New Year of Malaysian Chinese). 吉隆坡 (Kuala Lumpur): 馬來西亞國家博物館, 1983.

林榮洪, 風潮中奮起的中國教會 (Chinese Theology in Construction). 香港 (Hong Kong): 天道書樓, 1980.

林榮洪與溫偉耀, 基督教與中國文化的相遇 (Encounter between Christianity and Chinese Culture). 香港 (Hong Kong): 香港中文大學崇基學院, 2001.

金良年, 民間諸神 (The Deities of the Folk). 上海 (Shanghai): 三聯書店, 1991.

段琦, "對中國基督教本色化的兩點思考" ("Reflections on Indigenization of Christianity in Chin"), 於中華本色: 近代中國教會史論 (China's Indigenization: Essays on the History of Christianity in Modern China), 李金強,湯紹源,梁家麟編. 香港 (Hong Kong): 建道神學院, 2007, 49–63.

洪丕謨, 福祿: 民俗文化趣談 (A Discussion on Custom and Culture). 香港 (Hong Kong): 萬裡書店, 2006.

徐福全, 臺灣民間祭祀禮儀 (Taiwan Folk Sacrificial Etiquette). 新竹 (Hsinchu): 臺灣省立新竹社會教育館, 1996.

馬有藻, 神必救贖: 以賽亞書詮釋 (The Glory of Redemption – A Commentary on the Book of Isaiah). 臺北 (Taipei): 天恩出版社, 2005.

馬書田, 中國人的神靈世界 (Spiritual World of the people in China). 北京 (Beijing): 北京燕山出版社, 1990.

———. 冥間鬼神 (Deities in the Underworld). 臺北 (Taipei): 風格司藝術創作坊, 2012.

———. 華夏諸神 (Deities of China). 北京 (Beijing): 北京燕山出版社, 1990.

馬國棟和劉志良, 中國民間信仰揭秘 (Uncovering the Folk Beliefs of China), 增訂版. 香港 (Hong Kong): 香港基督徒短期宣教訓練中心暨佈道資源供應中心, 1997.

高明強, 神秘的圖騰 (The Mysterious Totem). 江蘇 (Jiangsu): 江蘇人民出版社, 1989.

高明發, "節日與信仰: 中國文化與基督教節期的融通芻議" ("Festivals and Faith: Comments on Chinese Culture and Christian Festivals"), 教牧期刊 (Pastoral Journal) 20 (2006): 165–193.

康新民, "民間節日文化價值初探" ("A Probe into the Cultural Value of Folk Festivals"), 於中國民間文化:民俗文化研究 (Folk Culture in China: Research on the Customs of China), 上海民間文藝家協會編. 上海 (Shanghai): 學林出版社, 1991.

張永信, 歌林多前書注釋 (Commentary on 1 Corinthians). 香港 (Hong Kong): 宣道出版社, 1997.

張君, 神秘的節俗: 傳統節日禮俗、禁忌研究 (Mystery of Festivals: Research on Traditional Festival Etiquettes and Taboos). 廣西 (Guangxi): 廣西人民出版社, 1994.

張鶴泉, 周代祭祀研究 (Research on Sacrificial Practices of Zhou Dynasty). 臺北 (Taipei): 文津出版社, 1992.

梁家麟, 今日歌林多教會: 歌林多前書注釋 (Today Corinthian Church: A Commentary on the First Corinthians). 香港 (Hong Kong): 天道書樓, 1992.

———. 超前與墮後: 本土釋經與神學研究 (Far Ahead and Lagging Behind: Studies in Contextual Hermeneutics and Theology). 香港 (Hong Kong): 建道神學院, 2003.

———. 愛主優先 (The Lord's Priority Over). 香港 (Hong Kong): 建道神學院, 2003.

梁燕城, 文化中國蓄勢待發 (Cultural China Is Developing). 臺北 (Taipei): 宇宙光, 2006.

梁燕城與徐濟時, 中國文化處境的神學反省: 中華福音神學人物研究 (Theological Reflections in the Context of Chinese Culture: A Study of Christian Scholars toward Their Evangelical Theologies). Burnaby: Culture Regeneration Research Society, 2012.

莊祖鯤, 契合與轉化: 基督教與中國文化更新之路 (Conformation and Transformation: The Renewal of Christianity and Chinese Culture). 多倫多 (Toronto): 加拿大恩福協會, 1997.

———. 宣教與文化 (Mission and Culture). 臺北 (Taipei): 道聲出版社, 2004.

莊雅棠, "本土神學的詮釋學輪廓" ("Hermeneutics of Local Theology"), 於基督生命長成: 現在中國本土基督教神學之發展 (Growth in Life: 2013 Symposium on Modern Chinese Theology). 新北市 (New Taipei): 聖經資源中心, 2014, 39–54.

莫福山編, 中國民間節日文化辭典 (Cultural Dictionary of China's Festivals). 北京 (Beijing): 中國勞動出版社, 1992.

許開明, "論趙紫宸先生的脈絡化基督論的神學意義" ("The Theological Meaning of T. C. Chao's Christology"), 於神學與中國: 紐約神學教育中心暨漢語網絡神學院二十周年紀念文集 (Theology and China: Essays Celebrating the 20th Anniversary of New York Theological Education Center and Chinese Online School of Theology), 劉永明編. 香港 (Hong Kong): 紐約神學教育中心, 2012, 195–237.

郭春梅與張慶捷, 世俗迷信與中國社會 (Superstitious Beliefs and Society of China). 北京 (Beijing): 宗教文化出版社, 2001.

陳守仁, 神功戲在香港: 粵劇、潮劇及福佬劇 (The Chinese Operas of Hong Kong's Hungry Ghost Festival). 香港 (Hong Kong): 三聯書店, 1996.

陳谷嘉, "中國傳統文化的基本精神" ("The Basic Spirit of Traditional Chinese Culture"), 於中國傳統文化導論 (An Introduction to Chinese Traditional Culture), 朱漢民編. 長沙 (Changsha): 湖南大學出版社, 2016.

陳美幸, 節、結、解:中國教會與祖先崇拜 (Churches in China and Ancestral Worship). 臺北 (Taipei): 大光宣教福音中心, 1993.

陳淑英編, 中國節日的故事 (Stories about China's Festivals). 臺北 (Taipei): 將門文物出版有限公司, 1997.

陳蒨, "香港的民間傳統風俗" ("Traditional Folk Customs in Hong Kong"), 於香港史新編, 下冊 (Hong Kong History: New Perspectives, vol. 2), 王賡武編. 香港 (Hong Kong): 三聯書店, 1997, 841–857.

陳潤棠, 破迷, 闢邪, 趕鬼, 第二集: 東南亞華人民間宗教 (Against Superstition, Witchcraft and Demon Possession), 第四版. 香港 (Hong Kong): 基道書樓, 2005.

———. 破迷, 闢邪, 趕鬼 (Against Superstition, Witchcraft and Demon Possession) 第十一版. 新山 (Johor Bharu): 人人書樓, 2008.

麥兆輝著, 顧瓊華譯, 尊天敬祖: 當代華人基督徒對祭祖的回應 (Revering God and Respecting Ancestors: A Contemporary Christian Chinese Response to Ancestral Practice). 香港 (Hong Kong): 浸信會出版社, 2014.

喬繼堂, 中國歲時禮俗 (Seasonal Etiquette in China). 天津 (Tianjin): 天津人民出版社, 1992.

———. 細說中國節: 中國傳統節日的起源與內涵 (The Origin and Connotation of Chinese Traditional Festivals). 北京 (Beijing): 九州出版社, 2006.

曾文星編, 華人的心理與治療 (Psychology and Therapy for the Chinese). 臺北 (Taipei): 桂冠圖書股份有限公司, 1996.

曾景來, 臺灣的迷信與陋習 (Superstitions and Customs in Taiwan). 臺北 (Taipei): 武陵出版公司, 1994.

程裕禎編, 中國文化攬萃 (The Collection of Chinese Culture). 北京 (Beijing): 學苑出版社, 1989.

週樹佳, 香港諸神: 起源、廟宇與崇拜 (Deities in Hong Kong: Origin, Temples and Veneration of Deities). 香港 (Hong Kong): 中華書局, 2009.

黃孝光, 與全人相遇 (The Holistic Encounter). 新北市 (New Taipei): 華宣出版, 2009.

廉正明, 龍的文化 (The Dragon Culture). 香港 (Hong Kong): 明窗出版社, 1999.

楊秀編, 中國風俗 (Customs in China). 蘇州 (Suzhou): 古吳軒出版社, 2010.

楊牧谷, "信徒皆祭司與神學處境化" ("The Priesthood of All Believers and Contextual Theology"), 於基督教與中國文化更新: 研討會匯報 (Conference

Essays on Christianity and the Renewal of Chinese Culture). 陳惠文編. Argyle, TX: 大使命中心, 2000, 128-137.

———. 復合神學與教會更新 *(Theology of Reconciliation and Church Renewal).* 香港 (Hong Kong): 種籽出版社, 1987.

———. 魔惑眾生: 魔鬼學研究 *(Study in Demonology).* 香港 (Hong Kong): 卓越出版社, 1995.

楊劍龍, "論非基督教思潮與中國教會本色化運動" ("The Anti-Christian Movement and The Chinese Indigenous Church Movement'"), 於基督教與中國社會文化: 第五屆國際年青學者研討會論文集 *(Studies in Christianity and Chinese Society and Culture: Essays from the Fifth International Young Scholars' Symposium),* 賴品超與吳小新編. 香港 (Hong Kong): 中文大學出版社, 2014, 25-38.

溫以諾, "榮耀的基督與人類文化" ("The Glory of Christ and Human Culture"), 於榮耀的基督與當代信徒 *(The Glorious Christ and the Contemporary Christian).* 加州 (California): 基督工人神學院, 2003.

———. 中色神學綱要 *(Sino-Theology: A Survey Study).* Scarborough: 加拿大恩福協會, 1999.

溫永生, "敬祖與喪禮處境化模式的建立" ("A Design for a Contextualized Model of Christian Ancestor Reverence and Funeral Ritual"), 建道學刊 *(Jian Dao)* 22 (2004): 57-98.

萬建中, 圖文中國民俗: 喪俗 *(A Pictorial Illustration of the Customs in China: Bereavement).* 北京 (Beijing): 中國旅遊出版社, 2004.

葉明翰, 祭祖與輪迴 *(Worship of Ancestors and Reincarnation).* 臺北 (Taipei): 大光傳播, 1999.

董芳苑, "就臺灣民間信仰之認識論基督教宣教的場合化" ("The Understanding of Taiwanese Folk Beliefs on the Contextualization of Christianity"), 臺灣神學論刊 *(Taiwan Journal of Theology* 3 (1981): 31-66.

———. 信仰與習俗 *(Beliefs and Customs).* 臺南 (Tainan): 人光出版社, 1994.

———. 探討臺灣民間信仰 *(Exploration of Folk Beliefs in Taiwan).* 臺北 (Taipei): 常民文化出版, 1996.

詹鄞鑫, 神靈與祭祀: 中國傳統宗教綜論 *(Spirit of God and Sacrifices: A View of China's Traditional Religion).* 南京 (Nanjing): 江蘇古籍出版社, 2000.

廖元威, "從基督教倫理和禮儀看祭祖問題" ("Christian Ethics and Etiquette View of Ancestral Worship"), 於歷史文化與詮釋學:中原大學宗教學術研討會論文集(二) *(History, Culture and Hermeneutics: The Religion Symposium of Chung Yuan Christian University),* 林治平編. 臺北 (Taipei): 宇宙光, 2001.

廖建裕, "亞細安華社與華族文化的變遷" ("ASEAN Chinese Society and the Changes of Chinese Culture"), 於中華文化之路: 中華文化邁向二十一世紀國際學術研討會論文集 *(The Road to Chinese Culture: An International Symposium of the 21st Century Chinese*

Culture), 林水檺與何國忠編. 吉隆坡 (Kuala Lumpur): 馬來西亞中華大會堂聯合會, 1995.

窪德忠著, 蕭坤華譯, 道教諸神 (The Taoist Deities). 成都 (Chengdu): 四川人民出版社, 1989.

趙世光, 撒母耳記上下 (1 & 2 Samuel). 香港 (Hong Kong): 靈糧出版社, 1970.

趙紫宸, "中國民族與基督教" ("Chinese and Christianity"), 於本色之探: 20 世紀中國基督教文化學術論集 (Indigenization: Essays on Chinese Christianity in 20th Century), 張西平與卓新平編. 北京 (Beijing): 中國廣播電視出版社, 1999, 18–33.

齊治平, 節令的故事 (The Tale of Festivals). 香港 (Hong Kong): 大方文化事業公司, 1979.

潛明茲, 中國神源 (The Origin of Chinese Deities). 重慶 (Chongqing): 重慶出版社, 1999.

蔡仁厚, 周聯華, 與梁燕城, 會通與轉化 (Transcend and Transform). 臺北 (Taipei): 宇宙光出版社, 1985.

蔡志祥, "香港的傳統中國節日: 節、誕、醮的比較研究" ("Traditional Chinese Festivals in Hong Kong: A Comparative Study of Festivals"), 華南研究 (The South China Research 1 (1994): 1–23.

鄭金明, 世界節日的故事 (Tales of World Wide Festivals). 臺中 (Taichung): 好讀出版, 2006.

鄭國治, 如何趕鬼 (How to Perform an Exorcism). Johor Bahru: 人人書樓, 1998.

餘喆編, 神鬼世界 (The Spiritual World). 香港 (Hong Kong): 中華書局, 1992.

盧建業編, 宗教世界 (A World of Religion). 香港 (Hong Kong): 中華書局, 1992.

蕭登福, 道教與民俗 (Taoism and Folklore). 臺北 (Taipei): 文津出版社, 2002.

———. 道教與佛教 (Taoism and Buddhism). 臺北 (Taipei): 東大圖書股份有限公司, 1995.

蕭遙天, "中華文化的本質特徵及對馬來西亞的貢獻" ("The Essential Characteristics of Chinese Culture and Its Contribution to Malaysia"), 於馬華文化探討 (Essays On Malaysian Chinese Culture), 賴觀福編. 吉隆坡 (Kuala Lumpur): 馬來西亞留臺校友會聯合總會, 1982.

賴觀福, 孟沙, 與鍾澤才編, 馬來西亞華人節日風俗 (Customs of Malaysian Chinese Festivals). 吉隆坡 (Kuala Lumpur): 馬來西亞中華大會堂, 1997.

韓盈和王上然, 節令風俗 (Festival Customs). 上海 (Shanghai): 上海古籍出版社, 1998.

鴻宇編, 節俗 (Festivals and Customs). 香港 (Hong Kong): 漢榮書局有限公司, 2006.

羅曼華編, 華人教會手冊 (Chinese Churches Handbook). 香港 (Hong Kong): 世界華人福音事工聯絡中心, 1981.

蘇慶華, 節令、民俗與宗教 (Festival, Folklore and Religion). 吉隆坡 (Kuala Lumpur): 華社資料研究中心, 1994.

龔天民, 諸佛、菩薩與鬼神真相 (A Study of Buddhas, Budhisattvas, Gods, and Ghosts). 臺北 (Taipei): 道聲, 1997.

THE STORY OF HANN TZUU JOEY TAN

Learn more about Hann Tzuu Joey Tan's story.

https://langhamliterature.org/joey-tan

Langham Literature, with its publishing work, is a ministry of Langham Partnership.

Langham Partnership is a global fellowship working in pursuit of the vision God entrusted to its founder John Stott –

> *to facilitate the growth of the church in maturity and Christ-likeness through raising the standards of biblical preaching and teaching.*

Our vision is to see churches in the Majority World equipped for mission and growing to maturity in Christ through the ministry of pastors and leaders who believe, teach and live by the word of God.

Our mission is to strengthen the ministry of the word of God through:
- nurturing national movements for biblical preaching
- fostering the creation and distribution of evangelical literature
- enhancing evangelical theological education

especially in countries where churches are under-resourced.

Our ministry

Langham Preaching partners with national leaders to nurture indigenous biblical preaching movements for pastors and lay preachers all around the world. With the support of a team of trainers from many countries, a multi-level programme of seminars provides practical training, and is followed by a programme for training local facilitators. Local preachers' groups and national and regional networks ensure continuity and ongoing development, seeking to build vigorous movements committed to Bible exposition.

Langham Literature provides Majority World preachers, scholars and seminary libraries with evangelical books and electronic resources through publishing and distribution, grants and discounts. The programme also fosters the creation of indigenous evangelical books in many languages, through writer's grants, strengthening local evangelical publishing houses, and investment in major regional literature projects, such as one volume Bible commentaries like the *Africa Bible Commentary* and the *South Asia Bible Commentary*.

Langham Scholars provides financial support for evangelical doctoral students from the Majority World so that, when they return home, they may train pastors and other Christian leaders with sound, biblical and theological teaching. This programme equips those who equip others. Langham Scholars also works in partnership with Majority World seminaries in strengthening evangelical theological education. A growing number of Langham Scholars study in high quality doctoral programmes in the Majority World itself. As well as teaching the next generation of pastors, graduated Langham Scholars exercise significant influence through their writing and leadership.

To learn more about Langham Partnership and the work we do visit **langham.org**

www.ingramcontent.com/pod-product-compliance
Lightning Source LLC
Chambersburg PA
CBHW061703300426
44115CB00014B/2548